AN ENCYCLOPEDIA OF

FISHING FLIES

In Memoriam
Alan Bramley

AN ENCYCLOPEDIA OF
FISHING FLIES

Malcolm Greenhalgh

Photography by Jason Smalley

FLIES TIED BY
Stuart Bowdin, Mick Hall, Chris Hosker,
Terry Jenner, Stevie Munn and friends

Collins

This edition produced for
The Book People Ltd
Parc Menai, Bangor LL57 4FB

HarperCollins Publishers
77–85 Fulham Palace Road
London W6 8JB
www.harpercollins.co.uk

Collins is a registered trademark of HarperCollins Publishers Ltd.

First published 2009

13 12 11 10 09
10 9 8 7 6 5 4 3 2 1

A catalogue record for this book is available from the British Library.

ISBN 978-0-00-785293-2

Edited and designed by Tom Cabot/ketchup
Cover design by Heike Schüssler

Colour reproduction by Colourscan, Singapore
Printed and bound in Italy by LEGO

Contents

Foreword

> The dressing of flies is one of the most delightful and at the same time one of the most impudently ambitious of human activities ... Perhaps the dresser of trout-flies is the most impudent of all, for he is ready to let a fly that he has dressed join a procession of real ones and expects a trout to accept it as one of those living insects that float before his eyes at the time.
>
> Arthur Ransome, *Mainly About Fishing*, 1959.

I first picked up a fly rod when I was in my teens 45 years ago and in the last 23 years fly-fishing and its associated natural history have dominated my life. Through my association with the hook-maker Partridge (now part of the Mustad empire) I have been lucky to tie flies at shows alongside the very best: people such as Peter Dunne, Oliver Edwards, Jack Gartside, Robert Gillespie, John Goddard, Hans de Groote, Preben Torp Jacobsen, Ed Jaworowski, Terry Jenner, Poul Jorgensen, Hans van Klinken, Lefty Kreh, Paul Little, Robert McHaffie, Frankie McPhillips, E. J. (Ted) Malone, Darrel Martin, Roman Moser, Marvin Nolte, Jack Norris, Hans Odegard, Marc Petitjean, Bob Popovics, Taff Price, Terry Ruane, Dave Whitlock and Davy Wootton. That this was possible was because of one man, the late Alan Bramley who, as Managing Director of Partridge of Redditch, did more than anyone in bringing together the top fly-tyers from around the world. I have dedicated this book to his memory.

I have also been very fortunate over the last 23 years in being able to travel widely with my fly-rods and to experience fly-fishing for many other species of fish besides the trout, grayling and salmon of my home waters. Species such as largemouth and smallmouth bass in Ontario; striped bass and bluefish off the shores of New England; bonefish, permit and tarpon on many a tropical 'flat'; steelhead and sea-run cutthroat in British Columbia; char, whitefish and ide in Scandinavia; and peacock bass and piranha in four Amazonian rivers. So I have had to learn a vast array of flies far removed from the handful of trout and salmon flies of my youth.

It is impossible to have too many books about fly-fishing and fly-tying! When you cannot go fishing, and have tied enough flies for the day, it is time for a book and, maybe, a glass of something. I am doubly fortunate in that my wife seems to be happy to live in a library-cum-fly-fishing den, and that Paul Morgan, proprietor of Coch-y-Bonddu Books, is a friend. Not only has Paul sold me almost enough books, but also he has used his database to check the thoroughness of the Bibliography.

Several fly-tying pals have helped with the tying of flies for this Encyclopedia: Stuart Bowdin tied most of the dry flies and loch flies, Terry Jenner the saltwater flies and Paul Little tied all the beautiful salmon flies. Other tyers who contributed flies are, Dave Bell, Brian Burnett, Ray Brown, the late Al Coen, Howard Croston, Oliver Edwards, Lawrence Finney, Wendy Gibson, Peter Greenhalgh, Les Gregory, Mick Hall, Geoff Haslam, Chris Helm, Chris Hosker, Ed Jaworowski, Peter Joest, the late Poul Jorgensen, Ian Kennedy, Torrill Kolbu, Ted Malone, Ken Maylor, Robert McHaffie, Stevie Munn, Dick Nelson, Wally Nowak, Steve O'Dea of Donegal Flies, Marc Petitjean, Bob Popovics, Terry Ruane, Roger Salomonsson, Riny Sluiter, Mikko Stenberg, Paul van den Driesche, Chris Wadmore, Bar Woodall and Terenzio Zandri.

I would also thank Partridge (Mustad) for providing hooks, and Steve Cooper (Cookshill), Flytec, Glasgow Angling Centre, Lakeland, Lureflash and Marc Petitjean for tying tools and materials.

Malcolm Greenhalgh,
Lowton, April 2009.

Introduction

> But nothing can compare with the moment that a fly of your own making … is accepted by the fish.
>
> Preben Torp Jacobsen, in Judith Dunham, *The Art of the Trout Fly*, 1988.

This *Encyclopedia* examines the whole range of fishing flies, from the smallest trout dry fly to the largest bait-fish imitation for catching huge predators. It also goes back in time to the first fly ever recorded for catching fish, almost two millennia ago, and includes some of the most recent fly designs. It also includes flies designed to catch fish in all the far-flung corners of Planet Earth: from the United States to New Zealand, from the British Isles to Patagonia, from Norway's North Cape to South Africa's Cape of Good Hope. Yet, though a fly may have been designed for one purpose (for example, catching peacock bass in an Amazon tributary), it may well be that the same fly might be useful in other situations (to continue our example – catching pike in a cool northern lake). So although a fly may be included in, say, the section on saltwater patterns, it may also be useful for catching freshwater predators, like pike and Nile perch. Thus, while this book is separated into sections, it is essential to remember that, to catch a particular species of fish, there may be relevant flies to be found in more than one section.

The great problem has been the selection of flies to include here: for it is impossible to include every fly that has been published somewhere (in magazine articles, books or on video/CD). The total number of published flies is quite likely to exceed 100,000 – it would be near impossible to account for them all – and the number increases every month. In his book *Flies*, published almost 60 years ago, J. Edison Leonard gave nearly 2000 different tyings that would catch most species of fish swimming in the rivers and lakes of the United States. But he was completely outgunned in 1960 by Donald Du Bois in his *The Fisherman's Handbook of Trout Flies*. Some 5939 trout flies are listed ... add to these the trout flies published since 1960 and the plethora of flies for catching salmon, steelhead and sea trout, bass and pike, and the full array of saltwater fish ... and the list could become endless.

One game played by many an amateur and a few professional fly-tyers, is to claim a fly invented by someone else as their own invention. Another is to change the dressing of a fly just slightly and then to rename the fly. When done deliberately, this is tantamount to theft. Lefty Kreh complained of such behaviour in the Introduction to his *Saltwater Fly Patterns*:

> During the past ten years many fly patterns, some developed generations ago, were renamed. Or someone sticks an extra feather on a new pattern, or changes the color slightly, and calls it by his or her name. This is something many people, including myself, find distasteful and unfair.

I agree.

One effect of this tendency has been that the number of published patterns has mushroomed needlessly. Consider just one category of fly, the Irish salmon shrimps (p. 324): there are now in excess of 130 published tyings, many of them only slightly different from earlier ones, with new ones being invented every year. Do we need so many? I don't think so.

Ed Jaworowski and Bob Popovics described (in their quite revolutionary book on saltwater flies, *Pop Fleyes*) how a trout angler had approached them to sing the praises of a new nymph he had invented. Its virtue was that it caught trout. 'Well, then, we probably don't need it,' they replied to the angler, who seemed taken aback by their response. 'If you had said that your fly sinks, floats, or casts better, acts differently, absorbs water, sheds water, anything, that's something else.' Ed and Bob continue:

> Thousands of flies are created annually, and it's only natural that their creators fall in love with them. But the fact remains that flies like Lefty's Deceiver, the Clouser Deep Minnow, the Muddler Minnow, the Dahlberg Diver, the Wulff drys, and some others are classics because they broke

> new ground. They redirected the course of fly tying and, as a result, fly fishing. They have a common element. They evolved from a need – a need to do something better. Note, we did not say they simply did something differently, rather, they answered a need. New fly designs should always strive either to do something previously not possible at all or to do something better than was previously possible, be it ever so small a difference.

By all means invent 'new' patterns for your own use, but don't go to the press and tell them that your 'new' fly is essential unless it is really different in its tying or the way that it fishes!

Even worse is the publication of flies that have never caught a fish. There is one professional fly-tyer who has invented several salmon flies and published their tyings. That fly-tyer never goes salmon fishing! Some years ago a semi-professional fly-tyer had published, in a book, an imitation of a pale watery dun, but the following year, when pale wateries were hatching out from a river, he asked his host what they were! He had invented a fly to match a real insect that he had never seen! Such flies are untruths.

The flies that have been selected for this book have all made a major contribution to the progress of fly-tying. They are proven catchers of fish, are good examples of a category of fly, and can be tied because the materials they incorporate are readily obtained. Above all else, the selected flies are for fishing and because many fishing flies have a short life span (sometimes only one cast in a piranha-infested river!) – they should not take too long to tie. Someone once said that if a fly takes more than five minutes to tie, time has been wasted! That may be a little hard … but imagine if you were to spend half an hour tying one fly, and the loss whilst out fishing was ten or more flies per day. Each day's fishing would require a full day spent in tying.

There are, of course, many books of fly-tying recipes. This *Encyclopedia* goes further, and includes details of the history of the flies, of who invented the different styles and categories, and where and when. So contained within it are many of the world's greatest fly-tyers. It also gives some brief notes on where and when and how flies should be fished. There are also many books, videos, CDs and DVDs on how to tie flies. The beginner should use them and join a fly-tying class, for there is no better way to learn than in the company of someone who is a good tyer and a qualified teacher of fly-tying.

Above all else this *Encyclopedia* is a celebration of the world of flies, an important part of the finest occupation that anyone in the world can have – that of a fly-fisher.

WHAT IS A FISHING FLY?

> One of the most apparent and widespread developments in American fly tying has been the increasing use of flies that do not imitate real flies. "Fly fishing" has come to mean, to most people, at least, the use of a fly rod and fly line to cast something we still call a fly but might imitate anything from blobs of stonefly eggs to a baby muskrat.
>
> Paul Schullery, *American Fly Fishing: A History*, 1987.

The fishing fly greatly predates the fly-fishing rod and heavy fly-fishing casting line. Until the eighteenth century artificial flies and baits were both used on the same rod and line. These early flies were attempts to imitate the flies that hovered over water and that, when they landed on the water's surface, were preyed on by trout. So when the angler spotted a trout (or other fish) rising to take real flies from the surface, bait tackle was cut from a fine horsehair line and an artificial fly that had some passing resemblance to the real one was knotted in place. Often, in these bygone days, the angler might take a bag of fly-tying materials to the waterside, and use them to produce an imitation of the type of fly the trout were eating as they watched. The fly could not be cast as we can today with the use of heavy fly-line – for the horsehair line was not weighty enough. Instead the fly-fisher used the breeze and a long fishing rod to dap or dib the fly on to the water's surface. That most (if not all) fishing flies back then were designed to match real species of fly is borne out by the writings of anglers in those far-off times (see pp. 14–44).

A further step in the development of the modern fishing fly was taken in the tying of fishing flies that did not imitate flying insects. Instead, other stages of aquatic insect life cycles were imitated: nymphs, larvae, pupae and, most recently, that remarkable and very short-lived stage, the emerger. Once that step had been taken, then it was logical to imitate other subsurface aquatic trout foods: crustaceans such as shrimps (scuds) and hog-lice (sow-bugs), water snails and fish fry. If these creatures are acceptable as flies, the argument continued, why not tie flies that imitate larger fish or frogs to catch predatory species such as pike and large-mouth and smallmouth bass? Go one step further, argued those anglers who lived by the shore. So a huge number of bait-fish imitations were concocted for catching species such as striped bass and bluefish, some very special shrimp imitations for catching bonefish, and crab imitations for casting to feeding permit. All these imitations – though far removed from a mayfly or stonefly imitation – we still call flies.

When a fly-fisher sets out to catch a fish, the important two questions usually are:

- What is the fish eating? And,
- What fly shall I use to match that food?

Such questions are irrelevant when it comes to catching species such as salmon, sea trout or steelhead, for they do not usually feed on their return to the river from their oceanic feeding grounds. It is true that sometimes such fish can be seen taking some sort of food and that they can sometimes be caught on food-imitating flies. To catch these fish, special flies have been designed that arouse aggression or curiosity. For example, in the autumn when cock Atlantic salmon are nearing the time to spawn, a fly with a lot of orange in its dressing is often most effective (see p. 291). Because shrimps and prawns turn some shade of orange when they are cooked we often refer to these flies as shrimp flies, but the salmon does not take the orange fly because it resembles something that it ate out at sea. It takes the fly because its vision is most sensitive to reds and oranges and because, with its high level of testosterone, the cock salmon is highly aggressive at that time of the year.

It is important to note that through the almost four centuries that flies have been tied for catching salmon, they have always been called 'flies', even though they imitate nothing living, and certainly not real flies. Because the salmon fly is usually not designed to imitate what the salmon is eating, some fly-fishers may prefer to call it a lure. This takes us into a second category of flies, for, besides feeding, most fish use their mouths to investigate what is, for them, new, and to attack intruders. Look at a range of tarpon flies, for instance (pp. 429–33). Many look nothing like the lesser creatures that tarpon eat. Yet, when fished in front of a tarpon, the tarpon looks and responds by giving such a fly a good chew.

Two large categories of flies may be taken by the fish as imitation food or as lures. These are streamers (pp. 255–85) and poppers (pp. 437–40). Some streamers are quite fish-like, so they may be taken as food. Others look nothing like something that has lived. Poppers, bobbling across the water surface, may suggest a meaty frog or injured bait-fish to a hungry largemouth bass or pike. But both streamers and poppers might just as easily be taken because they lure the fish to take out of curiosity or aggression.

Traditionally flies are 'tied' or 'dressed'. They are not 'made' or 'constructed'. The tying or dressing involves fixing the materials that go into the fly's construction – traditionally hair, fur and feather – onto a hook using nothing but thread. The majority of flies are still tied in this way. However, glues are increasingly being used in fly construction, and some flies are constructed, not dressed. One of the most primitive examples of this is the Wake Lure used to catch Atlantic sea trout in their natal rivers in the dead of night. This 'fly' simply consists of a piece of cork from a wine bottle, cut and trimmed to shape, lashed to the top of a hook shank. Painted a nice colour, or embellished with a couple of feathers, it's still just a bit of cork tied to a hook! The Wake Lure originates from the 1930s (see p. 360). Today similar flies are being constructed from deer hair or wool, that have all the properties of Rapallas and other wobbling plugs to catch saltwater species and pike. Cast them out and retrieve quickly: they dive and wobble from side to side in a way that predatory fish find so attractive.

There are some fly-fishers today who believe that fly-fishing should be solely about imitating real, winged flies and that to fish with 'flies' that do not (such as streamers, poppers and saltwater flies) is not fly-fishing but fishing with a fly-rod and line. Those controlling the fishing on some English rivers are perhaps the strictest, with 'dry fly only' or 'maximum hook size 10' rules. They are entitled to their opinions and to set whatever rules they want on their own waters. But does it matter? After all, fly-fishing and fly-tying for most people is a way of escaping for the day-to-day job of earning a living, of feeding the family, of maintaining a home. It is not about politics, argument and rules.

FLY-TYING MATERIALS

This book contains the dressings of a large number of flies and, consequently, a huge number of materials from which those flies are tied. In the fly-tying recipes as much detail as possible is given as to precisely what materials should be used.

HOOKS

A hook is the one essential ingredient in every fly. Since the 1960s the number of hook types designed for fly-tying has increased greatly, and some have been devised for the tying of one special style of fly. An early example of this came with the book *The Trout and the Fly* (1980) by John Goddard and Brian Clarke, and its accompanying TV/video spin-off. Though the first upside-down dry flies had been tied on ordinary dry fly hooks, hook-makers Partridge of Redditch were persuaded to produce special USD hooks that helped keep the point and bend of the hook pointing upwards, out of the water. Three decades on and the USD hooks are no longer made and consequently the flies promoted by Goddard and Clarke are rarely, if ever, tied. A current example is the Klinkhamer, a very popular emerger pattern devised by Hans van Klinken (p. 134). Originally the fly was tied on Partridge Long Shank/Caddis hooks code K12ST, later a special Klinkhamer hook code GRS15ST. Should Partridge (part of the Mustad company) cease the manufacture of these hooks, then it will become impossible to tie Klinkhamers … Well, not quite. Parachute emergers, of which the Klinkhamer is but one, can be tied on a range of hooks – just observe the commercially tied Klinkhamers available in tackle stores!

Many tyers who publish their fly recipes give quite precise instruction as to what hook should be used: manufacturer and hook code. Here, precise hook sizes are given, but other than that, usually only a general category is given: e.g. wet fly, size 14; dry fly, size 18; stainless steel streamer, size 2/0; midge, size 22–28; salmon low water, size 6–12. Readers may then examine tackle catalogues, or visit tackle shops or web sites and choose an appropriate hook by their favourite manufacturer. If a fly recipe specifies that a fly *must* be tied on one specific hook, it becomes defunct if that hook becomes unavailable or the manufacturer goes bust.

Perhaps the best piece of advice when it comes to choosing which hook to use comes from George Selwyn Marryat, the driving force behind the great and sadly maligned pioneer of the dry fly, F. M. Halford. A good hook, said Marryat, 'should have the temper of an angel and penetration of a prophet; fine enough to be invisible and strong enough to kill a bull in a ten-acre field.' In other words, buy the finest and strongest hooks you can find for the fly-tying bench and with an eye to the fishing situation in which it will be used.

Tip: With the increasing prevalence of 'catch-and-release' – either because of fishery rules or reduced fishing stocks – buy barbless hooks, or crush the barb before tying the fly.

THREADS

Up to the second half of the twentieth century the choice of threads (then mostly real 'silks') available to the fly-tyer was very limited – with Pearsall's Naples and Gossamer probably most popular. Today there are several manufacturers, producing ever stronger and finer threads. As with hooks, some writers specify precisely what thread (manufacturer and thread thickness) should be used to tie their flies. In general, this is unnecessary.

Tip: All fly-tyers are advised to find a brand and thickness of thread that they find they get on with for most of their small to medium-sized flies (hooks about size 10 and smaller). A thickness of approximately 10/0 to 12/0 is ideal. Buy several spools of every colour. Tune all your bobbin holders to the spool size of the brand of thread, by bending the bobbin arms so that the thread will run off the spool easily when pulled, but the spool will not turn unless the thread is pulled. Without different-sized spools of thread from several manufacturers, you avoid the need to re-tune your bobbin holders with every change of thread.

Buy some thicker and stronger threads for larger flies (size 8 and larger), and perhaps a very fine thread (Spider Web 20/0 is the finest currently available, though it comes only in white and must be coloured with a spirit-based pen) for the smallest of flies, and give them their own, tuned bobbin holder.

FUR AND FEATHER

There is of course some natural variation in the colour, shade and texture of natural materials, especially those taken from wild birds and mammals (e.g. hare's ear, speckled brown partridge). Fish seem not to notice. When it comes to other natural materials, there is a wider range of high-quality product now available to the fly-tyer than there has ever been. Half a century ago, cock hackles for dry flies came mostly from the Indian sub-continent and the best of them were grossly inferior to the specially bred 'genetic' capes available today.

Tip: The only problem with the genetic cock hackle is that it often has a thick stalk that, when the hackle is wound, twists around unless very tightly bound down with many turns of thread. Take the hackle from its cape and trim away the lower barbs. Then, before tying the hackle in, soften with stalk close to where it will be first wound, between the nails of thumb and forefinger.

Many flies were devised years ago, before there were worldwide concerns about endangered CITES (Convention on International Trade in Endangered Species of Wild Fauna and Flora) species. This Encyclopedia includes mention of no CITES species, other than in the sections dealing with historical fly-tyings (where the feathers used come from very old collections) or with species bred in captivity for fly-tying (e.g. jungle cock). There is no need to use CITES species when tying flies to catch fish.

Legislation varies from country to country when it comes down to owning and using feathers of birds that are protected. In the UK, the grey heron and waterhen are protected, but it is not unlawful to gather moulted heron quills from the riverside in summer or the feathers from a road-kill waterhen. Always check the legal situation – especially if planning to travel abroad – with fly-tying materials.

Synthetic materials have increasingly been used in the design of many fishing flies since the Second World War. They often have properties lacking in natural materials. They are usually consistent in colour and texture: contrast the variation of hare's ear or natural rabbit fur with a synthetic fur such as FlyRite. Sometimes they have properties not provided by any natural material: for example, no natural material provides such a soft, realistically segmented and translucent body for nymphs as Flexibody. However, there is a problem with synthetics. Rarely are they made solely for the fly-tying market and usually the fly-tying market is a tiny part of their sales. Consider Antron, made by the Dupont Corporation, which just about every fly-tyer in the world now uses. Almost 100 per cent of Dupont's production goes into carpet or similar manufacture and a fraction over zero per cent to fly-tying. So should furnishing fashions change and Dupont stop manufacturing Antron, fly-tyers could find many of their tying techniques compromised.

In 1924 J. W. Dunne published *Sunshine and the Dry Fly* (2nd edn, 1950), in which he described a new range of dry flies. These, he argued, were 'far more natural looking' than previous dry flies. Their bodies had a natural translucency brought about by winding 'cellulite floss' fibres over a hook shank that had been painted white. Cellulite flosses came in a variety of colours and shades that were given code numbers by their manufacturer, Wardle & Davenport. For the body of any fly, two or three strands of different shades had to be wound together according to Dunne's formulae. The angling wholesaler of these flosses, Messeena & Co, also sold cock hackles dyed to Dunne's instructions and special tying threads, and they too had their codes. The following is one typical tying, DUNNE'S DARK MAYFLY SPINNER (presented in modern form, but with quotes from Dunne's recipe):

Hook: Size 9.
Thread: Silk M2.
Tails: Cock pheasant tail herls, not dyed. 'Ends of whisks should be 1½ inches from eye of hook.'
Body: '2 (298A) + 2 (298) + 2(226). Thickness behind hackle, about 8/100 inch. Taper to half this thickness.'
Rib: Fine gold wire.
Outspread wings: Cut from hackle H2 (including plenty of brown markings). Total spread, 1½ inches.
Hackles: Four turns of N behind wings, and four turns of N in front. Maximum width across shank, ¾ inch.
Eyes: 'Unnecessary.'

Wardle & Davenport ceased production and so today we have no idea what M2, 298A, 298, 226, H2 or N were, we cannot obtain them, and Dunne's flies will never be tied again.

More recently, a material called Swannundaze, which was highly recommended in the 1970s for forming the segmented bodies of larvae and nymphs, has vanished from the fly-tying scene (see p. 75).

Many fly-tying recipes in this book include synthetic materials, such as Krystal Hair and Poly Yarn. It is likely, should such synthetics disappear from the market, that reasonable alternatives will become available.

TIP: One of the greatest pleasures in fly-tying is to gather materials for nothing. It may be a road-kill, or some distant aunt may have a fur coat that she wants to get rid of, or the local game dealer may have some rabbit or deer skins that he doesn't want, or a shooting friend may have a bag of mallard or pheasants that need plucking, or the family next door may have some hens and an aged cockerel with the most superb grizzle hackles! Never say no! Rub borax into skins and the cut ends of wings to prevent fungal and bacterial growth. If you are unsure that the material may hold parasites (e.g. feather mites or moth larvae) that could ruin a fly-tying collection, put the item in a plastic bag, knot the bag and put it in the deep freeze for a month. Store all natural materials in sealed plastic bags.

Often recipes require dyed fur or feather. Dyeing your own materials is good fun, provided the kitchen remains undyed! And when a colour is required for a tying recipe, consider a blend of material that gives that colour. For instance, if medium olive fur is needed, mix the fur from two or three sources (such as hare, rabbit and perhaps a synthetic) so that there is variety in texture. Perhaps also mix in a little yellow or red or orange to break up the flat tone of the olive. For a good example of this, see JC HATCHING BUZZER, p. 113.

DO WE NEED SO MANY DIFFERENT FLIES?

The answer is, of course, no! This *Encyclopedia* contains the tyings for nearly 250 different dry flies designed for catching trout and other fish that take insects from the water surface. By varying size and, sometimes, colour/shade, it would be possible to use one pattern to match several species of real fly, so from the practical fishing point-of-view, the 250 could become over a thousand flies in the box. If it were essential to carry so many imitations, the hatch would be over before a fly was cast! In *The Floating Fly* (2008), Malcolm Greenhalgh described just eleven different dry and emerger patterns that, he argued, would catch any fish eating any insect floating at the surface of any river or lake anywhere in the world! Seventy-five years earlier, Edward Hewitt listed ten dry flies (five winged and five hackled) in *Hewitt's Handbook of Fly Fishing* (1933) and added: 'Personally, I would not want any more patterns of dry flies than the above … Don't get a raft of patterns. They are not necessary *at all* [his italics].' Ray Bergman (in *Just Fishing*, also 1933) agreed, noting that: 'I think it is possible to get along with half a dozen [dry fly] patterns ranging from [sizes] 10 to 15.'

Life would, however, be incredibly boring if we tied and carried only a few patterns that we knew nearly always caught fish. Most of us do carry our favourite flies, the ones in which we have lots of faith. But we do enjoy tying and trying new ones. The worst scenario would be the discovery of the Holy Grail, the fly that catches every fish it is cast to. For then there would be no need to tie or carry any other fishing fly, there would be no challenge, and it would signal the end of fly-tying and fly-fishing.

THE PRESENTATION OF FLY-TYING RECIPES

There are two main ways of presenting fly-tying recipes.

The first is to list the parts of the fly in the order that they are tied in. So if the wing is tied in first, it appears after hook and thread detail, whereas if the wing is tied in last, it appears at the end of the recipe. This way lacks uniformity in that the order changes depending on what fly is being tied.

The second is to consider the finished flies (shown in this volume as photographs) and to list all the parts in order beginning with hook, then thread, then tail, body, rib, hackle and so on. In seeking to present the recipes in a clear uniform manner, this method will be used throughout this Encyclopedia.

PARTS OF A FLY

Hook: This may be one of several types (e.g. wet fly, dry fly, nymph, streamer, low-water salmon) and sizes. Some flies may also be tied on double and single hooks, tandem mounts, and tubes or Waddington shanks to which a separate hook is fixed. Note that often there may be restrictions as to what hooks may be used on particular stretches of water.

Thread: The ability to use thread well marks the difference between a good tyer and a poor one. The great tyer Terry Ruane used to say that, for the fly-dresser: 'the hook is the canvas, the thread the brush, and the materials the paint. A good artist is one who can use the brush.'

Tag (sometimes called 'butt'): Small amount of material (e.g. two or three turns of tinsel or floss silk) wound around the shank before the tail. But note that sometimes 'tag' means 'tail' (e.g. RED TAG, p. 226).

Tail: Represents the real tail in some flies based on insects and fish, but added simply to lend movement in, for instance, modern salmon and saltwater flies.

Butt (sometimes called 'tip'): At the base of the tail and immediately before the body, this is usually added to salmon flies and some loch/lough/sea-trout flies to add a hot spot that might attract the fish's attention (e.g. a turn of fluorescent floss).

Body: May be separated in insect imitations into abdomen and thorax.

Rib: Suggests segmentation in many imitative flies or, adds extra 'flash' (a tinsel rib) in salmon and other flies. Note that, when tying flies that imitate insects, the novice tyer is urged by the expert to rib evenly so that every segment is the same width. Yet in real larvae, pupae and adult insects, the segments will vary in width!

Body hackle: This is a hackle wound spirally around the body. It may be tied in at the end of the body, wound forward and then tied in at the front. Or, it is tied in at the front of the body, wound back around the body, and then fixed in place by bringing the tinsel ribbing forward through it. Note too that in some flies the body hackle is wound in touching turns (e.g. BIVISIBLES, p. 130), whereas in others it is wound in open turns (e.g. Troth's ELK HAIR CADDIS, p. 195).

Wing cases: In nymphs. Usually a slip from a feather, tied in on the dorsal surface between abdomen and thorax, and then brought forward over the back of the thorax after the thorax has been completed and legs tied in.

Shellback: In scud/freshwater shrimps. Usually some synthetic strip tied in at the end of the hook shank and then brought forward over the back of the fly just before completion.

Hackle: Wound at the front of the fly. In a false hackle, hackle fibres are tied in, in front of the body or in front of a fully wound hackle (e.g. GOLDEN-OLIVE BUMBLE, p. 232). In a parachute hackle, the hackle is tied in and wound around a 'posted' wing (e.g. KLINKHAMER SPECIAL, p. 135).

Legs: In imitative flies. May be a false hackle. Or a feather is tied in by its tip on top of the hook shank, pointing backwards, either before the body (in scuds/freshwater shrimps) or thorax (nymphs) is created. The feather is then brought over the back of the body or thorax and tied in. The fibres sticking out to either side to imitate legs.

Wings: In early flies represented the wings of real insects. Now also means feathers or hairs tied back over or alongside the body in streamers, salmon flies, many saltwater patterns etc. In parachute dry flies and emergers a single wing is tied in first, brought upright and then 'posted' with several turns of thread around its base. The parachute hackle is later wound around this posted base.

Topping: Fibres of herl or golden pheasant 'topping' feather etc. tied over the top of wings.

Cheeks: Small feathers, e.g. jungle cock eyes, tied in at sides of wings.

Head: Often not mentioned if only of tying thread.

THE EARLIEST FLIES

> The history of fly fishing is so long that we will never know who first had the inspired idea of tying feathers round a hook.
>
> Andrew Herd, *The Fly*, 2003.

THE MACEDONIAN FLY

The first recorded fly was published by a Roman called Claudius Aelianus in a manuscript book *De Animalium Natura* in about AD200. The fly was used to catch fish 'with speckled fins', which must have been trout. The trout rose to catch flies at the surface of a river then called the Astraeus in what was then Macedonia. Research by Andrew Herd and Dr Gorin Grubil has shown that the Astraeus is now known as the Arapitsa, and it flows through modern Greece. The real flies were known at the time as hippouros and they appear to have had combined characteristics of a midge, a wasp and a bee. Investigations by Fred Buller (in *The American Fly Fisher*, vol. 22, 1996) into the identity of hippouros indicated that it was either a horsefly *Therioplectes tricolor* or a drone-fly *Episyrphus balteatus*.

The imitation of the MACEDONIAN FLY was simple: 'They fasten red wool around a hook, and fix onto the hook two feathers which grow under a cock's wattle, and which in colour are like wax'. Or, to give it as a tyer's recipe:

Hook: Not given; suggest dry fly, size 14.
Thread: Not given; suggest red or brown.
Body: Red wool.
Wings: Two wax-coloured cock hackle points. [Wax coloured? Beeswax is a light creamy-buff.]

It seems clear that fly-fishing is a very ancient way of catching fish. Andrew Herd traced it back as far, perhaps, as the ninth century BC, and showed that by the early Middle Ages (late twelfth and early thirteenth century) fly-fishing was well established in Japan, in Spain, in central Europe and in Britain. The central European school is especially interesting for it produced an early fifteenth-century Bavarian manuscript, translated into English by Professor Richard Hoffmann, and called *Fisher's Craft and Lettered Art*. It included flies for catching several species of European freshwater fish, but the way the flies were tied and some of the terms used (for example, 'stingel') are not clear in their meaning.

Two examples are given below. The resultant flies were tied with a great deal of guesswork!

Bavarian Chub Fly

This is an imitation of a beetle called 'wengril'. 'The feathering should be black brown with the silks green and black and around the stingel green and brown.'

Bavarian Pike Fly

> The feathering should be of different sorts mixed together, with lead coloured and light blackish and ash coloured therein a black feather, with the silk pale coloured and around the heart black light blue silk, around the stingel pinkish coloured silk.

It is highly likely that many other manuscripts describing fly-tying and fly-fishing were produced in the early Middle Ages. Some will have been destroyed; others may be hidden deep in the vast library of the Vatican or in some other dust-gathering ancient corner. There can be no doubt, however, that the compiler of the first printed book on fishing used several of these manuscripts as sources.

THE FIRST FLIES TO APPEAR IN PRINT

William Caxton was born in Kent in about 1420. In 1441 he left England for Bruges and then Cologne, where he learnt the art and business of being a printer. In 1474 he published the first book ever to be printed in the English language, *The Recuyell of the Histories of Troye*. Two years later, Caxton returned to England and set up a printing press in London at Westminster, where he printed 96 books. One of these was *The Book of Hawking, Hunting and Blasing of Arms*, published in 1486, and also known as *The Boke of St Albans*. When Caxton died in 1491 his German assistant Wynkyn de Worde took over the press and, in 1496, he produced a new edition of *The Boke of St Albans*. This included the first slender volume on angling, *A Treatyse of Fysshynge with an Angle*. Many years later the authorship of the *Treatyse* was attributed to an abbess called Dame Juliana Berners, but there is no documentary evidence that

The opening page of the *Treatyse* of 1496. The gist of the introduction to the *Treatyse* is that fly-fishers live a long and happy life: 'Here begins the Treatyse of fishing with an angle [rod]. Solomon in his parables says that a good spirit makes for a flowering age, that is, a fair age and a long one …' Note that fishing vests and waders had not been invented in 1496!

Here begynnyth the treatyse of fysshynge wyth an Angle.

Salamon in his parablys sayth that a good spyryte makyth a flourynge aege/ that is a fayre aege & a longe. And syth it is soo: I aske this questyon/. Whiche ben the meanes & the causes that enduce a man in to a mery spyryte.: Truly to my beste dyscrecōn it semeth good dysportes & honest gamys in whom a man Joyeth wythout ony repentaunce after. Thenne folowyth it ẏ gode dysportes & honest games ben cause of mannys fayr aege & longe life. And therfore now woll I chose of foure good disportes & honeste gamys/ that is to wyte: of huntynge: hawkynge: fysshynge: & foulynge. The beste to my symple dyscrecōn whyche is fysshynge: callyd Anglynge wyth a rodde: and a lyne

she ever existed (see Fred Buller and Hugh Falkus, *Dame Juliana, the Angling Treatyse and its Mysteries*, 2001). What is certain is that Wynkyn gathered the material contained in the *Treatyse* from across Europe, something no fictitious abbess could ever have done.

The *Treatyse* outlined twelve artificial flies, but the way that they were tied is unknown. Sadly few, if any, actual flies tied before the middle of the nineteenth century have survived, for natural silk threads rot in light and humid conditions, and moth and mites move in quickly to devastate unprotected fur and feather. So any modern tyings of these flies may not be as they were tied more than 500 years ago. Two fly-tying historians produced plates of flies for Buller and Falkus (2001): Malcolm Greenhalgh and Jack Heddon. Examination of the plates in Buller and Falkus will reveal differences between their tyings – the set illustrated below were tied afresh by Greenhalgh without reference to his earlier tyings. Again there are differences in interpretation. It is quite likely that different tyers five centuries ago, having only the *Treatyse* as reference, would have tied the flies differently. The same applies to the other ancient flies illustrated in this section.

In the following, medieval spellings have been modernised.

FOR MARCH

The Dun Fly

The body of dun wool and the wings of the partridge.

Another Dun Fly

The body of black wool; the wings of the blackest drake and the jay under the wings and under the tail.

FOR APRIL

The Stone-Fly

The body of black wool and yellow under the wings and under the tail, and the wings of the drake.

IN THE BEGINNING OF MAY

A Good Fly

The body of red wool and ribbed with black silk; the wings of the drake and of the red capon's hackle.

MAY

The Yellow Fly

The body of yellow wool, the wings of the red cock's hackle and that of the drake dyed yellow.

The Black Louper

The body of black wool and ribbed with the herl of the peacock's tail and the wings of the capon with a blue head.

JUNE

The Dun Cut
The body of black wool and a yellow band along either side; the wings of the buzzard tied on with barked hemp.

The Maure Fly
The body of dusky wool; the wings of the blackest mail of the wild drake.

The Tandy Fly At St Williams's Day
The body of tandy wool and a pair of wings of the whitest mail of the wild drake.

JULY

The Wasp Fly
The body of black wool and ribbed with yellow thread; the wings of the buzzard.

The Shell Fly At St Thomas's Day
The body of green wool and ribbed with the herl from the peacock's tail; wings of the buzzard.

AUGUST

The Drake Fly
The body of black wool and ribbed with black silk; wings of the mail of the black drake with a black head.

Today we rarely tie and use flies that were devised over a hundred years ago. However the flies contained in the *Treatyse* were reprinted and recommended by several other writers up to and including Izaak Walton in *The Compleat Angler* (first published over 150 years later, in 1653).

A DOZEN EARLY FLIES FROM SWITZERLAND

In 1558 Conrad Gesner of Zurich published a large tome called *Historia Animalium*, the fourth volume of which was *De Piscum et Aquatilium Animatium Natura*, or *Of Fish and of Aquatic Animal Life*. He began his section on fishing flies with: 'Certain skilful fishers fabricate diverse kinds of worms and winged insects from the feathers of birds in various seasons of the year ...' (trans. Andrew Herd). 'Worms' probably included all sub-surface forms including larvae and nymphs. As in the *Treatyse* there were twelve patterns for catching trout and grayling. They lacked names, but were tagged to the months in which they were most effective, the first for each month being a grayling fly, the second a trout fly.

APRIL
Body: White [thread or wool?].
Wings: Whitish feather from the partridge belly.

Body: Red silk.
Wings: Red cock hackles.
Head: Green [thread?].

MAY
Body: Segmented black and white by twisting together black and white thread before winding down the hook shank [see **Dark Watchett**, p. 50; **Footballer Midge Pupa**, p. 111].
Wings: Varied (i.e. hooded) crow back feather.
Head: Blue.

Body: Red silk and gold [tinsel?].
Wings: Red cock hackles.
Head: Black.

JUNE
Body: Green 'from the feathers of the breast of the wild duck' [which are brown – were these wound round the hook shank?].
Wings: Dark heron tail.

Body: Blue silk and gold [tinsel?].
Wings: Partridge underwing coverts.
Head: Yellow.

JULY
Body: Blue silk.
Wings: Hooded crow belly feathers.
Head: Black silk.

Body: Green silk and gold [tinsel?].
Wings: Yellow feathers.
Head: Blue silk.

AUGUST
Body: 'Feathers of a crane's wing' [herl?].
Wings: Partridge.
Head: Green silk.

Body: Peacock herl, 'bound with a golden feather' [was the golden feather palmered as a body hackle?].
Wings: Back feathers of hazel hen.
Head: Yellow silk.

SEPTEMBER
Body: Blue silk.
Wings: Feathers from back of hooded crow.
Head: Red silk.

Body: Yellow and red silk [twisted, as for the first fly for May?].
Wings: Ptarmigan.
Head: 'Dark'.

When Gesner wrote his fly patterns, the *Treatyse* flies were in their pomp in England. It is clear that Gesner was unaware of the *Treatyse* flies, and that authors in England, up to and beyond Izaak Walton, were oblivious of Gesner's work.

ITALY'S VALSESIAN FLIES

The Sesia River flows from the Piedmont Alps of Italy. It has long been a great trout and grayling stream. So it is not surprising that it is one of the earliest centres of world fly-fishing and fly-tying, with its own special style of fly named after the valley, Valsesia, also published as Valasesiana. These flies have been traced back to 1570, 74 years after the *Treatyse* was published and only twelve years after Gesner's great book. Dr Nicola di Biase considered that they were fished much earlier (*Grayling Journal*, Summer 2007). The flies provided by Dr di Biase to illustrate her article show the flies to have a wound hackle, making them similar to the soft-hackles North Country style (p. 45), but (assuming that they were really tied that way in the sixteenth century) predating them by over a century. The hackling is, however, much heavier, and the hackle is forced forwards by several turns of thread immediately behind it. This method of hackling gives the fly more 'kick' than the conventional spider as the fly passes through turbulent mountain streams.

Different tyings of Valsesian flies were not, it seems, given different names. This was probably because tyers used what feathers were ready to hand, and what matched the real flies that the trout and grayling were taking. The following are three examples.

Body: Purple thread.
Hackle: Snipe upper wing covert.

Body: Orange thread.
Hackle: Brown speckled partridge.

Body: Olive thread.
Hackle: Starling neck.

SOME EARLY FLIES FROM NORTHERN SPAIN

The Danish fly-dresser Preben Torp Jacobsen was invited by Spain's president General Franco to dinner. After dinner Franco, who was a great fly-fisher and angling bibliophile, showed Preben his vast library. Among the collection was a hand-written manuscript, dated 1624, by Juan de Bergera, and called *El Manuscrito de Astorga*. Preben had photographs of the manuscript made and then, with a team from the Spanish Association for the Fly and Salmonids, produced a limited edition consisting of a facsimile of the original and translations into modern Spanish, French and English. Unfortunately a fire subsequently destroyed part of Franco's library, including the original manuscript.

Astorga is a small town not far from Leon in the Cantabrian Mountains. The rivers there have some very good fishing for brown trout, and it was to catch them that the flies in *El Manuscrito* were designed. The flies include in their dressings some of the most interesting wild birds to be found in Spain (such as pin-tailed sandgrouse and little bustard) and some very special hackles from cocks bred only in this region. These 'Coqs de Leon' are still available and, though expensive, are amongst the best material to use for tying upwinged fly (ephemerid) dun and spinner tails. There are two main types of Coq de Leon. 'Indios' are plain hackles, varying from the near white palometa to the blackish negrisco.

'Pardos' have a blackish centre (list) and coloured edges which vary from the creamy transparent crudo to a very dark grey corzuno, sometimes with black speckles.

El Manuscrito contains 49 different dressings, four of which are given here. Three are confusingly called Negriscos (they imitate a dark midge called enaguados), the fourth is one called Bermejo Crudo. Note that we do not know how these flies were tied. Hackles were then solely feathers and may not have been wound round the hook as we today wind hackles. However the last fly has one feather used as 'a wrapping', which presumably means that it was wrapped (i.e. wound) as we would wind a hackle, in which case, it seems likely that the others were not wound, but simply tied in. This is also suggested by the last of the four flies, where one feather was tied 'on top' of another. Whatever. The following tyings are one person's interpretation.

Negriscos (for January and February)
Thread: Grey.
Body: Dark silvery grey silk.
Rib: White silk.
Hackles: Two very dark blue dun.

Negriscos (for February and March)
Thread: Black.
Body: Black (linen) thread.
Hackles: Two extremely dark (almost black) blue dun.
Head: Fawn and white thread.

Negriscos (for sunny days in February and March)
Thread: Black.
Body: Black (linen) thread.
Rib: White thread.
Hackles: Two short barbed negrisco hackles.
Head: Black.

Bermejo Crudo (for the second half of March and April)
Thread: Purple-red.
Body: Tying thread.
Rib: Blue and white thread.
Hackles: 'It has a light blue dun negrisco [hackle]. Then a very fine textured pardo [hackle] that is not golden yellow; on top of the latter a king-

fisher's [feather]. Then another negrisco [hackle] identical to the first one. As a wrapping [wound hackle?] two turns of a bright vermilion [hackle] from a muladar cock.'

NOTE: Preben gave a footnote to the effect that 'muladar' meant dung, and that it was believed that the dung from mule stables gave cocks a very particular shade.

HOW TO TIE A FLY

In a small volume called *The Secrets of Angling*, by J. D. Esquire (1620), its author John D. Lawson gave us a fly that is of interest.

> The head is of black silk or haire, the wings of a feather of a mallart, teele, or pickled hen wing. The body of Crewel according to the moneth for colour, and run about with a black haire: all fastened at the taile, with the thread that fastned the hooke …

This indicates that the first part of the fly to be tied in after the hook had been lashed to the horsehair tippet is the wing. The next contributors would tell us more.

WALTON, BARKER AND COTTON

Izaak Walton (1593–1683) has been called 'the Father of Angling', but as a fly-fisher he is disappointing as his classic *The Compleat Angler* (1653) added little new to what was already on record with regard to fly-tying and fly-fishing. Two Englishmen who did make a major contribution were Thomas Barker, who published *Barker's Delight or the Art of Angling* (1651), and Charles Cotton, whose *Instructions How to Angle for a Trout or Grayling in a Clear Stream* appeared as a supplement to Walton's fifth edition of 1676. Cotton knew Walton well enough to have built an elaborate stone fishing 'temple' (hardly a hut!), called 'Piscatoribus Sacrum', in Walton's honour by the banks of his River Dove. Barker also knew Walton, so it likely that Cotton and Barker also knew each other and discussed their books during the writing.

Barker pointed out that there were two categories of flies when it came to trout fishing.

The first were what he called 'palmers'; they had a cock hackle wound or palmered down the hook shank. These have almost disappeared save for a group of flies known as Bumbles. They are still tied and used to catch,

Charles Cotton, in a portrait from the frontis of *The Compleat Angler* (above); the fishing hut, called Piscatoribus Sacrum, was built by Cotton in 1674 for a visit by Izaak Walton. It is on the bank of the River Dove, in England's Peak District.

mainly grayling, in the rivers of that part of England fished by Cotton (Staffordshire and Derbyshire). Two examples are the GRAYLING STEEL BLUE BUMBLE, p. 225, and GRAYLING WITCH, p. 227. They have also survived as trout flies in the loughs of Ireland and lochs of Scotland: examples include the GOLDEN-OLIVE BUMBLE and ZULU, pp. 232 & 243.

The second class of trout fly were winged flies and are still major trout flies today.

Now let us consult Cotton as to how to tie these flies and for some specific examples. It is important to understand that Cotton, like Walton, wrote in in a theatrical, lyrical style. He had two actors, one playing the part of the expert fly-fisher (Piscator), the other the novice who has come for instruction (Viator). First of all, Piscator must show Viator what materials can be used to tie flies, and in those days the fly-fisher took a huge bag of silks, fur and feather, some exotic and expensive, to the waterside so that the real fly being eaten by the trout could be imitated.

> PISCATOR. And now let me look out my things to make this fly. Boy! Come, give me my dubbing-bag here presently; and now, Sir, since I find you so honest a man, I will make no scruple to lay open my treasure before you.

VIATOR. Did ever any one see the like! What a heap of trumpery is here! Certainly never an angler in Europe has his shop half so well furnished as you have.

Piscator then gives Viator a verbal slap and points out that every item in his bag is indispensable. What would Viator think about our own twenty-first-century collections of 'essential' tying materials.

But then Cotton takes us through the tying of a fly. No vice …

PISCATOR. You see, first, how I hold my hook; and thus I begin. Look you, here are my first two or three whips around the bare hook; thus I join hook and line; thus I put on my wings; thus I twirl and lap on my dubbing; thus I work it up towards the head; thus I part my wings; thus I nip my superfluous dubbing from my silk; thus fasten; thus trim and adjust my fly. And there's a fly made; and now how do you like it?

VIATOR. In earnest, admirably well; and it perfectly resembles a fly.

And what modern category of fly has a body, upright wings and no hackle? Why, the most effective category of dry fly, the hackleless dry fly (see pp. 140–1, 167–9)!

Four of Cotton's flies have been selected to show the two styles, palmers and winged flies.

GREAT-HACKLE [a palmer], the body black, and wrapped with a red feather of a capon untrimmed; that is, the whole length of the hackle staring out …

WHITE HACKLE, the body of white mohair, and warped about with a white hackle-feather …

The artificial GREEN-DRAKE then is made upon a large hook, the dubbing of camel's hair, bright bear's hair, the soft down that is combed from a hog's bristles, and yellow camlet, well mixt together; the body long, and ribbed about with green silk, or rather yellow, waxed with green wax, the whisks of the tail of the long hairs of sable, or fitchet [polecat], and the wings of the white-grey feather of a mallard, dyed yellow …

Cotton then tells how to dye the mallard feather yellow. That fly would catch any trout eating large duns anywhere today.

> WHIRLING-DUN ... is commonly made of the down of a fox-cub, which is of ash colour at the roots next to the skin, and ribbed about with yellow silk; the wings of the pale grey feather of a mallard.

CHETHAM'S STRANGE CONTRIBUTION

James Chetham published his *Angler's Vade Mecum* in 1681, five years after Cotton's contribution to *The Compleat Angler*. His flies are very similar to Cotton's, but he insisted that, in addition to what the trout sees – what it smells or tastes like is also important.

> Next folow Ointments and Receipts which I have read and been informed of, by several knowing Anglers ... they'll not only allure, but even compel Fish to bite ... Take Man's Fat and Cat's Fat, of each half an Ounce, Mummy finely powdred three drams, Cummin-seed finely powdred one Dram, distill'd Oyl of Annise and Camphor four Grains, make an Ointment according to Art; and when you Angle anoint 8 inches of Line next to the Hook therewith ...

FRENCH CONNECTION

By the beginning of the eighteenth century French fly-tyers were producing flies with a similar structure to those made in Britain, though often the body was of plain silk whereas the British school mostly used dubbed fur for their bodies. These French artificial flies matched closely real flies. Louis Liger gave several examples in his book *Amusemens de Champagne* (1709), reprinted in 1714 as *Traite de toute sorte de Chasse et de Peche*. The following is typical entry:

> Dans le mois de May ils en fonte une, couverte aussi de soye, maise elle est de couleur rouge, et avec de filets tirans sur l'or: la tete en est noire, et on y joint les plumes rouge d'un capon.

This fly is an excellent imitation of the many species of upwinged fly spinner that have red or red-brown bodies.

TROUT FLY EVOLUTION INTO THE NINETEENTH CENTURY

During the 200 years following the publications of Barker and Cotton, three different styles of trout fly became established. The first was a winged fly that was an attempt to imitate real flies. This and the second style, the 'buzz' fly can best be seen in Alfred Ronalds' *The Fly-Fisher's Entomology*, which was first published in 1836 and was still in print in a new edition as late as 1921. His book was also the first to have fairly good illustrations of both the natural fly and corresponding imitative fly. The following are typical examples.

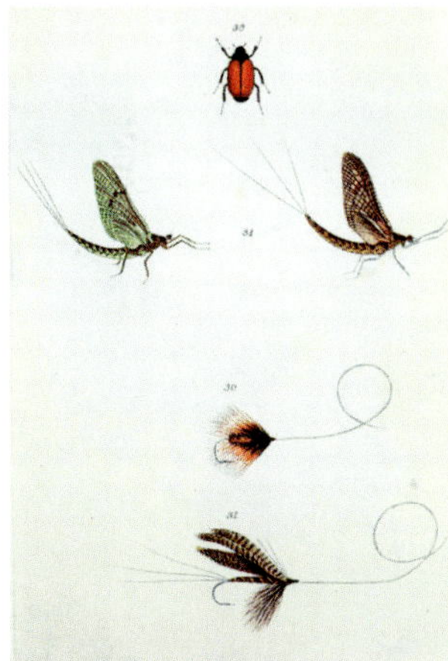

Plates from *The Fly-Fisher's Entomology*, showing some of the earliest coloured illustrations of real and artificial trout flies.

STYLE ONE – THE WINGED IMITATIVE TROUT FLY (SEE TOP PLATE, LOWER-LEFT FLY)

Example: Little Yellow May Dun
Hook: Size 15.
Thread: Not given; presumed yellow.
Tails: Two whisks from a dun hackle.
Body: Pale ginger fur from the back of a hare's ear.
Rib: Yellow silk.
Hackle (Ronalds called this 'Legs'): A light dun hackle lightly dyed yellow-green.
Wings: Drake mallard lightly dyed yellow-green.

STYLE TWO – THE BUZZ TROUT FLY (SEE BOTTOM PLATE, SECOND FLY FROM BOTTOM)

This was a fly with a palmered body hackle, like the Palmer flies of Cotton (p. 25). The term 'made buzz' indicated the palmered hackle.

Example: Marlow Buzz
Hook: Not given; size 12 suggested.
Thread: Red.
Body: Black ostrich herl and peacock herl twisted and wound together.
Wings and legs: 'Are made buzz with a dark furnace hackle.'

STYLE THREE – THE NORTH COUNTRY SPIDER (ALSO CALLED THE SOFT-HACKLED WET FLY)

Two Yorkshire men were instrumental in establishing this style, Michael Theakston, author of *British Angling Flies* (1853), and Francis M. Walbran, who edited a later edition of Theakston. This style of fly was later catalogued by T. E. Pritt in *Yorkshire Wet Flies* (1885), reprinted the following year as *North-Country Wet Flies*. These are still often fished today, on both sides of the Atlantic and in the Antipodes – they are therefore described more fully on pp. 45–54.

Spider wet flies have the simplest of bodies, often just of tying thread (silk), perhaps with a wisp of dubbing, and they have only two or two and a half turns of a soft hackle; a few also have very slender wings . They therefore suggest a fragile nymph or a waterlogged adult fly close to the surface.

Plate 8 of Pritt's book includes six that are not included in the later section on North Country Spiders, and they have been included here to illustrate this style of trout fly.

Old Master

Hook: Size 14.
Thread: Ash coloured.
Body: Tying thread, wrapped over with heron's herl.
Hackle (called 'Wings' by Pritt): Woodcock underwing covert.

Stone Midge

Hook: Size 15.
Thread: Ash coloured.
Body: Tying thread, dubbed sparely with heron's herl.
Hackle (called 'Wings' by Pritt): Pewit's [lapwing] neck, breast or rump.
Head: Magpie herl.

Grey Midge

Hook: Size 15.
Thread: Yellow.
Body: Tying thread.
Hackle (called 'Wings' by Pritt): Woodcock breast.
Head: Peacock herl.

Knotted Midge

Hook: Size 15.
Thread: Ash coloured.
Body: Tying thread, dubbed heron herl.
Hackle (called 'Wings' by Pritt): Back of a swift or a martin, or pewit shoulder.
Head: Magpie herl.

Sandy Moorgame

Hook: Size 15.
Thread: Dark brown.
Body: Tying thread.
Hackle (called 'wings' by Pritt): Reddish feather from the back of a grouse.

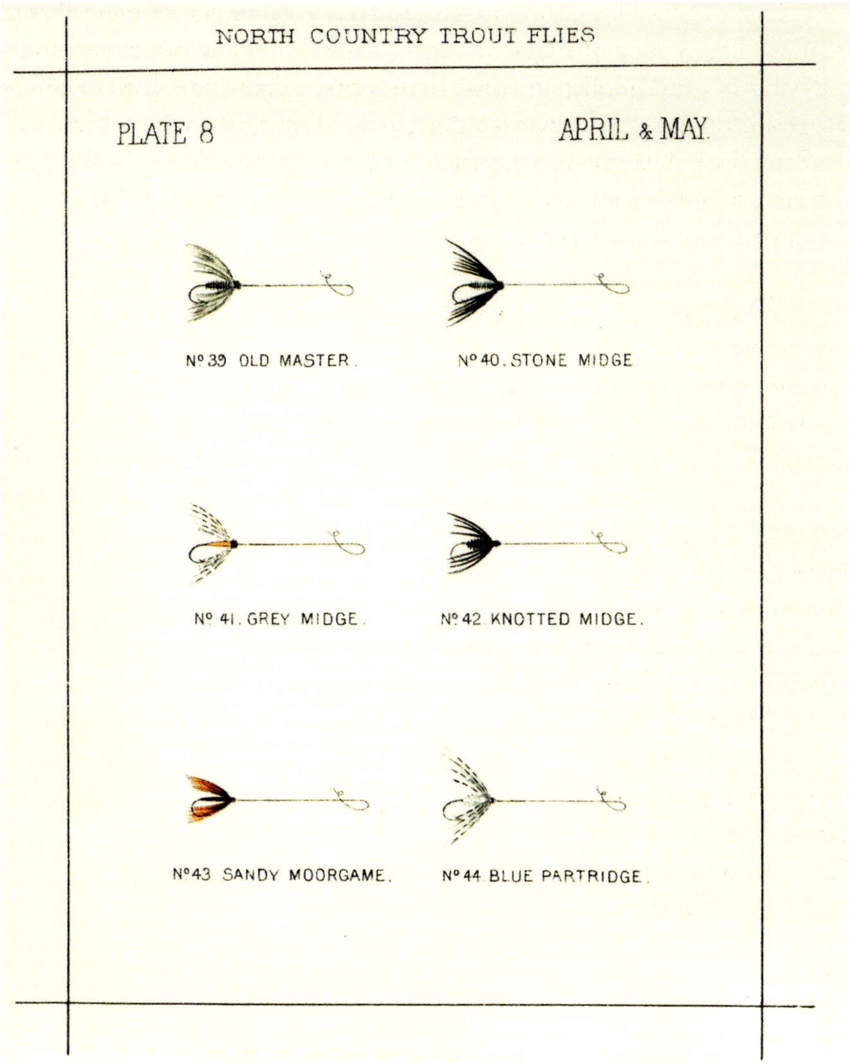

Plate 8 from T. E. Pritt's *Yorkshire Wet Flies* – note that in the 1880s, fly hooks were eyeless.

Blue Partridge

Hook: Size 14.
Thread: Blue.
Body: Tying thread, dubbed with a little blue lamb's wool.
Hackle (called 'Wings' by Pritt): Partridge back.

These styles of flies reached maturity in the Victorian era, at the height of British imperial power. As they travelled the empire, so the British took with them the brown trout that they loved to catch back at home – and to catch those trout they took their flies.

Captain G. D. Hamilton first visited New Zealand in about 1845 and he moved there in about 1860 to farm sheep, turning 40,000 acres of virgin country into 'English grasses'. In his book *Trout-Fishing and Sport in Maoriland* (1904), Hamilton relates how he stocked the river that flowed near to where he settled in the early 1870s, with brown trout. Ova were transported by ship on ice halfway round the world – with their journey completed on the backs of pack-mules. Others stocked the watercourses of New Zealand with rainbow trout from North America. Some of these stocked fish became migratory, swimming down to the ocean and returning to spawn as sea trout; others migrated into big lakes. The trout grew much bigger in New Zealand waters than they did back at home: 'It may be taken as a rule that all streams with sufficient water contain some exceptionally large trout, up to 8lb., 10lb., 11lb., and 12lb. in weight.'

Hooks for tying flies were imported from England, but the hooks sent out to New Zealand were not strong enough to hold these big trout. So Hamilton wrote to manufacturers in the then capital of hook-making, Redditch, requesting they make especially strong hooks for him. These, together with the five fly patterns that Hamilton came up with, were all that anyone needed to catch New Zealand trout.

> These flies are commonly known as red hackle, hare's-ear, black hackle, black spider, hare's-ear spider.
>
> No. 1, red hackle, light-brown mallard wing, yellow-silk body, is the most easily seen when the water is discoloured, and therefore best for use at that time.
>
> No.2, turn of brown partridge hackle, hare's-ear body, light woodcock wing, put together with yellow silk: A killing fly when the weather is clear and low.
>
> No. 3, black hackle, grouse wing, brown-silk body, put together with brown silk: Easily seen when the water is clear and low, and kills well then.
>
> No. 4, spider, black hackle, tied with brown silk, brown-silk body: Easily seen when the water is clear and low. A good fly to use as a tail fly when the trout are getting into high condition and shy, and when there is bright sunshine.
>
> No. 5, spider, brown partridge hackle, hare's-ear body, put together with yellow silk: Very killing, when the water is clear and low, among high-conditioned and shy trout. Used as a tail fly this is perhaps the most reliable of the whole, particularly among large trout of 2lb. and upwards.

Colour plate from Captain Hamilton's *Trout-Fishing and Sport in Maoriland*, showing his five fly patterns.

A similar influx of fly fishers occurred into the United States and Canada, though, because they had their own indigenous rainbow and cutthroat trout in the west, and a char that the colonists thought was a trout and that they called brook trout, the introduction of brown trout was later than many other parts of the English-speaking world. The first arrived in about 1880 – the fly-fishers had arrived much earlier. Paul Schullery provides excellent evidence that Richard Franck, author of *Northern Memoirs*, lived (and fly-fished?) in the United States between 1660 and 1687 (see below). Schullery also showed how many others took fly-fishing to the New World and that, until the second quarter of the nineteenth century, most fly-fishing tackle was imported from Britain. But then, because of the vast array of river, lake and saltwater habitats; the far larger number of fish species that can be caught with artificial flies; and a wealth of natural materials available for tying flies – fly-fishing and fly-tying in North America mushroomed. And because fly-fishers in North America have never been as constrained as fly-fishers in Europe (and especially England) by rules about what flies can or cannot be used, they eventually developed flies and techniques that could hardly have originated elsewhere. Can you imagine fishing a sculpin or minnow imitation on an English chalk stream? Or one of Gary LaFontaine's Deep Sparkle Caddis Pupae (see p. 97) on the Derbyshire Wye, where the rule is 'dry fly only' and even emergers are banned?

Thus far we have looked mainly at flies that imitate insects; flies that are designed for catching trout. Now we will look to some of the earliest flies for catching other species of fish.

EARLY ATLANTIC SALMON FLIES

It was only when the reel and rods with rings became readily available in the second half of the seventeenth century that fly-fishing for salmon became really possible. With a fixed, short line attached to the end of the rod, playing a salmon would have been well nigh impossible. Leonard Mascall pointed out the problem in *A booke of fishing with Hooke and Line* (1590): 'The Salmon is a gentle fish, but he is cumbrous to take.' Gervase Markham agreed, in *The Second Booke of the English Husbandman* (1614):

> Now, lastly, as touching the angling for Salmon, albe he is a fish which in truth is unfit for your Travaile, both because hee is too huge and cumbersome, as also in that he naturally delighteth to lie in the bottomes of the great deepe Rivers, and as neare as may bee in the midst of the Channell.

But with a rod and reel, a longer cast could be made and a large fish could be allowed to make long runs and tire itself out.

In his *Barker's Delight, or The Art of Angling* (1659), Thomas Barker described a rod with a ring at the tip, the reel and how to tie a salmon fly. The fly, he wrote, 'must be made of a large hook, which hook must carry six wings, or four at least'. The fly also had a palmered body hackle. Other than that, Barker's salmon fly was really an overgrown trout fly.

Colonel Robert Venables was perhaps the first person who could really be described as a salmon angler. He fought in the English Civil Wars and then, in July 1649, was sent by Oliver Cromwell, leader of the Parliamentarians, to subdue the Confederate–Royalist alliance in Ireland. From October 1649 to 1654 Venables was governor of Ulster and he took

The title page from *The Experienc'd Angler*. This was among the first published illustrations – albeit poor – of the artificial fly.

A plate of salmon flies from G. C. Bainbridge's *The Fly Fisher's Guide*. Besides dragonflies, it was thought that salmon ate other bright insects, like wasps and butterflies!

Herbert Howard, a renowned angler, fly-dresser and angling historian, states that he has seen a family Bible which belonged to a Newfoundland family named Stirling in which are handwritten entries dating back between the years 1720 and 1896. One of the entries, dating 1795, described a hair-winged fly called the Red Cow Fly and says that salmon were caught on it.

Red Cow Fly

Tying not known, alas. Perhaps a body of red cow underfur, and the wings from guard hairs or tail?

Although hair-winged flies had probably been in use for some time, this is the first published use of hair for winging flies.

ANCIENT PIKE FLIES

Like trout and salmon, pike are great fish to catch on rod and line, and (despite the many bones) they are very good to eat. So it is not surprising that early attempts were made to catch them on 'flies'. The earliest was a fifteenth-century fly from Bavaria (see p. 15).

PIKE FLY

> The fly must be larger than even those used for salmon; it must be made with a double hook formed of one piece of wire fastened to a good link of gimp; it must be composed of very gaudy materials, such as the feathers of the gold and common pheasant, peacock, mallard etc. With the brown and softest part of bear's fur, a little dark reddish mohair, with yellow and green mohair for the body, and four or five turns of gold twist slanting round the body; the head must be formed of a little

dark brown mohair, some gold twist, and two small black beads for the eyes; the body about three inches long, and made rough, full, and round; the wings not parted, but to stand upright on the back, and some smaller feathers continued thence all down the back to the end of the tail, so that where you finish they may be left a little longer than the hook, and the whole to be about the thickness of a tom-tit, and near three inches long.

Alexander Mackintosh, *The Driffield Angler*, 1806.

ANOTHER PIKE FLY

... pike rise tolerably freely to flys dressed very largely & of gaudy peacock feathers, sho'd be made up on large double, or even sets of hooks.

The Journal of A. J. Lane (1843, published by Medlar Press 1995).

ANOTHER PIKE FLY

... large size, with a pair of big, outspreading hooks, the body composed of divers coloured pig's wool, blue, yellow, and green as thick as a man's

little finger, with a large heron's or other hackle for legs; for the wings two eyes from a peacock's tail, with a few showy hackles, wide gold or silver foil, and a tail of various coloured hackles; at the head two glass beads are strung on to represent eyes. This which is more like a good sized hummingbird than anything else, is cast and worked like a fly.

Francis Francis, *A Book of Angling*, 1867.

THE FIRST SALTWATER FLIES

Flies dressed specially to catch saltwater fish are as old as the most ancient flies described here for catching freshwater fish. Again, we go back to Claudius Aelianus, in the second century AD (see also p. 14): '... one of the crew sitting at the stern [of the fishing boat] lets down on either side of the ship lines with hooks. [Each hook is] wrapped in wool of Laconian red, and to each hook attached to feather of a seamew [sea gull]'.

This is a very simple fly; but it would still take mackerel, pollock and even species like bluefish and striped and sea bass.

But though these are flies for catching sea fish, they were not fly-fished, and one of the difficulties when it comes to the early days of saltwater flies and fly-fishing is differentiating between 'feathering' and 'fly-fishing'. A good instance of this is found in a book *Fly-fishing in Salt and Fresh Water*, published in 1851 anonymously (though reputedly by one Mrs Hutchinson). Five patterns are given:

Hutchinson Fly One

Tag: ½-inch-long, oval gold tinsel.
Tail: Red feather of cock-of-the-rock.
Body rear half: Red wool.
Body front half: Blue wool.
Rib: Oval gold tinsel.
Body hackle: Orange or crimson.
Wing: Underwing of cock-of-the-rock tipped white; overwing mallard dyed yellow.
Head hackle: Blue jay.

Hutchinson Fly Two

Tag: ½-inch-long, oval gold tinsel.
Tail: Strips of red, orange, blue and green swan.
Body rear half: Red wool.
Body front half: Blue wool.
Rib: Oval gold tinsel.
Body hackle: Orange or crimson.
Wing: As tail, with white-tipped brown turkey over.
Head hackle: 0.

Hutchinson Fly Three

Tag: ½-inch-long, oval gold tinsel.
Tail: Strips of scarlet and blue swan and silver pheasant dyed orange.
Body rear half: Red wool.
Body front half: Blue wool.
Rib: Oval gold tinsel.
Body hackle: Orange or crimson.

Wing: Scarlet, blue and orange swan, with peacock over.
Head hackle: 0.

Hutchinson Fly Four

Tail: Strips of mixed colours of swan.
Body rear half: Red wool.
Body front half: Blue wool.
Rib: Oval gold tinsel.
Body hackle: Orange or crimson.
Wing: Mallard dyed green.
Head hackle: Blue hackle.

Hutchinson Fly Five

Tag: 2 Turns Of Gold Twist.
Tail: Blue Cock Hackle.
Body: Red Wool.
Rib: Oval Gold Tinsel.
Body hackle: Red.
Wing: Red, Yellow And Green Dyed Mallard.
Head hackle: Guinea fowl (gallina).

These five flies are quite gaudy and clearly reflect the then new craze of tying gaudy flies that was engulfing the salmon fly at the same time (p. 298). But how were they fished? Mrs Hutchinson gives us a clue:

> Most capital sea fly-fishing can be obtained off the coast of Connemara, viz., in Bertraghboy Bay, at the Skyard Rocks, at Deer Island, and off the Isle of Mweenish and the Isle of Arran. The whiting, pollack [sic] that are to be met there, take a large gaudy fly boldly. I have with a fly taken some in those parts, as large as nine pounds. I use seven flies at once, and have frequently taken seven fish at the same time.

Mrs Hutchinson was 'feathering', lowering her line with seven flies and jigging them up and down with the aid of a heavy weight. Her flies were not 'cast' as we fly-fishers cast a fly. It is still possible to catch several fish (such as pollock and mackerel) at once on a multi-fly jigged rig. But there is no need for such complicated flies when jigging or feathering.

It was also the method used by Sanez Reguart, *Diccionario Historico de las Artes de Pesca Nacionales* (1795), but his flies were dyed feathers (coloured hackles) tied on weighted (leaded) double hooks.

Theophilus South (real name Edward Chitty) did come up with a most simple fly that may have been cast in his *The Fly Fisher's Text Book* (1841):

Herring Fry

> The fly is a white feather, projecting considerably over the hook, and it resembles the herring fry, of which both mackerel and Pollock are very fond.

James Wilson gave a fly, which could be used today for catching sea trout, in *The Rod and the Gun* (1844).

Sea Trout Fly

> … a singularly successful fly for sea-trout, large or small, may be made with silver tinsel enwrapping the whole body from head to heel … the wings, of a narrow elongated form, composed either of pure white or pale grey [hackles], or a mixture of both.

Try that on a big hook or tandem mount instead of a Grizzle Sunk Lure (p. 357).

TWO FLIES FOR STRIPED BASS

> None is more killing than an orange body with peacock and bluejay wings and black hackle legs.
>
> Frank Forester (real name Henry William Herbert), *Fish and Fishing*, 1859.

> The best fly [for striped bass] is that with the scarlet ibis and white feathers mixed.
>
> R. B. Roosevelt, *Game Fishes of the North*, 1862.

But note: these may have been fished in rivers when the striped bass made their spawning runs.

In conclusion, over 100 years ago it was questionable whether it was necessary to have specific fly patterns for saltwater fishing (and black bass fishing), certainly in and around Florida. James Henshall (*Camping and Cruising in Florida*, 1884) advised that:

> Bright feathers are easily procured in Florida from the numerous gay-plumaged birds, so that the angler will be at no loss for materials for tying his flies. Two flies I remember as being particularly taking: one with upper wing of white ibis and lower wings of the mottled feather of chuck-will's-widow, another with top wings of white egret and lower ones of pink curlew [roseate spoonbill].

Not today, they aren't!

North Country Spiders or Soft-Hackled Wet Flies

> Old flies often seem to fade from popularity not so much because they lose their effectiveness as because they are replaced by more fashionable new flies, whether the new flies have proven more effective or not.
>
> Paul Schullery, *American Fly Fishing: a History*, 1987.

This category of fly evolved at least 200 years ago on the rivers of northern England and southern Scotland. They were first catalogued by T. E. Pritt (*Yorkshire Wet Flies*, 1885), later by Harfield H. Edmonds and Norman N. Lee (*Brook and River Trouting*, 1916) and by W. S. Roger Fogg (*The Art of the Wet Fly*, 1979). That these ancient flies travel well is borne out by three books about them by the American writer Sylvester Nemes: *The Soft-Hackled Fly* (1975), *The Soft-Hackled Fly Addict* (1981) and *Two Centuries of Soft-hackled Flies* (2004).

These are very simple flies to tie, many having a body of only tying thread (use a round thread – not flat thread, nor floss silk); if using real silk thread (e.g. Pearsall's Gossamer), wax the thread with solid tying wax. As one name for these flies indicates, the hackle is a soft one, usually from a game-bird, sometimes a hen barnyard fowl. Game-bird hackles usually have a very thick stalk, so they are tied in by the feather tip (stroke the hackle fibres back to expose the tip). The hackle should be sparse: two or two-and-a-half turns at most.

Hooks: wet fly, sizes 14–18, unless otherwise stated.

They are still very effective flies to use, in both rivers and lakes anywhere in the world, when trout, char, grayling or other fish are feeding on flies or emergers at, or close to the water surface. There are many recorded instances when these have out-fished more precise imitations of what the fish were eating. In rivers fish 'dead-drift', in lakes cast out and tweak or work back slowly.

SIMPLE HACKLE PATTERNS

In these the body consists of tying thread, wound from behind the hook eye to the end of the hook shank and then back to behind the hook eye in touching turns. Sometimes there is a rib, or a rib is optional.

Golden Plover & Orange

Thread: Orange.
Hackle: Golden plover upperwing covert, with gold markings.

Orange Partridge

Thread: Orange (traditionally a plain orange, though recently hot orange has been used).
Rib: Fine gold wire (optional).
Hackle: Brown speckled feather from the neck of a grey (English) partridge.

Probably the most famous of these flies, the Orange Partridge is a great catcher of fish and has even been known to catch salmon!

Greenwell's Glory (Spider Version)

Thread: Yellow waxed with dark cobbler's wax.
Rib: Fine gold wire.
Hackle: Furnace or coch-y-bonddu hen (black centred with natural red sides).

The original Greenwell's Glory, tied by James Wright for Canon William Greenwell in May 1854, had an upright wing of hen blackbird secondary feather fibres. It fishes better without the wing.

The Greenwell's Glory also makes a splendid dry fly for fishing during hatches of olive duns. Add tails (a few fibres from a cock furnace hackle) and use several turns of cock hackle instead of the 2½ turns of hen hackle.

The following five patterns are summer patterns, for when light-coloured flies are on the water.

YELLOW PARTRIDGE
Thread: Yellow.
Rib: Fine silver wire (optional).
Hackle: Grey speckled feather from the lower part of the neck of a grey (English) partridge.

LIGHT SNIPE
Thread: Primrose.
Hackle: Snipe underwing covert.

SNIPE BLOA
Thread: Straw.
Hackle: Snipe underwing covert.

POULT BLOA
Thread: Yellow.
Hackle: Grey underwing covert of a young (= poult) red grouse.

LIGHT WOODCOCK
Thread: Yellow.
Hackle: Woodcock underwing covert.

The following four flies are outstanding during a hatch of black midges or smuts, or during a fall of black land-bred flies such as black gnats.

BLACK GNAT
Thread: Black, brown, grey or olive.
Hackle: Feather from the neck or back of the starling.

Black Spider
Thread: Black or red.
Hackle: Black hen.

Williams's Favourite
Thread: Black.
Rib: Fine oval silver tinsel.
Hackle: Black hen.

Invented by the father of A. Courtney Williams, author of *A Dictionary of Trout Flies*, this can be turned into a very useful dry fly by the addition of tails (a few fibres of black cock hackle) and using a black cock instead of hen as hackle.

Ruz-Du
Thread: Black.
Body: Rear half orange thread, front half black thread.
Hackle: Black hen.

This is an extremely useful wet fly in rivers and lakes during a hatch of black midges. It comes from Brittany and was devised by André Ragot.

Snipe & Purple
Thread: Purple.
Hackle: Snipe upperwing covert.

Though originally used to match very dark upwinged flies in rivers, this is a most useful lake fly during a midge hatch.

Water Cricket
Thread: Yellow.
Rib: Black thread.
Hackle: Feather from the back of a starling.

A very useful pattern when strong winds are blowing a wide range of land-bred insects (beetles, dung flies, leaf hoppers etc.) onto the water.

DUBBED BODY PATTERNS

There are two types of dubbing: light and not light. In the latter, the usual method of dubbing, the thread becomes lost in the dubbing. In light, sometimes called 'touch', dubbing only the merest wisp of fur is used so that, when the dubbed thread is wound along the hook shank, every turn of thread is still visible through the haze of dubbed fur. To help keep the fur in place, use a solid rather than a liquid wax.

Waterhen Bloa
Thread: Yellow.
Body fur: Mole.
Hackle: Waterhen underwing covert.

Outstanding during a hatch of olives.

Snipe Bloa
Thread: Straw.
Body fur: Mole.
Hackle: Snipe underwing covert.

Good during a hatch of paler upwinged flies.

The following two wet flies are useful during a hatch of caddisflies, when the pupae are at or close to the surface, of a summer evening.

Woodcock & Hare's Lug
Thread: Orange.
Body fur: Hare's ear.
Hackle: Woodcock upper wing covert.

Hare's Lug And Plover
Thread: Primrose.
Body fur: Hare's ear.
Hackle: Golden plover upper wing covert.

Dark Watchet

Thread: Orange and purple (see below).
Body fur: Mole.
Hackle: Jackdaw throat or coot upperwing covert (otherwise, any small black soft hackle)

Use orange tying thread, tie in a separate length of purple, so that the two are tied in together at the end of the hook shank. Dub one of the threads very lightly. Then twist the two threads together and wind up towards the eye to create a segmented body. Cut off the excess purple and use the orange thread to tie in the hackle and finish off the fly.

Highly recommended during a hatch of darker water-bred flies, or a fall of dark land-bred flies.

HERL-HEADED FLIES

In these, the fly is completed with a couple of turns of herl in front of the hackle.The three described were devised as imitations of small stoneflies. They are most effective in fast, turblent streams.

Dark Needle

Thread: Orange, waxed so that it becomes quite dark.
Hackle: Tawny (brown) owl upperwing covert.
Head: Peacock herl.

Light Needle

Thread: Red, waxed so that it a deep red.
Hackle: Snipe underwing covert.
Head: Peacock herl.

Winter Brown

Thread: Orange, waxed so that it becomes quite dark.
Hackle: Woodcock underwing covert.
Head: Peacock herl.

THORAX SPIDERS

These are the latest soft-hackled wet flies to be devised, being pioneered by Harold Howorth and Frederick Mold in the 1940s and 1950s. The addition of a thorax gives the fly more of an insect profile. The first two are excellent during a hatch of dark midges or a fall of small black land-breds (e.g. black gnats).

BLACK MAGIC

Thread: Black.
Body: Tying thread.
Under thorax: Fine copper wire wound to create a small ball (optional, but is does help the fly penetrate the surface film).
Thorax: Peacock herl.
Hackle: Black hen.

HENTHORNE PURPLE

Thread: Purple.
Body: Tying thread.
Thorax: Peacock herl.
Hackle: Mallard upperwing covert.

This fly usually fishes in the surface film, held there by the mallard hackle. It is therefore a simple emerger pattern.

Trout appear to love eating tiny *Caenis* and trichos, but good imitations of these must be tied on very small hooks (see p. 171). Tie the following in size 18; it will catch fish eating those minute flies (or try GREY DUSTER, p. 137).

WHITE PTARMIGAN

Thread: White.
Body: Tying thread.
Thorax: Peacock herl.
Hackle: Upperwing covert of a white, winter-plumaged, ptarmigan (any small, soft white hackle will do).

Dave Hughes suggested giving the ORANGE PARTRIDGE a thorax; there is no reason why other soft-hackled spider patterns should not be given a thorax of dubbed fur or peacock herl.

Thorax Orange Partridge
Thread: Orange.
Body: Tying thread.
Thorax: Hare's ear.
Hackle: Brown speckled partridge.

SPIDER SEDGES (CADDISFLIES)

Most adult caddisflies are some shade of brown and the following two patterns will still deceive fish during a hatch or when the females have returned to lay their eggs on or below the water surface (note that many female caddisflies swim down under the surface to lay their eggs).

Dark Sedge
Hook: Wet fly, sizes 12–14.
Thread: Yellow.
Body: Dubbed medium brown fur.
Hackle: Tawny (brown) owl upperwing covert (a long-fibred brown hen is substitute).
Head: 2–3 turns cock pheasant tail herl.

Grannom or Greentail
Hook: Wet fly, sizes 12–14.
Thread: Grey.
Body: Two turns of green silk at rear, then hare's ear.
Hackle: Brown speckled partridge.

Female grannom carry a green sac of eggs at the tip of their abdomen, hence 'Greentail'.

THE RIDDLE OF THE MARCH BROWN

The real March Brown is a fairly scarce European fly (it occurs only on very rough, rocky rivers), though it has many near relations in North America and Europe. However the duns of most of these rarely occur on the water, for their nymphs crawl ashore for the dun emergence. So they usually do not figure highly in the trout diet. Nevertheless, the artificial, soft-hackled wet March Brown is an excellent fish catcher for, as G. E. M. Skues put it, the March Brown, 'is an excellent fly, and as generally tied, quite a poor imitation of the natural fly and quite a passable one of almost anything else'. It works in lakes (the real fly is a river insect) and rivers, for a wide range of fish.

March Brown
Hook: Wet fly, size 10–14.
Thread: Orange.
Tails: 2–3 fibres speckled partridge tail.
Body: Dubbed mix hare's ear and yellow mohair.
Hackle: Brown speckled partridge.
Wing: Bunch of fibres from speckled partridge tail or hen pheasant tail (optional).

Silver March Brown
As above, but body flat silver tinsel.

This tying is a very good fly for sea trout, salmon, when the rivers are low in summer, and large lake trout. It could be taken for a small fish (e.g. fry or minnow).

BUSTARDS

Though they are not soft-hackled flies, Bustards have the same origin. It is almost 200 years since Bustards first appeared in print (in G. C. Bainbridge, *The Fly Fisher's Guide*, 1816). They were devised for only a few trout rivers in north-west England, and yet they are great catchers of trout, anywhere in the trout world. They should be fished, in rivers, in high summer when the river is low and the weather hot, through the dead of night (provided the law permits night fishing). Then, large trout that have been hiding away by day emerge and seek food. Fish a strong leader. Cast the fly under the far bank and tweak the fly back. Takes are often explosive!

White Bustard
Hook: Wet fly, sizes 10–12.
Thread: White.

Body: White wool or chenille.
Hackle: White hen.
Wing: Palest barn owl wing (white goose as substitute).

Red Bustard
Hook: Wet fly, sizes 10–12.
Thread: Black.
Body: Red wool or chenille.
Hackle: Red hen.
Wing: Dyed red barn owl wing (white goose dyed red as substitute).

Brown Bustard
Hook: Wet fly, sizes 10–12.
Thread: Brown.
Body: Brown wool or chenille.
Hackle: Brown hen.
Wing: Darkest tawny (brown) owl wing (white goose dyed brown as substitute).

The following is a fairly modern fly, having been invented (or perhaps, more accurately, publicised) by T. C. Ivens in *Still Water Fly-Fishing* (1952). 'This fly', stated Ivens, 'is the best all-rounder in my box.' It will catch trout, and other lake fish, that are eating floating snails (they crawl along the underside of the surface film, sucking down trapped microscopic algae), black caddis pupae (on the surface at the point of hatch), and a wide range of land-bred insects from larger black gnats to black beetles (on some lakes over 90 per cent of surface foods are land-bred insects). The Black & Peacock Spider seems to have gone out of fashion in recent years (why?), but in the 1970s it was so well known that two fly-fishers, seeing trout feeding like pigs on a huge fall of black heather flies, reported that: 'There was a massive fall of Black and Peacock Spiders!'

Black & Peacock Spider
Hook: Wet fly, sizes 10–14.
Thread: Black.
Body: Peacock herl.
Rib: Fine or medium oval silver tinsel (optional).
Hackle: Black good-quality hen or henny-cock.

Nymphs

> With the actual natural nymph to be represented floating under one's eye … the length of the hook's shank necessary to give room for the thorax and abdomen can be exactly ascertained … In the representation, it is well to get the actual outline and taper as correct as possible.
>
> G. E. M. Skues, *Nymph Fishing for Chalk Stream Trout*, 1939.

Three major groups of aquatic trout foods have an incomplete life cycle consisting of a egg, followed by a nymph, followed by the adult: the upwinged flies (or mayflies), or Ephemeroptera; stoneflies, or Plecoptera; dragonflies and damselflies, or Odonata. The nymph is the growing stage, so that after hatching from the egg it is minute, whereas just before the adult emerges the fully grown nymph may be very large. Some *Ephemera* and *Hexagenia* mayfly nymphs attain length up to 1½ inches, or 4 cm, whereas the nymph of the huge stonefly *Pteronarcys calfornica*, of America's West, can exceed 2 inches, or 5 cm.

One feature of many nymphs is a slender abdomen and a thicker, rounder thorax. Thus the tying of the body is usually separated into these two components. Nymphs also develop wing buds or wing cases as they grow, and in the final stage the wing cases are very prominent and usually a darker colour than the body colour. They are often included in the tying of artificial nymphs.

While less bulky nymphs often sink fairly quickly, larger ones do not. It is therefore essential to have some weighting (provided the rules permit the used of weighted flies). If lead is permitted, wind fine lead wire down the hook shank in touching turns in larger nymphs, down the front half of the hook shank (i.e. under the thorax) in smaller patterns, or lash two or more strands of lead wire along the hook shank. If lead is not permitted, use tungsten or copper wire. Another alternative is to have a drilled metal bead fixed in place behind the hook eye (tungsten, brass, or silver or gold plated). Very heavy versions may be tied with body a lead wire underbody and a metal bead head. See also Goldheads, below.

Many of the more effective nymph patterns are general patterns and could be taken by the fish for a host of nymph species. There are also many more precise imitations.

GOLDHEADS

Goldheads are gold-plated brass beads with a hole through them so that they can be slipped over the point of the hook and pushed up against the eye. A goldhead should be held in place by several turns of thread soaked with Superglue, otherwise the bead may be forced backwards by the inertial forces during casting.

Goldheads achieved prominence in the 1980s, being promoted around the world by Dutchman Theo Bakelaar. Within a decade many flies were being tied goldhead style, as well as tungstenhead and silverhead style. The beads weighted the flies and, in the gold and silver versions (now also in colours like shocking pink!), added 'flash' that was said to simulate air bubbles associated with hatching nymphs. However it is clear that Goldheads are much older. The Samurai fished with Goldheads in Japan as early as 1650, their gold bead being real gold. More recently, three Goldhead flies were discovered in a box in an English stately home in 1996 that date from the end of the nineteenth century (note that the hooks are tied to gut). These flies come from an era when goldheads are absent from fly-tying literature. These mysterious three flies are tied as follows:

FLY I

Tail: Golden pheasant crest.
Body: In five sections: peacock herl-red floss-peacock herl-red floss-peacock herl.
Hackle: Natural light red henny-cock.
Wing: 3 strands green peacock herl (there is no sign of any other wing material).
Head: Goldhead.

This fly is particularly fascinating because of its body, red floss and peacock herl. It recalls the ROYAL COACHMAN (p. 139) that was invented by American John Haily and has a body of red floss with peacock herl at front and rear. The hackle is also the same, but the rest of the fly is completely different.

Fly 2

Body: Gold bead at tip; rear fifth green peacock herl, rest orange wool.
Hackles: Dirty cream-white and ginger henny-cock, wound together.
Wing: Two cock hackles and two hen hackles, all dirty cream-white.
Head: Goldhead.

Fly 3

Body: Gold bead at tip; middle crimson; front black fine dubbing.
Hackles: Rear green; middle crimson; front black.
Wing: A natural red cock hackle tied on either side.
Head: Goldhead.

The Hare's Ear Goldhead is a typical modern goldhead dressing and may be taken by trout as freshwater shrimps (scuds) or *Gammarus*, caddis pupae and caddis larvae (uncased).

Hare's Ear Goldhead

Hook: Wet fly, sizes 10–12.
Thread: Brown.
Body: Hare's ear, dubbed a bit straggly.
Rib: Fine oval gold tinsel.
Head: Goldhead.

Many of the following nymph patterns can be modified by fixing a goldhead, silverhead or tungsten bead on the hook just behind the eye.

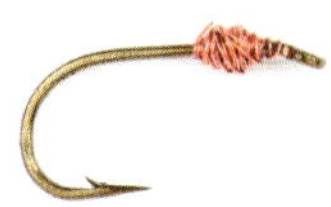

Bare Hook Nymph

Hook: Wet fly, sizes 14–16.
Thread: Red copper wire.
Body: A ball of wound copper wire behind the hook eye to simulate a thorax.

There is no simpler fly! Invented by Oliver Kite in the early 1960s, this is surprisingly effective. In one TV programme, Kite was seen to catch grayling with this fly while wearing a brown paper bag over his head! The problem is that the vast majority of fly-fishers either have no faith in such a simple tying, or they want more complex flies in their boxes.

Pheasant Tail-Less Pheasant Tail Nymph

Hook: Wet fly, sizes 14–16.
Thread: Red copper wire.
Body: Two layers of wire between eye and end of hook shank, with a built-up thorax just behind the eye.

Produced by *Field & Stream*'s Ed Zern, who noticed that a Pheasant Tail Nymph (below) that had had all the pheasant tail dressing removed by the teeth of several trout still caught fish.

The following tyings will catch trout that are feeding on many small nymphs and also on midge pupae (or 'buzzers', see pp. 109ff) in lakes. A fly devised by Malcolm Greenhalgh in Britain; the same idea was independently developed in the United States (see Two-Wire Brassie, below).

Two-Wire Nymph

Hook: Wet fly, sizes 14–16.
Thread: Fine red copper wire.
Abdomen: Tying thread.
Rib: Dark brown copper wire.
Thorax: Built-up tying thread under thorax, with dubbed hare's ear over.

Brassie

Hook: Wet fly, 12–18.
Thread: Black.
Abdomen: Red copper wire.
Thorax: Black dubbing (use a fine fur).

Devised by Ken Chandler and Tug Davenport on Colorado's South Platte River in the 1960s, the original Brassie had a short piece of black heat-shrink plastic tube for the thorax and the copper wire was also tying 'thread'. Rick Murphy, also of the South Platte River, also came up with the idea of using two colours of wire to give a segmented body in his Two-Wire Brassie.

Two-Wire Brassie

Hook: Wet fly, sizes 14–24.
Thread: Black.
Abdomen: Two wire colours to give segmentation.
Wing: Sparse, white synthetic (e.g. Saap, Z-lon, Antron).
Thorax: Peacock herl.
Head: Goldhead or silverhead (optional; not in original).

Ed Engle, who described the Two-Wire Brassie in his book *Tying Small Flies* (2004), also described John Barr's Copper John, a fly that leads on to the most famous of all nymphs. This has caught many trout, thousands of miles from its Colorado home.

Copper John

Hook: Wet fly, sizes 14–20.
Thread: Black.
Tail: 3–4 cock pheasant tail fibres.
Abdomen: Copper wire.
Wing case: Pearl Mylar or Flashabou or Crystal Hair.
Thorax: Peacock herl.
Legs: Brown speckled partridge, drake mallard breast dyed light brown, wood-duck (optional).
Head: Goldhead or silverhead.

The Pheasant Tail Nymph is probably the most famous of all the world's artificial nymphs. The original tying is by Frank Sawyer (1906–80), river keeper and author of *Nymphs and the Trout* (1958). Though originally an imitation of swimming *Baetis* nymphs in rivers, it will deceive trout that are eating any small nymph.

Pheasant Tail Nymph

Hook: Wet fly, sizes 12–18.
Thread: Copper wire (red or orange are most effective).
Underbody: Two layers of tying wire then a small ball built up under the thorax.

Tails: Tips of cock pheasant centre tail feathers.
Abdomen: Herls used to form tails, wound with the wire thread about 60 per cent up hook shank.
Thorax: As abdomen.
Wing cases: Dark parts of herls used to form tail and body, taken back and forth (two layers) over back of thorax and held in place with the trying wire.

Grey Goose Nymph

This is as Sawyer's Pheasant Tail Nymph except that grey goose herls are used. Sawyer devised this on a visit to Lapland, where he found trout feeding on summer mayfly (*Siphlonurus*) nymphs.

There are several other versions of the Pheasant Tail Nymph; the best are given below.

Pheasant Tail Nymph (Al Troth)

Hook: Wet fly, sizes 10–18.
Thread: Tan.
Tails: Tips of 3–5 cock pheasant tail fibres.
Abdomen: Wound fibres used for tails.
Rib: Fine copper wire.
Thorax: Under a ball of copper wire, with peacock herl over.
Wing cases: Dark parts of cock pheasant tail fibres.
Legs: Tips of cock pheasant tail fibres used to create wing cases.

Orange Spot Pheasant Tail Nymph

This is a similar tying, but has a thorax of fluorescent orange wool or fur and lacks legs. All fish seem very susceptible to orange, especially in dull light conditions, and this works in dirty water and late in the evening.

Pheasant Tail Nymph (Chris Hosker)

Hook: Wet fly, sizes 14–16.
Thread: Brown.

Tails: Tips of 4–6 cock pheasant tail fibres.
Abdomen: Cock pheasant tail.
Rib: Fine gold wire.
Thorax: Pink synthetic fur with some sparkle (e.g. Ice Dub).
Head: Gold head.

Chris uses this in cold water or in winter, when fish tend to be dour.

Pheasant Tail Nymph (Randall Kaufmann)

Hook: Wet fly or straight shank nymph hook, sizes 10–18.
Thread: Brown.
Tails: Tips of 4–6 cock pheasant tail fibres.
Abdomen: Cock pheasant tail.
Back: Pearl Flashabou.
Rib: Fine copper wire.
Thorax: Cock pheasant tail.
Wing cases: Pearl Flashabou.
Legs: Cock pheasant tail fibres.
Head: Copper wire or goldhead.

Pheasant Tail Nymph (Arthur Cove)

Hook: Nymph, sizes 8–14.
Thread: Brown.
Abdomen: Cock pheasant tail fibres.
Rib: Oval gold tinsel.
Thorax: Rabbit fur.
Wing cases: Cock pheasant tail fibres.

Cove fished this in trout lakes, at the end of a very long leader, slowly inching the nymph back close to the bottom. As in all nymph fishing, the end of the floating fly line must be heavily greased so that it floats and that takes (a twitch, or stop or dipping under of the floating tip) can immediately be noticed and the hook set.

Some natural fly-tying materials seem to have a magical property that attracts fish. One is fur from a hare's ear – the hare in question being the European brown hare *Lepus europaeus*.

Hare's Ear Nymph

Hook: Wet fly or nymph, sizes 6–16 (mostly 12–16).
Thread: Brown.
Tails: Sparse bunch of natural red (brown) or furnace hen hackle fibres, or few guard hairs from hare's mask.
Abdomen: Hare's ear.
Rib: Oval gold tinsel.
Thorax: Mix of hare's ear and mask, including plenty of guard hairs.
Wing cases: Grey goose or brown turkey quill slip.
Legs: A few guard hairs teased from the thorax with a dubbing needle.

Randall Kaufmann suggested three modifications to the basic Hare's Ear Nymph in *Tying Nymphs* (1994):

(a) Flashback Hare's Ear Nymph has wing cases of pearl Flashabou.
(b) Goldhead Hare's Ear has a goldhead in front of the dressing.
(c) Flashback Rubber Legs Hare's Ear has two rubber legs for tails, two rubber legs on either side of the thorax, and pearl Flashabou wing cases.

A

B

C

Red Fox Squirrel Nymph

Hook: Nymph, sizes 10–18.
Thread: Black.
Tails: Sparse tuft of guard hairs from the back of a red fox squirrel.
Abdomen: Fine red-buff fur from the belly of the red fox squirrel.
Rib: Fine oval gold tinsel (optional).
Thorax: Darker fur from the back of a red fox squirrel, including plenty of guard hairs.
Wing cases: Dark brown turkey tail.
Legs: Brown speckled partridge, 1 turn (optional).

Designed by Dave Whitlock, this is an essential nymph that could be taken for a wide range of aquatic invertebrates.

Mick's Pre-Emerger

Hook: Nymph, sizes 10–16.
Thread: Black.
Tails: Few fibres natural dark red (brown) cock hackle.
Body: Mix of 50:50 dark-brown and fiery-brown seal's fur (or substitute).
Rib: Fine copper wire.
Wing case: Black raffine.

A Mick Hall fly from Victoria, Australia, this is a useful pattern in rivers and lakes throughout the world when dark nymphs are moving to the surface or the shore to hatch into the adult flying stage. The next fly, also by Mick Hall, is what often typifies a great fishing fly. It matches nothing in particular, but might be taken by trout as a caddis larva, stonefly or mayfly nymph, small dark fry, etc.

Mick's Scruffy

Hook: Long shank nymph, sizes 12–14.
Thread: Black.
Tail: Bunch black squirrel tail hairs.
Body: Mix of olive and black rabbit fur.
Head: Chartreuse glass bead (slide this in place at the start).

Muskrat Nymph

Hook: Nymph, sizes 12–16.
Thread: Black
Tails: 2 brown goose biots (keep separate with a tiny ball of dubbing).
Abdomen: Muskrat.
Thorax: Fine black dubbing (e.g. rabbit or synthetic).
Head: Goldhead.

This is suggestive of a small stonefly nymph.

'Olives' and olive nymphs are important in all cool rivers and lakes, for these waters are habitat for many smaller species of upwinged flies (mayflies) that are some shade of that colour. The following are four typical olive tyings.

Olive Nymph

Hook: Nymph, sizes 12–14.
Thread: Olive.
Tails: 4–5 fibres drake mallard breast feather dyed olive.
Abdomen: Fine olive dubbing (e.g. rabbit).
Rib: Yellow floss.
Thorax: Hare's ear.
Head: Goldhead (optional).

PVC Nymph

Hook: Wet fly, sizes 12–16.
Thread: Brown.
Tails: Tips of 3 olive or brown goose herls.

Underbody: Fine copper wire.
Abdomen: Olive or brown goose herls, from tail.
Over-abdomen: 1/8 inch-wide strip cut from clear polythene bag.
Thorax: Olive of brown herls, from abdomen.
Wing cases: 4–6 cock pheasant tail fibres.

This is a modification of John Goddard's PVC Nymph (the original used dyed condor herls, that are now not readily available).

Dark Olive

Hook: Wet fly, sizes 14–16.
Thread: Yellow, well waxed with brown cobbler's wax.
Tails: 3 fibres guinea fowl (gallina) dyed olive.
Body: Dark olive seal's fur, tapering from tail to a pronounced thorax.
Rib: Fine old wire.
Hackle and wing cases: Bunch dark blue dun hackle fibres.

This is a very old tying by G. E. M. Skues, and dates from the first half of the twentieth century. Skues is considered the 'father' of nymph imitation and fishing.

Callibaetis/Baetis Fur Nymph

Hook: Nymph, sizes 12–18.
Thread: Olive.
Tails: Few fibres speckled brown partridge, dyed olive.
Abdomen: Fine olive fur (synthetic or natural e.g. rabbit).
Thorax: As abdomen.
Wing cases: Cock pheasant tail fibres or quill slip from grey goose.

The next two flies were designed by Chris Hosker for fishing deep in very dark or cold fast water. Chris uses them to great effect, catching grayling with them through winter.

Black Bead Baetis Nymph

Hook: Wet fly, sizes 12–16.
Thread: Brown.
Tails: Few fibres brown speckled partridge hackle dyed olive.
Abdomen: Heron herl dyed olive (or substitute).

Rib: Fine gold wire.
Thorax: Hare's ear.
Head: Black tungsten bead.

Green Bead Baetis Nymph

Hook: Wet fly, sizes 12–16.
Thread: Brown.
Tails: Few fibres brown speckled partridge hackle.
Abdomen: Brown herl (e.g. dyed goose).
Rib: Fine silver wire.
Thorax: Hare's ear.
Head: Fluorescent green tungsten bead.

Compara-Nymph

Hook: Nymph, sizes 12–18.
Thread: Grey.
Tails: 3 fibres drake mallard flank feather.
Abdomen: Rabbit underfur.
Thorax: As abdomen.
Wing cases: Grey goose quill slip.
Legs: Fibres of grey speckled partridge.

This pattern is by Al Caucci and Bob Nastasi, authors of *Comparahatch* (1973) and *Hatches* (1975).

The following five excellent catchers of trout and other nymph-eating fish utilise another magical natural material, peacock herl. See also: Black & Peacock Spider, p. 54. They are 'suggestive' of things like stonefly and stone-crawler upwinged fly nymphs, and the fact that trout often take them eagerly makes them good fishing flies.

Peacock Herl Nymph (Dave Hughes)

Hook: Nymph, sizes 8–14.
Thread: Black.
Tails: 0.
Body: Peacock herl.

Legs: Black hen hackle, either 1 turn or a bunch of fibres tied false.
Head: Black ostrich herl.

Prince Nymph

Hook: Nymph, sizes 10–16.
Thread: Black.
Tails: 2 brown goose biots, kept separate by a tiny ball of fine brown dubbing.
Body: Peacock herl.
Rib: Fine oval gold tinsel.
Hackle: Short-fibred brown hen, 2 turns.
Wings: 2 white goose biots, tied low over body.

Zug Bug

Hook: Nymph, sizes 10–16.
Thread: Black.
Tails: Tips of three green peacock sword feathers.
Abdomen: Peacock herl.
Rib: Fine oval silver tinsel.
Thorax: Peacock herl.
Wing cases: Slip of wood duck flank feather (or drake mallard flank dyed wood duck).
Hackle: Speckled brown hen or partridge, 2 turns.

Stimulator

Hook: Nymph, sizes 8–12.
Thread: Dark brown.
Tail: Bunch olive or olive-brown marabou.
Body: Peacock herl.
Body hackle: Natural red (brown) henny-cock, palmered in open turns.
Rib: Copper wire.

Kakahi Queen Nymph

Hook: Nymph, sizes 12–14.
Thread: Brown.
Tails: Tuft brown hen hackle fibres.
Abdomen: Peacock herl.
Thorax: Burgundy (brown) floss.
Wing cases: Dark mallard quill slip.
Legs: Two small bunches brown hen hackle fibres.

Although the KAKAHI QUEEN NYMPH was designed by Norman Marsh (in *Trout Stream Insects of New Zealand*) to match the spiny-gilled mayfly *Coloburiscus humeralis*, it is a good all-round catcher of trout elsewhere.

AUSTRALIAN HAIR NYMPH

Hook: Nymph, sizes 12–16.
Thread: Brown.
Tail: 4–5 fibres speckled brown partridge.
Body: Rabbit underfur tied slender.
Rib: Fine oval silver tinsel.
Thorax: Hare's mask.
Wing cases: Slip from speckled partridge tail.
Legs: Guard hairs teased from thorax.

TOM JONES

Hook: Nymph, sizes 8–14.
Thread: Black.
Tails: A few fibres black squirrel tail.
Body: Kangaroo, either natural buff-brown or dyed olive.
Wings: As body.

Many Australians use kangaroo fur in their flies. It is a lovely fur to use, but not often available elsewhere in the world. This fly was devised by John Lanchester to match the red fin fly in the rivers of Victoria, but should be a useful general nymph anywhere.

The following two nymphs are by Jean-Paul Pequegnot, author of *Repertoire des Mouches Artificielles Francaises* (1984).

PRECIEUSE (PRECIOUS)

Hook: Nymph, sizes 12–16.
Thread: Grey.
Tails: Grey (light-blue dun) hackle fibres.
Abdomen: Light fine grey fur (e.g. rabbit or synthetic).
Rib: Fine silver wire.
Thorax: Slightly darker grey fur.
Hackle: Dark grey, short-fibred.

Lievre Et Perdrix (Hare And Partridge)

Hook: Wet fly, sizes 12–16.
Thread: Brown.
Tails: Fibres of speckled brown partridge.
Abdomen: Buff-yellow wool.
Thorax: Hare's mask and ear, well mixed.
Wing cases: Slip from speckled partridge tail.
Legs: Speckled brown partridge fibres, tied in false.

Following, a fly by Malcolm Greenhalgh that matches a wide range of tiny upwinged fly nymphs that go under the umbrella name 'pale wateries'.

Oppossum Pale Watery Nymph

Hook: Nymph, sizes 14–18.
Thread: Brown.
Tails: 3–4 short tips of cock pheasant tail fibres.
Abdomen: Cream oppossum.
Rib: Brown thread.
Thorax: Cream oppossum.
Wing cases: Cock pheasant tail fibres (from tails).

March Brown Nymph (Poul Jorgensen)

Hook: Nymph, sizes 10–12.
Thread: Brown.
Tails: Tips of 3 cock pheasant tail fibres.
Abdomen: Amber seal's fur (or sub.) and tan fox fur well mixed.
Rib: Thick brown embroidery cotton.
Thorax: As abdomen.
Wing cases: Cock pheasant tail fibres.
Legs: Brown speckled partridge hackle tied in at base of thorax and palmered over thorax in 2–3 turns.
NOTE: Poul recommended, whenever tying dubbed fur bodies, soaking the initial turns of thread along the hook shank with cement.

American-Dane E. H. 'Polly' Rosborough was one of the great fly-tyers of the second half of the twentieth century. Of the following fly, Poul wrote: 'This is one of my favourite impressionistic nymphs.'

Rosborough wrote a book *Tying and fishing the Fuzzy Nymphs* that went through several editions (1st edn, 1965; 4th edn, 1988). Two of his greatest inventions were the NONDESCRIPT and the NEAR ENOUGH.

Both are very good catchers of trout in rivers throughout the world.

Nondescript

Hook: Nymph, sizes 8–16.
Thread: Mid brown.
Tails: Tips of 3 cock pheasant tail or red-brown marabou fibres.
Body: Deep fiery brown synthetic yarn; it must have a fuzzy outline.
Rib: Bright yellow thread.
Body hackle: Furnace cock.
Head: Black thread, very large.

The technique is to tie the tails, rib and hackle in at the end of the hook shank, take the thread back to the front of the shank and there tie in the yarn. Wind this tightly down the shank, soak this layer with tying cement, and wind the yarn back before tying this off. Soak again with cement. Now flatten the body with forceps. Wind the hackle forward in open, but close, turns; then the rib. Trim all upward- and downward-pointing hackle fibres. Again, with the cement-soaked body still sticky, flatten. Wind a large thread head and soak with cement. Flatten with forceps. The result is a crude, though effective imitation of a stone-clinging heptagenid (mayfly) nymph.

Near Enough

Hook: Nymph, sizes 8–16.
Thread: Pale grey.
Tails: Mallard drake flank fibres, dyed light tan.
Abdomen: Grey fox underfur.
Thorax: Grey fox underfur.
Wing cases: Mallard drake flank, dyed light tan.
Legs: Tips of mallard drake flank fibres, dyed light tan.

Rosborough suggested that the sides of the abdomen might be roughed up to simulate gills, but added: 'this addition does not seem to enhance its fish-taking qualities; it's a killer any way you look at it.'

The following two patterns attempt to match the pattern of coloration in most nymphs, which have a darker dorsal surface and paler ventral surface, by using a slip of dark feather fibres over the back of the paler body. This dark feather strip is held in place by the ribbing.

Poxyquill
Hook: Nymph, sizes 12–18.
Thread: As body.
Tails: Tips of 3 cock pheasant tail fibres.
Dorsal surface of abdomen: Narrow section of brown turkey tail fibres.
Abdomen: Light tan Antron.
Rib: Pearl Flashabout, 1 strand, which also ties down the turkey tail section.
Thorax: As abdomen.
Wing cases: Very dark turkey, epoxied.
Legs: Grouse hackle palmered along the thorax in three turns.
Head: As abdomen.

Shell-Back Nymph
Hook: Nymph, sizes 14–20.
Thread: Light brown or olive.
Tails: Tips of 3 cock pheasant tail fibres.
Dorsal surface of abdomen: Medium or dark dun goose quill slips.
Abdomen: Fine, light tan or light olive fur (e.g. rabbit).
Rib: Thread, darker than abdomen.
Thorax: As abdomen.
Wing cases: Goose quill slips, continued from dorsal surface of abdomen.
Legs: Brown speckled partridge or dyed olive grey partridge.

The large cream-coloured mayfly nymphs live their lives in burrows in lake- or river-beds until the moment comes when they must swim to the surface where the dun emerges. So for most of the year trout are unlikely to encounter these nymphs and, from autopsies of feeding trout, it seems that during a hatch they prefer to eat the emerged duns rather than the nymphs. Nevertheless, these large burrowing nymphs have been imitated and, remarkably, they do catch trout the year round, and in waters where the real nymph does not live!

Mayfly Nymph
Hook: Nymph, sizes 8–10.
Thread: Brown.
Tails: Tips from 4–5 cock pheasant tail fibres.
Abdomen: Cream-yellow angora wool.
Rib: Thick brown thread.

Thorax: As abdomen.
Wing cases: Cock pheasant tail fibres.
Legs: Tips of cock pheasant tail fibres used to form wing cases.
Note: This fly, designed by Richard Walker, should be heavily weighted, and fished very close to the bottom.

Real nymphs are usually well camouflaged and blend into their habitat, the bed of rivers and lakes. However, some, like the next four patterns, are much brighter and are great attractor patterns.

Orange Nymph

Hook: Nymph, sizes 12–14.
Thread: Brown.
Tails: Few fibres brown speckled partridge.
Abdomen: Orange wool or fur.
Rib: Fine silver wire.
Thorax: Brown wool or fur.
Wing cases: Brown speckled partridge.

Though this imitates New Zealand's pepper-winged olive, it will take trout in rivers on the other side of the planet. It is very good when the water has a slight peat tinge. The same can also be said of the following – another New Zealand pattern.

Red-Tipped Governor

Hook: Nymph, sizes 12–14.
Thread: Black.
Tails: Dyed red hackle fibres.
Abdomen: Red floss.
Thorax: Peacock herl.
Wing cases: Hen pheasant tail slip (dark section).
Legs: Few fibres red hen hackle.

Faisan et Orange (Orange and Pheasant)

Hook: Wet fly, 10–12.
Thread: Brown.
Tails: Tips of about 5 cock pheasant tail fibres.
Underbody: Copper wire.
Body: Orange floss.
Rib: Finest oval gold tinsel.
Shellback: About 10 cock pheasant tail fibres.

Besides trout and grayling, this nymph, by Raymond Rocher, has also accounted for several Atlantic salmon.

The next four are New Zealand patterns and imitate upwinged fly nymphs found in the rivers there. They can also be usefully used in North American and European streams and lakes, as they match several natural nymphs in those continents.

Sulphur Nymph

Hook: Nymph, sizes 12–14.
Thread: Brown.
Tails: Grey partridge fibres dyed yellow.
Abdomen: Yellow seal's fur (or substitute).
Thorax: Hare's ear.
Wing cases: Brown goose quill slip.
Legs: Grey partridge, dyed yellow.

Striped Nymph

Hook: Nymph, sizes 12–16.
Thread: Black.
Tails: Pale ginger or honey hen hackle fibres.
Abdomen: Stripped peacock quill (the best marked come from the 'eye' feather).
Thorax: Hare's ear.
Wing cases: Grey mallard quill slip.
Legs: Ginger hen hackle fibres.

Sepia Nymph

Hook: Nymph, sizes 12–14.
Thread: Black.
Tails: Black cock hackle fibres.
Abdomen: Black and dark brown fur, mixed (use a fine synthetic fur).
Rib: Black thread.
Thorax: As abdomen.
Wing cases: Black quill slip (e.g. crow).
Legs: Black hackle fibres.

Tellico Nymph

Hook: Wet fly, sizes 8–14.
Thread: Black.
Tails: Few fibres of guinea fowl (gallina).
Body: Yellow floss.
Rib: Peacock herl.
Shellback: Peacock herl.
Hackle: Brown hen.
Head: Black.

STONEFLY NYMPHS

Stonefly nymphs live only in the cleanest of rivers and lakes and in many parts of the world of trout fishing they are far less important in the diet of the fish than caddisflies and upwinged flies. However stoneflies are very popular among fly-tyers, partly because of their solid build that makes them good to imitate, partly because some species grow very large. Further, in some North American rivers, there are very large populations of big stonefly species, such as the giant stonefly *Pteronarcys californica* and the golden stoneflies *Acroneuria pacifica* and *A. californica*. So there the pleasure of tying big stonefly nymphs is closely linked with the pleasure of catching trout with them. Across the Atlantic, Europe has some big stoneflies (*Perla* and *Dinocras* species) but only in a relatively few rivers are the populations big enough to warrant carrying imitations of their nymphs or adults. It is interesting to note, however, that in the nineteenth and early twentieth centuries the large nymphs were collected and fished as bait in some rough British rivers. Not surprisingly most stonefly imitations have their roots in North America. They are worth trying in any cool, clean trout stream.

The first three, fairly simple tyings, are by Polly Rosborough (see p. 68).

Dark Stone

Hook: Nymph, sizes 4–14.
Thread: Tan.
Tails: 4–6 dark brown feather fibres (e.g. pheasant church window feather).
Body: Light cream synthetic fur.
Shellback: Slip from dark mottled turkey tail.
Rib: Tan thread, doubled.
Wing cases: Dark brown feather slip (e.g. pheasant church window dyed dark brown).
Legs: Dark brown feather fibres.

Brown Stone

Hook: Nymph, sizes 12–16.
Thread: Brown.
Tails: Few fibres brown feather fibres (e.g. dyed partridge).
Body: Medium brown fur or wool.
Shellback: A dark brown quill slip (e.g. dyed goose).
Rib: Brown thread, doubled.
Wing cases: Dark brown quill slip.
Legs: Tips of cock pheasant tail fibres.

Yellow Stone

Hook: Nymph, sizes 10–14.
Thread: Amber.
Tails: Few fibres mallard dyed yellow-buff or wood duck.
Body: Dull yellow-orange fur or wool.
Shellback: Mallard dyed yellow-buff or wood duck.
Rib: Amber thread, doubled.
Wing cases: Mallard dyed yellow-buff or wood duck.
Legs: Tips of feathers used for wing cases.

Montana Nymph

Hook: Nymph, sizes 2–12.
Thread: Black.
Tails: Black crow quill fibres.
Abdomen: Black chenille.
Thorax: Yellow chenille.
Wing cases: 2 strands of black chenille.
Legs: Soft black hen hackle wound through thorax.

The Montana Nymph is perhaps the best-known artificial stonefly, and catches trout where there are no stoneflies! It is also an excellent catcher of small Atlantic salmon (grilse) in Norway and Scotland. Ted Trueblood's Stone is very similar, but includes brown instead of black chenille, orange instead of yellow chenille, and has two dark brown goose biots as tails.

Randall Kaufmann devised three great stonefly imitations in which the rib was Swannundaze. This is no longer available, but at the time of writing (2009) the similar Vinyl Rib (US) or Magic Glass (UK) is available. Like Swannundaze, this has a D-shaped cross-section and is ideal for ribbing large nymphs. A natural alternative is to take a dyed goose or swan feather quill and to peel, using a sharp knife or razor blade, a thin section of the outer core. Then trim this to the required width before tying in.

Kaufmann's Black Stone

Hook: Nymph, sizes 2–12 (Kaufmann recommended 12X long).
Thread: Black.
Tails: 2 black turkey biots.
Abdomen: ½ black Antron, ½ black, purple, claret, red, amber, fiery brown, blue and hot orange angora, well mixed.
Rib: Black Swannundaze (see above).
Thorax: As abdomen.
Legs: 2 pairs black rubber (optional).
Wing cases: Dark turkey, 3 sections coated in Fexament (or other clear flexible glue), tied in with thorax.
Head: As abdomen.
Antennae: 2 black turkey biots.

Kaufmann's Brown Stone

Hook: Nymph, sizes 2–12 (Kaufmann recommended 12X long).
Thread: Tan.
Tails: 2 ginger goose biots.
Abdomen: ½ golden-brown fur, ½ claret, rust, black, blue, ginger and purple angora, well mixed.
Rib: Amber Swannundaze (see above).
Thorax: As abdomen.
Legs: 2 pairs black rubber (optional).
Wing cases: Mottled turkey, 3 sections coated in Fexament (or other clear flexible glue), tied in with thorax.
Head: As abdomen.
Antennae: 2 ginger goose biots.

Kaufmann's Golden Stone

Hook: Nymph, sizes 8–14.
Thread: Brown.
Tails: 2 brown turkey biots.

Abdomen: ½ hare's ear (or the synthetic Haretron), ½ gold, amber, rust, blue and orange angora, well mixed.
Rib: Amber Swannundaze (see above).
Thorax: As abdomen.
Legs: 2 pairs black rubber (optional).
Wing cases: Dark turkey, 3 sections coated in Fexament (or other clear flexible glue), tied in with thorax.
Head: As abdomen.
Antennae: 2 brown turkey biots.

Kauffmann also recommends tying some with a goldhead (see p. 56) behind the eye.

Charles Brooks, author of *Nymph Fishing for Larger Trout* (1976), devised several excellent, simple-to-tie stonefly nymphs that should be in every nymph-fisher's fly box. He insisted on a lead wire underbody to take the nymphs deep; otherwise use a goldhead or tungstenhead.

Brook's Stonefly Nymph

Hook: Nymph (3X), sizes 4–10.
Thread: Black.
Tails: 2 black goose biots.
Body: Black fur dubbing, with slightly fatter thorax.
Hackle: Grizzle, tied in at base of thorax section and palmered forward to head.

Brown Stonefly Nymph

Hook: Nymph (3X), sizes 6–12.
Thread: Brown.
Tails: 2 brown goose biots.
Body: Brown fur dubbing, with slightly fatter thorax.
Hackle: Brown hen hackle, tied in as base of thorax section and palmered forward to head.

Olive Stonefly Nymph

Hook: Nymph (3X), sizes 10–16.
Thread: Olive.
Tails: 2 olive goose biots.
Body: Olive fur dubbing, with slightly fatter thorax.
Hackle: Olive hen, tied in at base of thorax and palmered forward to head.

Little Yellow stonefly

Hook: Nymph (3X), Sizes 10–14.
Thread: Light brown.
Tails: 2 Yellow-buff goose biots.
Body: Golden-yellow or yellow-brown fur dubbing, with slightly fatter thorax.
Hackle: Ginger hen, tied in at base of thorax and palmered to head.

Someone asked Jack Dennis, author of *Western Trout Fly Tying Manual Vol. II* (rev. edn, 1995), what was his most successful fly:

> I gave some thought to the flies I used in lakes, creeks, and streams and had produced well, under a variety of conditions. One pattern kept flashing through my mind – Bitch Creek Nymph.

Bitch Creek Nymph

Hook: Nymph, sizes 4–12.
Thread: Yellow.
Underbody: Lead wire.
Tails: 2 rubber legs.
Abdomen: Yellow chenille.
Shellback: Black chenille.
Rib: Yellow thread.
Thorax: Black chenille.
Legs: Blue dun hen hackle plus a grey ostrich herl palmered through thorax.
Antennae: 2 rubber legs.

The following is probably the best specific imitation of the *Pteronarcys* nymph, sometimes called the salmon fly, though Al Troth's tying is very effective.

Black Ugly Nymph

Hook: Nymph, sizes 3–4.
Thread: Black.
Underbody: At least one layer of lead wire wound in touching turns.
Tails: 2 black goose biots.
Abdomen: Black knitting wool.
Rib: Black Swannundaze (see above).
Thorax: Dull orange dubbing.

Wing cases: Black goose quill slip.
Legs: Black hen hackle, palmered though thorax.

Troth's Terrible Stonefly Nymph

Hook: Nymph, sizes 1–4.
Thread: Dark brown.
Tails: 2 black turkey biots, ½ inch long.

Body: Dark brown chenille, with two layers at the front as a thorax.
Overbody/rib: Mix of black and brown seal's fur (or substitute), put in a dubbing loop, spun and then wound up body between the turns of chenille. Clip back along the top and bottom.
Legs: Trimmed dark brown hackle stalks.
Antennae: Two black turkey biots, 1 inch long.

Woven bodies are relatively new, and seem to have developed mostly in Eastern Europe (especially Poland) and in Norway (where Torrill Kolbu produced several patterns for her Mustad Collection of flies). Weaving is a special technique, but not too difficult to master. Darrel Martin's *Fly Tying Methods* (1987) gives an excellent account, while there are several DVDs and CDs illustrating the technique.

Woven-Bodied Stonefly Nymphs

Hook: Nymph, sizes 6–12.
Thread: Brown or black.
Tails: 2 goose biots dyed the colour of the fly's dorsal surface.
Abdomen: Woven, with darker dorsal side, paler ventral surface; e.g. black dorsal, warm brown ventral; dark brown dorsal, tan ventral; orange-brown dorsal, yellow ventral.
Thorax: Fur dubbing, as ventral surface of abdomen.
Wing cases: Goose quill slips, dyed to match dorsal surface of abdomen.
Legs: Grouse for the black version, brown speckled partridge for the brown version, and partridge dyed golden-olive for the orange-brown version.

Olive Woven-Bodied Nymph

Hook: Nymph, sizes 14–18.
Thread: Brown.
Tails: Sparse bunch bronze mallard.

Abdomen: Olive and grey-olive silk, woven.
Thorax: Fine olive fur.
Wing cases: Light grey duck quill slip.
Legs: Light furnace or ginger hen hackle.

Brown Woven-Bodied Nymph
Hook: Nymph, sizes 12–18.
Thread: Orange.
Tails: Sparse bunch bronze mallard.
Abdomen: Black and orange silks, woven.
Thorax: Fine brown fur.
Wing cases: Light grey duck quill slip.
Legs: Light furnace or ginger hen hackle.

Swannundaze Stonefly Nymph
Hook: Curved nymph, sizes 6–12.
Thread: Brown.
Tails: 2 Dyed brown goose biots.
Abdomen: Brown Swannundaze.
Thorax: Brown rabbit fur.
Wing cases: Speckled turkey slip or synthetic.
Eyes: Lead.

DAMSELFLY NYMPHS

Dragonflies and damselflies belong to the great Order of insects, the Odonata. Some have devised imitations of dragonfly nymphs, but trout and panfish are unlikely to encounter more than the occasional real dragonfly nymph because they crawl slowly and cannot swim, and they often hide away in thick weed or debris on the bottom. They are exceedingly rarely found in autopsies.

In contrast damselfly nymphs do swim with a vigorous undulation of the body, and they tend to occur in much higher densities in lakes and slow weedy rivers than dragonfly nymphs. They are sometimes found in numbers in autopsies. So damselfly nymph imitations are important fishing flies.

The Olive Marabou Damsel is a good imitation simply because the long marabou 'tail' imitates the undulating tails and abdomen of the real insect.

Olive Marabou Damsel

Hook: Wet fly, sizes 10–12.
Thread: Olive.
Tails and abdomen: Bunch of olive marabou.
Thorax: Fur dubbing, slightly darker than the tails/abdomen.
Legs: Partridge dyed olive.
Wing cases: Goose quill slip dyed dark olive.

Tie Brown Marabou Damsel in the same way, using medium-brown marabou, fur and goose quill slip, and an undyed brown speckled partridge hackle.

Floating Foam Backed Damsel Nymph

Hook: Long shank, sizes 10–12.
Thread: Olive.
Tails: Olive marabou, plus 4 strands Crystal Hair/Krystal Flash.
Abdomen: Olive dubbing, e.g. seal's fur, or Antron or other synthetic.
Rib: Fine oval gold tinsel.
Wing case: 3 mm-wide green foam strip, extended back to abdomen.
Thorax: Olive dubbing, e.g. seal's fur, or Antron or other synthetic.
Legs: 6 knotted olive goose biots.
Eyes: 2 red glass beads, lined with mono that is burnt at either end to give black centres to eyes.

A fly by Wendy Gibson for lake fishing. Fish this just below the surface using a slow-sink or fast intermediate line. When the fly is retrieved it will bobble below the surface, but swims up when the retrieve is stopped.

Extended Body Damsel Nymph

Hook: Wet fly, sizes 12–14.
Thread: Brown.
Tail: Tips of olive marabou fibres.
Abdomen: Marabou fibres from tails wound around piece of olive floss tied in at end of hook shank (an extended body).
Thorax: Fine olive fur.
Rib: Fine oval gold tinsel.
Legs: Tips of a few dark blue dun cock hackle fibres, tied to each side.
Wing cases: Cock pheasant tail herls.
Eyes: Lead eyes.

Goldhead Damsel

Hook: Nymph, size 12.
Thread: Olive.
Tail: Olive marabou.
Abdomen: Olive ostrich herl.
Rib: 10lb clear mono.
Thorax: Goldhead.
Wing cases: Brown speckled partridge feather, dyed olive, tied over back of thorax.
Head: Fine olive dubbing, with thread painted red at front.
Eyes: Green beads.

Doug Jorgensen's Damsel Nymph is fairly similar in style.

Damsel Nymph

Hook: Streamer or nymph, size 12.
Thread: Olive.
Tail: Olive marabou.
Abdomen: Olive Antron.
Rib: Fine gold wire.
Thorax: As abdomen.
Wing cases: Duck or goose quill dyed olive.
Legs: Olive marabou tips tied in at sides.

Rumpf Damsel Fly Nymph

Hook: Nymph, sizes 12–14.
Thread: Black.
Tails: Tips of 3–4 cock pheasant tail fibres.
Body: Mix of olive and golden-olive synthetic fur or seal's fur, with a little twinkle (e.g. Laser Light and Lightbrite).
Rib: Fine copper wire.
Wing cases: Cock pheasant tail fibres.
Eyes: Burnt mono.

Invented by John Rumpf of South Australia, this should be fished in lake margins where real damsel fly nymphs abound.

Gene Kugach gave, in *Fly Fisher's Pattern Book* (2000), George Cik's excellent pattern. This is tied front to back: tie in the eyes first, then dub the thorax, then tie in the wool on top just behind the eye of the hook and take that back to the rear of the hook shank/thorax. There, whip finish leaving the remains of the wool sticking back. Trim to length to make the abdomen, and tease the tip to create a suggestion of the three tails.

Damsel Nymph (George Cik)

Hook: Wet fly, size 8–10.
Thread: As body colour.
Extended abdomen/tail: Wool strands, olive, green or brown.
Thorax: Olive, green or brown dubbing.
Wing cases: Strand of olive, green or brown wool.
Eyes: Bead chain or burnt 25lb mono.

Green Damsel

Hook: Nymph, sizes 10–14.
Thread: Olive.
Tail: 3–4 tips dyed olive goose quill herls.
Abdomen: Olive goose herls.
Rib: Fine oval gold tinsel.
Thorax: Olive ostrich herl.
Wing cases: Goose quill slip, dyed olive.

This pattern is by Dave Collyer, author of *Fly Dressing* (1975).

Larvae and Pupae

Several Orders of aquatic insects have a life cycle consisting of complete metamorphosis in which, instead of a nymph, a larva hatches from the egg. The larva is the feeding and growing stage. In some species it may last only a few weeks (e.g. mosquitoes) whereas in others it lasts about a year (e.g. caddisflies). The larva usually looks nothing like the adult and in some species it looks more like a worm than an insect (e.g. the larval bloodworm that gives rise to the adult chironomid midge). When the larva reaches maximum size it enters a resting stage, the pupa, when its tissues are reorganised into the adult form. A special case, or cocoon, is sometimes constructed in which the pupa hides away from potential predators. Then, when the time is right for the adult to hatch, either the adult emerges from the cocoon and swims to the surface (e.g. reed smults), or the pupa swims to the surface and the adult emerges there (e.g. chironomid midges). In that very important group of trout foods, the caddisflies (or sedges), the pupal cocoon is enclosed in a caddis case, even in those species in which the larvae lack cases (see below). The adult breaks free of its case and cocoon and swims to the surface enclosed in a skin-like sheath that was part of the pupal structure. To entomologists, this is known as a 'pharate adult' or 'clothed adult' and was brought to the attention of the fly-tying world by the American angler-entomologist Gary LaFontaine. Many fly-tyers and fly-fishers, however, still call this stage a 'pupa'. This is not unreasonable, for the pharate adult is quite different in its shape and behaviour from the adult standing or flying above the water. Once at the surface, the adult caddisfly rapidly takes flight, leaving the sheath behind.

In some aquatic insects the fully grown larva crawls ashore to pupate in damp waterside sand or silt (e.g. aquatic beetles and alderflies). The trout never encounter the pupae nor the hatching adults of these species.

Note: Some writers have included larvae and pupae, and other subsurface aquatic invertebrates such as water boatmen (back swimmers) and freshwater shrimps (scuds), with nymphs. Scientifically this is incorrect. In years to come even the word 'nymph' may slowly vanish, for freshwater biologists now call nymphs, 'larvae', thus ceasing to differentiate between the incomplete and complete growing stages of metamorphosis life cycles.

CADDIS LARVAE

There are two categories of caddis larvae: those that are protected by a case made from sand, small pebbles, bits of twig or pieces of leaf, held together with silk – and those that do not have a case, though they acquire one just before pupation. Both categories are imitated with fishing flies.

CASED CADDIS

Because these live on the river- or lake-bed it is important to add weight to the dressing (rules permitting). This can be done by:

- Lashing lead wire or foil strips to the top of the hook shank (this helps the finished fly fish 'point up' so that it avoids snagging).
- Winding lead wire around the shank. More weight can be added with this method – but the hook point is more likely to snag bottom.
- Fitting a tungsten bead (or goldhead or silverhead) to the hook behind the eye.
- Fitting a piece of split shot to the hook just behind the eye. To do this, fix a split shot (BB is about right) onto a loop of 3lb leader material, and then bind the loop to the top of the hook shank, with the shot tight against the shank behind the eye. Paint the shot black to suggest the head of the caddis larva protruding from its case. Note too that, with the shot fixed in this way, the fly will tend to fish upside-down.

Cased caddis larvae have a very soft, dirty white, cream or palest olive body. It is well worth imitating this in all cased caddis flies by winding a thin layer of cream, or palest olive floss or wool over the shank (and any ballast). This will show through any gaps in the case and may act as a trigger to the trout. Several patterns have been called Peeking or Peeping Caddis because they have a smidgen of cream or pale yellow wool between the case and the head, suggesting that the larva is partially out and having a good look round! This feature ought to be included in all cased caddis imitations.

Fur-Bodied Cased Caddis

Hook: Nymph or long shank, sizes 8–14.
Thread: Black.
Case: Coarse brown or sandy dubbing with plenty of guard hairs (e.g. hare's ear or mask).
Rib: Fine silver wire.
Thorax: A tiny amount of cream dubbing or wool at front of case.
Legs: 2 turns of short-fibred black hen hackle.
Head: Black thread or black split shot (see above).

Especially useful where the bottom is sand or silt. In Spain this is tied with hare's fur and a thick black rib.

Feather-Bodied Cased Caddis

Hook: Nymph or long shank, sizes 8–14.
Thread: Black.
Case: Take several large coarse hackles (e.g. mallard, grouse, grey partridge, upper wing coverts). Tie one in by its tip at the end of the hook shank and palmer it forward in touching turns; tie it off when almost run out. Then tie in and palmer a second, and so on until the length of the case is correct. After ribbing, trim back the feather fibres to give a case that resembles a mass of tiny bits of twig.
Rib: Fine gold wire.
Thorax: A tiny amount of cream dubbing or wool at front of case.
Legs: 2 turns of hen furnace hackle.
Head: Black thread or black split shot (see above).

A caddis to use in well-wooded streams and lakes, or where there is plenty of detritus on the bottom.

Herl-Bodied Cased Caddis

Hook: Nymph or long shank, sizes 8–14.
Thread: Black.
Case: Wound herl (see below); if using goose quill or pheasant tail, about five or six fibres will be needed.

Rib: Fine gold wire.
Thorax: A tiny amount of cream dubbing or wool at front of case.
Legs: 2 turns of brown or black hen hackle.
Head: Black thread or black split shot (see above).

NOTE: Use dyed green goose herl to imitate a case constructed from the leaves or stems of water weeds, brown or grey goose to simulate a case made from silt, cock pheasant tail to match a case made from sand. If fishing crystal clear limestone rivers (such as Slovenia's Soca) a case made from white goose quill matches the white limestone sand cases of the local caddis.

PHRYGANEA CASED CADDIS

Hook: Nymph or long shank, sizes 8–14.
Thread: Black.
Case: Bright green herls (e.g. goose, swan), tied in by their tips at end of hook shank, then brought forward and tied in at the front of the hook shank, so that the herls run parallel to the hook shank.
Rib: Black thread.
Thorax: A tiny amount of cream dubbing or wool at front of case.
Legs: 2 turns furnace or natural red (brown) hen.
Head: Black thread or black split shot (see above).

Caddis in the Family Phryganidae live mostly in weedy lakes and make beautifully crafted cases from sections of green waterweed, formed in a spiral arrangement. This pattern imitates those cases.

The next caddis imitation is tied back-to-front, in that the head of the insect is at the end of the hook shank. By fixing the shot in place on top of the hook shank, the fly tends to fish upside-down, with hook point uppermost. This reduces the chance of the fly snagging on the bottom.

PEEPING CADDIS

Hook: Nymph, sizes 12–14.
Thread: Light brown.
Peeping head/thorax: Fluorescent green floss.
Legs: Brown speckled partridge.
Body: Hare's ear and mask fur, mixed well.
Weight: A split shot (BB) fixed to fine mono which is then tied to the top of the hook shank, just behind the eye.

In the 1980s Roman Moser produced a video made on his native Austrian River Traun, *New Ways of Fishing the Caddis*, in which he introduced many new imitations of every stage of the caddis life cycle. Many materials used were synthetic and some (e.g. 'Body Gills') are now not too easy to obtain. Nevertheless, he has made a major contribution to the imitation of caddis.

Cased Caddis (Roman Moser)

Hook: Wet fly, sizes 10–12.
Thread: Brown.
Abdomen: Light brown fine synthetic dubbing and brown deer hair mixed. After dubbing and winding down the shank, the hair/fur is clipped to give a caddis case shape.
Thorax: A little light yellow deer hair, dubbed, wound and trimmed.
Hackle: Sparse, black henny-cock.

Deer Hair Cased Caddis

Hook: Nymph, sizes 8–12.
Thread: Black or brown.
Body: Roughly chopped and dubbed brown deer hair, suggesting a case of bits of fine twig and detritus.
Rib: Yellow thread.
Thorax: A little yellow fur to suggest a 'peeping' caddis.
Hackle: Black hen.

This is a modification of Paul Young's Strawman Caddis.

The following are New Zealand patterns and feature in Keith Draper's *Trout Flies in New Zealand.* The first is a splendid fly for rivers and lakes throughout the world.

Horn Caddis

Hook: Nymph, sizes 10–14.
Thread: Black.
Body: Grey darning wool.
Rib: Fine silver wire.
Thorax: White wool.
Legs: Few grizzle hackle fibres.

Bragg's Caddis Larva

Hook: Curved grub/sedge, sizes 12–14.
Thread: Yellow.
Body: Golden-yellow floss.
Rib: Fluorescent yellow floss.
Hackle: Ginger hen.

This matches the caddis larva *Olinga feredayi*.

Many attempts have been made to create cased caddis with the real materials that caddis use in the construction of their cases, such as bits of twig, sand and pebbles. The only problem is that the resultant flies can sometimes be a bit too heavy to cast unless a meaty rod and line are used.

Sand Cased Caddis

Hook: Nymph or streamer, size 10.
Thread: Black.
Underbody: Cream wool or floss.
Body: Sand. Soak the underbody with Superglue and cover with dry sand. Leave to set before continuing.
Thorax: The front of the underbody showing.
Hackle: Black hen.

The Twig Cased Caddis is dressed in exactly the same way, using bits of dry twig and leaf.

Innes Stick Caddis

Hook: Nymph, sizes 12–14.
Thread: Yellow.
Tail and body: Mix of synthetic furs (e.g. BMS, Antron, SLF) or seal's fur: 20 per cent of each of yellow, olive and orange; and 40 per cent dark brown.
Head: Tying thread.

Devised by Rick Innes of Melbourne, and useful on both lakes and rivers.

Black & Peacock Caddis

Hook: Nymph or long shank, sizes 8–14.
Thread: Black.
Case: Peacock herl.
Rib: Fine silver or gold wire.
Legs: 2 turns black hen hackle.
Head: Black thread.

This is really a long shanked version of the Black & Peacock Spider (p. 54), and exploits the magic appear that peacock herl has to trout. When tied with a short thorax of fluorescent green, yellow or orange floss or wool, this is known as the Stick Fly. This variation is especially effective for Arctic char in northern lakes (e.g. Arctic Canada, Greenland, Iceland).

Caseless Cased Caddis Larva

Hook: Curved grub or shrimp hook, sizes 8–16.
Thread: Black.
Body: Cream wool or dubbed fur over the rear two-thirds, with black-brown wool or fur over the front third.

Note: Poul Jorgensen, who invented this pattern, often gave the cream part of the body an overbody of natural latex, to suggest segmentation. 'It's not really needed', he said. In any case, latex tends to rot after a while, especially in a warm, humid fly box.

CASELESS CADDIS LARVAE

During a flood, when boulders are being carried downstream, some caddis lose their cases as they are swept away. Autopsies suggest that trout look out for these caseless caddis and quickly mop them up. Fish as the river is fining down.

There are two main groups of caseless caddis larvae:

- *Rhyacophila* is a group of free-living larvae that wander amongst the river-bed boulders and mosses seeking lesser creatures to devour. These may include other nymphs and larvae, fish eggs, and trout and salmon alevins.
- *Hydropsyche* and their allies is a group of net-spinning larvae. They build tents and tubes from silk in which they take cover and which they also use to filter the water of food items. Trout are unlikely to encounter them in their hideaways – but they are very territorial, and

as the *Hydropsyche* larvae grow, they each need more space and, as the stronger individuals retain territories, the weaker are forced to leave. Thus, throughout spring and summer, small numbers of larvae drift away downstream and may be eaten by trout.

Weight: While some may be tied without ballast for shallower water, most should have a layer of fine lead wire wound in touching turns along the hook shank. Where the use of lead is prohibited, tungsten wire or foil, or copper wire might be used.

Quill Larva

Hook: Nymph or curved caddis hook, sizes 12–14.
Thread: As abdomen.
Abdomen: Ginger or green cock hackle stalk.
Thorax and legs: Brown ostrich herl, with the top fibres trimmed away. It is worth strengthening the top of the thorax with a good, slightly thickened head cement.

The ginger stalk version matches *Hydropsyche*, the green *Rhycophila*. This simple pattern is a modification of A. K. Best's Caddis Quill Larva (in *A. K.'s Fly Box*, 1996).

Bread Crust

Hook: Nymph, sizes 10–14.
Thread: Black.
Body: Orange, cream or green floss
Rib: Dark brown hackle stalk.
Hackle: Grizzle hen.

A popular US pattern by Larry Solomon and Eric Leiser (in *Caddis and the Angler*, 1977), the latter two body colours seem more effective in Europe.

During the late 1940s and 1950s C. F. Walker made a special study of the trout insects in British lakes and rivers. The following fly is perhaps the earliest imitation of a *Rhyacophila* larva.

Caseless Caddis

Hook: Nymph, sizes 12–14.
Thread: Olive.
Body: Seal's fur (or substitute), ½ olive, ½ green, well mixed.

Rib: Oval gold tinsel.
Hackle: Woodcock underwing covert.
Head: Cock pheasant tail herl.

Fur-Bodied Rhyacophila

Hook: Curved caddis hook, sizes 12–14.
Thread: Olive.
Abdomen: Green, olive green or light green fur (a mix of, for example, rabbit and seal's fur is better than only one type).
Rib: Fine gold wire or finest oval tinsel.
Thorax: Hare's ear.
Legs: Few fibres brown speckled partridge hackle (optional).
Essentially a lake pattern that is very effective in the evening – fished along shores onto which waves are breaking.

Fur-Bodied Hydropsyche

Hook: Curved caddis hook, sizes 12–14.
Thread: Light brown.
Abdomen: Grey or light buff fur.
Rib: Fine gold wire.
Thorax: Hare's ear.
Legs: Few fibres grey partridge hackle (optional).

These two flies are most effective in fairly shallow, turbulent, bouldery water where the trout are most likely to find washed-out or drifting natural larvae.

Gorjan Franko lives in Tolmin, a small town on the Soca River (Slovenia). The Soca is full of trout, grayling and *Hydropsyche*, and the three come together well with Gorjan's imitation.

Hydropsyche (Gorjan Franko)

Hook: Wet fly, sizes 10–12.
Thread: Brown.
Body: Mix of ⅓ brown and ⅔ cream fur (fine textured).
Rib: Fine gold wire.
Hackle: Brown speckled partridge.

Upstream of Tolmin there are some very rapid stretches of river. To fish there, tie some with a tungsten bead at the head to get the fly down to the fish!

The following is a slight modification of one of Roman Moser's caddis larvae for the River Traun.

Hydropsyche

Hook: Wet fly, sizes 10–12.
Thread: Brown.
Tails (to represent the short tassel-ended 'prolegs' at the end of the body): Few fibres grey partridge hackle, cut short.
Body: Light grey or buff wool.
Shellback: Brown raffine.
Rib: Thick brown thread.
Legs: Brown speckled partridge hackle fibres.
Head: Hare's ear.

Gary LaFontaine wrote the important textbook, *Caddis Flies* (1981), in which he explored North American caddis species and their life cycles, and created some fine imitations. The following is a useful general pattern – change the abdomen colour to buff, grey, brown and olive to match other species.

Bright Green Free-Living Caddis

Hook: Curved grub/shrimp, sizes 10–12.
Thread: Brown.
Underbody: Fine lead wire.
Abdomen: Mix of 50 per cent olive and 50 per cent bright green fur or wool.
Rib: Brown cock hackle stalk.
Thorax: Dark olive-brown fur.
Hackle: Speckled grouse hackle fibres.

The next two tyings are by Oliver Edwards, whose book *Fly Tyers' Masterclass*, videos/DVDs and tying demonstrations have inspired many around the world of fly-tying, from Japan, through Europe to the United States.

Rhyacophila Larva
Hook: Curved grub/shrimp, sizes 10–12.

Weight: Lead foil.
Thread: Yellow.
Abdomen and thorax: 4-ply knitting yarn (preferably including Antron), bright mid-green. Darken dorsal surface with medium olive waterproof pen; give two black dots to dorsal surface of first three segments.

Rib: 3–5lb clear nylon mono.
Legs: Grey partridge hackle fibres, dyed yellow-olive.
Head: Tying thread.

Hydropsyche Larva

Hook: Curved grub/shrimp, sizes 8–12.
Thread: Light brown or grey.
Abdomen and thorax: 4-ply knitting yarn (preferably including Antron), fawn, drab grey-yellow, grey-olive.

Back: Speckled turkey section.
Ribs: Fine gold wire and 3lb clear nylon mono.
Legs: Partridge hackle, dyed black.
Dorsal surface of thorax and head: Tint black with waterproof pen.

During the 1990s the use of woven bodies in fly-tying grew in popularity (see also p. 170), but recently it seems to have fallen out of favour. The following are useful examples.

Woven-Bodied Rhyacophila

Hook: Curved grub/shrimp, sizes 12–14.
Tying thread: Brown.
Body: Woven, dark green-olive dorsally, lime-green ventrally, with a tiny amount of hare's ear dubbing at the front as thorax.

Legs: Few fibres brown speckled partridge dyed olive.
Wing cases: Brown herl (e.g. goose).

Woven-Bodied Hydropsyche

Hook: Curved grub/shrimp, sizes 12–14.
Tying thread: Light brown.
Body: Woven, drab grey or beige-brown dorsally, lighter brown or tan ventrally, with a tiny amount of fine olive fur dubbing at the front as thorax.

Legs: Few fibres ginger hen.
Wing cases: Light olive or tan raffine.

CADDIS PUPAE

The following flies imitate the adult caddisfly after it has left its pupal case and cocoon, but is still enclosed in a pupal skin, drifting deep in the water before it makes its way to the surface. They should mostly be well weighted, so that they get down to the depth of natural pupae and the feeding fish. A few unweighted ones can be used in shallower, slower-moving water.

Most adult caddis hatch from their nymph shuck in the later afternoon and through into the darkness (in sub-arctic waters, in summer, hatches of different species may occur throughout the short summer twilight night). These deep pupae are best fished in the hours before adult emergence is expected to occur.

DEEP PUPAE

This first pattern, by John Goddard, is hardly a good imitation, but it is an extremely good catcher of trout. It is one of those very effective fishing flies that look like no living thing!

Persuader

Hook: Wet fly, sizes 8–10.
Thread: Orange.
Abdomen: 4–5 strand white ostrich herl.
Rib: Fine oval silver tinsel.
Thorax: Orange seal's fur (or substitute).
Wing Cases: Slip from turkey tail.

Brown Pupa

Hook: Wet fly, sizes 8–10.
Thread: Brown.
Body: Brown ostrich herl.
Rib: Fine oval gold tinsel.
'Horns' (antennae): 2 peacock herls tied back over body.
Head: Peacock herl.

This was devised by Tom Ivens for use on reservoirs.

Amber Nymph [Pupa]

Hook: Wet fly, sizes 10–12.
Thread: Black.

Body: Amber seal's fur (or substitute).
Hackle: Ginger hen, tied false.
Wing cases: Grey or brown goose quill slip.

Invented by Dr Bell, pioneering deviser of imitative trout flies for still waters, who fished Blagdon Reservoir in southwest England.

Goldhead Pupa

Hook: Wet fly, sizes 8–10.
Thread: Brown.
Body: Grey-brown wool.
Head: Goldhead.

An alternative is the Hare's Ear Goldhead (p. 57), whereas the following, by Roman Moser, uses wound copper wire instead of the goldhead.

Grey Pupa

Hook: Curved shrimp or sedge, sizes 8–12.
Thread: Brown.
Body: Mix of grey polypropylene with a few silver Crystal Hair fibres.
Head: Copper wire; large.

Phryganea

Hook: Nymph, sizes 8–12.
Thread: Black.
Abdomen: Fine green fur (natural e.g. rabbit, or synthetic).
Rib: Black thread.
Thorax: Drab cream fur.
Legs: Brown speckled partridge hackle fibres.

This matches the pupae of several large lake caddis that are especially abundant in weedy areas.

The following two patterns are by one of the greatest freshwater anglers of the second half of the twentieth century, Richard (Dick) Walker. They are especially effective in weedy lakes.

Shorthorn
Hook: Wet fly, sizes 10–14.
Thread: Brown.
Abdomen: Dark olive herl (e.g. dyed heron, goose).
Rib: Yellow thread.
Thorax: Yellow-green fluorescent wool.
Wing cases: Black lurex.
Legs: 2 small bunches of brown speckled partridge, tied on either side.

Longhorn
Hook: Wet fly, sizes 8–12.
Thread: Pale yellow.
Abdomen: Amber wool or seal's fur (or substitute).
Rib: Fine oval gold tinsel.
Thorax: Chestnut brown fur.
Hackle: 2 turns brown speckled partridge.
Antennae: 2 cock pheasant tail fibres tied long over back.

The following pattern, by Frank A. Johnson of New Zealand, will catch trout anywhere that are eating caddis pupae.

Swannundaze Sedge Pupa
Hook: Curved shrimp or sedge, sizes 8–10.
Thread: Brown.
Abdomen: Transparent yellow Swannundaze (see p. 75) wound over an under-abdomen of fluorescent red floss.
Rib: Peacock herl, following the turns of Swannundaze.
Thorax: Brown Antron.
Wing cases: Cock pheasant tail slip.
Hackle: Brown speckled partridge.
Antennae: 2 cock pheasant tail fibres, tied back over body.

The following are not individual fly patterns but recipes that enable several colours of pupae to be tied.

Sparkle Sedge Pupa
Hook: Wet fly, sizes 8–14.
Underbody: Lead wire in touching turns.
Thread: Black.

Abdomen: A sparkling mix of furs, e.g. seal's fur (or a good substitute), Antron, dyed or natural hare's fur, dyed or natural rabbit fur), with some chopped pearl and silver Crystal Hair. Mix in also a very little hot orange and hot yellow fur (e.g. seal). The basic underlying colours to be green, olive, brown and grey.
Thorax: Hare's ear.

When trout are feeding ravenously on pupae deep in the water, they will savage these until there is hardly any dressing left!

Deep Sparkle Caddis Pupae

Hook: Wet fly, sizes 10–14.
Underbody: Fine lead wire in touching turns.
Thread: As body.
Body: 50:50 mix of Antron and coarse natural fur in green, olive, tan, brown and grey.
Overbody, or body veiling: Antron fibres, as body colour. These are tied in at the end of the hook shank. Then, after the body has been tied, the fibres are brought forward all round the body so that they provide a veil over the body. This simulates the pupal skin that surrounds the caddis after it has left its case and cocoon.
Hackle: Brown speckled partridge or grouse upper wing covert, 2 turns.
Head: Brown ostrich herl.

Gary LaFontaine produced this style of fly to imitate the pharate adult beginning its journey to the surface. The body is that of the adult caddis, the hackle its legs; the overbody is the pupal shuck.

Seal's fur has long been a popular fly-tying material and, despite the moves to ban the killing of young seals, it is still available. Its chief virtue is that it sparkles when held against the light, so that a fly tied properly with seal's fur (not wound too tight, with fibres sticking out) has a life-like appearance. Eventually politics will outlaw the use of seal's fur; in which case, use a coarse sparkling synthetic fur.

Seal's Fur Pupa

Hook: Curved sedge hook, sizes 10–14.
Thread: As thorax.

Abdomen: Coarse fur, e.g. seal or a good substitute, wound so that plenty of fibres stick out to create a haze round the fly. Colours: green, olive, tan, brown, grey.
Rib: Oval gold tinsel.
Thorax: Ostrich herl a little darker than the abdomen.
Hackle: 1 turn of long-fibred brown speckled partridge.

Caddis Pupa

Hook: Grub or shrimp, sizes 8–16.
Thread: Brown.
Abdomen: Medium brown seal's fur (or substitute).
Thorax and legs: Brown rabbit fur, spun in a dubbing loop.
Wing cases: Medium grey mallard quill slip.

A Poul Jorgensen fly. Other colours might be tried, including green, olive and grey (natural rabbit).

One very effective use of very heavy caddis imitations (both larvae and pupae) and other weighted 'bugs' evolved in what is now the Czech Republic and is known as 'Czech Nymphing'. Two heavy flies are fished on a simple leader on a very short line under, or just beyond, the tip of the extended rod. The flies are flicked upstream in fast water and led downstream by the current and guided by lifting the rod tip as they drift past and lowering the rod tip as they continue downstream. It is a very effective way of fishing for grayling and trout. Chris Hosker is a master of the Czech nymph technique, and the following twelve patterns are from his cold-water, winter fly boxes. They can, of course, be fished singly in more traditional nymphing.

All have at least one layer of lead wire as an underbody.

Cream Bug

Hook: Curved grub or shrimp, sizes 10–12.
Thread: Red.
Body: Fine cream wool.
Shellback: Pearl strip.
Rib: Fine gold wire.
Head: Red cement.

Amber Bug

Hook: Curved grub or shrimp, sizes 10–12.
Thread: Black.
Abdomen: Amber wool or seal's fur.
Shellback: Dark amber raffine.
Rib: Fine gold wire.
Thorax: Grey fur.
Wing cases: Black poly strip.
Head: Black cement.

The next two patterns each come in two colours, giving four fishing flies. They may not look like a real larva or pupa, but they do catch lots of fish, especially in dark, very fast, or cold water.

Pink Reflections

Hook: Curved grub or shrimp, sizes 10–12.
Thread: Red or black.
Body: Pink fur dubbing.
Shellback: Silver or red-orange fluorescent strip cut from a road-mender's safety jacket.
Rib: Fine gold wire.
Head: Red or black cement.

Emergency Exit!

Hook: Curved grub or shrimp, sizes 10–12.
Thread: Red or black.
Body: Either peacock herl or peacock synthetic dubbing, or hare's ear or Haretron synthetic dubbing.
Shellback: Strip cut from the luminous material used in hotels and other public buildings to show the way to emergency exits in the dark.
Rib: Fine gold wire.
Head: Red or black cement.

The next 'fly' is really added weight to use in very deep or fast water where the other patterns do not sink quickly enough. This is used on a dropper, with one or two others on the point (and a second dropper).

Get It Down!

Hook: Curved grub or shrimp, sizes 6–8.
Thread: Black.

Underbody: Many layers of lead or tungsten wire.
Tail: Fluorescent red wool.
Body: Any fine tan dubbing.
Head: Black cement.

Hosker's Rhyacophila No. 1

Hook: Curved grub or shrimp, sizes 10–12.
Thread: Black.
Abdomen: Fine golden-olive fur dubbing.
Shellback: Golden-olive poly strip.
Rib: Fine gold wire.
Thorax: Brown fine fur dubbing.
Wing cases: Black poly strip.
Head: Black cement.

Hosker's Rhyacophila No. 2

Hook: Curved grub or shrimp, sizes 10–12.
Thread: Black.
Abdomen: Fine olive fur dubbing.
Shellback: Clear poly strip.
Rib: 3lb clear mono.
Thorax: Synthetic green sparkling dubbing (e.g. Antron).
Wing cases: Black poly strip.
Head: Black cement.

Hosker's Hydropsyche No. 1

Hook: Curved grub or shrimp, sizes 10–12.
Thread: Black.
Tails: Tuft brown speckled partridge fibres.
Abdomen: Fine buff fur dubbing or hare's ear.
Shellback: Brown poly strip.
Rib: Fine gold wire.
Thorax: Brown fine fur dubbing.
Wing cases: Black poly strip.
Head: Black cement.

Hosker's Hydropsyche No. 2

Hook: Curved grub or shrimp, sizes 10–12.
Thread: Red.
Body: Fine cream fur dubbing with plenty of sparkle (e.g. Antron).

Shellback: Pearl Flashabou.
Rib: Fine gold wire.
Head: Black cement.

Chris's final offering was devised for catching grayling in coloured, turbulent water when the river was fining down after a spate in autumn. It does catch grayling (and trout), but to its inventor's surprise it is also consistently taken by salmon!

Salmon Bug

Hook: Wet fly, sizes 10–12.
Thread: Tan.
Tail: Fluorescent red floss.
Body: Fine pink fur dubbing, built up at the front to suggest a thorax.
Rib: Fine gold tinsel.
Head: Goldhead.

The difficulty with fishing Czech-nymph style is getting the flies close to the river-bed in deep, very turbulent water. In such circumstances, extra heavyweight flies are needed. One of these is fixed to either the point or dropper of a two-fly leader, and a more conventional weighted nymph or pupa is also attached to the leader. The heavily weighted fly takes the other down to the fish. Occasionally the large, weighted fly might be taken.

Hooks are all large, sizes 6–8.

Heavyweight Cased Caddis

Thread: Black.
Body: A tapering cylinder of lead, longer than the hook, that is dipped in glue and then sand to give a realistic case appearance.
Thorax: Light olive or yellow dubbing.
Legs: Speckled partridge.
Head: Black fur.

When fished on the point, the end of the body of this fly hits the bottom and can be bounced through a lie without the hook point touching the bottom. The risk of snagging is thus reduced.

Lead Bug
Thread: Black.
Body: Lead, lacquered black.
Head: Goldhead.

With its smooth body and lack of any real dressing, this sinks quickly.

Heavyweight Hare's Ear Goldhead
Thread: Black or brown.
Tail: Speckled partridge.
Underbody: Lots of lead or tungsten wire or foil.
Body: Hare's ear.
Rib: Copper wire.
Head: Goldhead.

This looks a bit more like an edible item.

Heavyweight Pupa
Thread: Black or brown.
Underbody: Lots of lead or tungsten wire or foil.
Body: Yellow fur.
Rib: Copper wire.
Legs: Rubber.
Head: Copperhead.

Heavyweight Bug
Thread: Black or brown.
Underbody: Preformed lead.
Body: Latex sheet.
Head: Fluorescent red.

Most of the flies were specially tied for this book. These heavyweights were not. They were taken from the fishing fly-box of Howard Croston, who has fished them throughout the world. They are practical, fishing flies.

SURFACE CADDIS PUPAE (EMERGERS)

(For other Emergers, see pp. 107, 135, 159ff.)

When the adult is ready to leave the water the 'pupa', which is really a pharate adult (see p. 83), swims to the surface and rests there for anything between seconds and several minutes. Then, the adult quickly rises through the water's meniscus, shedding its pupal sheath, and in a split second takes to the air. This is quite unlike the more leisurely emergence of mayflies, where it takes a some seconds for the dun to escape the nymphal shuck and stand on the surface film, and then for the dun to prepare to take flight (they may stand on the surface for many minutes). So whereas in a dun hatch we see the duns standing on the water and trout taking them, in a caddisfly hatch it is unusual to see the adult caddisfly standing on the water, so rapid is their emergence.

The air is full of flying caddis, there seems to be nothing on the water, and yet trout are feeding on something at the surface – what are they feeding on? The answer is caddisfly emergers. Imitations of adult caddisflies, if they imitate anything, imitate female caddisflies that have returned to the water to lay their eggs. However, from hundreds of sessions fishing caddisfly hatches (backed up by autopsies) it is clear that many adult caddisfly imitations (especially hackleless ones, such as the Cul De Canard and Hackleless Elk Hair Caddis) are effective because their bodies, sitting in the surface film, suggest to the trout the emerger stage, resting at the surface, and not a hatched adult caddis. For adult caddisfly imitations, see p. 193.

Several of the deep pupal imitations given above can easily be turned into emerger patterns by simply tying without any added weight and by waterproofing the fly with Gink or other semi-solid floatant (good examples would be Phryganea, Sparkle Sedge Pupa, Seal's Fur Pupa, Caddis Pupa).

Deer Hair Pupa Emerger

Hook: Dry fly, sizes 10–14.
Thread: Brown.
Abdomen: Olive or grey or brown deer hair, spun tightly on the rear ⅔ of the shank.
Thorax: Brown deer hair, spun tightly on the front ⅓ of the shank.
The deer hair body is then trimmed to produce a chunky abdomen and broader thorax outline.

This pattern comes from Sweden and it is very effective on summer nights on the Gim River, where huge grayling dine lustily on immense populations of caddis emergers. It is, of course, barely visible on the surface film, especially in the crepuscular glimmer of 1 a.m. in July, just south of the Arctic Circle. It can be made more visible by the addition of a white Poly-yarn or Antron 'wing', sticking up between abdomen and thorax.

Sparkle Sedge Emerger

Hook: Wet fly, sizes 8–16.
Thread: Brown.
Body: 50:50 Antron (or another sparkling synthetic fur) and a natural soft fur (e.g. rabbit), in olive, grey and brown.
Wing and head/thorax: Deer hair. Tie one sparse bunch with the tips back to form the wing, and then spin another one or two sparse bunches in front. Tie off and trim the head/thorax.

This pattern blends ideas of LaFontaine with that of the Muddler Sedge (p. 199). The deer hair helps the fly float in the surface (grease also with Gink).

Floating Pupa (Roman Moser)

Hook: Dry fly, sizes 10–14.
Thread: Brown.
Body: Natural or dark brown dyed deer hair.

A scruffy body simulating the body, legs and shuck of the real insect in the surface film.

Floating Pupa

Hook: Wet fly, sizes 14–18.
Thread: Brown.
Abdomen: Green or olive or grey seal's fur (or substitute).
Rib: Dark brown thread.
Thorax: Brown seal's fur (or substitute).

By Luis Antunez. The dubbing should be fairly 'slack' so that the completed fly has lots of straggling hair fibres. Grease well.

MIDGE LARVAE

Midge larvae often feature in the diet of trout and other insect-eating fish. They are very simple in appearance, resembling well-segmented worms and are often bright red, hence their common name – 'bloodworms'. Not all are red, however – green and olive also being common. A major problem when it comes to fishing imitations is that the naturals live in the river- or lake-bed – so imitations need to be fished very deep. The problem is that it is very difficult to weight artificial larvae sufficiently as this tends to produce too bulky an imitation of such slight beasts. There are two solutions. First, pinch a piece of split shot on the leader close to the fly. Second, fish a very heavy fly (such as a nymph pattern) on a dropper, with the slender bloodworm imitation on the tippet point.

This first pattern rivals the Bare Hook Nymph (p. 57) as the world's simplest artificial fly! Also usefully tied with lime-green floss.

Floss Bloodworm
Hook: Wet fly, sizes 14–16.
Thread: Red.
Body: Length of red floss, knotted at the end.

The next three tyings are not that much more complicated!

Bloodworm (Dave Hughes)
Hook: Curved caddis/shrimp, sizes 12–22.
Thread: Red.
Body: Red floss
Rib: Fine silver wire.

Bloodworm
Hook: Longshank sedge, sizes 12–14.
Thread: Red floss (used in body).
Body: Red floss wound along hook shank, with extra turns behind the eye.
Rib: Red copper wire.

Bloodworm

Hook: Curved grub, size 12.
Thread: Red.
Body: Length of twisted floss, through a gold, silver or other metallic bead, that is fixed in place over a foundation of tying thread soaked with Superglue.

The five bloodworm patterns that follow all have heads of peacock herl. Some larger bloodworms do have keratinised darker patches at the head; peacock herl does attract trout.

Red Larva

Hook: Nymph, sizes 10–14.
Thread: Brown.
'Tail': 2–3 swan or goose herls dyed bright red..
Body: As tails, wound over hook shank.
Rib: Fluorescent red floss.
Head: Peacock herl.

Can be tied with green herls and floss.

Rubber Band Larva

Hook: Wet fly, sizes 12–14.
Thread: Red.
'Tail': Red rubber band.
Body: Goose herl dyed red.
Rib: Fine oval silver tinsel.
Head: 2 turns of peacock herl.

Swannundaze Midge Larva

Hook: Curved sedge, sizes 12–14.
Thread: Black.
Body: Red, amber or olive Swannundaze (see p. 10).
Head: Peacock herl.

Poly Midge Larva

Hook: Curved sedge, sizes 12–14.
Thread: Black.
Body: Red floss.
Overbody: Narrow strip cut from polythene bag.

Rib: Fine silver wire.
Head: Peacock herl

Disco Midge Larva

Hook: Wet fly or nymph, sizes 14–24.
Thread: White for underbody, black for head.
Abdomen: Red Krystal Flash or similar translucent flashy material wound over white thread.
Thorax: Peacock herl.

Can be tied in other colours of both underbody and Krystal Flash, but red is the most effective.

MIDGE PUPAE

Midge pupae develop deep in the water and, as the time approaches for the adults to emerge at the surface, they slowly float upwards until they come to rest, hanging down from the surface film. Then, at the point of hatching, the body of the pupa swings round so that its body lies parallel to and immediately below the water's surface. The pupal shuck now splits and the adult emerges. Like adult caddisfly emergence, while the pupa may rest for several minutes at the surface, the adult is out and away in a split second. So newly hatched adults are rarely seen on the surface.

During a hatch, research has shown that large numbers of pupae move upwards simultaneously so that feeding fish cannot pick them off one by one. Also, during an afternoon or evening hatch, more than one wave of nymphs may reach the surface. So, when there is no sign of activity at the surface, imitations should be fished deep, whereas when there are lots ot adult midges in the air (indicating that a hatch is occurring) and trout are feeding in the surface, an emerger fished in the surface is needed.

It is very easy to convert any midge pupa imitation into an emerger:

1. Before tying the rest of the fly, enclose a small ball of Plastazote (or similar floating foam) in a piece of ladies' tights material and tie this on to of the hook shank, immediately behind the hook eye, before dressing the rest of the fly.

2. Before tying in the thorax, tie in two cul de canard feathers (see p. 163) backwards, by their tips, with the rest of the feathers sticking back over the abdomen. Complete the thorax and then bring the two cul de canard feathers forward, tying them down at the head so that they form a veil over the thorax. Do not trim any straggling cul de canard fibres away for tidiness sake. The cul de canard veil or bubble will hold the pupa in the surface film.
3. Take a narrow, square cross section, piece of white Plastazote or similar dense-celled foam, and tie this in tightly with touching turns of thread along the hook shank. Leave a small piece of foam at the head and tail to match the breathing tubes found at either end of the natural pupa's body. Tie the pupa imitation between the two white ends.
4. After completing the thorax, dub a small ball of polypropylene or similar synthetic dubbing and fix this in place on top of the thorax. A cock hackle can then be tied in under this ball and then wound parachute-style. The fur ball (and parachute hackle if used) are well greased with a semi-solid floatant such as Gink.
5. Tie in a wing of Poly Yarn or Antron on top of the hook shank roughly halfway along where the thorax will be later formed, and post the wing base with several turns of thread. Take a grizzle or blue dun cock hackle and tie this in at the base of posted wing. Now tie the pupal dressing and, having completed that, make three or four turns of hackle around the wing, tie it off, snip away waste and whip-finish. See also p. 159 for other parachute flies. This is a far more difficult tie than the first three, and no more effective.

All five methods are illustrated with the first pattern, the Herl Buzzer.

Alternatively, provided rules permit the use of more than one fly on the leader, fish pupal imitations on short droppers with a large dry fly on the point. Grease up the end of the fly line. The dry fly and tip of the fly line hold the pupae just below the surface. This method, known as the 'washing line technique', is ideally used on lakes.

The other artificial buzzers are for fishing deeper, and their sinking rate may be enhanced by fixing a tungsten bead on the hook behind the eye. Tie the thorax over this bead.

Note on terminology: A commonly used fly-fisher's alternative name for the midge pupa is the 'buzzer' or 'buzzer pupa'.

Note on breathing tubes: These little white tufts, found on the natural, seem often not to be noticed by the trout. However, very occasionally, a deeply fished artificial with breathing tubes will out-fish the same tying where they have been left out. They can be ignored in surface emergers.

Herl Buzzer

Hook: Curved grub or wet fly, sizes 12–16.
Thread: Brown or black
Breathing tubes at end of body (optional): Few fibres white Antron.
Abdomen: Goose herl, dyed olive, grey, tan or black.
Rib: Oval gold tinsel.
Thorax: Peacock herl.
Breathing tubes at head (optional): Few fibres white Antron.

This is a good workhorse of a fly in all types of water. With a Plastazote bead enclosed in ladies' tights material tied at the head, emerger style, it makes a great Suspender Buzzer (see also below).

A

B

C

D

E

(A) Herl Buzzer; Herl Suspender Buzzer with **(B)** Plastazote ball enclosed in tights material as float, **(C)** CDC veil as float, **(D)** Plastazote at head and tail as float, **(E)** polypropylene wing and hackle as float.

The Reverse Buzzer is tied in exactly the same way but on the wet-fly hooks and with the thorax at the end of the hook shank, the abdomen at the eye end. Some fly-fishers have argued that buzzers tied the 'wrong way round' are more effective. No good documentary evidence of this is presently forthcoming!

Black Beauty Thread Midge Pupa

Hook: Wet fly, sizes 14–24.
Thread: Black.
Abdomen: Tying thread.
Rib: Fine copper wire.
Thorax: Fine synthetic fur.

This is an excellent and simple pattern to use at the start of a midge hatch. It can also be used as point fly, with an emerger pattern, such as the next, on a dropper.

Clive Perkins came up with the idea of using several cul de canard (see p. 163) feathers at the head of the fly to act as a 'float', keeping the fly hanging from the surface film. Several of the patterns listed here could be given the 'shuttlecock-treatment'. One example is given.

Shuttlecock Emerger Buzzer

Hook: Curved sedge, sizes 12–18.
Thread: Black.
Abdomen: Stripped black cock hackle stalk.
Thorax: Peacock herl.
Wing cases and float: Several small cul de canard feathers or a bunch of fibres from a large cul de canard feather.

The following, by Charles E. Brooks of the United States, was among the earliest 'suspender' tyings to imitate the pupa hanging from the surface film.

Brooks's Suspender

Hook: Wet fly, sizes 10–16.
Thread: Black.
Breathing tubes at end of body (optional): Tuft of white wool.
Body: Black seal's fur (or substitute).
Rib: Fine silver wire.
Wing buds: A slip of orange goose quill tied as wing case.
Thorax: Peacock herl.
Head: Foam bead enclosed in ladies' tights material.

Marabou Poly Pupa

Hook: Curved grub, sizes 12–16; wet fly, sizes 12–16 for emerger.
Thread: Black or as abdomen.

Breathing tubes at end of body (optional): Few white Antron fibres.

Abdomen: Olive, black or red marabou wound over wet cemented thread.

Rib: Silver lurex.

Over-abdomen: Narrow strip from clear polythene bag.

Thorax: Peacock herl.

Breathing tubes at head (optional): Few white Antron fibres.

Footballer Midge Pupa

Hook: Wet fly, sizes 12–18.

Thread: White.

Abdomen: Black and white horsehair, wound together to give segmented effect.

Thorax: Mole fur.

This is from Geoffrey Bucknell's fly-tying stable. Geoffrey has been one of Britain's leading professional tyers for the past half century.

Red & White Midge Pupa

Hook: Wet fly, sizes 12–16.

Thread: Black.

Breathing tubes at end of body (optional): Bunch white cock hackle fibres, clipped short.

Abdomen: One crimson swan or goose herl and two black swan or goose herls, twisted and wound to give a segmented effect.

Rib: White hackle stalk.

Thorax: Peacock herl.

Breathing tubes at head (optional): Bunch white cock hackle fibres, clipped short.

Floss Buzzer

Hook: Curved grub, sizes 12–16; wet fly, sizes 12–16 for emerger.

Thread: As abdomen.

Breathing tubes at end of body (optional): White cock hackle fibres, tied short.

Abdomen: Floss silk in black or olive or grey or brown.

Rib: White hackle stalk.

Thorax: Dark brown turkey tail herls.

Breathing tubes at head (optional): White cock hackles, tied short.

Quill Buzzers

Hook: Wet fly, sizes 12–20.
Thread: As abdomen.
Abdomen: Stripped cock hackle stalk, black, or cream, or ginger, or olive.
Thorax: Fine fur dubbing, black, or buff, or brown or dark brown.

These were devised by A. K. Best, a leading tyer in the United States.

Also from the United States, the following, devised by Carl E. Richards, will deceive trout that are feeding anywhere on buzzers.

Midge Pupa

Hook: Wet fly, sizes 12–28.
Thread: Finest olive.
Abdomen: Finest olive dubbing.
Thorax: As abdomen, but tied thicker.

In sizes bigger than 14, it will be worth adding breathing tubes of white Antron. Richards tied these only in smaller sizes (18–28).

The same simple pattern can also be tied in black, brown, grey and orange.

Thompson's Delectible Chironomid Pupa

Hook: Nymph, sizes 12–16.
Thread: Black.
Body: Fine black fur dubbing, built up at thorax.
Rib: Fine oval silver tinsel.
Collar: White ostrich herl, 1 turn to suggest breathing fibres.

Dick Thompson of the Department of Fisheries in Washington State also tied this in olive, tan and grey.

Kaufmann's Suspender

Hook: Wet fly, sizes 10–20.
Thread: Black.
Breathing tubes at either end of body: white plastazote (see (3) on p. 109).
Abdomen: Black or olive herl, or stripped quill from peacock eye.
Rib: Fine gold wire.
Thorax: Peacock herl.

By Randal Kaufmann, this pattern lies horizontally in the surface film and suggests a pupa from which the adult will take flight at any time.

Some fly-tyers have noticed the wing buds in a midge pupa and observed that when starting to open they appear orange or fluorescent orange. So they have added wing buds to their imitations. These wing buds may be orange floss, orange plastic, orange herl or orange crisp packet.

Crisp Packet Buzzer

Hook: Curved grub, sizes 10–12; wet fly, sizes 10–16 for emerger.
Thread: Black.
Breathing tubes at end of body (optional): Few fibres white Antron.
Abdomen: Stripped well-marked peacock quill from eye feather.
Wing buds: Two narrow slips cut from an orange crisp packet.
Thorax: Built up with tying thread.
Breathing tubes at head (optional): Few fibres white Antron.
Overbody: Several layers of clear cement (Sally Hansen's 'Hard as Nails' is ideal), allowing each to dry before the next is applied.

If available, Dorito's Tangy Cheese flavour corn chips packet provides an excellent very hot orange.

Epoxy Buzzer

Hook: Curved grub, sizes 12–16.
Thread: Black.
Body: Floss; red, black or olive.
Rib: Fine pearl Crystal Hair or Flashabou.
Wing buds: Red lurex.
Breathing tubes: Short tuft white Antron.
Overbody: Clear epoxy resin.

JC Hatching Buzzer

Hook: Nymph, sizes 12–16.
Thread: Black.
Abdomen: Mix of fur (see below).
Rib: Pearl Flashabou or Crystal Hair.
Wing buds: Jungle cock eye, one either side, tied so that when the thorax has been completed, they peep out at its base.

Thorax: Peacock herl (as alternative, two short slips goose dyed orange).
Fur mixes: 70 per cent black seal's fur (or substitute) and 5 per cent each of red, orange, claret, blue, green and yellow seal's fur; or 70 per cent medium olive seal's fur and 5 per cent each of red, orange, claret, blue, green and yellow seal's fur. The aim is to suggest air bubbles separating the adult body from the pupal shuck.

Devised by Malcolm Greenhalgh. In clear water the jungle cock wing buds are visible for many yards when the rest of the fly is not. If they suddenly disappear, tighten immediately, for a fish must have taken the fly into its mouth!

Shipman's Buzzer

Hook: Wet fly or nymph, sizes 10–16.
Thread: As body.
Breathing tubes at either end of body: White Poly Yarn (tie a length in the full length of the shank plus extra at either end at the start; cut away excess leaving a tuft at the tail and a tuft at the head end).
Body: A good fur mix (as in the last pattern, the JC Hatching Buzzer).
Rib: Pearl Flashabou or tinsel.

A slight modification of Dave Shipman's simple, yet most effective, lake pupa imitation for fishing during a hatch and when the trout are feeding in the surface.

Devised by Ross Marigold for the Madison River, the Serendipity series of flies are said to match midge pupae, though they could equally match caddis pupae. The Beadhead version matches the pupa drifting deep in the water, whereas the Emerger version matches the pupa on point of adult hatch. They are very useful patterns.

Beadhead Serendipity

Hook: Curved shrimp or caddis, sizes 14–18.
Thread: Brown.
Abdomen: Brown Antron yarn, tied in and twisted into a tough rope before being wound up the hook shank. There should be a well segmented effect.

Thorax: Hare's mask.
Head: Goldhead.

Emerger Serendipity
Hook: Curved shrimp or caddis, sizes 14–22.
Thread: Black.
Abdomen: Dark olive Antron yarn, tied in and twisted into a tough rope before being wound up the hook shank. There should be a well-segmented effect.
Thorax: Spun and clipped deer hair, with the hair tips sticking up and back.

Both types of Serendipity can usefully be tied with abdomens of olive, tan, grey, brown, black and red.

Mick Hall has developed his Aussie Midge Trilogy to cope with fish taking midge pupae at different depths: deep, just below the surface and emerging onto the surface. In waters in the British Isles, where it is quite usual to fish three flies on the one leader, the Deep Midge may be fished on the leader point, the other two on droppers.

Deep Midge
Hook: Curved grub hook, sizes 14–16.
Thread: White.
Underbody: White thread.
Body: White Super Floss or similar elastic floss, marked with light olive pen.
Thorax: Olive rabbit.

Subsurface Midge
Hook: Curved grub hook, sizes 14–16.
Thread: White.
Underbody: White thread.
Body: White Super Floss or similar elastic floss, marked with light olive pen.
Wing buds: Pearl Krystal Flash (or similar), 3 fibres.
Thorax: Olive rabbit.

Emerging Midge

Hook: Curved grub hook, sizes 14–16.
Thread: White.
Underbody: White thread.
Body: White Super Floss or similar elastic floss, marked with light olive pen.
Thorax: Olive rabbit.
Hackle: Very short fibres grizzle, 3 turns.
Wing cases: Fine olive foam (e.g. Evasote or Larve Lace).

CORIXIDS, WATER BOATMEN AND BACKSWIMMERS

This category of real insects comprises two main families: the water boatman (Notonectidae) and the lesser water boatman (Corixidae). Because the former swim on their backs, they are also called backswimmers. Although generally they are not a major component of the trout diet, the occasion may still arise when the fish are hooked onto them (as when there has been a population explosion, for some reason). So several imitations have been devised.

The real insect has markedly different ventral and dorsal surfaces, the back (wings) being dark, the underside pale – there may also be a conspicuous silvery air bubble at the end of the body. Also two of the legs are enlarged and act as oars (paddles) which are used for swimming vigorously. These are the chief characters to include in any imitation.

A smooth rugby/American football shaped underbody should be formed, ideally of lead or tungsten foil or wire to aid sinking.

Corixa

Hook: Wet fly, sizes 10–14.
Thread: Brown or black or red (imitates red eyes).
Body: White floss.
Rib: Fine silver wire.
Wings (back): Dark brown squirrel tail.
Legs/paddles: Grouse hackle fibres; a small bunch to either side.

Plastazote Corixa

Hook: Wet fly, sizes 10–14.
Thread: Brown.
Body: Tip flat silver tinsel. The rest – Plastazote (see note below).

Wings (back): Dark brown goose herl.
Legs/paddles: A cock pheasant tail fibre tied back on either side.

Note: For the body, make a small block of white Plastazote, the length just less than that of the hook shank. Make a cut midway down its length and slip the Plastazote onto the shank, next to the silver tinsel tip and the tied-in and sticking backwards goose herls, with the cut uppermost. Put in the cut a drop of Superglue and set aside for it to set. (Make another couple in the meantime.) When set, cut the body to shape with sharp scissors. Next fix the thread on the eye side of the Plastazote body, bring the herls forward over the back and tie off; tie in the two paddles. Whip finish.

This is a great still-water fly, fished on a fast-sinking fly-line. When the line is pulled in quickly the fly dives, and when the pulling stops the fly swims back upwards. Just like the real thing! That's tying-in behaviour!

Yellow Corixa

Hook: Wet fly, sizes 10–14.
Thread: Olive.
Body: Primrose floss.
Wings (back): Olive-green dyed goose herls.
Legs/paddles: A pair of crow or peacock herls (optional).

Some lesser water boatmen are not blackish and whitish like water boatmen.

Water Boatman

Hook: Wet fly, sizes 2–14.
Thread: Red.
Body: Flat silver tinsel.
Wings (back): Crow quill slip.
Legs/paddles: a pair of peacock herls tied to either side.

Pale Moon-Winged Backswimmer

Hook: Wet fly, sizes 12–20.
Thread: Pale olive.
Body: Pale olive floss.
Wings (back): Pale grey duck quill slip.
Legs/paddles: A pair of grey duck quill fibres, tied ⅓ back from the head.

This American pattern by Dave Hughes has a most appealing name – it is also very effective.

Caryl's Water Boatman
Hook: Wet fly, sizes 10–14.
Thread: Black.
Body: Red-tan fox, or cream or white synthetic fur.
Wings (back): Metallic blue mallard speculum slip.
Legs/paddles: Tips of grey goose herls.

By Everett Caryl Sr.

SHRIMPS (OR SCUDS) AND HOG-LICE (OR SOW-BUGS)

Trout, as well as the other fly-fisher quarry species, char and grayling, love to eat small crustaceans, and two of the commonest forms of small crustaceans are freshwater shrimps (in Europe) or scuds (in North America), and hog-lice (in Europe) or sow-bugs (in North America). Sometimes they are referred to by the scientific names *Gammarus* (shrimp/scud) or *Asellus* (hog-louse/sow-bug).

Both live on the river- or lake-bed, or clamber amongst weed or detritus, and they are never found swimming in mid-water or at the surface. Thus artificials ought to be weighted, and the weighted underbody can be formed in such a way that it helps create the correct underlying shape: a flattened side-to-side body (in shrimps), and a flattened top-and-bottom body (hog-lice).

FRESHWATER SHRIMP/SCUD
This first pattern is not weighted.

Gerroff
Hook: Wet fly, sizes 10–14.
Thread: Brown.

Body: 3 parts olive-brown and 1 part fluorescent orange seal's fur (or substitute), well mixed.
Shellback: Clear PVC strip.

This simple pattern, by John Goddard, was given its name from an occasion when small trout would nip in and grab hold as the fly was slowly sinking towards a bigger trout. 'Get off!' became 'Gerroff!'

Killer (Or Grayling) Bug

Hook: Wet fly, sizes 10–14.
Thread: Fine red copper wire.
Body: Fine pinkish-grey darning wool.

A fly by the great river keeper and nymph expert Frank Sawyer. He insisted that only one brand and shade of wool was good enough: Chadwick No. 477. It has been many years since this wool was manufactured (see note on pp. 9–10), but occasionally a card of it appears at auction (usually at the Grayling Society AGM) and fetches a high price, often in excess of £40 ($60). However, despite what Sawyer said, any fine pinkish-buffish-greyish wool will succeed! Grayling (and trout) certainly take this for freshwater shrimps, for they are a major food source on Sawyer's River Avon in autumn and early winter.

Shrimper

Hook: Wet fly, sizes 10–14.
Thread: Orange.
Underbody: Fine copper wire (colour not stipulated, but red is best).
Body: Olive-brown seal's fur; mix in a little fluorescent orange for spring and summer when the shrimps are in mating colour.
Legs (body hackle): Olive cock.
Shellback: Clear PVC strip.

Another John Goddard pattern, and one of the earliest attempts to imitate freshwater shrimps.

Shrimp

Hook: Wet-fly, 12–14.
Thread: Brown.
Underbody: Lead foil built up to give a humped outline.
Body: Mix of fawn, pink and olive-green wool. For spring and summer fishing, add a little bright orange wool to the mix.
Legs (body hackle): Buff or dull ginger hen; trim sides and top.
Shellback: Several layers of clear tying cement, allowing time for each layer to dry before adding the next.

Many tyers of *Gammarus* imitations stress the orange hue of the real shrimps during the mating season. The following are instances of this. Incidentally, the following are similar to several other published scud/freshwater shrimp imitations.

Gammarus In Winter Plumage

Hook: Wet fly, sizes 10–18.
Thread: Grey.
Underbody: Fine lead wire strips on top of hook shank, or wound wire flattened side-to-side with snipe-nosed pliers.
Tails: Few grey or blue dun hen hackle fibres (optional).
Body: Mix of 50 per cent hare's ear, with 10 per cent each of grey, orange, red, olive and claret seal's fur or Antron.
Legs: After completing fly, teased out strands of body material.
Shellback: Pearl Flashabou under a strip of clear plastic bag material.
Rib: Thick black thread.
Antennae: Few grey or blue dun hen hackle fibres (optional).

Note: The fly is equally effective with or without tails and antennae.
Note on hook sizes: While the sizes given here match most species of freshwater shrimp/scud, Ed Engle has pointed out, in *Tying Small Flies*, that one common species of scud found in North America is smaller. *Hyalella azteca* is better matched by the same tyings in sizes 18–24.

Gammarus In Summer Plumage

Hook: Wet fly, sizes 10–18.
Thread: Orange.
Underbody: Fine lead wire strips on top of hook shank, or wound wire flattened side-to-side with snipe-nosed pliers.
Tails: Few orange hen hackle fibres.
Body: Mix of 50 per cent orange seal's fur or Antron, with 10 per cent each of grey, olive, brown and claret seal's fur or Antron and hare's ear.
Legs: After completing fly, teased out strands of body material.
Shellback: Pearl Flashabou under a strip of clear plastic bag material.
Rib: Thick red thread.
Antennae: Few orange hen hackle fibres.

Grey Shrimp

Hook: Curved grub/shrimp, sizes 12–14.
Thread: Light grey.
Underbody: Lead foil on top of the hook shank.
Tails: Barbs from grey partridge hackle.
Body: Medium grey-olive synthetic fur.
Legs: Grey partridge hackle barbs.
Shellback: Clear thick polythene strip.
Rib: 4–6lbs clear mono.
Antennae: Sparse clump grey partridge hackle barbs.

This is Oliver Edwards' imitation. For his Mating Shrimp Oliver uses ginger-orange-dyed grey partridge for tails, legs and antennae, ginger-orange synthetic fur for the body, and uses a rib of fine gold wire.

Cul De Canard Shrimp

Hook: Wet fly or curved grub/shrimp, sizes 12–16.
Thread: Black.
Body: Grey cul de canard wound over a wire underbody.
Legs: Fibres of cul de canard sticking out from body.
Rib: Dark copper wire.

A simple though very effective fly by the great cul de canard expert Marc Petitjean. Marc tied a mating version using rust-red cul de canard and red copper wire.

The next three very effective patterns are by Chris Hosker.

Pink-Spot Shrimp

Hook: Curved grub/shrimp, sizes 12–14.
Thread: Black.
Body: Fine grey synthetic fur dubbing with a pink wool tuft halfway along on either side.
Shellback: Clear poly strip.
Rib: Olive or tan thread.

The Orange-Spot Shrimp has an orange rather than a pink wool tuft halfway along either side of the body. Many *Gammarus* scuds become infected by a parasite that gives them the bright spot on the body.

Tungsten Shellback Scud No. 1
Hook: Curved grub/shrimp, sizes 12–14.
Thread: Red.
Body: Green ostrich herl.
Shellback: Olive tungsten shellback to match hook size (see note).

Tungsten Shellback Scud No. 2
Hook: Curved grub/shrimp, sizes 12–14.
Thread: Red.
Body: Fine pink-buff synthetic fur dubbing.
Shellback: Gold tungsten shellback to match hook size (see note).

Note: These commercially produced tungsten shellbacks add a great deal of weight to the shrimp pattern. Tie the body and whip finish. Then make sure that the dorsal side of the body is smooth (trim away the herl fibres in Scud No. 1). Put a layer of gel superglue over the back and then put in place the tungsten shellback. Hold firmly down until the glue has set.

HOG-LICE/SOW-BUGS

Hog-Louse
Hook: Wet fly, sizes 14–16.
Thread: Brown or olive.
Underbody: Lead wire wound along hook shank in touching turns, then flattened top and bottom with snipe-nosed pliers.
Tails: Speckled brown partridge hackle fibres.
Body: Hare's ear.
Legs and antennae: Speckled brown partridge hackle.
Shellback: PVC strip.
Rib: Fine silver wire.

An alternative tying is identical except for the shellback of grey goose quill slip; another tying is identical other than the body is of grey synthetic dubbing.

American Sow-Bug

Hook: Wet fly, sizes 16–18.
Thread: Grey.
Tails: 2 grey goose quill biots, forked.
Body: Muskrat and grey squirrel furs, mixed.
Legs: Guard hairs from body teased out after the fly has been completed.
Shellback: PVC strip.
Rib: Fine gold wire.

A Dave Whitlock pattern that is excellent in European lakes!

Dry Flies and Floating Flies

> It is generally accepted that an angler can get along with four or five different [dry] fly patterns and catch trout anywhere. You can do a very competent job with an Adams Quill, a Light Cahill, Brown Bivisible and Royal Coachman (hairwing), for instance, provided the fly behaves like an insect after you throw it on the water.
>
> A. J. McClane, *The Practical Fly Fisher*, 1953.

It is very difficult to define the term 'dry fly' for, after a few casts, most dry flies will be moist. Furthermore, most dry flies do not float completely on the water surface: part – perhaps the hook bend and point or maybe the tail – will sink into and through the surface film. In patterns that have no tail, the rear of both hook and body are likely to dip under the surface. Thus dry flies would better be called 'floating' flies. However floating flies would also include emergers, that match the transient and very vulnerable stage in the life cycle of many water-bred insects where the dun or adult-winged fly is emerging from the pupal or nymphal shuck at the surface.

The definitions of dry fly and emerger become more difficult when dealing with adult flies that have failed to escape fully from their nymphal or pupal shucks and will never fly from the water. The fly-fisher sees flies drifting downstream over one trout, but notices that the trout takes only a proportion of the real flies. A quick survey of the flies drifting downstream reveals that some have the end of their abdomen stuck in the nymphal shuck. An imitation with a shuck to the rear of the body (two or three strands of pearl Crystal Hair or some similar material is ideal, see below) catches the trout and its stomach contents are examined. This reveals that most, if not all, of the flies eaten by the fish were incapacitated. So here we have what appears to be a natural dry fly, but what is really a fly trapped in its (later) emerger stage.

Note: This problem seems to be greatest in upwinged flies, where the long tails of the duns are prone to sticking inside the shuck. Some of these unfortunates manage eventually to escape, but often with twisted or broken tails.

Incapacitated Imperial

(See p. 145 for the conventional dressing)

Hook: Dry fly, sizes 14–18.
Thread: Purple.
Tails: 0. Instead 3 strands of pearl Crystal Hair are tied in at the end of the hook shank, very slightly round the bend so that the dip down into the water, to simulate the near empty nymphal shuck.
Body: Grey heron herl.
Rib: Fine gold wire.
Hackle: Ginger or blue dun cock hackle.

All imitations of hatched but incapacitated surface flies might be tied in this way. Take any suitable artificial fly pattern, leave out the tails if there are any, and tie a shuck simulation extended back from the rear of the body.

Rene Harrop devised a very similar method of imitating duns that have the tip of their abdomen or tails stuck in their nymphal shuck.

Cripple Dun

Hook: Dry fly, sizes 12–22.
Thread: As thorax (e.g. olive).
Tails: Z-lon fibres to match shuck, under a few fibres wood duck flank.
Abdomen: Rabbit fur, colour as natural fly (e.g. olive).
Wing tied in front of abdomen: White cul de canard, with a few fibres Z-lon at sides.
Thorax: Rabbit fur, colour as abdomen (e.g. brown olive).

The following is another style that may be fished when trout are suspected of feeding on duns that are stuck in their nymphal shucks.

Sangre De Cristo Emerger (Modified)

Hook: Dry fly, sizes 14–20.
Thread: As body colour.
Tails: Grey Z-lon or 3–4 strand pearl Crystal Hair.
Body: Rabbit fur or a fine synthetic (olive, grey and tan are the essential colours).
Hackle: Olive or blue dun, wound parachute around the wing base.
Wing: Close-cell foam. This is tied in at the beginning and the base 'posted'. After completing the fly, cut the foam to a short length.

When fish are feeding in crystal clear water, in good lighting, below the surface (what Oliver Edwards has called, 'eye ball to eye ball with the fly') their view of both natural and artificial flies is likely to be excellent. Rarely, however, is the water clear and light good. Even in clear rivers, where trout are feeding in rough turbulent water, the view of a subsurface fly will be quite poor and, because of the velocity of the flow, trout will not have much time to examine our artificial nymphs, larvae etc. They must take the fly as soon as it appears, or they will be too late. So, as the previous sections have shown, most of our very effective soft-hackled North Country wet flies, and artificial nymphs, larvae and pupae are not precise imitations. In some cases, outrageous tyings that the fish can hardly fail to see may be far more effective than good imitations (see p. 99 for good examples).

When it comes to the dry fly/floating fly the trout is at a disadvantage in that it looks up to the fly it is going to take. The trout sees the fly pretty much in silhouette, so that colour is unlikely to be very important most of the time and of no importance under certain circumstances (for instance, in very bright dazzling sun, during very dark cloudy weather and towards the end of the evening rise).

Note that in the evening it becomes dark under the water's surface earlier than above. This is because, as the sun becomes low in the sky, increasingly it's light is reflected off the surface so that eventually none penetrates the water. A trout looking up in darkness maybe caught by the fly-fisher still enjoying the twilight above the water's surface.

So, while trout will almost certainly be able to differentiate between a black dry fly and a lightly coloured fly, they are highly unlikely to be able to differentiate between various shades of olive and brown and grey. Examples of evidence supporting this are:

- Trout feeding in one of the great limestone loughs (lakes) of Ireland on the large mayfly *Ephemera danica*, that has a cream, or pale olive-yellow body with tiny black markings, will take a Green Wulff (p. 140) or Grey Wulff (p. 139) that looks nothing like the real thing.
- Trout that are feeding on a host of emergers will take a grey-bodied Klinkhamer or a Pink Klink (p. 139–40) no matter what the body colour of the real insect.
- Trout eating a wide range of duns, with body colours varying from almost white to almost black, will take a grey-bodied artificial, such as an Imperial (p. 145), Adams (p. 154) or a Dark Hendrickson (p. 157–8) – *provided that the size is correct.*

It is for that reason that many great fly-fishers have argued that we do not *need* many kinds of dry flies (Art Flick recommended just three in his *Streamside Guide* (1947): Dun Variant, Cream Variant, Grey Fox Variant). Of course, the further we travel and the greater the diversity of waters we fish, the more dry flies we may need. Visit an Irish lough in May and you need will some big Mayflies (p. 174). Make a trip to the big rough Patagonian rivers or to Yellowstone in summer and you will need some Hoppers and Crickets (p. 220). Have a day in summer by a forest lake and you may need some ant imitations (p. 214).

At the same time, some tyers like to make more precise imitative dry flies. And why not? After all, we tie flies and fish them for our own pleasure, and if some like to have a minimalist's fly box, fine, and if others like to carry a huge portfolio of several hundred different patterns, then that too is fine!

DRY FLY HACKLES

The traditional dry fly has several turns of stiff cock hackle wound around the hook shank just behind the head and hook eye, or wound (palmered) down the body/hook shank. This hackle aids floatation and, supposedly, simulates the legs of the real insect. However, such a hackle detracts from the imitative properties of the fly. With several turns of hackle at the head, the front of the fly's body is held in the air, whilst the tip of the abdomen and tails rest on the surface. In a real dun, caddisfly, midge or stonefly, the six legs are held out at either side, the underside of the front of the body (thorax) rests on or a minute distance off the surface, and the tip of the abdomen and any tails are held in the air. So a good imitation will lack tails and have a short body touching the water.

Such a fly may be hackleless and therefore lack legs, but rarely if ever do trout seem to notice this despite the fact that some fly-fishers have described how the feet of the real fly appear, when looking from the point of view of a trout up towards the surface, as dimples or spots of light on either side of the body. The best hackle, when it comes to imitating floating flies, is the parachute hackle (see p. 132, 159). Otherwise, mostly forget the hackle.

Trout do, of course, take traditionally hackled dry flies, which shows how unobservant they are! And for that reason alone, they are worth tying and fishing. However, if fishing a conventionally hackled dry fly and the trout ignores it, cut away the lower hackle fibres so that the fly body rests on the surface.

DRY FLY WINGS

Three of the most important books on the subject of the trout's view of a dry fly are *A Modern Dry-Fly Code* (1950) and *In the Ring of the Rise* (1976) by Vincent C. Marinaro and *What the Trout Said* (1982) by Datus Proper. They suggested that the wing is probably the most crucial feature in the image of the dun as seen by the trout. Their analysis was 100 per cent correct.

The dry fly wing is also important to the fly-fisher, for it helps in making the fly visible on the surface. Why not tie in a wing that makes the fly even more visible? Tie a paler wing for use when the water surface is dark, or a darker wing when the surface is shimmeringly light. For evening fishing, why not add a white top wing on a sedge imitation, or a white tuft on top of the thorax of a spent spinner?

HOW MINIMALIST CAN WE BE?

The One-Fly

Hook: Dry fly, size 18.
Thread: Grey.
Tails: 2 microfibetts or coq de Leon hackle fibres.
Body: Yellow round thread (e.g. Pearsall's Gossamer) very lightly dubbed (touch-dubbed, see Waterhen Bloa, p. 49) mole fur.

Hackle: Blue dun cock, parachute.
Wing: Lime-green Aerowing or other synthetic hair, posted.

Chris Hosker decided to fish only this pattern in this one size on his home British rivers (that lack bigger stoneflies, mayflies and caddisflies) through one whole year. He reported that his catch was no smaller than in previous years when he had fished a large number of imitative dry flies.

GENERAL DRY FLIES

Dry flies in this category can be used to match a wide range of real flies or they may be used profitably to search the water when fish are not rising or rising sporadically.

Palmers are amongst the oldest trout flies – in 1813 Thomas Best wrote, in *The Art of Angling*: 'the Angler should always try the palmers first'. They should be well oiled so that they float high on the water, or they should not be oiled at all so that they fish in the surface film.

Badger Palmer
Hook: Dry fly, sizes 10–16.
Thread: Brown.
Body: 50:50 mix of hare's ear and blue rabbit furs.
Rib: Brown thread.
Hackle: Badger cock, palmered.

Black Palmer
Hook: Dry fly, sizes 10–16.
Thread: Black.
Body: Black ostrich herl.
Rib: Fine gold wire.
Hackle: Black cock, palmered.

Brown Palmer
Hook: Dry fly, sizes 10–16.
Thread: Brown.
Body: Dark brown seal's fur (or substitute).

Rib: Fine oval gold tinsel.
Hackle: Natural red (brown) cock, palmered.

The following is an excellent French Palmer.

Tricolore
Hook: Dry fly, sizes 12–14.
Thread: Black.
Tails: Few ginger cock hackle fibres.
Body: None.
Hackle: Rear – black cock; middle – ginger cock; front – blue dun cock.

The Bivisibles were devised by E. R. Hewitt, author of *A Trout and Salmon Fisherman for Seventy Five Years*). They are Palmers with a white hackle wound at the front to aid visibility, and are excellent on turbulent water.

Grey Bivisible
Hook: Dry fly, sizes 10–16.
Thread: Black.
Tails: Dark blue dun cock hackle fibres.
Body hackle: Dark blue dun cock, palmered.
Head hackle: White cock.

Black Bivisible
Hook: Dry fly, sizes 10–16.
Thread: Black.
Tails: Black cock hackle fibres.
Body hackle: Black cock, palmered.
Head hackle: White cock.

Brown Bivisible
Hook: Dry fly, sizes 10–16.
Thread: Black.
Tails: Brown cock hackle fibres.
Body hackle: Brown cock, palmered.
Head hackle: White cock.

Trivisible

Hook: Dry fly, sizes 14–16.
Thread: Finest brown.
Tip: 3 turns fine flat silver tinsel.
Body hackles: Rear yellow, middle orange, front light blue dun.

Jack Norris invented this colourful fly for evening fishing when the trout are taking egg-laying female caddisflies in the margins of trout lakes.

Garrett's Marong

Hook: Dry fly, sizes 10–12.
Thread: Light brown.
Body: Furnace cock hackle wound in touching turns up the hook shank.
Hackle: Bright orange cock.

This Australian pattern is a slightly different form of 'bivisible'.

The following five flies are all Australian and, though devised to match insects found on the surface of Australian/Tasmanian streams, they are excellent general patterns for use elsewhere in the trout world.

Movie Star

Hook: Dry fly, sizes 12–16.
Thread: Black.
Body: Peacock herl.
Hackle: Natural red (brown cock) wound both sides of wing.
Wing: Pink Antron or Poly Yarn tied upright.

Could represent a beetle, or a caddisfly.

Dr Wark

Hook: Dry Fly, sizes 12–14.
Thread: Black.
Tail: White feather fibres with black markings.
Body: Green Mylar.
Body hackle: Short-fibred natural red (brown) cock.
Hackle: Natural red (brown cock) wound both sides of wings.
Wings: Blue dun (light grey) hackle points.

Useful during a hatch of any green-bodied water-bred flies.

Guide Tag

Hook: Dry fly, sizes 12–14.
Thread: Black.
Tail: Tuft pink Antron.
Body: None.
Body hackle: Short-fibred black cock.
Rib: Pearl Mylar.
Hackle: Black cock.

Very much an attractor pattern: it looks black and edible!

Superba

Hook: Dry fly, sizes 12–14.
Thread: Black.
Tail: Few natural red (brown) cock hackle fibres.
Body: Orange synthetic dubbing.
Body hackle: Short-fibred natural red (brown) cock.
Hackle: Natural red (brown cock) wound in front of wings.
Wings: Hen pheasant or woodcock quill slips.

This, and the next pattern, could be taken as a dun or spinner, or a caddisfly. They are typical of good all-round dry flies. Not great imitations of anything, but might be anything!

Arthur's Dun

Hook: Dry fly, sizes 12–14.
Thread: Brown.
Tail: 4 cock pheasant tail fibres.
Body: Cock pheasant tail.
Rib: Fine gold wire.
Hackle: Natural red (brown cock) with a brown speckled partridge hackle in front, wound in front of wings.
Wings: Hen pheasant or woodcock quill slips.

PARACHUTE-HACKLED FLOATING FLIES

Parachute flies have a long history. It was thought that they were invented by the Scottish tackle company Alex Martin in the 1930s, and that Martin's patented them to prevent others from profiting from the idea. In the original flies the hackle was wound around an upright pig's bristle. To get around this patent, the hookmakers Partridge of Redditch produced the Aero Hook that had an upright piece of wire behind the eye around which the hackle could be wound. Hardy Bros. (now House of Hardy) retailed flies tied on these hooks as Aero Flies. However, research by Jack Heddon has shown that the patent (No. 379343), which gave Alex Martin an apparent monopoly on the parachute fly, had, in fact, been granted to an American called William Avery Brush in August 1932.

Flies tied with parachute hackles were slow to gain popularity. However, starting in the 1970s, investigations into what trout actually saw of a fly on the surface were being made – and the findings began to affect the design of floating flies. One of the greatest changes was the increased use of the parachute hackle accompanied by an upright, 'posted' wing of synthetic hair (e.g. Poly Yarn and Antron) or natural hair (e.g. mink) or the bases of feather wings (e.g. hackle points). The wing is tied in first. Sometimes the hackle is then tied in at the base of the wing, but not wound until later. The rest of the fly is then tied, and finally the hackle is wound around the wing base before the fly is completed.

Peter McKenzie-Philps introduced his 'Pensioner' series during the late 1970s. Its name derives from the fact that its white mink wing is highly visible, even to us senior citizens whose eyesight may be not what it was half a century ago! Excellent for searching the water.

Black Pensioner

Hook: Dry fly, sizes 12–14.
Thread: Black.
Tails: A few fibres of black cock hackle.
Body: Black herl (e.g. dyed goose).
Rib: Fine gold wire.
Hackle: Black cock, parachute.
Wing: Bunch of white mink tail, tied upright and posted.

May also be tied in olive or brown, but always with the white wing.

The following fly was devised by Hal Jansen in the early 1970s and is tied upside-down so that the hook point and bend stick up in the air and do not penetrate the water surface. As in all parachute flies, the wings are tied in first, with the hackle points sticking upwards in front of the hook point. The hackle stalks are bound together (posted) on the other side of the hook shank and the hackle later wound around them. Thus the fly rides very high on the surface.

Stalking Fly

Hook: Dry fly, sizes 12–14 (must be a down-eyed hook).
Thread: Grey.
Tails: Few fibres blue dun (grey) cock.
Body: Fine grey fur (natural or synthetic).
Rib: Fine silver wire.
Hackle: Grizzle cock.
Wings: 2 grizzle cock hackle points.

The use of curved hooks in conjunction with a posted wing and parachute hackle goes back to at least the early 1980s, but it was not until Hans van Klinken popularised his tying that the combination became widely popular. The original Klinkhamer Special was tied on a large hook and was intended for big grayling in brawling Norwegian rivers (where it also caught salmon). Originally Hans used a Partridge K12ST sedge hook and bent the wire of the hook just behind the thorax to give a different shape to the body. Then Partridge produced a special Klinkhamer hook (GRS15ST) with the added bend. This latter seems to lose fish because the long shank helps the hook point lever out of the trout jaw. Now many tyers dress their Klinkhamers on shorter-shank, curved hooks, and now just about any parachute fly tied on a curved hook on sale in a tackle shop has been given the name Klinkhamer.

The 'real' Klinkhamer tying has a change of thread, from black to the finest white Spiderweb, before the hackle is wound, and the whip-finish is around the wing base and not behind the eye of the hook. There is no need for this complication. After winding the hackle, tie off the hackle behind the hook eye, cut away the waste, and then whip finish in the normal place. Then pull the wing fibres gently but firmly apart to bed down the turns of hackle.

Klinkhamer Special

Hook: Curved, fine-wire, sedge or shrimp hook, sizes 8–20.
Thread: Finest black.
Abdomen: Fine fur dubbing.†
Rib: Fine oval silver tinsel.
Thorax: Peacock herl.
Hackle: Cock hackle, colour dependent on body.†
Wing: White or grey Poly Yarn or Antron yarn or similar synthetic.

† Black and grey are two essential shades. A black hackle goes with a black body, and a grizzle or blue dun with the grey body. Frequently tied also in olive, tan, brown.

Chris Hosker has devised an outrageous version of the Klinkhamer that is a great catcher of fish in arduous conditions:

Pink Klink

Hook: Short-shanked curved hook, sizes 12–16.
Thread: Finest black.
Abdomen: Fine pink dubbing.
Thorax: Peacock herl or synthetic Peacock Ice Dub.
Hackle: Grizzle cock, dyed pink.
Wings: Pink Aerowing, Poly Yarn or Antron.

To us, this looks nothing like a real emerger, but the trout seem to think otherwise!

Bernie's Buzzer

Hook: Short-shanked curved hook, sizes 14–18.
Thread: Finest black.
Tail: 2–3 short fibres pearl Crystal Hair.
Abdomen: Stripped blue dun (grey) hackle stalk.
Thorax: Peacock herl.
Hackle: Grizzle cock, dyed pink.
Wings: White Poly Yarn or Antron.

An Australian pattern imitation a midge emerger.

FLYMPHS

Vernon S. Hidy devised a style of fly that could match an emerger or a semi-waterlogged sedge or land-bred fly. It floats, but is fairly damp! The body fur is fixed in a dubbing loop and should be fairly straggling, with lots of fibres sticking out to create movement and the suggestion of a struggling insect. In slow water the hackle is hen, in fast water cock. This style is the Flymph, a hybrid between a fly and a nymph.

Hare's Ear Flymph

Hook: Dry fly, sizes 12–16.
Thread: Red.
Tails: Brown or furnace hackle fibres.
Body: Mix of hare's ear and mask fur, with plenty of guard hairs.
Rib: Fine oval foil tinsel.
Hackle: Furnace.

Olive Flymph

Hook: Dry fly, sizes 12–16.
Thread: Olive.
Tails: Blue dun hackle fibres.
Body: Olive fur (e.g. dyed rabbit).
Rib: Fine oval gold tinsel.
Hackle: Blue dun.

Other variations might be tied. For example, a black tying might be used to imitate waterlogged beetles or black land-bred flies.

SOME OTHER GENERAL DRY FLIES

Gold-Ribbed Hare's Ear

Hook: Dry fly, sizes 14–16.
Thread: Yellow.
Tails: Few hare's guard hairs.
Body: Dark fur from hare's ear, made thicker at the thorax.
Rib: Fine flat gold tinsel.
Legs: Few hairs teased out of the thorax.

This very old fly is still very efficient, despite the fact that it looks an absolute mess in the fly box, when compared with other neatly tied flies.

Yet grease it up and fish it in the surface film and it will often out-fish modern, more nicely tied dry flies!

Grizzle Mink

Hook: Dry fly, sizes 14–18.
Thread: Brown.
Tails: Bunch grizzle cock hackle fibres.
Body: Mix of grey mink underfur and guard hairs, tied roughly.
Rib: Fine gold wire.
Hackles: Grizzle cock, then a natural red (brown) cock wound through the grizzle. In summer use a ginger cock instead of the red.

This concoction comes from Neil Patterson who wrote, in *Trout Fisherman*, that: 'Few flies can claim to be as downright scruffy as the Grizzle Mink ... If it has nothing else going for it, a roughly tied Grizzle Mink lives. It has life!'

The next two flies are both ancient – but are greatly improved by a little modification.

Grey Duster

Hook: Dry fly, sizes 10–18.
Thread: Black.
Tails: Few badger cock hackle fibres (optional).
Body: Blue-grey rabbit fur.
Hackle: Badger cock.

The modernised tying has a white Poly Yarn or Antron posted wing and the hackle is wound parachute-fashion around the wing base.

This will take trout that are feeding on a wide range of natural flies, and in size 18 is one of the best general flies to use during a hatch/fall or caenis and tricos (see p. 171).

John Storey

Hook: Dry fly, size 14.
Thread: Black.
Body: Peacock herl.
Rib: Red thread (optional).

Hackle: Rhode Island red cock.
Wing: Mallard breast feather tied in as a bunch, sticking out over the hook eye.

Steve Rhodes devised an outstanding modernisation that is one of the world's greatest dry flies (as far as catching trout is concerned):

Hook: Dry fly, sizes 14–22.
Thread: Black.
Tails: Few fibres natural red (brown) cock hackle.
Body: Peacock herl.
Hackle: Natural red (brown) cock, tyed parachute.
Wing: White Antron or Poly Yarn, tied upright and posted.

Trout will take this fly for land-bred beetles and black gnats, for midges and reed-smuts … in fact, for anything black that floats on the water. Especially good on a hot summer's day when things are very difficult. Incidentally, John Storey was a river keeper in the northeast of England.

Members of the Coachman series are highly visible because of their white wings. These wings were originally tied with white duck quill slips, but these are fragile. Most are now tied with white hair wings. They are great 'searching' flies.

Hackle-Point Coachman (Dave Collyer)

Hook: Dry fly, sizes 10–16.
Thread: Red.
Tails: 0.
Body: Peacock herl.
Hackle: Ginger cock, with underside trimmed so that the fly sits lower on the water.
Wings: White cock hackle-points, tied semi-spent.

Coachman Trude (A. S. Trude)

Hook: Dry fly, sizes 10–16.
Thread: Brown.
Tip: Flat gold tinsel.
Body: Peacock herl.

Rib: Fine gold wire.
Hackle: Natural red (brown), wound entirely in front of the wings.
Wings: White calf tail.

Royal Coachman

Hook: Dry fly, sizes 12–20.
Thread: Black.
Tails: Golden pheasant tippets.
Body: Peacock herl, with a central band of red floss.
Hackle: Natural red (brown) cock.
Wings: White calf tail.

The Royal Coachman was devised by John Haily of New York as far back as 1878 – yet it is still a great fish-catcher.

Lee Wulff was one of the most influential fly-fishers of the twentieth century, and not just in his North American home range. Like so many of the patterns in this section, his range of Wulff dry flies can be seen as imitative or simply general 'searching' flies.

Royal Wulff

Hook: Dry fly, sizes 4–14.
Thread: Black.
Tails: Brown bucktail.
Body: Peacock herl, with a central band of red floss.
Hackle: Natural red (brown) cock.
Wings: White calf tail.

This is one of the all time great salmon dry flies, as well as a very good trout fly. The body is, of course, borrowed from the Royal Coachman (but see also the ancient Goldhead on p. 56). Dave Hughes (in *Trout Flies*, 1999) gets rid of the peacock herl in his Beetle Bug and the body is entirely red floss. It is, as he says, a 'searching dry fly'.

Grey Wulff

Hook: Dry fly, sizes 4–14.
Thread: Black.
Tails: Brown bucktail or (F. M.) squirrel.

Body: Blue-grey wool.
Hackle: Blue dun (grey) cock.
Wings: Brown bucktail or (F. M.) squirrel.

Yellow Wulff (F. M.)

Hook: Dry fly, sizes 4–14.
Thread: Yellow.
Tails: Grey squirrel.
Body: Yellow floss.
Hackle: Yellow cock.
Wings: Grey squirrel.

Green Wulff

Hook: Dry fly, sizes 4–14.
Thread: Brown.
Tails: Brown bucktail or (F. M.) squirrel.
Body: Green wool or (F. M.) seal's fur or substitute seal's fur.
Rib: Lime-green floss.
Hackle: Green-olive cock.
Wings: Brown bucktail or (F. M.) squirrel.

Note: lower hackle fibres trimmed

F. M. above refers to Ireland's great fly-dresser Frankie McPhillips. His tyings of the Grey, Yellow and Green Wulffs are outstanding during a mayfly hatch on the famous Irish loughs. Note, however, that they are made more effective by trimming away the hackle fibres sticking down under the hook so that the body of the fly rests on the surface. Otherwise they are great during dun hatches (choose the correct size) or for searching the water.

Elk Hair Caddis

Hook: Dry fly, sizes 12–24.
Thread: Tan.
Body: Fine synthetic fur; colour fairly irrelevant, but grey, brown and olive are fine.
Wings: Bleached elk hair, with the butts sticking out at the front to create a square head.

This is Malcolm Greenhalgh's simplification of Al Troth's Elk Hair

CADDIS (see p. 195). It will catch fish that are eating a wide range of foods from small midges, to duns to biggish caddisflies. Grease it with Gink and let it sit in the surface film. On the night of 21–22 June 1992, two fly-fishers on Norway's River Gloma (one of whom was M. G.) had 154 grayling and five large trout to this pattern!

THE MOP

Hook: Dry fly (fairly wide in gape), sizes 12–16.
Thread: Black.
Body: Tying thread over wing base (see Note).
Wing: Arctic fox tail, in black, brown and olive.
NOTE: Having wound the thread down the hook shank to the bend, take a bunch of arctic fox hair and tie this in with the tips forward over the eye of the hook as the thread is wound forwards to the eye. Then pull the bunch of hair back over the hook shank and bind it down with several turns of thread. Whip finish and cut the wing to length.

This ultra-scruffy fly was devised by Les Gregory and will take fish that are rising to the surface of both lakes and rivers. Its effectiveness lies in its simplicity – to a feeding fish it could mimic a wide range of insect foods.

HUMPY (ALSO KNOWN AS THE GOOFUS BUG)

Hook: Dry fly, sizes 8–16.
Thread: Black.
Tails: Moose body hairs.
Body: Deer body hair.
Hackles: Grizzle and natural red (brown) cock, tied together.
Wing: Deer body hair.

Humpies may also be tied with red, brown and black deer hair. They are great searching flies and, because so much deer hair is used in their tying, very buoyant.

IRRESISTIBLE

Hook: Dry fly, sizes 8–14, salmon hooks, sizes 4–10.
Thread: Black.
Tails: Brown deer hair.
Body: Deer hair spun along the shank and trimmed to a slender cigar shape.

Hackle: Dark blue dun cock.
Wings: Brown deer hair.

This is a notable salmon dry fly (also excellent for sea trout) as well as a river trout fly. The Rat-Faced Macdougal is similar but has two grizzle hackle points for wings and a dark ginger cock hackle wound in front of the wings.

AN ASIDE: FLOATING SNAILS

Most fly-fishers probably think of aquatic snails as living on the bottom or in weed. However some do float to the surface of lakes – and when they do, fish find them easy to mop up. It seems that planktonic algae accumulate in the surface film on sunny warm days and that this encourages members of one family of snails to take in air so that they can float along the underside of the surface film and suck down this plankton soup. A black Cul De Canard Sedge (p. 168) with a thickish body that rests in the surface will deceive the trout. So too will a chunky black wet fly such as the Black & Peacock Spider (p. 54), with the leader greased up so that the fly is fished just beneath the surface. The following are two more precise 'imitations'.

Floating Snail (Bob Church)
Hook: Dry fly, sizes 10–12.
Thread: Black.
Body: Ball of black chenille.

Floating Snail
Hook: Dry fly, sizes 10–12.
Thread: Black.
Body: Piece of black Plastazote (or other dense foam) or cork, sculptured to snail shape.
Eye stalks: 2 short lengths of black mono (optional).

MORE PRECISELY IMITATIVE FLIES:

UPWINGED FLIES or MAYFLIES

The trout-fishing dry fly world has long been dominated by the imitation of the two flying stages of the upwinged flies. The first of these stages is the dun, that flies from the water to adjacent vegetation. The second of these stages is the spinner, that emerges from the shuck of the dun. This is the sexually mature stage and, after emergence, mating occurs in the air and often over dry land. The males die almost immediately after mating, and so often the spent male spinners fall on land and not the water. The gravid female spinners return to the water and there lay their eggs, either by crawling below the surface to stick their eggs onto solid objects (e.g. bridge piers, boulders) or in flight by touching the tip of their abdomen onto the surface as they release eggs. The spent female spinners almost always die on or in the water.

Though the species of upwinged flies are different in different parts of the world, they are so superficially similar that a pattern that matches an American species can be used to match a European species, and vice versa. For examples:

North America	Europe
American blue-winged olive	Large dark and medium olives
March brown (*Maccaffertium*)	March brown (*Rhithrogena*); False march browns (*Ecdyonurus*)
Sulphur duns (*Ephemerella*); Yellow evening dun (*Ephemerella*)	Yellow dun (*Heptagenia*)
Trico (*Tricorythodes*)	Angler's curse (*Caenis*)
Drakes (*Ephemera, Hexagenia, Litobrancha*)	Mayfly (*Ephemera*)

Note: Because tricos and caenis are so tiny and often hatch in vast numbers, they have their own section (pp. 171–4); also the drakes and mayfly because they are both large and seasonal (pp. 174–82).

The following are useful references for readers wishing to know more of American and European upwinged flies:

Ted Fauceglia, *Mayflies: Major Eastern and Midwestern Flies* (Mechanicsburg, PA: Stackpole, 2005).

Malcolm Greenhalgh & Denys Ovenden, *The Fly-Fisher's Handbook: Natural Flies and their Imitation* (Coch-y-Bonddu Books, 2nd rev. edn, 2004).

HACKLED DUN IMITATIONS

These are the simplest dry flies in that they lack wings, though the image of the upper part of the hackle, above the level of the body, may well appear as an upright wing to a trout that is taking duns. These are mostly very old dry flies and, because hackleless and parachute hackled flies are currently in vogue, these have lost their early popularity. Note, however, that they are still often very effective.

The first three are Art Flick's essential dry flies (see p. 127).

Dun Variant
Hook: Dry fly, 12–16.
Thread: Olive.
Tails: Dark blue dun hackle fibres.
Body: Rhode Island red (natural red) cock hackle stalk.
Hackle: Dark blue dun cock.

Grey Fox Variant
Hook: Dry fly, sizes 12–16.
Thread: Primrose.
Tails: Gold-ginger cock hackle fibres.
Body: Cream cock hackle stalk.
Hackles: Golden-ginger, dark ginger and grizzle mixed.

Cream Variant
Hook: Dry fly, sizes 12–16.
Thread: Yellow.
Tails: Cream cock hackle fibres.
Body: Cream or white cock hackle stalk.
Hackle: Cream cock.

Art Flick noted: 'If I had one fly to fish, the Gray Fox Variant would be my choice.'

Imperial

Hook: Dry fly, sizes 14–18.
Thread: Purple.
Tails: Few ginger cock hackle fibres.
Body: Grey heron herl (or any light grey herl as substitute).†
Rib: Fine gold wire.
Hackle: Ginger cock.

† Suitable heron quills can often be found by rivers and lakes, especially in summer when the birds are moulting.

This pattern by Oliver Kite was first published in 1962 and is almost identical to an older fly called the Usk Nailer. Kite had previously fished the Usk, a south Wales river, and may have 'met' the fly before he (re) invented it. Initially Kite insisted that the tails and hackle should be of honey dun cock, echoing the pernickety nature of late nineteenth- and first half of the twentieth-century fly-dressers when it came to hackle colour. When Kite could no longer obtain honey-dun, he wrote that ginger or blue dun hackles would do just as well! Kite also insisted that the herl used to create the body of the fly should be 'doubled and redoubled' on top of the front of the body to simulate the thorax of the real fly. He called this the 'Netheravon style' – Netheravon being the village by the chalk stream Avon in southern England where he lived. The fact that trout would never see the top of the body of the fly as it floated on the water seems to have evaded Kite. Nevertheless, devised to match the large dark olive dun, the Imperial is excellent in any dun hatch, no matter what the body colour of the natural fly. Highly recommended!

Olive Dun

Hook: Dry fly, sizes 12–18.
Thread: Olive.
Tails: Few fibres blue dun cock.
Body: Originally, heron herl dyed olive in picric acid; today goose herl dyed olive [picric acid is a now prohibited explosive chemical].
Rib: Fine gold wire or finest oval gold tinsel.
Hackle: Blue dun cock.

Outstanding in an olive dun hatch. By using sandy-brown herl instead of the olive, a useful march brown imitation results. The following is an alternative when duns with brown bodies are on the water.

Olive Dun

Hook: Dry fly, sizes 14–16.
Thread: Olive.
Tails: Dark olive cock hackle fibres.
Body: Dark olive wool or fine fur dubbing (rabbit or synthetic are ideal).
Rib: Fluorescent white thread.
Hackles: Dark blue dun and dark olive cock, wound together.

This fly is from the stable of the great tyer, the late Thomas Clegg.

Pheasant Tail

Hook: Dry fly, sizes 12–18.
Thread: Black.
Tails: Either a few fibres natural red (brown) cock hackle fibres or 3–4 tips of cock pheasant tail herls.
Body: Cock pheasant tail.
Rib: Fine gold wire.
Hackle: Natural red (brown) cock.

This same pattern also serves as a goodish spinner pattern, made more effective by trimming away all downward pointing hackle fibres so that the fly lies flat on the water (see p. 140).

Diaphane

Hook: Dry fly, sizes 14–18.
Thread: Olive.
Tails: Few fibres dark blue dun cock hackle.
Body: Tying thread, varnished with fly-head cement.
Hackle: Dark blue dun cock.

Another great dun imitation by Guy Plas. Tie several up to the end of tying the body and give the bodies a good soaking with cement. Allow to dry, then reattach the thread and complete the flies.

Beacon Beige

Hook: Dry fly, sizes 14–18.
Thread: Brown.
Tails: Few fibres grizzle cock hackle.
Body: Stripped quill from the peacock eye.
Hackles: Grizzle and natural red (brown) cock.

According to John Roberts (*New Dictionary of Trout Flies*) this was originally called the Beige and had been invented by a member of the Wills family when on leave from the Somme during the First World War. It was resurrected by the great fly-tyer Peter Deane who rated it as: 'the best-ever olive dun imitation'.

It is very similar to a fly used in South Africa called the Grizzle Hackle, in which the tails are natural red cock hackle fibres and the hackles either two grizzle or one grizzle wound in front of a natural red.

Tup's Indispensable

Hook: Dry fly, sizes 16–18.
Thread: Yellow.
Tails: Few fibres blue dun cock hackle.
Body: 2–3 turns of tying thread and then sparsely dubbed with the following fur mix: cream fur from a ram's scrotal sacs, lemon fur from a Welsh spaniel, cream seal's fur, and red and yellow mohair.†
Hackle: Light blue dun cock.

† The photographed fly has the authentic fur dubbing (the vital ingredient obtained by a veterinary surgeon!). First devised by R. S. Austin in 1900 and named by G. E. M. Skues, the unusual body ingredient had been used before. In *The Driffield Angler* (1806), Alexander Makintosh wrote: 'Take a little fine wool from the ram's testicles, which is a beautiful dusty yellow …' Though several substitutes for the fur mix have been marketed, tying with the original mix has become popular at fly fairs and conclaves.

Tup's Indispensable matches the pale watery and other light-bodied upwinged flies.

Many duns have quite dark-coloured bodies, and many attempts have been made to imitate them. The following three are examples.

Claret Dun

Hook: Dry fly, sizes 14–16.
Thread: Claret.
Tails: Few fibres very dark blue dun cock hackle.
Body: Very dark claret dubbing (fine synthetic is ideal).
Rib: Fine gold wire.
Hackle: Very dark blue dun cock.

Sepia Dun
Hook: Dry fly, sizes 12–16.
Thread: Dark brown.
Tails: Dark brown cock hackle fibres.
Body: Dark heron herl.
Rib: Fine gold wire.
Hackle: Black-brown cock.

Iron Blue Dun
Hook: Dry fly, sizes 16–18.
Thread: Crimson.
Tails: Few fibres very dark blue dun (iron blue) cock hackle fibres.
Body: Two turns tying thread, then darkest heron herl.
Rib: Tying thread.
Hackle: Very dark blue dun (iron blue) cock.

Neil Patterson introduced a new style of hackled dry flies in his book *Chalkstream Chronicle* (1995). He called the style Funneldun because the way the body and wound hackle appears resembles a funnel, the fibres funnelling forwards over the eye of the hook. Though his book was published in both the United States and UK, the Funneldun style has been little taken up. This is a pity, for it is a simple-to-tie yet outstanding fishing style. Briefly, the tying is as follows:

1. Fix the thread behind the hook eye and there dub a small ball of fine fur.
2. Tie in a cock hackle behind the fur ball, with concave (underside) of feather facing forwards, towards the eye.
3. Make several turns of hackle tight behind the fur ball, then tie off the hackle with turns of thread that force the hackle fibres forward. Cut away waste.
4. Tie in the body, including a thorax at the base of the hackle, ending up at the beginning of the hook bend.
5. There tie in a bunch of stiff cock hackle fibres so that they stick out slightly round the bend. Make sure they splay out (a turn of thread under the tail bases is useful). Then whip finish at the tail.
6. Cut a V in the hackle fibres that stick up on top of the hook shank. This will ensure that the fly lands on the water upside-down.

Any of the hackled dry flies can be tied Funneldun but: use one size smaller hook (e.g. a 16 instead of a 14). The two great advantages of this style are that the flies fish upside-down (there is no heavy hook point threatening to pierce the surface) and that larger hackles are used that would normally be wasted … and a good inexpensive Indian cape is more than adequate.

The following are three examples of hackled dry flies tied in the Funneldun style:

[A] Imperial Funneldu [B] Olive Herl Funneldun [C] Claret Funneldun

	A	B	C
Hook: (Dry fly)	14–18	12–18	12–16
Thread:	Purple	Olive	Brown
Tails:	Pale blue dun cock	Pale blue dun or olive cock	Natural red cock
Body:	Grey fur	Medium olive fur	Claret fur
Hackle:	Blue dun cock	Blue dun or olive cock	Natural red cock

A B C

SPLIT-WINGED DUN IMITATIONS

Split-winged dry flies were the most popular form of dry fly during the sudden boom of the dry fly in the latter years of the nineteenth and first half of the twentieth centuries. Almost all the dry flies devised by the so-called 'High Priest of the Dry Fly', Frederick M. Halford, and his associates were of this type (see, for example, F. M. Halford, *Floating Flies and How to Dress Them*, 1886). The same fly-dressers also considered that they were tying precise imitations of duns and spinners, matching the colour of

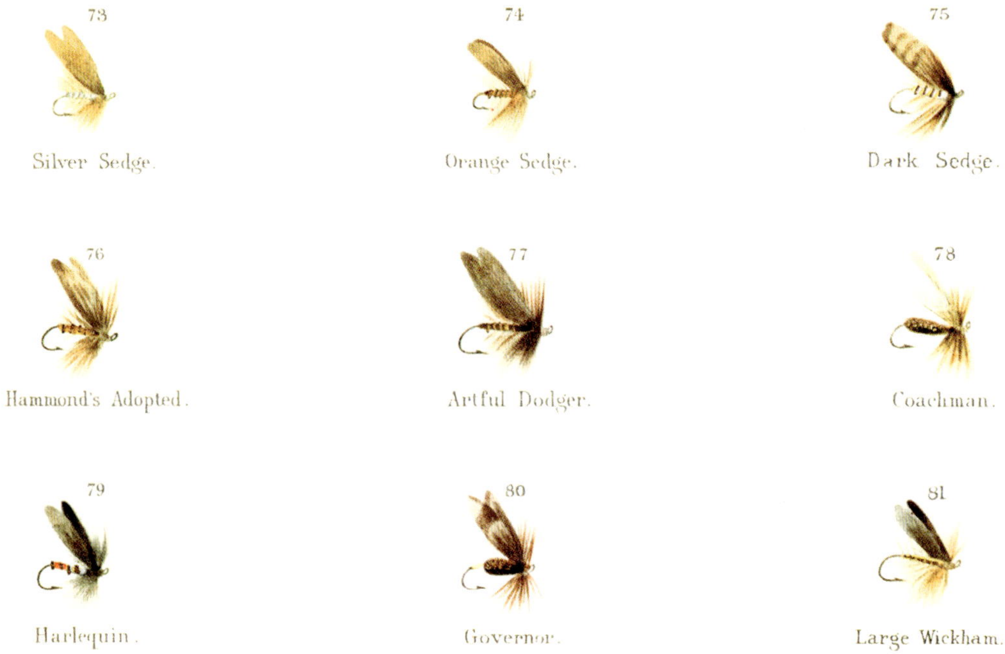

Plate VII from Halford's *Floating Flies* (1886). Note how Halford used upright split wings even in flies that imitated species that do not have upright wings, e.g. sedges (caddisflies).

the insect legs and tails with hackle shade, body with various meticulously dyed herls, furs and quills, and even, in some, the eyes of the real fly with things like dyed horsehair wound at the head of the artificial fly.

Like the classic salmon fly (p. 298), these classic trout dry flies are rarely dressed for fishing. Instead they are dressed to demonstrate the tyer's ability and to preserve their inherent beauty. There are almost always subtle differences in the same flies tied by different tyers – and often it is possible to look at a fly and say with confidence: 'Oh! So-and-so tied that!'

Most of the flies in this category were single split-wings, in that there was a single pair of wings. Others were double split-wings, so that there were two wings on either side. These wings were a major problem, for they were fairly difficult to tie properly and were very fragile; the teeth and slime from the first-caught trout often ruined the fly. So today these old flies are rarely tied to be fished, and they have mainly become 'classic flies' for display, like the old salmon flies of the same era.

Because few modern books on fly-tying techniques include split-winged dry flies, the following tips are included for those who wish to tie some up. Either for display or for fishing:

- Halford and his team mostly used slips taken from the flight feathers of the starling. This is a very difficult material, splitting easily. Some tyers have sprayed the quills with some form of adhesive to prevent splitting, but that is not very satisfactory (it could be considered cheating!). Instead use a similar feather in which the fibres making up the slip are well hooked together: teal or mallard.
- A slip from a quill from the right wing and one from the left wing are needed. These must be taken with precision: take the same width of slip (number of feather fibres) from precisely the same position on exactly the same feather from the same bird. In other words, take the first flight feather from each of the wings of a teal. Pull away the same length of rubbish from the base of each feather. Now take the same width of slip from each feather for the two wings. And so on until all the first flight feathers are used up; after that take flight feathers number two. And so on. The reason for this precision? The curve of each of the flight feathers on each wing varies along their length and from each other. Precision gives a pair of wing slips with the same curve, which will differ from any other pair of wing slips from the same bird.
- Use a very fine thread. The late Jack Norris, whom dry-fly doyen Dermot Wilson rated the neatest tyer of a dry fly during the 1960s and 1970s, used a strand taken from a 16-denier ladies' real silk stocking!

The following are a sample of split-winged dry flies tied by Stuart Bowdin.

Blue Dun

Hook: Upwinged dry fly, sizes 14–16.
Thread: Yellow.
Tails: 2 rabbit or hare whiskers.
Body: Tying thread dubbed lightly with mole.
Hackle: Blue dun cock.
Wings: Teal wing slips.

Blue-Winged Olive

Hook: Upwinged dry fly, sizes 14–16.
Thread: Olive.
Tails: Pale blue dun hackle fibres.
Body: Tip flat gold tinsel, the rest green-olive seal's fur (or substitute).

Hackle: Medium olive cock.
Wings: Teal quill slips, darkest available.

Flight's Fancy

Hook: Upwinged dry fly, sizes 14–16.
Thread: Primrose.
Tails: Gallina dyed green or green-olive (dyed mallard is sometimes used).
Body: Primrose floss.
Rib: Narrow flat gold tinsel.
Hackle: Light ginger cock.
Wings: Teal quill slips, pale.

Ginger Quill

Hook: Upwinged dry fly, sizes 14–16.
Thread: Light brown.
Tails: 'Pale brown ginger' (i.e. a good ginger or light natural red).
Body: Stripped peacock quill.
Hackle: 'Pale brown ginger' cock.
Wings: Teal quill slips, pale.

Orange Governor

Hook: Upwinged dry fly, sizes 14–16.
Thread: Orange.
Tails: Few natural red cock hackle fibres.
Body: Tip of orange thread, then peacock herl from the eye.
Hackle: Natural red cock.
Wings: Teal quill slips.
Note: Though devised in the UK, this was once one of the most popular dry flies in the United States.

July Dun

Hook: Upwinged dry fly, sizes 12–14.
Thread: Olive.
Tails: Light olive cock hackle fibres.
Body: Yellow-olive herl (originally heron herl dunked in picric acid.
Rib: Fine gold wire.
Hackle: Light olive cock.
Wings: Teal quill slips.

Little Marryat

Hook: Upwinged dry fly, size 16.
Thread: Cream.
Tails: Palest olive or cream cock hackle fibres.
Body: Fine cream fur (opossum).
Hackle: Cream cock.
Wings: Teal quill slips, palest.
Note: Named after George Selwyn Marryat, Halford's friend and mentor.

Lock's Fancy

Hook: Upwinged dry fly, sizes 14–16.
Thread: Primrose.
Tails: Pale honey or ginger cock hackle fibres.
Body: Tying thread.
Rib: Fine gold wire.
Hackle: Pale honey or ginger cock.
Wings: Teal quill slips.

Red Quill

Hook: Upwinged dry fly, sizes 12–16.
Thread: Brown.
Tails: 3 fibres of the brightest natural red cock.
Body: Stripped peacock quill.
Hackle: Brightest natural red cock.
Wings: Teal quill slips.
Note: Halford rated this as the best all-round dry fly!

These last two patterns are by the late Jack Norris.

Sepia Dun

Hook: Down-eyed dry fly, size 14.
Thread: Finest brown (see notes above).
Tails: 6 natural red cock hackle fibres.
Body: Rear 60 per cent a stripped natural red hackle stalk; front 40 per cent black crow herl as thorax.
Hackle: Natural red cock.
Wings: Mallard quill slips, choosing the darkest section.

Pale Evening Dun

Hook: Down-eyed dry fly, size 16.
Thread: Finest brown (see notes above).
Tails: 6 cream cock hackle fibres.
Body: Rear 60 per cent a stripped cream or white cock hackle stalk; front 40 per cent pale buff herl (e.g. dyed goose).
Hackle: Cream cock.
Wings: Mallard quill slips.

HACKLE-POINT DUN IMITATIONS

It is difficult to understand why relatively few dun imitations have been tied with hackle-point wings, for they are so much easier to tie than the split wing (above) and far more durable. They are more often found on spinner imitations (p. 182, 184). Originally hackle points were taken from cock hackles. Today, hen hackle points are probably better to use in all hackle-point dry flies than hackle points from a cock cape. Hackle points from the 'new genetic' capes are far narrower than from the Indian capes used up to the 1980s. Feathers from hen capes give wider hackle points.

There is no reason why any dun imitation should not be tied with hackle-point wings.

Olive Hackle Point Dun

Hook: Dry fly, sizes 12–20.
Thread: Olive.
Tails: Blue dun cock hackle fibres.
Body: Finest olive fur (e.g. rabbit or synthetic).
Rib: Fine oval gold tinsel (optional).
Hackle: Blue dun cock.
Wings: Blue dun hackle points (originally cock, but today use hen).

Adams

Hook: Dry fly, sizes 12–20.
Thread: Black.
Tails: A few grizzle and natural red (brown) cock hackle fibres.
Body: Grey muskrat.
Hackles: Grizzle and natural red (brown) cock.
Wings: Grizzle cock hackle points, tied upright or semi-spent.

This fly, by Ray Bergman, was created in approximately 1930 and is still going strong, 80 years later. Any trout, intent on taking a medium-sized or small dun from the surface of any river or lake, may well be fooled by this magnificent fly.

Kossie Dun

Hook: Dry fly, sizes 12–16.
Thread: Finest black.
Tail: Pale ginger cock hackle fibres.
Body: Fine pale ginger dubbing (natural or synthetic).
Hackle: Natural red (brown) cock.
Wings: Cree hackle points.

An Australian dry fly that can be used to match a wide range of light-brown-bodied duns, including the march browns of the Northern Hemisphere.

A. K. Best is a leading North American fly-tyer. In his book *A. K.'s Fly Box* (1996) he gives us several dun imitations with hackle-point wings. Often his tyings require some materials to be specially dyed, and for this purpose his book *Dying and Bleaching Natural Fly-Tying Materials* (1993) could come in handy. The following is one of his most effective patterns.

Quill Dun

Hook: Dry fly, sizes 14–18.
Thread: Grey.
Tails: A few medium blue dun hackle fibres.
Body: Medium blue dun hackle stalk (one stalk for hooks <#18, two for hooks >#18).
Hackle: Light grizzle cock.
Wings: Light medium dun hen hackle points.

In his book *A Modern Dry-Fly Code* (1950), Vincent Marinaro came up with the idea of 'thorax duns'. He suggested that the trout may clearly see the thorax of the dun touching or almost touching the water surface, with feet around the thorax making pin-points of light at the water surface. Thus, he shortened the body to only the thorax and, because the wings stick up from the dun's thorax, he tied the wings midway along the hook shank.

Olive Thorax Dun
Hook: Dry fly, sizes 12–20.
Thread: Olive.
Tails: 2 microfibetts or coq de Leon hackle fibres, tied as outriggers.†
Body: Fine olive fur (e.g. rabbit or synthetic).
Hackle: Blue dun cock, works equally behind and in front of the wings.
Wings: 2 blue dun hen hackle points.

† Dub a whisper of fur on the thread and use this the make a tiny ball at the end of the hook shank. Then tie the tails, one on each side, immediately in front of this tiny ball. The fur ball will help hold out the tails so that they adequately support the heavy hook bend.

Harry Darbee devised a way of using a single feather to imitate both tails and body of a dun. The following is an example of this style that, by changing the shade of the materials being used, can be adapted to match any dun species.

Olive Dun
Hook: Dry fly, sizes 12–16.
Thread: Grey or black.
Tails and body: Take an olive cock hackle and cut away the tip. Leaving 2 or 3 fibres in either side of the cut in their natural position, pull the rest of the hackle fibres forward in the same way that a 'wonder-wing' is created (see p. 202). Tie this to the mid-point of the hook shank to make 2 tails and the body.
Hackle: Blue dun cock.
Wings: 2 blue dun hen hackle points.

FEATHER-FIBRE WING DUN IMITATIONS

This includes some of the oldest and best dun imitations. The wings are very easy to tie: after fixing the thread to the shank a couple of eyes diameter behind the eye, tie in a bunch of feather fibres forward over the eye of the hook. Then bring the bunch into an upright position with a couple of turns of thread before splitting the bunch into two and separating them with two figure-of-eight turns of thread around their bases. Now go to the end of the hook shank and tie the rest of the fly.

The two Cahills are excellent during a hatch of medium to small duns of nondescript appearance. They take their name from Daniel Cahill, who worked on the New York railroad in the 1880s.

Dark Cahill

Hook: Dry fly, sizes 12–18.
Thread: Grey or black.
Tails: Dark ginger cock hackle fibres.
Body: Muskrat.
Hackle: Dark ginger cock.
Wings: Lemon wood duck flank feather fibres.

Light Cahill

Hook: Dry fly, sizes 12–22.
Thread: Pale yellow.
Tails: Cream cock hackle fibres.
Body: A fine cream or cream-yellow dubbing.
Hackle: Cream.
Wings: Lemon wood duck flank feather fibres.

Theodore Gordon is one of the most revered names in the history of trout fishing in the United States and his fly remains a great catcher of trout the world over.

Quill Gordon

Hook: Dry fly, sizes 12–16.
Thread: Black.
Tails: Blue dun cock hackle fibres.
Body: Stripped peacock quill (those from near the eye are the ones to use for they are better marked).
Hackle: Blue dun cock.
Wings: Wood duck flank feather fibres.

Roy Steenrod of Liberty, NY, devised the following as long ago as 1916. It still catches trout.

Hendrickson

Hook: Dry fly, sizes 12–16.
Thread: Tan.
Tails: Blue dun cock hackle fibres.
Body: Fawn fur from a fox's belly.
Hackle: Blue dun (originally 'rusty blue dun', but such hackles are very rare).
Wings: Wood duck flank feather fibres.

The Dark Hendrickson is identical, but has a body of muskrat fur.

March Brown
Hook: Dry fly, size 12.
Thread: Orange.
Tails: Dark ginger cock hackle fibres.
Body: Fawn or light yellow-brown fur (dyed rabbit or synthetic).
Rib: Tying thread.
Hackle: Grizzle and ginger cock, tied together.
Wings: Wood duck flank feather fibres.

Kakahi Queen
Hook: Dry fly, sizes 12–14.
Thread: Grey.
Tails: Ginger cock hackle fibres.
Body: Stripped peacock quill.
Hackle: Ginger cock.
Wing: Bunch of mixed drake mallard flank and dyed yellow partridge hackle fibres.

This is a fly from the Antipodes that will catch trout on the other side of the world.

CUT- OR BURNT-FEATHER WINGS

In these the wings are cut from a pair of matching feathers, or they are held in a special tool that is the shape of the wings and excess feather is burnt away. The wing therefore consists of feather fibres and the central feather stalk. Such wings have varied in popularity and they have two main drawbacks. Firstly, if not tied perfectly, they cause the fly to spin in the air like the falling fruits of plane and sycamore trees. This causes the leader to twist and become kinked. Secondly, the stiff feather stalk running through the centre of the feather may hinder the hook entering the mouth of the fish. For these reasons, relatively few use this style of winging today.

Cut-Wing Olive
Hook: Dry fly, sizes 12–18.
Thread: Olive or light brown.
Tails: Blue dun cock hackle fibres.

Body: Fine olive dubbing (e.g. rabbit or synthetic).
Hackle: Blue dun cock.
Wings: Blue dun cut-wings (or burnt-wings).

Any other dun imitation can be modified with this style of wing.

PARADUNS

Paraduns are dun imitations with a parachute wings (parachute hackles were introduced on p. 108 with some emerger dressings). Any dun dry-fly dressing can be easily converted into a parachute fly by giving the fly an upright posted wing (this is done first, before the rest of the fly is tied), then winding the hackle around this wing instead of around the hook shank as in conventional tyings. Such flies will often out-fish the conventional parent fly.

The choice of wing material: Some tyers have chosen a clump of hair (e.g. white mink), others a clump of white feather fibres (e.g. turkey), but the simplest to use is a one of the synthetic yarns such as Antron or Poly Yarn. After fixing the thread in place around the hook shank, a length of yarn is tied in about one third the way back from the hook eye, with the length that will become the wing pointing over the hook eye. Waste to the rear is cut away. Then the wing is lifted vertically, several turns of thread are made to hold it upright, and then about six turns made around the base of the wing to 'post' it. When the fly is finished, cut the wing to the required length.

Note on tails: Cock hackle fibres are often used, tied in as a clump and then splayed. However, the use of outrigger tails is perhaps more effective. Dub a tiny amount of body fur on the thread and use that to create a tiny ball at the end of the shank. Now tie in a couple of Microfibbets or coq de Leon hackle fibres immediately forward of this ball on either side. The tiny ball will hold them out at an angle from the body.

Olive Paradun

Hook: Dry fly, sizes 12–16.
Thread: Olive.
Tails: Few fibres blue dun cock hackle fibres, or dun Microfibbets or coq de Leon hackle fibres, tied outrigger-style.

Body: Fine olive fur (natural, e.g. dyed rabbit, or synthetic).
Rib: Finest oval gold tinsel (optional).

Hackle: Blue dun cock.
Wing: Grey Antron or Poly Yarn.

This will match all olive duns and blue-winged olives.

Yellow Paradun

Hook: Dry fly, sizes 12–16.
Thread: Yellow.
Tails: Few fibres yellow cock hackle fibres, or buff-yellow Microfibbets or coq de Leon hackle fibres, tied outrigger-style.
Body: Fine yellow fur (e.g. dyed rabbit or synthetic).
Rib: Finest oval gold tinsel (optional).
Hackle: Yellow cock.
Wing: Yellow Antron or Poly Yarn.

This matches yellow dun, yellow evening dun and sulphur duns.

March Brown Paradun

Hook: Dry fly, sizes 12.
Thread: Orange.
Tails: Few fibres ginger cock hackle fibres, or brown Microfibbets or coq de Leon hackle fibres, tied outrigger-style.
Body: Sandy-brown fur from hare's ear and mask, or dyed light brown natural (e.g. rabbit), or synthetic.
Rib: Orange thread (optional).
Hackle: Ginger and grizzle cock, wound together.
Wing: Brown Antron or Poly Yarn.

A good match for all march browns and false march browns.

Many of the world's duns are very pale in colour, with cream, almost white abdomens with perhaps a tinge of olive. The name 'Pale Watery' matches them perfectly.

Pale Watery Paradun

Hook: Dry fly, sizes 12–18.
Thread: Pale grey.
Tails: Few fibres cream dun cock hackle fibres, or dun Microfibbets or coq de Leon hackle fibres, tied outrigger-style.
Body: Fine textured cream fur (e.g. opossum or synthetic).

Hackle: Cream cock.
Wing: White or cream Antron or Poly Yarn.

Other duns are very dark in colour: blackish-purple or black-brown. These can all be mimicked by the DARK GREY PARADUN – trout will not notice subtle differences in shade.

DARK GREY PARADUN

Hook: Dry fly, sizes 14–18.
Thread: Black or dark grey.
Tails: Few fibres dark blue dun cock hackle fibres, or dun microfibetts or coq de Leon hackle fibres, tied outrigger-style.
Body: Very dark grey ('iron blue') fur (e.g. dyed rabbit or synthetic).
Hackle: Very dark dun or iron blue cock.
Wing: Dark grey Antron or Poly Yarn.

SOME AUSTRALIAN PARACHUTES

The great Australian fly-dressers Mick Hall and the late Warryn Germon have adapted the Klinkhamer style to match several of the flies that emerge at the surface of Tasmanian and Victorian rivers and lakes. The following will also work well in the Northern Hemisphere.

BLACK WARRYN

Hook: Curved grub hook, sizes 12–16.
Thread: Black.
Abdomen: 4–5 goose herls dyed black.
Rib: Fine silver wire.
Wing: Black synthetic, posted.
Thorax: Rear half peacock herl, front half fine black dubbing
Hackle: Black cock, 4 turns.

This pattern by Australia's Warryn Germon, is a very useful all-round emerger and is used on the waters of Tasmania's highlands when the lambda dun is hatching (see following fly).

LITTLE GREY EMERGER

Hook: Curved grub hook, sizes 14–18.
Thread: Blue-grey.
Body: Fine blue-grey dubbing.
Wing: Silver-grey EP Trigger Point, or Antron or Poly Yarn.
Hackle: Grizzle cock; four turns.

Matches the little grey sedge during emergence, but just as useful in smaller sizes during a hatch of pale watery duns.

Aussie March Brown

Hook: Curved fairly long shank sedge hook, size 18 (see Note).
Thread: Tan.
Tails: Pardo coq de Leon fibres (note that Microfibbets are also excellent).
Emptying shuck (rear 1/3 of abdomen): A warm brown synthetic fur blend (see note).
Abdomen (front 2/3): Mix hare's ear and warm brown blend.
Wing: Mix brown and black synthetic hair, posted.
Thorax: Larva Lace Dry Foam.
Hackle: Medium or dark champagne cock.

Note: Mick Hall, who devised this fly, uses a very long shank Partridge 15BN Klinkhamer hook. This tends to lever out of a trout's jaw, so a shorter shank is preferable when tying the fly for fishing. Mick also uses Spirit River brand of synthetic fur for the body and wing. This can be difficult to find. Instead use very fine natural/synthetic furs, as the trout may not notice the difference! A great fly, and not only for Australia/Tasmania. The Aussie March Brown is also called the Lambda Dun.

Rusty Dun

Hook: Straight or slightly curved emerger, or long shank dry fly hook, sizes 14–16.
Thread: Tan.
Tail: Medium pardo coq de Leon (see note above).
Body: Warm brown mix of synthetic fur (see note above).
Wing: Dark grey (or blue dun) synthetic hair, posted.
Hackle: Golden badger cock, 4 turns.

Mick Hall's excellent imitation of a dun that hatches on the streams of northern Victoria throughout the season.

All Rounder Baetid

Hook: Straight or slightly curved emerger, or long shank dry fly hook, sizes 12–18.
Thread: Tan.

Tail: Medium pardo coq de Leon.
Body: Mix of hare's ear and a fine brown fur, synthetic or natural (see note above).
Wing: Dark grey (or blue dun) synthetic hair, posted.
Hackle: Golden badger or medium champagne cock, 4 turns.

Baetids are one of the staple families of upwinged flies (or smaller mayflies). This pattern by Mick Hall matches the 17 known Australian species, but it will equally match the larger number of species found in North America and Europe.

Kossie Dun

Hook: Dry fly, sizes 8–10.
Thread: White.
Tails: 4–5 strands moose mane.
Body: Medium hare's fur (natural or synthetic), with terracotta spirit-pen markings on back.
Wing: Palest grey (or pale morning dun dun) synthetic hair, posted.
Hackle: Light tan cock, 4 turns.

See note, previous page. There are four species of Kossie Dun (Kosciuszko Dun) in the mountain streams of south-eastern Australia, one of them discovered recently by the late Warryn Germon and Mick Hall (who designed this imitation).

CUL DE CANARD DRY FLIES

The most revolutionary recent development in the design of dry flies, and perhaps in the entire world of fly-dressing, began in the late 1970s in the centre of Europe. That development was based on the use of the few quite distinctive feathers found around the preen gland of ducks. Those feathers were named 'cul de canard' by the great French fly-dresser Henri Bresson. This can be translated as the duck's bum and is often abbreviated as CDC. The huge growth in the popularity of CDC as a fly-tyer's feather comes in part from the properties of the material, and in part from the work of one man, Marc Petitjean, who brought together all the different uses of CDC that were scattered around central Europe and added his own major contribution in 1985–6, the CDC body (for full details, see Leon Links, *Tying Flies in CDC*, 2003).

Cul de canard feathers.

CDC has the following properties that make it an ideal material for dry flies and emergers:

- It is light and very strong. Most CDC dry flies can easily face the teeth of ten trout. Many CDC dry flies have caught over 30 fish without falling apart and some over 50 without disintegrating. That cannot be said of most small, imitative dry flies.
- It is highly buoyant. There are two reasons for this. First of all floatation is enhanced by a very thin film of oil coating the feather, from the preen gland of the duck. This oil is hydrophobic: it repels water. Secondly, the feather structure is water repellent. Each CDC feather fibre is coated with microscopic barbules that are tightly coiled. These coils hold air and this air helps keep the CDC fly afloat. Should some of these minute air-holding coils take in water, then a couple of quick false casts will usually get rid of the water and put air back in its place. Sometimes a CDC fly will become waterlogged and seemingly impossible to dry (as after catching a hard-fighting fish, especially when coated in lots of slime). For most normal dry flies, that is their end. For a CDC dry fly, wash the fly well in the river or lake and set it aside. It will then dry out as new.†
- CDC fibres are extremely soft so that, in the cast, they collapse in a streamlined fashion and offer little resistance to the air as the line pulls them through it. Then, as the forward cast ends, the CDC fibres open up and the fly gracefully floats down to the water. So more precise yet gentler casts are possible with CDC dry flies than most others.

† Floatants should not be used on CDC because they fill those little air-filled coils. There is one exception: in CDC bodies (see below) the feather structure is somewhat damaged as the body is tied, so Marc Petitjean recommends giving the underside of the body a thin smear of CDC floatant.

Two people vie for who was the first to use CDC in fly-tying, in the 1920s: one was Maximilian Joset who used the feather in his Moustique series; the other Charles Bickel who marketed his dry flies under his own name.

Moustique

Hook: Dry fly, sizes 14–20.
Thread: Fine black.
Tail: Sparse bunch cock hackle fibres.
Body: Pearsall's Marabou floss silk, the colour to match that of the natural fly's body.
Rib: A darker shade of the same floss.
Hackle: Grey-brown CDC feather wound as a hackle.

Bickel's Dry Fly

Hook: Dry fly, sizes 14–16.
Thread: Fine black.
Tail: None.
Body: Pearsall's Marabou floss silk, the colour to match that of the natural fly's body, or peacock herl.
Hackle: Grey-brown CDC feathers wound as a hackle.

Both types of fly would almost certainly fish with their bodies hanging down from the underside of the surface film, held there by the CDC hackle holding position in the surface film. They were, therefore, early forms of 'emergers'.

It was late in the 1970s that Slovenia's Marjan Fratnik produced what is still the most famously named CDC dry fly, the F-Fly. It is very easy to tie and it is extremely effective; and by varying size and colour it can be used to match any real fly from the tiniest of midges to the largest mayflies and caddisflies.

F-Fly

Hook: Dry fly, sizes 10–22.
Thread: As body.
Body: Tying thread, the colour to match that of the natural fly's body. Originally Marjan used round silks like Pearsall's Gossamer (it can still be bought).
Wing: Grey CDC feathers: 3 for hook sizes 10–12, 2 for 14–16, 1 for 18–20.
Note: The feathers are tied back, on top of the hook shank, and when then fly is completed they are cut back to the required length (a fraction beyond the bend of the hook).

The German fly-dresser Gerhard Laible, author of *Cul de Canard Flies* (1993), made two major contributions to the further development of CDC flies. The first was the technique of using a thread loop to form a false hackle of CDC feather fibres.† He employed this technique in his Parachute Emerger.

CDC Parachute Emerger

Hook: Dry fly, sizes 12–18.
Thread: Black.
Tails: Brown or grey hackle fibres.
Body: Fine natural brown or grey fur (e.g. rabbit, mink, muskrat).
Float/wing case: Ball of fine cell foam (e.g. Polycelon) in yellow or white for visibility.
Hackle: CDC fibres.

† Petitjean has designed a 'Magic Tool' (with accompanying DVD) that makes the production of these false hackles very easy.

CDC Bubble Emerger

Gerhard Laible was also the first to use CDC feathers to form a 'bubble' over the thorax of emerger patterns to keep them afloat at the surface film.

Take any unweighted nymph or pupa that you want to fish hanging down from the surface film of the river or lake so that it matches a real nymph or pupa that is on the point of hatching, and give it a CDC bubble. Tie the abdomen. Now take two CDC feathers (white or grey) and tie them in by their tips. With the feather stalk pointing backwards over the back of the abdomen. Now tie the thorax. Then bring the two CDC feathers forward over the back of the thorax and tie them down at the head in such a way that they form a CDC bubble over the thorax. Finish the fly. The CDC bubble will hold the thorax under the surface film.

Two examples:

CDC Bubble Buzzer Emerger

Hook: Dry fly, sizes 12–16.
Thread: Black or brown.
Abdomen: Heron or goose herl, dyed black, grey or olive.
Rib: Fine oval gold tinsel.
Bubble: Two white or light grey CDC feathers.
Thorax: Peacock herl.

CDC Bubble Mayfly Emerger

Hook: Dry fly, sizes 10–16.
Thread: Black or brown.
Abdomen: Heron or goose herl dyed grey or olive or tan or cream.
Rib: Fine oval gold tinsel.
Bubble: Two white or light grey CDC feathers.
Thorax: Peacock herl or fine synthetic dubbing a shade darker than the abdomen.

Marc Petitjean brought all the virtues of CDC together in the middle of the 1980s, adding two other techniques that were made easy by his own sourced large CDC feathers. The first was a wing made, not from whole feathers, but from soft CDC feather fibres. The second was the twisted CDC body, where a CDC feather is tied in at the end of the hook shank, the fibres dubbed (or twisted) round the feather stalk into a CDC rope, and the rope wound forward to create the body.

Basic CDC Dry Fly

Hook: Dry fly, sizes 8–28.
Thread: As body.
Tails: Three coq de Leon hackle fibres or, larger sizes, three cock pheasant tail fibres (optional).
Body: CDC feather, with the fibres twisted round the feather stalk.
Wing: CDC feather fibres.

This is one of the greatest dry flies, for by manipulating size and colour, *any* floating insect can be imitated. For instance, to match a tiny black midge, use black CDC for the body and white or grey for the wings, on a size 18–28 hook, whereas to match a large *Ephemera* mayfly use pheasant tail for the tails, buff or pale yellow or light olive CDC for the body and for the wings, on a size 8–10 hook.

[A] CDC Black Gnat [B] CDC Brown Caddis [C] CDC Blue-Winged Olive [D] CDC Ephemera Mayfly

A

B

To tie: Take the thread to the end of the hook shank and there trap in an appropriate large CDC feather by its tip. Take the thread two-thirds of the way back to the hook eye. Now twist the feather fibres around the stalk and wind the CDC rope forward to the hanging thread to create an abdomen. Tie off, but do not cut away the rest of this feather. Now take CDC feather fibres for the wing and tie them in over the abdomen. Always make the wing bulkier than you initially think: for a size 8–10 mayfly you will need the fibres from 2–3 large CDC feathers; for a small size 16–18 1–1½ feathers. Go back to the remains of the feather that you used to form the abdomen, and use it to form a distinct thorax in front of and over the bases of the wings. Whip finish. Trim away any CDC fibres sticking downwards from the body, but do not be too tidy! Finally, cut the wing to length.

Tip: If tying a dark wing (e.g. brown to match evening caddisflies), tie a bunch of white CDC fibres on top of the wing. That will make it more visible in the gloaming.

C

D

Cdc Mayfly Dun (Marc Petitjean)

Hook: Dry fly, sizes 8–10.
Thread: Brown.
Tails: coq de Leon.
Body: Mix of brown and olive CDC.
Wing: Mix of olive, brown and natural black CDC fibres.

From the stable of the master of CDC, this is an oustanding pattern.

CDC SPENT SPINNER

Hook: Dry fly, sizes 8–28.
Thread: As body.
Tails: Three coq de Leon hackle fibres or, larger sizes, three cock pheasant tail fibres.
Body: CDC feather, with the fibres twisted round the feather stalk.
Wing: CDC feather fibres.

The tying is similar to the last one, but here the CDC used to wing the fly is separated into two bunches, one on either side. The CDC feather 'rope' used to form the thorax is then wound figure-of-eight also to keep the wings in place. Two examples are given below.

CDC ORANGE SPINNER/CDC EPHEMERA MAYFLY SPINNER

The CDC Orange Spinner, matches many smaller species, while the Ephemera Mayfly Spinner is fished during a fall of the layer white or cream-bodied spinner.

The final CDC dry fly is by Chris Hosker. It is a very effective catcher of trout and grayling.

PINK CDC

Hook: Dry fly, sizes 14–18.
Thread: Black.
Tails: 2 coq de Leon hackle fibres on each side.
Body: Finest synthetic pink dubbing.
Wing: Pink CDC fibres.

WOVEN-BODY EMERGERS AND DRIES

The use of woven bodies (see also p. 79) can produce very beautiful dry flies, though from the fish-catching point-of-view they are certainly inferior to, say, CDC flies.

Woven-Body Emerger

Hook: Curved grub or emerger hook, sizes 10–18.
Thread: As thorax.
Tail filaments: Few fibres grizzle hackle (optional).
Abdomen: Two strands floss or other thick thread, woven (see Note 1).
Emerging wing: Tuft white or grey Poly Yarn or Antron.
Thorax: Fine-textured synthetic dubbing (see Note 1).
Hackle: Grizzle cock, parachute.
'Wing': White or grey synthetic fibres (see Note 2), with some darker fibres included.
Note 1: Use a lighter shade for the underside of the abdomen. Useful colours: olive, yellow, brown, tan, grey, black. For the thorax use the same shade as the back of the woven abdomen.
Note 2: There is a wide range of suitable fibres, including Poly Yarn, Antron, Z-lon. This wing is for the fly-fisher and not the fish! Tie this wing in first. Post its base and then tie in the hackle. Now wind the thread to the end of the shank and tie the rest of the fly. Finish off by winding the hackle and whip-finishing.

This matches emerging olive duns, black midges, etc.

Woven-Body Polydun

Hook: Dry fly, sizes 10–18.
Thread: As thorax.
Tail: Few fibres blue dun (grey) or ginger cock hackle.
Abdomen: Two strands floss or other thick thread, woven (see Note 1).
Thorax: Fine-textured synthetic dubbing (see Note 1).
Hackle: Blue dun (grey) or ginger cock hackle, parachute.
Wing: White synthetic fibres (see Note 2).
Note 1: Use a paler shade for the underside of the abdomen. Useful colours: olive, cream, yellow, tan, grey.
Note 2: See Note 2 above.

Woven-Body Spinner
Hook: Dry fly, sizes 10–18.
Thread: As thorax.
Tail: Few white or pale blue dun (grey) cock hackle fibres.
Abdomen: Two strands floss or other thick thread, woven (see Note).
Wings: Tuft white or grey Poly Yarn or Antron.
Thorax: Fine-textured synthetic dubbing (see Note).
Wings: Two bunches white or grey synthetic fibres, tied spent or semi-spent.

Note: Orange, yellow and white/cream are the most useful colours.

CAENIS AND TRICOS

These are the smallest of the upwinged flies and the dry flies that match them require a special section. Caenis occur throughout much of Europe, tricos North America. They are closely related (both have three tails and only one pair of wings). They are tiny: ideally matched on a size 22–26 hook, though it is often possible to get away with a larger one (18–20). They have the shortest flying period of all upwinged flies; while the larger ones may survive for three or four days. In these the spinner emerges from the dun within a few minutes of landing in cover (they will use anglers and car windscreens as moulting spots and leave them covered with empty shucks), and mating and egg-laying occur soon afterwards. They often occur in immense hatches (and spinner falls), and trout can be sometimes almost impossible to catch (hence the English name, 'anglers' curse').

One artificial fly that looks nothing like a caenis or trico but will deceive trout when they are gorging on these curses is the Grey Duster (p. 137). The following look more like the real thing.

Note on hooks for tiny dry flies: The hooking power of tiny hooks is not great unless the trout takes the hook well inside its mouth. This is because of the narrow gape. Vince Marinaro designed a hook that is still manufactured by Partridge (now part of the Mustad Company) that bears his name and is coded K1A. It has an offset point, which increases the gape and thus the hooking power. It is important, when using this hook, to hold the hook by the extreme rear of the bend in the tip of the vice jaws. To push the hook in further will flatten this offset and weaken, if not break, the hook. This applies to all hooks with an offset point.

Both dun and spinner in caenis have whitish abdomens and darker thoraces, the only clear difference between them being the much longer tails in spinners.

Paythorne Caenis

Hook: Dry fly, sizes 18–24.
Thread: Finest black.
Tails: Three white or grey microfibetts or coq de Leon hackle fibres.
Abdomen: Stripped white cock hackle stalk.
Thorax: Peacock herl.
Hackle: Blue dun cock.
Wings: Originally 2 white cock hackle points, but white Antron or similar synthetic hair-wing is more robust. Tie the wings spent or semi-spent.

Before fishing, trim the hackle fibres that stick down below the body. This fly by Malcolm Greenhalgh was designed to catch trout making pigs of themselves on a species of *Caenis* that hatches at dawn. It has since caught trout, grayling and char throughout Europe.

Anglers' Curse (J. R. Harris)

Hook: Dry fly, sizes 18–24.
Thread: Finest black.
Tails: Few cream cock hackle fibres.
Body: Cream herl or floss silk.
Hackle: Pale cream cock.

Deer-Hair Caenis

Hook: Dry fly, sizes 18–22.
Thread: White or grey.
Tails: 3 strands white deer hair.
Body: White thread.
Thorax: Dot of black head cement at front of body.
Wings: White deer hair, spent.

This next pattern attempts to imitate a clump of caenis on the water surface.

Alphonse (Richard Walker)

Hook: Long shank, 12–14.
Thread: Brown.
Body: White swan or goose herl.
Hackles: 4 tiny cream cock hackles spaced out along the body.

In tricos, the female dun has a light-grey abdomen with an olive hue and the female spinner a pale green-grey abdomen. The male dun has a brown-black abdomen, the male spinner a blackish abdomen. They have darker thoraces, and the legs and tails are light, so many tyers produce four matching imitations. However, to get the best out of the trico hatch it is essential to be out before first light, just as the hatch starts. Then the trout will fall for any small general imitation, including the caenis patterns. Later in the morning, with masses of real flies about, it is time for breakfast!

Ed Engle's book *Tying Small Flies* (2004) contains several excellent trico imitations. Two are given below.

Trico Spent

Hook: Dry fly, sizes 18–26.
Thread: Black.
Tails: White microfibetts, flaring out.
Abdomen: Black thread.
Thorax: Finest black synthetic dubbing.
Wings: White polypropylene or Antron, tied spent.

CDC Trico Spent

Hook: Dry fly, sizes 18–26.
Thread: Black.
Tails: White or dun microfibetts, flaring out.
Body: Tying thread.
Wings: Few strands of white CDC, with a strand of Crystal Hair or Krystal Flash on each side.

Marinaro's Trico

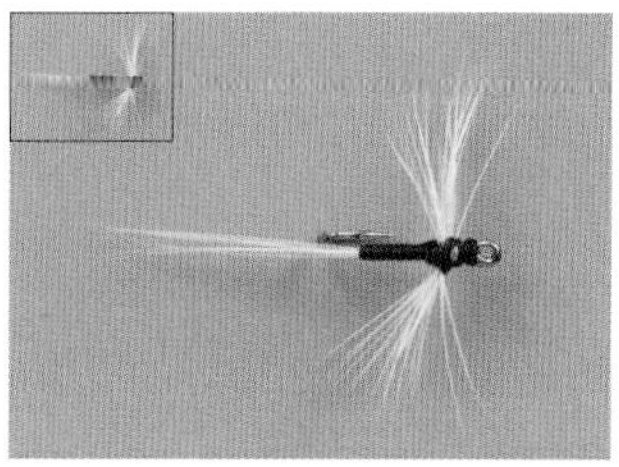

Hook: Dry fly, sizes 20–26.
Thread: Black.
Tails: White cock hackle fibres.
Body: Tying thread.
Wings: A white cock hackle wound over the front third of the hook, the fibres being brought up to splay out either side with figure-of-eight turns of tying thread (this also thickens the front of the body to suggest a thorax).

Black Polypro Trico Spinner (Dave Hughes)

Hook: Dry fly, sizes 18–24.
Thread: Black.

Tails: White cock hackle fibres.
Body: Fine black fur (natural or synthetic).
Wings: White Polypro or Antron, spent.

Olive Polypro Trico Spinner (Dave Hughes)
Hook: Dry fly, sizes 18–24.
Thread: Brown.
Tails: White cock hackle fibres.
Abdomen: Very light, fine olive dubbing (natural or synthetic).
Thorax: Dark brown dubbing (natural or synthetic).
Wings: White Polypro or Antron, spent.

MAYFLIES

Every spring in parts of northwest Europe – most notably the great limestone loughs of Ireland, the famous chalk streams of southern England and Normandy, and the weedy lime-rich rivers of England's Peak District – the fly-fishing highlight is the 'mayfly season'. On Irish lakes like Corrib, Conn, Arrow and Erne the hatch usually starts in early May and continues into June. On chalk streams the main hatch lasts for up to two weeks and is usually over by June. On the more northerly mayfly rivers the mayfly season is more of a June event. Fly-fishers from around the world try to fish an Irish lough and a southern chalk stream, at mayfly time, at least once during their lives! The main mayfly is *Ephemera danica*; there is a second species, the dark mayfly *Ephemera vulgata*.

North America has several very similar species. The eastern green drake *Ephemera guttulata* hatches in late May and June, the brown drake *E. stimulans* in May–June (it more closely resembles the dark mayfly of Europe), the yellow drake *E. varia* in June–August, the great olive-winged drake *Hexagenia limbata* in mid-June–August and the dark green drake *Litobrancha recurvata* from May through July.

So special is the large mayfly that hundreds of tyings have been devised to match its emerger, dun and spinner stages. Malcolm Greenhalgh's book *The Mayfly and the Trout* (2009) gives many patterns and describes fishing in the mayfly season.

Hooks for mayfly imitations: Because these mayflies are quite long insects it became the fashion, during the first half of the twentieth century, to tie imitations on very long-shanked, special 'Mayfly Hooks'. The two problems with these are that they are very heavy, and that because of the long shank and small gape a good proportion of hooked fish become detached. The hook gets levered out. Today most fly-fishers tie their mayfly imitations on standard dry-fly hooks, mostly in size 10 (sometimes 8). Even though this gives a fly with a short body, the trout do not mind and fewer hooked fish are 'lost'.† Unless otherwise stated, the following should be tied of size 8–10 standard dry fly hooks.

† Izaak Walton rightly pointed out to his readers that no angler ever 'loses' a fish, for 'how can any man lose what he never had!'

Though this section of this book deals with dry flies, there are some very special Irish wet flies used during a hatch of duns. They are called 'Straddlebugs' or 'Goslings'; for the origin and meaning of those names see Greenhalgh (2008). Three of these will be described first (there are scores of other patterns).

French Partridge Straddlebug

Thread: Black.
Tails: 3–4 cock pheasant tail fibres.
Body: Light beige seal's fur (or substitute).
Rib: Finest oval gold tinsel.
Head hackles: 1. Yellow cock, 2. Brown speckled partridge, 3. French partridge.

E. J. Malone states that this very old fly was invented for fishing Lough Erne (*Irish Trout & Salmon Flies*).

Lough Arrow Green Straddlebug

Thread: Black.
Tails: 3–5 cock pheasant tail fibres.
Body: Natural raffia (raffine is the synthetic equivalent).
Rib: Finest oval gold tinsel.
Body hackle: Short-fibred white cock.
Head hackles: 1. Grey partridge dyed golden-olive, 2. French partridge dyed green-olive, 3. Grey partridge dyed green olive.

Lough Arrow is famed for the large brown trout that rise to the mayfly.

Grey Gosling

Thread: Black.
Tails: 3–5 cock pheasant tail fibres.
Body: Natural raffia.
Rib: Finest oval gold tinsel.
Body hackle: White cock.
Head hackles: 1. White henny-cock, 2. Grey partridge.

Some form of Grey Gosling has been designed for most of the great Irish mayfly lakes.

Stevie Munn is one of the great fly-dressers, and the following is his outstanding mayfly pattern.

Munn's May

Thread: Olive.
Tail: Few fibres cock pheasant tail.
Body: Yellow Flashabou or Lite Brite dubbing.
Rib: Fine silver wire.
Body hackle: Light or medium blue dun (grey) cock.
Hackles: 2 turns orange cock, then in front grey partridge dyed yellow-olive.
Wing: Light green-chartreuse deer hair (optional).

Mayfly Emerger

Hook: Curved sedge or grub, sizes 8–12.
Thread: Black.
Abdomen: Cream dubbing (natural or synthetic).
Ribs: Black thread, fine oval silver tinsel.
Thorax: Peacock herl.
Hackle: Blue dun cock.
Wing: White or cream Antron or Poly Yarn, tied upright and posted.

See Klinkhamer Special for tying notes. This fly, by Malcolm Greenhalgh, is effective in both rivers and lakes and has accounted for wild brown trout in excess of ten pounds in both types of water. It may be used in conjunction with dry dun imitations in a three-fly cast for lake fishing.

The following are dun imitations (see also Wulff series, p. 139–40).

Conn Mayfly

Thread: Tan.
Tails: 4–5 cock pheasant tail fibres.

Body: Yellow floss.
Rib: Fine gold wire.
Hackle: Grizzle cock dyed yellow.
Wings: Two French partridge feathers dyed yellow.

Lough Conn is one of the great Irish mayfly lakes. This pattern has fan wings, though tied more upright than most other fan wings. Though they look good to us, from the fishing point-of-view they are not so good in that they spin in the air and after a few casts the leader becomes twisted.

Cul De Canard Mayfly Dun

Thread: Tan.
Tails: Few fibres cock pheasant tail.
Body: Cul de canard in beige, yellow-olive or dull yellow.
Wings: Cul de canard fibres, as body colour.

The body is tied using the Petitjean technique (see p. 167). Primarily a river fly, it will however catch trout that are rising keenly in lakes (after many casts, fishing the water, it tends to become waterlogged). Great for both European and American waters.

Green Paradrake
Thread: Yellow.
Tails: 3 moose tail hairs.
Body: Yellow deer hair (extended).
Rib: Tying thread.
Thorax: Fine yellow dubbing.
Hackle: Dark blue dun, wound parachute style.
Wings: Natural deer hair, tied upright and posted.

This pattern exploits the buoyancy of deer hair. Again, this has caught trout on both sides of the Atlantic.

O'Connor's Mayfly Dun
Thread: Grey.
Tails: 3–4 cock pheasant tail fibres.
Body: Cream floss.
Overbody: Clear polythene or plastic.
Rib: Fine red copper wire.
Hackle: Grizzle dyed yellow.
Wings: Mallard flank feather fibres, dyed yellow.

USD Mayfly Dun
Hook: Partridge Swedish Upside-Down, size 8–10.
Thread: Tan.
Tails: Few fibres cock pheasant tail.
Body: Fine yellow wool.
Rib: Brown thread.
Thorax: Peacock herl.
Hackles: Blue dun and olive cock, wound together.
Wing: Bunch mallard flank fibres, dyed yellow.

The Swedish Dry Fly Hook is the best of the special hooks designed to fish upside-down.

The following are examples of very effective mayfly spinners (curiously called 'spent gnat' in Ireland).

Mayfly Spinner
Thread: Black.
Tails: 3–5 cock pheasant tail fibres dyed black.
Body: Natural raffia.

Rib: Fine gold wire or finest oval gold tinsel.
Body hackle: Short-fibred badger or grizzle cock.
Head hackles: Blue dun, the fibres being bound with tying thread so that they extend out sideways with the wings.
Wings: Either black cock hackle points, or a long-fibres black hackle, wound and then with the fibres separated into two spent wings.

Cul De Canard Mayfly Spinner
Thread: Black.
Tails: Cock pheasant tail fibres.
Abdomen: White cul de canard, tied Petitjean style (p. 167).
Thorax: Peacock herl, wound figure-of-eight round wing bases.
Wings: Grey or natural black cul de canard fibres.

The following is based on patterns in Ted Fauceglia's *Mayflies*, where he uses deer hair for the body. It allows for all large mayflies/drakes to be matched, in both dun and spinner stages.

[a] Drake Dun [b] Drake Spinner
Hook: Dry fly, sizes 6–10.
Thread: Dark brown.
Tails: Black moose mane.
Abdomen: Deer hair (see Note 1).
Rib: Tying thread.
Thorax: Fine textured synthetic fur, in duns. In spinners the hackle simulates the thorax.

Hackles:

In duns: Brown or olive or blue dun and grizzle cock, wound together, parachute style (see Note 2).

In spinners: Blue dun and grizzle cock, wound conventionally on either side of the wings (see Note 3).

Wing:

In duns: White or cream calf or Antron, tied upright and posted (see Note 2).

In spinners: Grey Antron or Poly Yarn, or grey/blue dun hen hackle points (see Note 3).

Note 1: It was suggested that a paler deer hair should be used for the underside of the body and a darker colour for the dorsal side. However, trout cannot see the upper side, so that is not essential. For the underside, dyed yellow or olive matches most species pretty well, for spinners white or cream. Tie the deer hair in by its tips at the rear of the hook shank, bring the deer hair forward tightly, and bind it down with the ribbing thread.

Note 2: As in Paraduns (p. 159), tie in and post the wing before the rest of the fly is tied. Tie in the hackles and wind them together round the wing base before completing the fly.

Note 3: After completing the body, tie in the wings, one on either side, spent or semi-spent. Note that sometimes trout taking these large flies will select ones that have died with one wing sticking up in the air. So tie some with one wing up and one wing down. Then tie in the hackles and wind with several turns on either side of the wings. In rough rivers the trout will often take a fully hackled fly, but in calmer water they may refuse a fly that has not had the lower hackle fibres cut away so that the body rests in the surface.

A

B

Mayfly Spinner (E. J. Malone)
Thread: Black.
Tails: 3–5 cock hackle fibres dyed black.
Body: Tip of red seal's fur (or substitute), rest palest dun.
Rib: Fine oval silver tinsel.
Hackle: Badger cock.
Wings: Black cock hackle points, tied spent.

The following is a French pattern that seems to work whether duns or spinners are on the water. It is also said to be successful when large stoneflies are about.

Panama
Hook: Long shank dry fly, sizes 8–14.
Thread: Black.
Tails: Bunch golden pheasant tippets.
Body: Natural raffia.
Rib: Black thread.
Body hackle: Short-fibred natural red (brown) cock.
Hackle: Natural red (brown) cock.
Wings: A grizzle and a red cock hackle point on either side, red in front of grizzle.

WHY ARE DRY FLIES ALWAYS TIED THE SAME WAY ROUND?

All the dry flies described so far have been tied with the tails at the end of the hook shank, and the wing and hackle at the eye end of the shank. Davis Jaques was watching some mayfly duns when he noticed that the tails and tip of the abdomen were held up in the air, whilst the front of the fly was lower, closer to the water. From this basic observation he suggested that we should tie duns the other way round so that the tip of the leader would hold the tails higher. Was this something new? The great professional fly-dresser Geoffrey Bucknall said that two flies were sometimes tied that way round, the Leckford Professor and Blanchard's Abortion. Their dressings are as follows, and they have been tied here 'the wrong way round'.

Leckford Professor

Hook: Up-eyed dry fly, sizes 12–14.
Thread: Brown.
Body: Dark fur from hare's ear.
Rib: Fine flat gold tinsel.
Hackle: Natural red and then white cock.

Leckford is a beat on the 'Hallowed River Test'.

Blanchard's Abortion

Hook: Dry fly, sizes 12–14.
Thread: Olive.
Tail: Natural medium red (brown) cock hackle fibres.
Body: Rabbit fur.
Rib: Fine oval or flat gold tinsel.
Hackle: Natural medium red (brown) cock.
Wing: Bunch ginger cock hackle fibres.
Note: Dave Blanchard fished the rivers of the Peak District of northern England, south of Manchester.

However, such tying was not new. Fosters of Ashbourne (then a north of England fly-fishing company) dressed flies in reverse in 1882 and on 4 May 1886 Wakeman Holberton took out a US Patent for his Fluttering Fly, again tied reverse-style.

Upwinged Fly Spinners

Spinners are the sexually mature stage of the upwinged fly life cycle, and they may end up on or in the water in two ways. In most species the females lay their eggs while flying over the water by touching the water surface with the tip of the abdomen (in blue-winged olives the female carries one large egg ball at the end of her abdomen). These females die 'spent' after laying all their eggs, usually with wings and tails outstretched, with the body, *in* and not *on* the surface film. Trout can sometimes be quite selective, taking only those naturals that are flat in the surface, and they will often refuse an artificial that stands on the surface. We must consider this when tying spinner imitations.

Some females, in the family Baetidae (this includes the olives, but not the blue-winged olive), lay their eggs underwater. They crawl down masonry or rocks or wooden structures and when they have deposited all their eggs they get washed away. So to imitate them we must fish a spinner under the surface. The Red Spinner (below) is designed to imitate washed-out olive spinners (that have a rich brown or reddish body).

Many old spinner imitations were given a hackle, partly to help them float (this was the early days of floatants, when a bit of deer fat or butter from the sandwiches were the only readily available floatants) and partly because they were designed when hackled flies reigned supreme! They will catch some fish, but they are improved by either leaving out the hackle or, perhaps preferably, cutting away any hackle fibres pointing down so that the body lies flat in the surface film.

Spinners are always brighter in colour than their dun stage, but they often fall onto the water in the evening when the sun is low or at dusk, when the trout can see only black, white and shades of grey. Then, colour is pretty irrelevant, though we enjoy putting the colour into our flies.

Note: for imitations of the spinners of caenis and trico, see p. 171, and for the large mayflies, see p. 180.

Lunn's Particular

Hook: Dry fly, sizes 14–16.
Thread: Crimson.
Tails: Bunch Rhode Island red cock hackle fibres.
Body: Stripped Rhode Island red cock hackle stalk.
Hackle: Rhode Island red cock.
Wings: Medium blue dun cock hackle points.

Invented by William Lunn, River Keeper to the Houghton Club on the River Test, in 1917. This is still a very good fly when red-brown spinners are falling on the water.

Orange Quill

Hook: Dry fly, sizes 12–16.
Thread: Orange.
Tails: Dyed orange or bright natural red cock hackle fibres
Abdomen: White hackle stalk, dyed orange.
Thorax: Few goose or swan herls dyed orange and wound figure-of-eight round the wing bases (optional, for use when there is no hackle).
Hackle: Bright natural red cock (optional).
Wings: Blue dun hackle points or grey Antron or Poly Yarn, tied spent.

Here we have Spinners ancient and modern. The hackled form, with hackle-point wings and no thorax is by the great G. E. M. Skues and dates from early in the twentieth century. Discard the hackle, give the fly a thorax, and use the more durable synthetic hair wing, and you have a very effective modern spinner. The bodies of many spinners are some shade of orange, red – or a glowing orange-brown in the evening sunlight. This pattern matches them all and is one of the best all round spinner patterns. The following is a good alternative.

Orange Spinner

Hook: Dry fly, sizes 12–16.
Thread: Orange.
Tails: Natural red cock hackle fibres or ginger coq de Leon hackle fibres.
Abdomen: Fine orange fur.
Rib: Fine gold wire.
Thorax: As abdomen, wound figure-of-eight round wing bases.
Wings: Grey Antron.

Pheasant Tail Spinner

Hook: Dry fly, sizes 12–16.
Thread: Brown.
Tails: Few blue dun hackle fibres
Body: Cock pheasant tail herls.
Rib: Fine gold wire (optional, but protects the herls).
Hackle: Ginger cock.
Wings: Light blue dun hackle points, spent.

There is more than one tying for the Pheasant Tail Spinner – this one is by M. Riesco.

Blue Spinner

Hook: Dry fly, sizes 14–16.
Thread: Black.
Tails: Blue dun cock hackle fibres.
Body: Stripped peacock quill.
Hackle: Blue dun cock.
Wings: Blue dun cock hackle points.

This New Zealand pattern imitates *Deleatidium vernale*, but away from its native rivers is a very good all-round dry fly.

Cream Spinner [Light Cahill Spinner]

Hook: Dry fly, sizes 12–16.
Thread: Pale yellow.
Tails: Light ginger microfibetts or coq de Leon hackle fibres.
Body: Mix of yellow and cream fine synthetic or soft natural furs.
'Thorax cover' (separating wings): light ginger Poly or Antron yarn.
Wings: Light blue dun cul de canard fibres.

This and the next pattern are by Ted Fauceglia, whose book *Mayflies* (2005) should be on the bookshelf of all fly-tyers.

Grey Fox Spinner

Hook: Dry fly, sizes 10–14.
Thread: Light tan.
Tails: 2 fibres blonde elk hair.
Abdomen: Stripped ginger hackle stalk.
Thorax: Light tan fox dubbing, wound round wing bases.
Wings: Blonde elk body hair.

Black Spinner

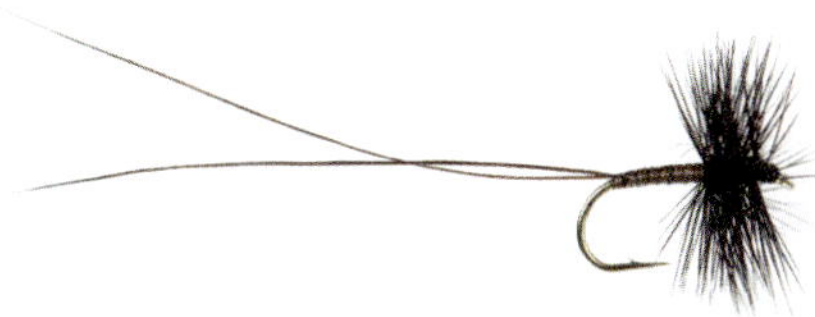

Hook: Dry fly, sizes 12–14.
Thread: Black.
Tails: 2 long black thick hairs (e.g. bucktail).
Body: Stripped peacock quill dyed black.
Hackle: Black cock.

An Australian/Tasmanian imitation of the black spinner.

Cream Spinner (Pale Watery)

Hook: Dry fly, sizes 14–18.
Thread: Finest cream or white.
Tails: Cream cock hackle fibres.
Body: Stripped cream hackle stalk.
Hackle: Cream.
Wings: Light blue dun hackle points.

A Jack Norris fly from the 1970s – modernise with grey Antron yarn wings and with a thorax of cream herl or fur wound figure-of-eight round the wing bases.

White Spinner (Iron Blue)

Hook: Dry fly, sizes 14–18.
Thread: Red.
Tails: White cock hackle fibres (microfibetts are better).
Body: Tip of tying thread, then white silk.
Overbody: White horsehair.
Hackle: White cock (1 turn).
Wings: White cock hackle points.

This is a pattern from early in the twentieth century by the great professional fly-dresser Roger Woolley.

Claret Spinner

Hook: Dry fly, sizes 12–14.
Thread: Black.
Tails: Badger cock hackle fibres.
Body: Dark claret floss.
Rib: Fine gold wire.
Hackle/wings: Badger cock, wound and then with fibres bunched on either side to give the wings.

Red Spinner (Subsurface)

Hook: Wet fly, sizes 12–14.
Thread: Black.
Tails: Few natural red cock hackle fibres.
Body: Red floss.
Rib: Fine gold wire or finest oval gold tinsel.
Hackle: Light blue dun or a soft hackle such as waterhen.

Fish this in the late afternoon or evening on rivers where there is a good hatch of 'olive' duns. Their female spinners oviposit underwater and many die there when all their eggs have been deposited.

Stoneflies

In the Western and Midwestern United States many large dry stonefly imitations have been devised to match the great hatches there. Elsewhere in the trout world, stonefly imitations are relatively few in contrast to those for upwinged flies and caddisflies. The reason for this is that small to medium-sized stoneflies can be matched well by general patterns, including small caddis imitations. Furthermore, in many regions hatches of stoneflies are dwarfed by other hatches. But the main reason that adult stoneflies are often ignored is that the adults are usually not found on the water's surface in big numbers. Stoneflies do not hatch at the water surface, as do most upwinged flies, caddisflies and midges. Their nymphs crawl ashore and the adults emerge at the water's edge. So the only stoneflies that do occur naturally on the water are egg-laying females.

There are occasions when newly hatched adults find themselves on the water and the fish gorge on them – for instance, when strong wings blow them from riverside vegetation. The first pattern, devised in Finland, matches windswept stoneflies, struggling against the wing on a rough river.

Windswept Stonefly

Hook: Dry fly, sizes 10–14.

Thread: Brown.

Body: Fine brown fur, or yellow fur (natural or synthetic).

Rib: Fine gold wire.

Body hackle: Ginger or natural red (brown), or yellow cock.
Head hackle: As body hackle, with several turns in front of the wings.
Wings: Brown, or yellow deer hair tied not too tidily (the original had quill slip wings, but the deer-hair wings are more durable).

This matches the wide range of both brown and yellow stoneflies.

Dave Hughes gave an alternative tying for a stonefly struggling to get off the water after being blown there.

Fluttering Stone
Hook: Long shank dry fly, sizes 6–12.
Thread: Orange.
Extended body: Orange polypropylene yarn (synthetic wool), twisted so that it doubles on itself, tied to rear.
Hackles: 3–4 natural red (brown) cock hackles wound along shank in front of wings.
Wings: Bleached elk.
Note: By varying body, hackle and wing colour (to yellow, brown and black) other windswept stoneflies might be matched.

Quill Stonefly
Hook: Dry fly, sizes 12–16.
Thread: Black.
Body: Stripped peacock quill.
Hackle: Black or dark brown, clipped underneath so that the fly rests low on the surface.
Wings: Narrow slip of black crow or dark brown dyed goose, varnished and tied low over body.

Needle Fly
Hook: Dry fly, size 14.
Thread: Olive.
Body: Tying thread dubbed lightly with a fine dirty yellow fur (e.g. rabbit or synthetic).
Hackle: Grizzle or blue dun cock.
Wings: 2 blue dun cock hackle points, tied flat over body.

Needle flies are very slender stoneflies, and other than the hackle the tied fly should likewise be very slender. A John Veniard pattern, the following is an alternative imitation these stoneflies – often abundant through much of the summer and autumn.

Many stoneflies are yellow or olive-yellow and the following pattern matches them well.

Yellow Sally

Hook: Dry fly, sizes 8–14.
Thread: Yellow.
Body: Fine yellow fur (ideally synthetic that does not change colour when wet).
Rib: Fine gold wire.
Hackle: Dull yellow or golden-olive cock, clipped underneath so that the fly rests low on the surface.
Wings: Yellow quill slip, varnished, and tied low over the body.

Dark Stonefly

Hook: Dry fly, sizes 8–14.
Thread: Black.
Tails: 2 peacock herl tips (optional).
Body: Tip of red fluorescent floss (optional), the rest peacock herl.
Rib: Fine copper wire.
Body hackle: Black cock, the lower fibres clipped short.
Wings: Varnish black quill slip (e.g. dyed goose, crow), tied low and clipped to length.
Head: Peacock herl.

Large Stonefly

Hook: Long shank dry fly, sizes 4–12.
Thread: Black.
Tails: 2 black goose or turkey biots.
Abdomen: Dull orange fur (synthetic).
Rib: Fine gold wire.
Wings: 2 brown or brown-black varnished quill slips, tied very low over body.
Head/thorax: Dark brown deer hair spun and clipped to shape, with several fibres pointing backwards at rear unclipped.

Many imitations have been made of the huge stonefly, known as the salmon fly, of America's West. Pat Barnes devised one called the Sofa

Pillow, which was superseded by the Improved Sofa Pillow ('... my favourite pattern during salmon fly time', wrote Dave Hughes). The Jug Head is said to be a further improvement.

Jug Head

Hook: Long shank dry fly, sizes 4–10.
Thread: Black.
Tails: Elk hair.
Body: Orange 2-ply yarn or synthetic fur dubbing.
Body hackle: Short-fibred natural red (brown) cock palmered.
Underwing: Elk hair.
Overwing: Red fox squirrel tail.
Head: Deer hair spun and clipped.

Troth's Salmon Fly

Hook: Long shank dry fly, sizes 4–8.
Thread: Orange for the body, then brown for the head.
Tails: Brown or black deer hair.
Underbody: Orange polypropylene yarn.
Overbody: Orange bucktail.
Rib: Thick orange thread.
Underwing: Brown or black elk or deer hair.
Overwing: Fluorescent or bright orange bucktail.
Head and legs: Dark brown elk or deer. The bunch is tied in with the tips forward; it is then brought back all around the front of the fly and there tied down to give a head and, the tips, legs.

Al Troth is one of the legendary fly-tyers from Yellowstone.

Caddisflies, or Sedges

The name 'caddisfly' derives from the larval case, whereas the name 'sedge' comes from the behaviour of the adult fly – fluttering, as it does, amongst waterside vegetation such as willows, reeds, rushes and sedges.

Compared with the upwinged flies and stoneflies, the number of caddisflies species in vast: over 900 in Europe, maybe in excess of 1200 in North America. It is true that many species are quite rare, or occur in habitats where there are few or no fish. But there are still a lot of species that fish such as trout do eat. Thus there are a many imitative caddisflies and two books that deal especially with them. Gary LaFontaine's *Caddis Flies* (1981) includes imitations that have built into them some aspect of the behaviour of real caddisflies, while Taff Price's *The Angler's Sedge* (1989) includes many imitations from across the trout and caddisfly world.

While adult caddisflies do (mostly) emerge from their pupal shucks at the water surface, they do so very rapidly. Consequently, during a hatch few if any adults will be seen standing on the surface though many will be seen in flight. So during a hatch the fish feed, not on hatched caddis, but on pupae resting at the surface or emergers (see p. 103). Those adult caddisflies seen on the surface will mostly be egg-laying females. Some of these crawl across the surface film and then dive or climb under to lay their eggs. Others scuttle across the surface as they lay their eggs and this movement must be matched, as well as the appearance of the real caddisfly.

Compared with upwinged flies and stoneflies, caddisflies are relatively long lived, for, unlike members of those groups, they can drink nectar from waterside flowers in addition to water from the river. The majority of adult caddisflies spend most of the daylight hours under cover and only emerge in the very late afternoon and evening, continuing on the wing well into the dark. And in most species hatching and egg-laying occur from dusk into the night. At this time of day the trout are completely colour-blind, though they may be able to discern extremes of shade or tone. So for late-evening or night fly-fishing, the size, shape and behaviour of the artificial flies are far more important than colour.

Some species are more active by day, and this includes the grannom (caddisflies in the genus *Brachycentrus* that has similar species in both Old and New Worlds).

Note on hackles: Some tyings have a palmered body hackle. Front or head hackles in winged caddisfly imitations are tied in and wound after and in front of the wings. Whereas previously it has been suggested that the underside of the hackle in dry flies should be clipped away to bring the body of the fly low over the water, keep the full hackles at least until the trout have ignored the fully hackled fly. Then attack the underside of the fly with scissors.

Grannom

Hook: Dry fly, sizes 12–14.
Thread: Green.
Body: Yellow-brown fur (natural or synthetic).
Hackle: Ginger cock.
Wings: Bronze mallard.
Antennae: 2 fibres wood duck flank (optional).

This is the American imitation; the following matches the European species.

Grannom

Hook: Dry fly, size 14.
Thread: Green.
Body: Tip of green wool, the rest hare's ear.
Hackle: Blue dun cock.
Wings: Hen pheasant quill slips.

CDC Sedge

Hook: Dry fly, sizes 10–14.
Thread: Black or brown.
Abdomen: Cul de canard, brown, olive, black or grey. This is formed using the Petitjean method (p. 167).
Wing: Cul de canard fibres, brown, black or grey.†
Head/thorax: As abdomen, but a little wider.
† A tuft of white cul de canard on top of the wing makes the fly visible well into the gloaming. If the white disappears, tighten, for the white is hidden away in a trout's mouth!

This is from the Petitjean school and an outstanding catcher of fish.

Elk Hair Caddis

Hook: Dry fly, sizes 10–18.
Thread: Tan.
Body: Fine olive fur (synthetic).
Body hackle: Natural red (brown) cock, palmered.
Wing: Elk hair.
Head: Roots of wing, cut square.

Al Troth's great dry caddis. At dusk this matches any medium-small caddisfly. See p. 141 for the hackleless version.

Grey Flag

Hook: Dry fly, sizes 12–14.
Thread: Grey.
Body: Grey seal's fur (or substitute).
Rib: Fine silver wire.
Hackle: Grizzle cock.
Wings: Grey squirrel tail.

Grey Flag is a name given to many species of small-medium, grey caddisflies.

G & H Sedge

Hook: Dry fly, sizes 8–12 (sometimes tied on long-shank hooks).
Thread: Brown.
Body and wings: Having wound thread to the end of the hook shank, leave a long waste end (put out of the way in a materials spring). Now

spin deer hair the length of the shank, but leaving room at the front to wind a hackle and form a head. Trim this to caddisfly shape. Then take the waste end and dub green seal's fur onto it. Bring this forward under the clipped deer hair body and tie off at the front. This gives a simulation of the soft green body. It is often left out of commercially tied G & H Sedges, and the trout never notice.

Hackle: Natural red (brown) cock. If two are used, the tips of the stalks can be tied forwards to simulate antennae (again the trout never notice if there are no antennae).

This tying is by John Goddard and Cliff Henry, and is known as the Goddard Caddis in North America. Karsten Fredrikson has produced similar patterns but with brown or mixed deer hair, and with other colours of hackle.

Murrough or Great Red Sedge

Hook: Dry fly, sizes 8–10 (sometimes tied on long-shank hooks).
Thread: Brown or black.
Body: Grey fur or wool.
Body hackle: Natural red (brown) cock, palmered.
Rib: Fine gold wire.
Hackle: Natural red (brown) cock.
Wings: Brown turkey slips.
Antennae: 2 cock pheasant tail fibres (optional).

This matches the large *Phryganea grandis* of the great trout lakes of the British Isles and Scandinavia. Late on a summer's evening (between 11 p.m. and 3 a.m. close to the Arctic Circle) the big female caddisflies scuttle rapidly across the weedy lake as they lay their eggs. Trout (and char) hit them hard – use a strong leader! In size 10 the same tying can be taken for several smaller species in the same Family.

The following is an alternative for late in the evening.

Scuttling Caddis

Hook: Dry fly, sizes 8–12 (perhaps also on long-shank hooks).
Thread: Brown.
Body: 0.
Body hackle: Natural red (brown) cock, with many touching turns. It may be necessary to use two or more hackles.
Wings: Bunch brown deer hair.

Antennae: Two stalks from body hackles (optional).

The following pattern is also for the evening/darkness when pale sedges and moths go crashing about on the water surface. It is based on two earlier flies, the White Sedge by Austria's Norbert Eipeltauer and the American White Miller, and given by Taff Price.

White Caddis

Hook: Dry fly, sizes 12–14.
Thread: Black.
Body: White wool or synthetic yarn.
Body hackle: White cock.
Wing: White duck or goose quill slip, varnished and cut to shape.

Voljc Sedges

The following style of caddisflies was devised by Dr Bozidar Voljc of Slovenia and is based on this method of winging. The wings are made by stretching a large piece of ladies' tights material over a frame (a saucepan is ideal). Give the tights material a coating of dope. Then take feathers: crow, grey hen, grouse, woodcock, partridge etc., and trim away the waste at the butts. Now coat the underside of each feather with a waterproof adhesive and stick them down on the tights material. Allow to dry.

Now for the tying …

Hook: Dry fly, sizes 12–16.
Thread: Brown (or black for Black Sedges).
Body: 0.
Body hackle: Palmered cock hackles. Use touching turns so get a dense hackling.
Hackle: As body hackle, tied in front of wing.
Wing: Cut out one feather and trim it to size and shape for the fly you are tying. Put a very few drops of adhesive on the tips of the up-pointing hackle fibres, then tie in the wing. The adhesive, plus dense hackle fibres, plus the wing, trap air bubbles and aid floatation.

You can vary the colour to match the commoner caddisflies found on and around the water that you fish. For instance, use black hackles and a crow wing to match Black Sedges, natural red hackles and a grouse wing to match Grouse Wing Caddis, grizzle hackles and a grey partridge wing to match Grey Sedges. And so on.

The following are two caddis imitations devised by Roman Moser for fishing Austria's River Traun. They are both excellent floaters.

Moser Sedge

Hook: Dry fly, sizes 8–12.
Thread: Brown.
Body: Deer hair, bound down shank by the rib.
Rib: Brown thread.
Wings: Synthetic, cut-out (see above).
Head/hackle: Deer hair, tied forward, then brought back and bound down to give the head, and with the tips as the legs.

Moser's Balloon Sedge

Hook: Dry fly, sizes 10–14.
Thread: Brown.
Body: Fine synthetic fur (brown, though can be tied with olive).
Wing: Brown or natural deer hair.
Head: Yellow close-celled foam.

Note that Alan Airey uses white close-celled foam for the head at dusk because it is more visible.

Fluttering Caddis

Hook: Dry fly, sizes 12–20.
Thread: Brown.
Body: Cock pheasant tail fibres.
Rib: Fine gold wire.
Hackle: Natural red (brown) cock.
Wings: Brown mink tail.

This is Leonard Wright's pattern. In his book *Fishing the Dry Fly as a Living Insect*, Wright argued that the behaviour of the fly should be as the natural, and he explained that this fly should be twitched on the surface to match the behaviour of the egg-laying female. An alternative, the Fluttering Hackle Caddis is precisely the same, except that, instead of having wings, the fly is heavily hackled and well greased so that, when twitched, it creates a nice wake.

Dancing Caddis

Hook: Swedish Dry Fly, sizes 10–16.†
Thread: Black.
Body: Fine synthetic dubbing (see below).
Hackle: Cock, see below.
Wings: Deer hair (see below).

† This is an upside-down hook, manufactured by Partridge (part of the Mustad Company). At the time of writing it is still available.

This is a style of artificial caddis by Gary LaFontaine, where colour is tied to match the natural. The following are as useful as any:

	Body	Hackle	Wing
1.	Grey	Blue dun	Natural
2.	Olive	Ginger	Natural
3.	Green	Natural red (brown)	Dyed brown

1.

2.

3.

Many caddisflies end up on the water dead or dying. To imitate this last stage in the natural fly's life Larry Solomon invented the Delta Caddis.

Delta Caddis

Hook: Dry fly, sizes 10–16.
Thread: Olive.
Body: Fine olive fur (natural or synthetic).
Hackle: Natural red (brown) cock.
Wings: Natural red (brown) hen hackle points, set out at 45 degrees from body.

Note that this is a style of tying. Simply vary the size and colours of body, hackle and wings to match any natural fly.

Wonderwing Caddis

Like so many flies in this section, this is a style based on a method of winging, in this case devised by Chauncy Lively. A feather (usually a cock hackle, but others might be used) is taken and the waste removed from the base of the stalk. Then the hackle fibres are carefully pulled downwards towards the stalk base to form of oval or rounded wing. This is tied in with the stalk central to the also tied-in hackle fibres. One fly used to illustrate this style was tied with two wonderwings by the late Jack Norris, the other has one wonderwing and antennae.

Hook: Dry fly, sizes 14–16.
Thread: Finest brown.
Body: Brown, grey or black herl.
Rib: Finest pearl tinsel.
Hackle: Natural red, blue dun or black cock, wound in front of the wings.
Wings: Wonderwing, natural red, blue dun or black.
Antennae: Hackle stalks (optional).

Deer-Hair Caddis

Hook: Dry fly sizes 8–12.
Thread: Brown.
Body: Olive, grey or buff synthetic dubbing (e.g. Antron).
Head and wing: Natural deer hair (tie forward and then bring back, tying down to create a round head).
Legs: Rubber.

A very buoyant pattern that is ideal for big brawling rivers; useful for fishing from a drifting boat, when the fish have only a split second in which to grab a fly.

The last two caddis patterns are not dry flies, though they do imitate adult caddisflies: females that have gone underwater to lay their eggs. Again, the precise tying can be modified to match different species. However, the tyings given will match many species.

Diving Goldhead Caddis

Hook: Wet fly, sizes 12–14.
Thread: Brown.
Body: Fine grey synthetic fur, or hare's ear.
Hackle: Grey partridge or brown speckled partridge.
Head: Goldhead.

Diving Caddis

Hook: Wet fly, sizes 10–14.
Thread: Orange or black.
Body: Black, grey, brown or olive seal's fur or substitute, with a few strands pearl Crystal Hair mixed in.
Hackle: Black hen, or grey partridge, or brown speckled partridge.
Wings: Few strands pearl Flashabou (or similar material).
Head: Tungsten bead or goldhead.

Fish either of the above flies between late spring and late autumn when there are lots of small caddisflies over the water.

Adult Midges

Adult midges are not as important in the diet of trout as are midge larvae and pupae. However trout do sometimes feed keenly on midges, and patterns that imitate midges also match many other tiny flies that appear on the water from time to time, such as mosquitoes, thunderflies (or thrips) and reed-smuts (or buffalo gnats).

For note on using tiny hooks, see p. 171.

La Petite Merde

Hook: Dry fly, sizes 18–24.
Thread: Finest black.
Body: Natural black cul de canard.
Wing: Natural black, grey or white cul de canard.

A Petitjean pattern, using his winging and body tying techniques.

Herl Midge

Hook: Dry fly, sizes 20–28.
Thread: Black.
Tails: Few fibres black cock hackle.
Body: Black ostrich herl.

A pattern by Ed Koch, author of *Fishing the Midge* (1972). As long ago as 1885, T. E. Pritt was fishing a similar pattern … it just lacked the tails of Koch's tying! Real midges (in the family Chironomidae) vary widely in colour. The following takes account of that.

Herl-Bodied Midge

Hook: Dry fly, sizes 18–24.
Thread: Finest black.
Body: Herl, tied thicker at the front to simulate a thorax. Goose herl is ideal, dyed black, grey, green, olive, orange and red.
Hackle: Blue dun cock, wound in front of the wings.
Wing: 2 white cock hackle points or goose biots or tuft Z-lon or white Antron.

Blagdon Reservoir, in southwest England, just outside the city of Bristol, was one of the first lakes where trout foods were intensively studied. It has a green-bodied midge that hatches in large numbers in April. The following imitates that midge.

Blagdon Green Midge

Hook: Dry fly, sizes 18–24.
Thread: White.
Body: Emerald green wool.
Hackle: White cock, no more than three turns.

Phantom flies are midges that have transparent floating larvae in lakes. There have been many attempts to imitate the larvae, but such imitations cannot behave like the real larva, and in any case trout take these larvae (as they take all planktonic crustaceans in lakes) by filtering the water. Practical imitation is just 'not on'! However the adult is worthy of imitation in any productive lake, where, on a summer's evening, large numbers of spent adults die on the surface. The following is the ideal imitation.

Phantom Midge

Hook: Dry fly, size 14.
Thread: Orange.
Body: Grey herl (condor originally, but now grey heron or dyed goose).
Rib: Narrow strip of clear polybag,
Hackle: 2 turns ginger cock, with the underneath fibres either cut away or tied so that they splay out sideways.
Wings: White cock hackle points, tied spent.

Griffith's Gnat
Hook: Dry fly, sizes 16–24.
Thread: Black.
Body: Peacock herl.
Hackle: Grizzle cock, palmered along body.

This fly, devised by George Griffiths, is a good eye-opener for those who believe that trout have a Master's degree in entomology! It looks like nothing living, yet takes trout after trout after trout anywhere in the world.

Cluster Midge
Hook: Dry fly, sizes 14–22.
Thread: Black.
Tail: A few fibres grizzle cock.
Body: Tying thread.
Body hackle: Grizzle cock, palmered.
Hackle (in front of wings): Grizzle cock.
Wing: Grizzle hackle points, upright.

This is a cluster of Griffith's Gnats!

Knotted Midge
Hook: Dry fly, sizes 14–16.
Thread: Black.
Body: Tying thread.
Hackles: Black cock, one at either end of the body.

This is a very old pattern, devised when it was impossible to find hooks smaller than size 18. The answer to imitating tiny midges, it was then argued, was to tie two of them on one hook. It remains a useful catcher of trout.

Stillborn Midge
Hook: Dry fly, sizes 20–26.
Thread: Black.
Shuck: Tuft soft white hair (e.g. muskrat or opossum underfur).
Body: Peacock herl.
Hackle: Grizzle cock.

This pattern, by R. Hill, imitates a midge that has been unable to free itself fully from its pupal shuck.

Peacock Midge
Hook: Dry fly, sizes 18–22.
Thread: Black.
Abdomen: Stripped peacock quill (from eye).
Thorax: Peacock herl.
Hackle: Black or grizzle cock.

This could match so many tiny blackish flies, from mosquitoes to midges.

Damselflies

Very occasionally – so very occasionally that you, the reader, may never encounter it – trout and other insectivorous fish will be seen eating adult damselflies. Should this happen, an imitation damselfly might be useful.

Blue Damselfly
Hook: Long shank dry fly, size 12.
Thread: Blue.
Extended rear of body ('tail'): Bunch blue cock hackle fibres.
Underbody: Blue fluorescent floss.
Overbody: Blue fur, fine texture.
Wings: 2 pairs cock badger or blue dun hackle points, spent.

Tie this also in bright red to match red damselflies. Note, however, that only male damselflies are so brightly coloured and a drab light brown or brown-olive version might be tied to match females that have laid their eggs and died of old age.

Blue Damselfly
Hook: Dry fly, sizes 10–12.
Thread: Black.
Body: Blue bucktail, extended.
Rib: Tying thread.

Hackle: Blue dun cock, parachute style.
Wing and back of thorax: Blue bucktail from body.

A Dave Hughes fly. After completing the body, the forward 'waste' of blue bucktail is lifted to make an upright wing and then 'posted'. The hackle is tied in and wound round the wing base. The wing is then brought forward and tied in behind the hook eye. The rest of the wing is then cut off, a head wound and the fly finished off.

This again may be tied in red and other colours to match other species.

Red Damselfly
Hook: Dry fly, sizes 10–12.
Thread: Black.
Abdomen: Fine, flexible, red tubing.
Thorax: Rusty-red fine dubbing.
Legs: Black monofilament.
Hackle: Grizzle cock.
Wings: Grizzle or cree cock hackle points.

A Jack Norris fly. Jack would cast this so that it landed on a lilypad – and when a fish cruised by he would pull it off and onto the water!

Terrestrials ... or Land-Bred Insects that Fall Onto the Water

Many fly-fishers overlook terrestrials, yet they are vitally important in the diet of trout and other insectivorous fish. Frequently a fish will be seen rising, perhaps to a hatch of duns. A dun imitation takes that fish and its stomach contains, besides lots of duns, three or four black flies (houseflies or bluebottles) and a bee. Frequent observations like that suggest that trout will often turn aside what they appear to be selectively eating to take a land-bred food item.

Studies on some northern lakes have shown that over 90 per cent of the surface foods taken by trout and char – and in some cases the percentage may reach 99 per cent – are land-bred. Trout living in lakes surrounded by pine forests will often eat small green and brown beetles or wood ants, blown onto the water from the trees. The percentage of land-bred insects in the diet of river trout is never so high, but there are days, where the river meanders through grasslands, that grasshoppers are keenly sought.

Beetles vary greatly in size, shape and colour, but almost always the most abundant can be matched on a size 14–16 hook and have a black ventral surface (the surface that the fish can see as they look up). They are commonly blown onto the water, but are difficult to see because they sink well into the surface.

Black Beetle

Hook: Dry fly, sizes 14–18.
Thread: Black.
Body: Peacock herl.
Back (the elytra or the two hard front wings): Black deer hair.
Legs: 6 pieces of knotted black thread.
Head: Hair butts from back, cut square.
Note: Tie the deer hairs in by their tips at the end of the shank, wind the body and then bring the hairs over, binding them down just behind the hook eye. Whip finish and then cut the hairs to create a head.

Black Beetle

Hook: Dry fly, sizes 12–16.
Thread: Black.
Body: Peacock herl.
Back (elytra or the two hard front wings): Black herl (e.g. crow).
Hackle: 2 turns black cock.
Note: A similar tying, using herl instead of deer hair.

A John Veniard pattern.

Eric's Beetle

Hook: Dry fly, sizes 10–12.
Thread: Black.
Underbody: Yellow wool.
Overbody: Peacock herl, leaving a little wool at the rear.
Hackle: 2 turns black cock.

Eric Horsfall Turner's pattern. This can profitably be modified with an underbody of fluorescent red, pink or orange wool and becomes an excellent, though simple, searching fly.

Coch-y-Bonddu

Hook: Dry fly, sizes 12–14.
Thread: Black.
Body: Tip of flat gold tinsel, then peacock herl wound chunky.

Rib: Red thread (optional).
Hackle: Coch-y-bonddu cock.

This is a fly from Wales that imitates a very common beetle that lives in the countryside around the rivers there. The name of the beetle and hackle means red and black, the hackle being the black-centred natural red more often called 'furnace'. Note that some consider the coch-y-bonddu hackle to also have black tips, but this is not strictly speaking correct. This will catch trout thousands of miles away from its Welsh fatherland.

Foam Beetle

Hook: Dry fly, sizes 12–14.
Thread: Black.
Body: Black foam.
Hackle: Black or dyed red, sparse.

Another easy-to-tie, but very effective fishing fly.

Shark Beetle

Hook: Dry fly, sizes 8–10.
Thread: Yellow.
Body: Orange seal's fur (or substitute).
Back: Yellow Plastazote.

An Australian beetle pattern. When the real beetle is on the water, big trout approach rather like silently hunting sharks!

Gum Beetle

Hook: Dry fly, size 12.
Thread: Olive.
Body: Yellow-olive dubbing.
Wing cases: Yellow thin foam (Mick Hall, who devised this fly, uses Evasote), marked with olive and burnt orange permanent pen.

'During the summer in Tasmania's High Country, gum beetles may hatch out in billions. Many end up on the water and the trout gorge on them. At times the wind blows so many into the shoreline that mounds develop up to a few inches thick and can spread out as a band a couple of feet wide in the margins' (Mick Hall).

Tea-Tree Beetle

Hook: Dry fly, sizes 12–14.
Thread: Black.
Body: Black seal's fur (or substitute).
Back: Tan raffine.
Hackle: Black cock.

Another Australian beetle imitation, which will catch trout anywhere where trout swim.

Jassid

Hook: Dry fly, sizes 14–22.
Thread: Black.
Body: Tying thread.
Body hackle: Black cock, palmered in touching turns along the shank and then with all upward and downward pointing fibres cut away to leave only the fibres sticking out remaining.
Wing: A jungle cock eye feather tied low.

This, again simple yet great, fly was devised by Vince Marinaro to match the very common black land-bug, the jassid. True jassids do not occur out of North America, though there are plenty of brown and olive land-bugs that are close relations. However Marinaro's pattern does match so many other black land-bred insects that it is successful throughout the world. Chris Lee modified Marinaro's pattern to match these other land-bugs.

Green Land-Bug

Hook: Dry fly, sizes 12–14.
Thread: Green.
Body: Tying thread.

Body hackle: Grizzle cock dyed green, palmered in touching turns along the shank and then with all upward and downward pointing fibres cut away to leave only the fibres sticking out remaining.
Wing: Section of goose quill dyed green or olive, varnished and cut to shape.

The Brown Land-Bug is identical, but has light-brown thread, hackle and wing. Both green and brown versions are excellent in streams bordered by heavy and overhanging vegetation, as the natural insects feed on sap from leaves and stem tips.

Ants commonly occur by every river and lake and, as they climb high into vegetation, many are blown onto the water – especially in high summer and on hot autumn days. Some years they seem not to appear on the water at all, but in others they can be seen in myriad numbers. So it is essential to carry at least two or three imitations – just in case!

Black Ant

Hook: Dry fly, sizes 14–22.
Thread: Black.
Body: Two small balls of fine black fur, the rear ball larger than the front one.
Hackle: Black cock, wound with 3 turns between the two fur balls. Trim away the hackle fibres sticking down.
Wings: Two white cock hackle points, tied back low but splayed apart from the rear of the front fur ball (optional).

A Red Ant is tied similarly, but with red fur and a natural bright red cock hackle.

Red Ant

Hook: Dry fly, sizes 16–18.
Thread: Red.
Abdomen: Ball of tying thread, varnished with clear cement.
Hackle: Ginger cock.
Wings: Blue dun hackle points (optional).
Thorax: Tying thread, small ball.

Deer Hair Ant

Hook: Dry fly, sizes 12–16.
Thread: Black.
Body: Black deer hair.
Legs: Black deer hair.
Note: The deer hair is tied in by its tips at the end of the shank. The tying thread is then wound to create a rounded under-abdomen and the deer hair brought over this and tied down. The thread is then wound forward over the deer hair to just behind the eye, leaving the deer hair pointing forward over the eye. Now the thread is wound to create a small under-thorax and the deer hair brought back over this and tied down. The thread is then whip finished behind the thorax and most deer hairs cut away to leave just a few sticking out on either side to simulate legs.

Use red thread and deer hair to tie a Red Deer Hair Ant.

Foam Ant

Hook: Dry fly, sizes 14–18.
Thread: Black.
Body: Black foam, with larger abdomen than thorax.
Legs: Either knotted thick black thread.
Or 2–3 turns black cock hackle.
Wings: 2 white cock hackle points.

One of the most common groups of insects found in waterside vegetation is the aphid. Some of these minute insects are black or dark brown, but usually they are green – hence their common name, 'greenfly'. Greenfly occur in huge densities in overhanging trees, especially the maple/sycamore group, and in autumn, when their leaves are turning yellow, brown and red, many greenfly fall onto the water. Later, at leaf fall, the greenfly fall with the leaves. In clear water it is sometimes possible to watch trout and grayling sucking greenfly from leaves being washed down the river. Then a tiny imitation will catch them. The following three patterns are ideal. The first two are by Malcolm Greenhalgh.

Aphid

Hook: Dry fly, sizes 18–28.
Thread: Finest olive or green.
Body: Fluorescent lime-green floss.
Hackle: White or light olive cock, 2 turns.

Greenfly

Hook: Dry fly, sizes 18–22.
Thread: Yellow.
Body: Finest synthetic green fur or wool.
Hackle: Light blue dun cock.

Green Insect

Hook: Dry fly sizes, 16–22.
Thread: Black.
Tag or tail: Very short piece of red floss (fluorescent red is a useful variant to carry).

Body: Green peacock herl from a sword feather.
Hackle: White hen.
Note: This latter is an ancient pattern, but still a very successful one when trout are 'greenflying'.

Black land-flies include black gnats, hawthorn and heather flies, bluebottles, houseflies and so on. Occasionally the fall of these may be so large that trout feed on them quite selectively. One of the following ought always to be carried.

Hawthorn Fly

Hook: Dry fly, sizes 12–18.
Thread: Brown.
Body: Black herl (originally condor, but dyed goose or pheasant tail is equally effective), tied in at end of shank and twisted with tying thread before being wound down hook shank.
Hackle: Black cock.
Legs: 2 herls tied back, one on either side at base of hackle.

This is by Denmark's Preben Torp Jacobsen and imitates a fly special to northwest Europe, the hawthorn fly. This is out in late April and May, is matched by a size 12 hook, and has a pair of long, trailing rear legs. Take away these legs and you have a black gnat, a large group of insects whose members can be found flying through most of the year and which vary greatly in size.

The same also applies to the next two flies.

Hawthorn Fly (John Henderson)

Hook: Dry fly, sizes 12–18.
Thread: Black.
Body: Fine black fur.
Rib: Fine gold wire.
Body hackle: Black cock palmered in open turns and trimmed to about 1/16th of an inch.
Hackle: Black cock.
Wings: Pale blue dun hackle points.

Tie some with the wings spent and hackle trimmed underneath so that the fly will rest in the surface film just like a dead one that has fallen onto the water.

Hawthorn (Greenhalgh)

Hook: Dry fly, sizes 12–18.
Thread: Black.
Abdomen: Black floss.
Rib: Peacock herl.
Thorax: Peacock herl (continued from rib).
Hackle: Black cock.
Wings: 2 pale blue dun hackle points.

Blossom Fly

Hook: Dry fly, sizes 14–16.
Thread: Black.
Body: Peacock herl.
Body hackle: Short-fibred black cock hackle.
Hackle: Black cock.

Designed in New Zealand to match tiny black flies that abound at blossom-time, this simple fly works anywhere when small black flies are on the water.

Daddy long-legs (also called craneflies) are large flies with long, slender legs. Traditionally, the legs are formed by knotting cock pheasant tail fibres. In recent years many have attempted to find alternative materials for the legs, such as knotted fishing line. However, though these may look good, they are stiffer than the pheasant tail and tend to prevent the hook from getting into the mouth of the fish. So keep with the old-fashioned pheasant tail! These fibres are easiest knotted using a crochet hook.

Some patterns of daddy long-legs used long-shank hooks. These often lever out of the jaw of the fish – instead use standard shank hooks (see also note on p. 174).

Daddy Long-Legs (Greenhalgh)

Hook: Dry fly, sizes 8–10.
Thread: Brown.

Body: Brown herl (e.g. cock pheasant tail, cinnamon turkey).
Rib: Fine gold wire.
Legs: 8 knotted cock pheasant tail herls, or six pairs of double pheasant tail herls.
Hackle: Natural red (brown) or ginger cock.
Wings: 2 pale blue dun cock hackle points.

Daddy Long-Legs (Greenhalgh)

Hook: Dry fly, sizes 8–10.
Thread: Brown.
Body: Piece of cork, cut roughly to shape, and bound on top of the hook shank with tying thread.
Legs: 8 knotted cock pheasant tail herls, or 6 pairs of double pheasant tail herls.
Hackle: Natural red (brown) or ginger cock.
Wings: Grey Antron, tied spent.

Note that this lands with a 'plop' on the water and when cast directly over the head of a trout, sea trout or salmon (fish that at the time have no interest in real daddy long-legs) the plop will sometimes induce a savage take. Don't worry if the cork body is a bit bulky.

Detached Latex Body Daddy Long-Legs

Hook: Dry fly, size 12.
Thread: Black.
Body: Preformed latex body, tied on bare hook one third back from eye.
Legs: Cock pheasant tail, knotted.
Hackle: Pale blue dun cock, with 3 turns behind and 67 turns in front of wings.
Wings: Hackle points, cree or speckled ginger.

By Wendy Gibson, this highly buoyant fly is excellent on lakes when real daddies are being blown onto the water.

The great Irish fly-tyer E. J. (Ted) Malone has exploited the attraction of the long-legged daddy by producing two colour variations.

White Daddy

Hook: Dry fly, sizes 8–10.
Thread: Black.

Body: Extended, white (see Note below).
Legs: 6 pairs of double pheasant tail herls, dyed black.
Hackle: Badger cock, tied in front of the wings.
Wings: Black cock hackle points.

Red Daddy

Hook: Dry fly, sizes 8–10.
Thread: Brown.
Body: Extended, orange.
Legs: 2 pairs of double pheasant tail herls, dyed red.
Hackle: Ginger cock, tied in front of wings.
Wings: Natural red cock hackle points.
Note: At the time of writing, synthetic bodies are available. Alternative: suede chenille.

Wherever there is a high density of livestock close to the river or lake, there will be a high density of deposits of dung and therefore lots of dungflies. Trout love wind-blown dungflies.

Dungfly

Hook: Dry fly, sizes 12–14.
Thread: Red.
Body: Yellow chenille.
Rib: Peacock herl.
Hackle: Ginger cock.
Wings: 2 white or pale blue dun hackle points.

On a hot summer day, when fishing is at its hardest, try a bee imitation.

Bee

Hook: Dry fly, size 12.
Thread: Black.
Body: Banded yellow and black-brown fine-textured synthetic fur.
Hackle: Natural red (brown) cock.
Wings: 2 blue dun hackle points.

Provided the local rules/law permits it, on hot summer days the best fishing begins at dusk and continues well into the night. The caddisflies and spinner falls may induce the trout to rise, but moths will be out and, when these fall and splutter about on the water surface, trout will grab them violently. A very old series of flies, the Bustards, are ideal (see p. 53). The following are recent inventions.

Hoolet

Hook: Dry fly, sizes 8–10.
Thread: Black.
Underbody: A slither of cork.
Body: Peacock herl.
Hackle: Natural red (brown) cock.
Wings: Woodcock upper wing coverts.

A Geoffrey Bucknall pattern. Hoolet is an old name for the hooting owl.

White Moth

Hook: Dry fly, sizes 12–14.
Thread: Black.
Body: White synthetic dubbing.
Body hackle: White cock, palmered.
Wings: White duck or goose quill slip, cut to shape.

An Australian pattern that works at the other end of the planet.

Grasshoppers and crickets are found in highest densities in grasslands. For that reason, more imitations of these have been devised in regions where rivers meander through extensive grasslands, such as the Midwest of the United States, Australia, and in Patagonia. There are, however, other parts of the trout world where a stretch of a river flows through lush grasslands and where, from late spring to autumn, trout and other surface-feeding fish become accustomed to grasshoppers and crickets accidentally leaping onto the water.

Green Grasshopper

Hook: Long shank, dry fly, size 12.
Thread: Green.
Body: Green or olive deer hair, spun down shank and trimmed to shape.
Wings: Swan or goose quill, dyed green.
Hopping legs: 2 pairs cock pheasant tail fibres, knotted.
Head: Olive or green ostrich herl.

A Brown Grasshopper is tied similarly, but with brown thread, deer hair and ostrich herl. These are slightly modified versions of patterns by Taff Price.

Many Hoppers are tied with a dense foam that makes them unsinkable.

Foam Hoppers

Hook: Long shank, dry fly, sizes 8–12.
Thread: Darker than body, or black.
Body: Dense, fine-grained white foam trimmed to shape and coloured green or olive or light brown with permanent felt-tip pen, OR, yellow, buff, light brown or olive foam, cut to shape and tied in to give the three body sections of head, thorax and abdomen.
Rib: Tying thread.
Wings: Green or olive or light brown swan or goose, cut to shape, perhaps with a few strands of Crystal Hair or similar.
Legs: Long herls as used in wings, knotted, OR brown rubber, marked with black felt-tip pen.
Head: Large, foam or deer hair or wool, perhaps with eyes. For very turbulent water, a sight-marker on top (e.g. orange or white or green foam) may be useful.

[A] Lime green foam and legs. [B] Green foam and brown legs. [C] Yellow foam with deer-hair head and brown legs. [D] Beige foam with rubber legs, brown herl wing and orange sight-marker. [E] Buff foam body (extended) and wool head with lime-green sight-marker, brown herl wing and rubber legs.

A

B

C

D

E

These are great to tie; make your own variations on the theme! They are popular in the very rough rivers of Patagonia, America's West, Australia and Fenno-Scandinavia. They float well, without the need for frequent drying and oiling, and they are very resilient to the trout teeth. It is possible to catch a dozen and more trout on one of these without having to change fly.

Ed Shenk of Pennsylvania came up with two easy-to-tie patterns to match the crickets and grasshoppers he found on the banks of the Letort. These will catch fish far from Pennsylvania.

Letort Hopper

Hook: Dry fly sizes, 6–12.
Thread: Yellow.
Body: Yellow-tan fur (synthetic of fine natural).
Rib: Dark brown thread.
Wings:
Under: Brown mottled turkey, varnished, set flat.
Over: Natural deer hair.
Head: Butts from overwing, cut square and varnished.

Letort Cricket

Hook: Dry fly, sizes 10–14.
Thread: Black.
Body: Fine-textured black fur.
Wing:
Under: Dyed black quill slip (e.g. goose), varnished.
Over: Black deer hair.
Head: Butts from overwing, cut square and varnished.

Maurice's Hopper

Hook: Dry fly, sizes 12–14.
Thread: Grey.
Abdomen: Lime-green Plastazote, extended and ribbed tying thread.
Wing: Golden pheasant tippets.
Head and hackle (beard): Deer hair. Tie this forward, then bring it back so that tying in creates a round head and the tips the beard hackle.
Legs: Orange, rubber.

This is an Australian pattern. The very similar Augusta Hopper is tied on #8–10 hooks, has a buff Plastazote abdomen, and the wing of tippets dyed yellow plus a few strands pearl Crystal Hair.

The final four Hopper patterns are by a trio of great American tyers and one Australian.

Dave's Hopper

Hook: Long shank dry fly, sizes 6–14.
Thread: Brown.
Tail: Dyed red deer hair with a tuft of the wool used to tie the body over.
Body: Yellow wool or synthetic yarn.
Rib: Natural red (brown) cock hackle palmered down body and trimmed short.
Wings:
Under: Pale yellow deer hair.
Over: Section of mottled turkey.
Legs: Yellow grizzle hackle stems, knotted (optional).
Collar and head: Deer hair, spun and trimmed to shape.

This is Dave Whitlock's Hopper pattern. Trout love it!

Troth's Hopper

Hook: Dry fly or long shank dry fly, sizes 10–16.
Thread: Yellow.
Body: Yellow bucktail.
Legs: 2 dyed red goose quill fibres.
Wings: White tail deer flank hair, spun and clipped to shape.

Al Troth's Hopper was tied for Yellowstone, but has caught trout as far away as Slovenia.

Gartside's Pheasant Hopper

Hook: Long shank dry fly, sizes 8–14.
Thread: Yellow.
Tails: Dark moose.
Body: Grey, light olive, tan or yellow polypropylene yarn.
Body hackle: Furnace cock.
Wings:
Under: Deer hair, colour as body.
Over: Cock pheasant 'church window' feather.
Hackle and head: Deer hair spun and clipped to shape.

Jack Gartside is one of the greatest eccentrics in the world of fly-tying and a great tyer.

Chopper Hopper

Hook: Dry fly, size 10.
Thread: Brown.
Body: Soft foam trimmed to shape.
Overwing: Green rump feather from a cock pheasant, treated with vinyl cement.
Rear legs: Thin slip of dyed yellow goose shoulder, treated with vinyl cement and marked with orange, brown and olive marking pens.
Frong legs: Tan rubber legs, marked with brown marker pen.
Head: Deer hair tied bullet fashion.

Australia has almost 3000 species of grasshopper and when they start leaping onto the water, Mick Hall (who devised this pattern) says that: 'the fishing can be simply awesome'. This Hopper pattern will work anywhere, and might profitably be tied in slightly larger sizes.

Dry Flies for Grayling

Through must of Europe and eastwards into Asia the grayling (*Thymallus thymallus*) is a revered fish. North America has its grayling, the arctic grayling (*Thymallus arcticus*) that, though it has a restricted range, is highly sought. These grayling have their own international society, The Grayling Society.

While grayling readily fall to weighted nymphs and bugs and to dry flies and emergers already described, there are some patterns specially devised to catch them (which trout will also take!). They are mostly quite old patterns.

Grayling Steel Blue Bumble

Hook: Dry fly, sizes 14–18.
Thread: Orange.
Body: Tip of flat silver tinsel, then 3 turns of tying thread, then peacock herl.
Hackle: Sparkling blue cock, palmered in touching turns down the peacock herl part of the body.

A 'palmer' pattern (see p. 25) by Roger Woolley, that fishes at the surface.

Double Badger

Hook: Dry fly, sizes 14–18.
Thread: Black.
Body: Peacock herl.
Hackles: Badger cock, one at either end of the body.

Orange Otter

Hook: Dry fly, sizes 14–16.
Thread: Orange.
Tail: Natural red (brown) cock hackle fibres.
Body: Otter throat fur dyed orange (substitute with seal's fur or a seal's fur substitute).
Hackle: Natural red (brown) cock tied in the middle of the body.

Invented by the Reverend Edward Powell, Courtney Williams described it as 'phenomenal'.

Red Tag

Hook: Dry fly, sizes 14–18.
Thread: Black.
Tail (tag): Red wool.
Body: Peacock herl.
Hackle: Natural red (brown) cock.

Also tied with a hen hackle as a wet fly. This is a great 'searcher fly' in rough water for trout.

Treacle Parkin

Hook: Dry fly, sizes 14–18.
Thread: Black or brown.
Tail (tag): Should be orange wool, but more usually tied with yellow.
Body: Peacock herl.
Hackle: Natural red (brown) cock.

Treacle parkin is a delicious cake that includes treacle (black mollases syrup) and oatmeal in its recipe. It originates in the north of England, where grayling have long been revered, and is enjoyed late in the autumn when the trout season is over and the grayling season in full swing.

Sturdy's Fancy

Hook: Dry fly, sizes 14–18.
Thread: Purple.
Tail (tag): Red wool.
Body: Peacock herl.
Hackle: Off-white cock.

Invented by the 'keeper of the Tanfield beat' on the Yorkshire Ure, this is perhaps the best of all grayling dry flies.

Grayling Witch

Hook: Dry fly, sizes 14–16.
Thread (tag): Red floss.
Body: Green peacock herl from a sword feather.
Rib: Fine silver wire.
Hackle: Blue dun cock, palmered along body.

This is another pattern by Roger Woolley. With a white hackle it becomes the White Witch.

Gloire De Neublans

Hook: Dry fly, sizes 16–20
Thread: Dark brown.
Tails: White cock hackle fibres.
Body: Tying thread.
Hackle: White cock.

A pattern that Charles Ritz placed at the head of his list of grayling flies for European rivers (in *Pris sur le Vif*, 1953).

Fancy Wet Flies or Loch/Sea Trout Flies

There is one category of fishing flies that is still very popular in one part of the world but today hardly used elsewhere. They are flies that are used to catch brown trout, sea trout and salmon from a drifting boat in the great lakes of Scotland (lochs) and Ireland (loughs). Many of them are also used to catch sea trout and salmon in rivers in the same regions, and it is as river flies that they are fished more widely in northern Europe. Although some new patterns have been devised in recent years (e.g. Dabblers, p. 233, and several flies specially designed for the wonderful lochs of the Outer Hebrides, p. 243), most are very old, with a history going back 200 years or more. It is surprising, perhaps, that this style of fly has not flourished in other parts of the world (with the notable exceptions of New Zealand and South Africa), though in the past, North America has contributed some commendable patterns, such as Parmachene Belle and Cardinal. Yet for any wild-trout lake, and for any migratory fish – whether sea trout or steelhead, or Pacific salmon or Atlantic salmon, or any sea-run char – they are extremely useful.

When used in their native lakes it is normal practice to fish a team of three flies, one on the leader point, two on droppers. The fly on the uppermost dropper is usually a bushier fly than the other two and, during the end of the retrieve, it should create a wake in the surface and then be bobbed or dibbled up and down on the surface prior to the next cast; this fly is known as the 'bob fly'. Of course, in some areas the use of more than one fly on the leader is not permitted, so this traditional method of fly-fishing cannot take place.

When used in rivers they are fished 'down-and-across' the flow as with other salmon, sea trout and steelhead flies. It will be noted which of the following patterns are most useful for this type of fishing; while for lakes sizes 10–12 are most useful, for migratory fish it is worth tying them up to size 6.

All the flies illustrated were tied on single hooks. They are sometimes tied also on double and small treble hooks. Not only does this increase hooking-power; the heavier hook helps sink the fly that bit deeper. Choice of hook is very important. The best wet-fly hooks when it comes to landing fish have a very short point, a tiny barb (which should be completely flattened when catch-and-release is being practised), a round bend, and a shank length that is about 2½ times the hook gape. It should also be made of not too thick a wire, for the thicker the wire the less rapid hook penetration and more fish become disconnected.

The old patterns stipulated cock hackles for many of these wet flies, but the hackles were then not as stiff as modern genetic hackles. A better term would be henny-cock, and the ideal source for these is Indian cock capes. They are inexpensive. For those who wish to dye their own, don't dye white capes unless you are after primary colours (pure red, orange, yellow, green, blue): for clarets dye ginger capes, for black dye the darkest brown you can find (a tip from the late Gordon Griffiths).

Alexandra

Hook: Wet fly, sizes 8–14.
Thread: Black.
Tail: Narrow strip of red ibis (dyed swan or goose as substitute).
Body: Flat silver tinsel.
Rib: Fine oval silver tinsel (optional).
Hackle: Black hen.
Wings: Green peacock sword fibres, with a strip of red ibis (substitute) on either side.

This old fly was originally called the Lady of the Lake, but was renamed in about 1863 when Princess Alexandra of Denmark married Prince Albert Edward who, on the death of Queen Victoria in 1901, became Britain's King Edward VII. It is still a very useful fly to use when trout are feeding on tiny bait-fish such as minnows and sticklebacks. Such was its reputation at one time that its use was prohibited in some fisheries. Many fly-fishers have dressed this on much larger hooks (to 1/0) and caught larger predatory fish with it.

Black Pennell

Hook: Wet fly, sizes 10–14.
Thread: Black.
Tails: Few golden pheasant tippet fibres.
Body: Black floss (occasionally seal's fur).
Rib: Oval silver tinsel.
Hackle: Black henny-cock.

A fly from the stable of H. Cholmondeley Pennell, a wealthy gentleman from Edwardian England who spent his life fishing in northern Europe in summer and wintering on the French Riviera. A good variant has the tippet fibre tail dyed hot orange. For migratory fish, a body of flat silver tinsel is sometimes very effective (the Silver Pennel). Despite its simplicity, this is a very good fishing fly for lake trout and for sea trout and Atlantic salmon in rivers.

Blae and Black

Hook: Wet fly, sizes 10–14.
Thread: Black.
Tails: Golden pheasant tippet fibres, or none.
Body: Black floss.
Rib: Fine oval silver tinsel.
Hackle: Black hen.
Wings: Grey teal or mallard quill slips.

This winged version of the Black Pennell is very useful during a midge hatch.

Butcher

Hook: Wet fly, sizes 8–14.
Thread: Black.
Tail: Narrow strip of red ibis (substitute).
Body: Flat silver tinsel.
Rib: Fine oval silver tinsel.
Hackle: Black hen.

Wings: Slips from the mallard's blue speculum.

This fly was originally called the Moon Fly after an English butcher called Mr Moon, but then it was renamed the BUTCHER. It is still an outstanding catcher of fish, and is worth tying in sizes 4 and 6 for catching migratory salmonids when there is a touch of water on the river. The equally good BLOODY BUTCHER has a crimson hackle. For peaty lakes in dull light the following pattern is very good.

KINGFISHER BUTCHER

Hook: Wet fly, sizes 8–14.
Thread: Black.
Tails: Blue cock hackle fibres or kingfisher.
Body: Flat gold tinsel.
Rib: Fine oval gold tinsel.
Hackle: Orange henny-cock.
Wings: Slips from the mallard's blue speculum.

CAMASUNARY KILLER

Hook: Wet fly, sizes 8–14.
Thread: Black.
Tail: Royal blue wool.
Body:
  Rear ½: Royal blue wool.
  Front ½: Fluorescent red wool.
Rib: Medium oval silver tinsel.
Hackle: Long-fibred black hen.

This fly is named after the famous Camasunary fishery on the Isle of Skye, off the western coast of Scotland. The fishery was an outstanding fishery for salmon and sea trout in the 1930s and 1940s and is described in Stephen Johnson's book *Fishing From Afar*. Johnson's family owned the fishery and Steve Johnson, whose plane was shot down in the Second World War, wrote his book in a Prisoner of War camp in Germany.

CINNAMON AND GOLD

Hook: Wet fly, sizes 8–14.
Thread: Black.
Tails: Golden pheasant tippet fibres.
Body: Flat gold tinsel.

Hackle: Hen, either dyed light cinnamon or natural light ginger.
Wings: Hen quill dyed light cinnamon, or cinnamon slips from an owl's flight feathers.

The main use of this fly is for catching sea trout in both rivers and lakes.

Bumbles are palmer-hackled flies, and the following two are essential for anyone going to fish an Irish lough. They were devised in the middle of the twentieth century by High Court Judge T. C. Kingsmill Moore, author of one of the finest books on fly-fishing in Ireland (*A Man May Fish*). They are bob flies, for use on the top dropper.

Claret Bumble

Hook: Wet fly, sizes 8–14.
Thread: Black.
Tails: Golden pheasant tippet fibres.
Body: Medium claret seal's fur (or substitute).
Rib: Oval gold tinsel.
Body hackles: Medium claret and black henny-cock, wound together up the body.
Head hackle: Blue jay.

Tying tip from Davy Wootton: Fix the thread behind the hook eye and first tie in the jay. Strip the blue barred fibres from the feather and tie them in so that the fibres stick out forward around the eye rather like an inside-out umbrella. Tie the rest of the fly and then bring the jay fibres back, holding them in place by the turns of thread used to make the head and whip finish.

The Claret Bumble is a great lake bob fly for salmon and sea trout. The following is a better brown trout fly, especially through spring.

Golden-Olive Bumble

Hook: Wet fly, sizes 8–14.
Thread: Black or olive or light brown.
Tail: Golden pheasant crest feather.
Body: Golden-olive seal's fur (or substitute).
Rib: Oval gold tinsel.
Body hackles: Golden-olive and natural red henny-cock.
Head hackle: Blue jay (see Tip, above).

Connemara Black

Hook: Wet fly, sizes 8–14.
Thread: Black.
Tag: Fine silver wire and yellow floss (optional; may have an effect for salmon and sea trout).
Tail: Golden pheasant crest feather.
Body: Black seal's fur (or substitute).
Rib: Oval silver tinsel.
Hackle: Black henny-cock, with a bunch of blue jay fibres in front.
Wings: Bronze mallard.

Connemara is a wonderful part of Ireland's west, where loughs with plenty of trout, salmon and sea trout abound. Yet this fly can have a far wider impact, provided it is used. It has caught fish from the rivers draining to America's West Coast to the rivers of Arctic Russia.

Dabbler

Hook: Wet fly, sizes 8–12.
Thread: Brown.
Tails: Up to 10 cock pheasant tail fibres.
Body: Golden-olive seal's fur.
Rib: Fine oval gold tinsel.
Body hackle: Natural red (brown) cock.
Wing: Bronze mallard feathers arranged along the top and sides of the fly, rather like a cloak.

This very new fly was created by Donald McClarn in the early 1990s. It was an instant success. Subsequently many older patterns have been tied Dabbler-style. Two examples by Lawrence Finney are given below.

Cock Robin Dabbler

Hook: Wet fly, sizes 8–12.
Thread: Black.
Tails: Bronze mallard fibres.
Body:
  Rear ½: Golden-olive seal's fur (or substitute).
  Front ½: Red seal's fur (or substitute).
Rib: Oval gold tinsel.
Body hackle: Natural red (brown) cock.
Wing: Bronze mallard.

Red Dabbler
Hook: Wet fly, sizes 8–12.
Thread: Black.
Tails: Several cock pheasant tail fibres.
Body: Red seal's fur (or substitute).
Rib: Fine red lurex.
Body hackle: Dyed red cock.
Wing: Bronze mallard.

Donegal Blue
Hook: Wet fly, sizes 8–14.
Thread: Black.
Body: Dark blue seal's fur (or substitute).
Rib: Flat gold tinsel.
Hackle: Long black henny-cock. Sparse.

Donegal, a county in the north-west corner of Ireland, has some fabulous sea trout streams and it was here that the Donegal Blue was devised. It is a great fly for migratory fish anywhere. For instance, for migratory Arctic char in the streams of northern Iceland.

Doobry
Hook: Wet fly, sizes 8–14.
Thread: Black.
Tail: Fluorescent fire-red wool.
Body: Flat gold tinsel.
Rib: Fine Oval gold tinsel.
Body hackle: Black henny-cock.
Hackles: Hot orange henny-cock with a turn of black hen through it.

A fly designed by Stan Headley, guru of Scottish loch fishing, for peat-stained lochs in poor light. Great for salmon and sea trout.

Dunkeld
Hook: Wet fly, sizes 8–14.
Thread: Black.
Tail: Golden pheasant crest.
Body: Flat gold tinsel.
Rib: Fine gold wire or fine oval gold tinsel.
Hackle: Hot orange hen.

Wings: Bronze mallard.
Cheeks: Jungle cock eyes.

Dunkeld is a village on Scotland's River Tay and this fly is a simplification of an old classic salmon fly of the same name. It is good for any migratory salmon or trout in rivers, especially clearing ones with a slight peat tinge. It is good in peat lakes, especially in overcast conditions.

Fiery Brown

Hook: Wet fly, sizes 8–14.
Thread: Black.
Tag: Yellow floss (optional).
Tails: Golden pheasant tippet fibres.
Body: Fiery brown seal's fur (or substitute).
Rib: Oval gold tinsel.
Hackle: Henny-cock, either dyed fiery brown or natural red.
Wings: Bronze mallard.

Rogans of Ballyshannon were the oldest trading fly-tying company (founded in 1830) until they closed in the 1990s, following the death of the last of the Rogans, Rita, on 6 April 1989. In her obituary in *Salmon, Trout & Sea Trout* magazine, Malcolm Greenhalgh wrote:

> Rita and Michael [Rogan] were superb hosts to the many pilgrims who visited their shop from around the world. Many are the Rogan's Fancy, Ballyshannon, and Fiery Brown, tied by Michael and Rita, that have been carried to North America, New Zealand, Australia, Europe and Japan … and framed and hung over fly-tying benches as a tribute to traditional flies tied with traditional materials.

Their company typified international fly-tying.

The Fiery Brown was invented by an earlier Michael Rogan who used stale donkey urine as mordant for his fiery-brown dye. The urine was kept in an open barrel in a yard at the back of the shop. Many were the protests about the resulting stench!

Grouse and Claret

Hook: Wet fly, sizes 8–14.
Thread: Black.
Tails: Golden pheasant tippet fibres.

Body: Dark claret seal's fur (or substitute).
Rib: Oval gold tinsel.
Hackle: Black henny-cock.
Wings: Slips from the tail of a red grouse.

This is a great sea-trout fly for night fishing, often tied on double hooks. There are several other flies in the 'Grouse Series', for instance:

Grouse And Green
Hook: Wet fly, sizes 8–14.
Thread: Black.
Tails: Golden pheasant tippet fibres.
Body: Green seal's fur (or substitute).
Rib: Oval gold tinsel.
Hackle: Dark ginger henny-cock.
Wings: Slips from the tail of a red grouse.

Heckham Peckham
Hook: Wet fly, sizes 8–14.
Thread: Black.
Tails: Golden pheasant tippet fibres.
Body: Red seal's fur (originally hare's ear).
Rib: Oval silver tinsel.
Hackle: Red henny-cock.
Wings: White-tipped slips from the mallard's blue speculum.

Invented by William Murdock of Aberdeen.

Invicta
Hook: Wet fly, sizes 8–14.
Thread: Black.
Tails: Golden pheasant crest.
Body: Yellow seal's fur (or substitute).
Rib: Oval gold tinsel.
Body hackle: Natural red cock, palmered.
Hackle: Natural red cock, with blue jay fibres in front.
Wings: Hen pheasant tail slips.

Invented by James Ogden (author of *Ogden on Fly Tying*, 1879) this is, beyond doubt, one of the best flies in this category for catching migratory

trout and char. Yet it is at least 130 years old! Will any of our most modern creations last that long? Tied with a flat silver tinsel body, this becomes the SILVER INVICTA, which is an excellent fly for lake and river trout that are feeding on tiny bait-fish, and for sea trout and small summer salmon.

KEHE

Hook: Wet fly, sizes 8–14.
Thread: Black.
Tails: Golden pheasant tippet fibres and red wool.
Body: Peacock herl.
Rib: Fine ocal gold tinsel (optional).
Hackle: Dark ginger or bright natural red henny-cock.

Invented in the 1930s by Mr *Ke*mp and Mr *He*ddle, this was a fly for the lochs of the Isles of Orkney, off the northern coast of Scotland. It and the BLACK KEHE, which is identical other than for a black hackle, are very good brown trout flies.

KINGSMILL

Hook: Wet fly, sizes 8–14.
Thread: Black.
Tail: Golden pheasant crest.
Tag: Blue floss (optional, but recommended when sea trout are the quarry species).
Body: Black ostrich herl
Rib: Oval silver tinsel.
Hackle: Black henny-cock.
Wings: Rook (or crow) secondary quill slip, rolled and tied low over the body.
Sides: Jungle cock eye feather.
Topping: Golden pheasant topping.

An alternative to the CONNEMARA BLACK as a very sound and versatile fly for all trout, whether resident or migratory in both lakes and rivers. By T. C. Kingsmill Moore (see above).

MALLARD AND CLARET

Hook: Wet fly, sizes 8–14.
Thread: Black.
Tails: Golden pheasant tippet fibres.

Body: Claret seal's fur or (substitute).
Rib: Fine oval old tinsel.
Hackle: Most usually tied with either black or dyed claret henny-cock; sometimes natural red.
Wings: Bronze mallard.

A. Courtney Williams stated that the Mallard and Claret (probably devised by William Murdock from Aberdeen), 'is one of the best all-round general-utility patterns'. It is! Also outstanding is the Mallard and Silver, which is identical other than for a flat silver tinsel body with an oval silver rib. This, tied in a wide range of sizes from 2–14, is a great fly for salmon, migratory trout (the great writer and film-maker Hugh Falkus had three steelhead on this during his one and only visit to Canada) and resident trout. Why fish go for it we just do not know … but they do!

March Brown

Hook: Wet fly, sizes 8–14.
Thread: Orange.
Tails: A few fibres from a partridge's speckled tail feather.
Body: Hare's ear.
Rib: Orange or yellow thread.
Hackle: Brown speckled partridge.
Wings: Slips from a partridge's speckled tail feather.

This is a fly that is meant to imitate the real flies called march brown (see also p. 143). However it is a great catcher of salmon, migratory trout and resident trout in both lakes and rivers. Hardy's Favourite is fairly similar, with a peacock herl body ribbed with red thread and brown turkey wing. The Silver March Brown, that has a flat silver tinsel body is equally good, and also can be used to imitate small bait-fish.

Mini-Muddlers

Mini-muddlers are lake flies with a deer-hair muddler head (see p. 000):

Hook: Wet fly, sizes 8–12.
Thread: As body.
Tail: A few fibres of Crystal Hair or other 'flash' fibres.
Body: Seal's fur or Fritz (a sparkle chenille).
Collar: Henny-cock hackle.

Head: Deer-hair spun and trimmed muddler-style.
Colours: Black, brown, claret, olives and orange are useful.

Stan Headley has described one with a body of hare's ear:

Muddler Hare's Ear

Hook: Wet fly, sizes 10–16.
Thread: Brown.
Tail: Lemon wood duck.
Body: Hare's mask/ear.
Rib: Fine oval gold tinsel.
Hackle: Brown speckled partridge.
Wing: Lemon wood duck.
Eyes: Jungle cock.
Head: Fine deer-hair, spun and clipped muddler-style.

The advantage of these compared with other bob flies is that they are very difficult to sink, so that they readily fish in the surface. Thus they are easy to bob and dibble in the surface, and they may be pulled across the surface as small 'wake-lures'.

Professor

Hook: Wet fly, sizes 8–14.
Thread: Black.
Tails: 2–3 fibres of red ibis.
Body: Primrose silk.
Rib: Flat or oval gold tinsel.
Hackle: Ginger henny-cock.
Wings: Mottled grey mallard.

A very old pattern from about 1820 invented by Professor John Wilson of Edinburgh University. In his *Dictionary of Trout Flies*, Courtney Williams noted that it is 'a great fly for sea-trout and big brown trout,' and that, 'in America … it is a tremendous favourite.'

Soldier Palmer

Hook: Wet fly, sizes 8–14.
Thread: Red.
Tail: Red wool, short.
Body: Red wool or seal's fur (or substitute).

Rib: Flat or oval gold tinsel.
Hackle: Bright natural red henny-cock palmered along body.

A very useful wet fly for peaty lakes or rivers that are fining down after heavy rain.

Teal, Blue and Silver

Hook: Wet fly, sizes 2–14.
Thread: Black or red.
Tails: Golden pheasant tippet fibres.
Body: Flat silver tinsel.
Rib: Fine silver wire or finest oval tinsel.
Hackle: blue, or kingfisher blue, henny-cock.
Wings: Teal.

The wing consists of a full barred drake teal feather, not feather slips. Fix the feather in place behind the eye and on top of the hook shank, and pull back on the end of the stalk until you have the right length of wing. The Teal, Blue and Silver is really a scaled-down version of some more complex 'classic' salmon flies and is a great fly for all migratory salmonids anywhere in the world. For larger sizes the teal feathers may be too small – use pintail as an alternative. Ian Kennedy gives his a fluorescent yellow tail, and it catches a lot of big sea trout and salmon in Hebridean lochs (see also p. 243).

Teal and Green

Hook: Wet fly, sizes 8–14.
Thread: Black.
Tails: Golden pheasant tippet fibres.
Body: Green seal's fur (or substitute).
Rib: Fine oval gold tinsel.
Hackle: Black henny-cock.
Wings: Teal.

Vary the fly by varying the body colour. This is a fly for resident lake trout.

The next two flies are part of a historically interesting trio. Go back and look at Franck's Glittering Fly (p. 34). Now continue.

Teal and Red

Hook: Wet fly, sizes 8–14.
Thread: Black.
Tails: Golden pheasant tippet fibres.
Body: Red seal's fur (or substitute).
Rib: Oval silver tinsel.
Hackle: Black (or mixed black and dyed red) henny-cock.
Wings: Teal.

This is an early nineteenth-century 'improvement' on Franck's fly, while the next was an improvement made by a man named Peter Ross, from Killin in Perthshire (1873–1923).

Peter Ross

Hook: Wet fly, sizes 8–14.
Thread: Black.
Tails: Golden pheasant tippet fibres.
Body: Rear ½: Flat silver tinsel.
  Front ½: Red seal's fur (or substitute).
Rib: Fine oval silver tinsel.
Hackle: Black henny-cock.
Wings: Teal.

On the eastern side of the Atlantic this is usually rated a major fly for lake trout and sea trout, but it is virtually unknown on the western side of the Big Pond. But it has caught fish in several western salmon and steelhead rivers. Fish it also in larger sizes (2–8), using hairs from the tail of a grey squirrel as wing. Tie some with a gold tinsel body for slightly coloured water. This is a typical example of a very old, but very effective fly that is still being tied and fished! When tied with a bronze mallard wing, it is then called the Silver Knight.

Watson's Fancy

Hook: Wet fly, sizes 8–14.
Thread: Black.
Tail: Golden pheasant crest feather.
Body: Rear ½: Red seal's fur (or substitute).
  Front ½: Black seal's fur (or substitute).
Rib: Fine gold wire.
Hackle: Black henny-cock.

Wings: Black crow quill.
Cheeks: Jungle cock eye feathers.

When fishing for any migratory trout or salmon, that have no interest in feeding, it is important that the fly catches their attention. Sometimes it pays to give one or two tiny points rather than make the entire fly a gaudy 'Here I am, come and grab me!' (see also p. 291–2). Watson's Fancy is a typical example: it is a drab fly with three points of attraction, the glowing yellow tail, the red rear to the body, the stark orange-white jungle cock. Salmon love it!

Waup and Yellow

Hook: Wet fly, sizes 8–14.
Thread: Black.
Tails: Golden pheasant tippet fibres.
Body: Yellow seal's fur.
Rib: Oval gold tinsel.
Hackle: Ginger henny-cock.
Wings: Waup secondary wing slips.

'Waup' is the Scottish name for the curlew, and this fly, that was devised for fishing the River Esk which forms the border between England and Scotland, is a great sea trout fly. The Esk has long been famed for its sea trout (though in very recent years runs have declined somewhat) … so two plus two make four!

Woodcock and Green

Hook: Wet fly, sizes 8–14.
Thread: Black.
Tails: Golden pheasant tippet fibres.
Body: Green seal's fur.
Rib: Fine silver wire or finest oval tinsel.
Hackle: Ginger or red or dyed green henny-cock.
Wings: Woodcock quill slips.

Like the grouse, mallard and teal, a series of flies have developed with slips from the flight feathers of woodcock as wings. This is a very good lake fly for summer evenings.

Zulu

Hook: Wet fly, sizes 8–14.
Thread: Black.
Tails: Red wool, short.
Body: Black wool or seal's fur (or substitute).
Rib: Fine flat or oval silver tinsel.
Body hackle: Black henny-cock, palmered in close turns.

A simple bob fly beloved by the wild brown trout in Scottish lochs. In peaty water try the Blue Zulu, that has a blue hackle in front of the black body hackle.

A VISIT TO THE HEBRIDES

The Outer Hebrides, set far out in the Atlantic off the west coast of Scotland, has some fabulous fishing. Close to the sea are the 'machair lochs' that, their fertility raised by gale-blown oceanic shell-sand, produce big wild brown trout. A little further inland are some of the best lakes in the world for catching Atlantic salmon and sea trout. The fishing is from drifting boats and to catch the fish the locals have devised some great flies.

Pin Fry

Hook: Wet fly, sizes 10–14.
Thread: Bright orange.
Tails: Golden pheasant crest feather.
Body: Pearl Flashabou.
Rib: Fine silver wire.
Wings: Slips from a mallard's blue speculum.
Eyes: Jungle cock.

The machair lochs have lots of tiny sticklebacks and the trout take this as a small fry.

Dusty

Hook: Wet fly, sizes 10–14.
Thread: Black or red.
Tails: Fluorescent red and yellow floss.
Body: Flat silver tinsel.
Rib: Fine silver wire.
Hackle: Red and golden-olive henny-cock wound together.

Dan O'Donovan's fly for bright sunny days and clear water.

Gentian Blue
Hook: Wet fly, sizes 8–14.
Thread: Black.
Tails: Blue wool.
Body: Aquamarine seal's fur (or substitute).
Rib: Blue lurex.
Hackle: Gallina dyed aquamarine.

Reverend Mother
Hook: Wet fly, sizes 10–14.
Thread: Black.
Tails: 2 jungle cock eye feathers tied in toward the front of the hook shank.
Body: None.
Hackle: Black henny-cock.

The similar Blue Nun has a deep blue hackle and is a sea trout fly for a bright day. Ireland's famed Delphi fishery has a fly called Delphi, which has a similar style:

Delphi
Hook: Wet fly, sizes 8–12.
Thread: Black.
Tails: 2 jungle cock eye feathers, but tied in at the end of the shank.
Body: Flat silver tinsel, in two halves.
Hackles: A black henny-cock tied and wound halfway down the body, and another in front of the body.

Both are great trout and sea trout lake flies.

O'Donovan's Fry
Hook: Wet fly, sizes 10–14.
Thread: Black.
Tails: Fluorescent yellow floss.
Body: Orange seal's fur at the rear ('the arse'), the rest grey.
Rib: Fine silver wire.
Body hackles: Natural red (brown) and golden-olive henny-cock, wound together.
Hackle: Natural red (brown) henny-cock.

Another Dan O'Donovan fly for salmon and sea trout on grey wet days.

Clan Chief

Hook: Wet fly, sizes 10–14.
Thread: Black.
Tag: Fine silver wire or finest oval tinsel.
Tails: Red and yellow fluorescent floss (red on top).
Body: Black seal's fur (or substitute).
Rib: Fine silver wire.
Body hackles: Carmine red and black henny-cock wound together.
Hackle: Black hen.

This and the next two flies are by John Kennedy of the Island of South Uist. This and the following are primarily for sea trout and salmon, the third for big brown trout.

Brigadier

Hook: Wet fly, sizes 10–14.
Thread: Black.
Tail: Golden pheasant crest feather.
Body: Black seal's fur (or substitute).
Rib: Fine silver wire.
Body hackle: Dark claret henny-cock.
Hackle: Blue peacock neck hackle.

This has some characters of the Goat's Toe (see below).

Machair Claret

Hook: Wet fly, sizes 10–14.
Thread: Black.
Tag: Fine gold wire or finest oval tinsel.
Tails: Jungle cock eye feather.
Body: Dark claret seal's fur (or substitute).
Rib: Fine gold wire.
Body hackles: Claret and black henny-cock.
Hackle: Black hen.

Jungle Bunny

Hook: Wet fly, sizes 10–14.
Thread: Hot orange.
Body: Banded black, then hot orange, then black seal's fur (or substitute).
Rib: Fine silver wire.

Body hackle: Black henny-cock, 3–4 turns.
Hackle: Black hen.
Eyes: Jungle cock.

Another excellent fly for migratory salmonids (see note on p. 242, WATSON'S FANCY).

GOAT'S TOE

Hook: Wet fly, sizes 8–12.
Thread: Black.
Tail: Red wool.
Body: Peacock herl, one strand wound in touching turns, then a second wound in open turns.
Rib: Red wool.
Hackle: Blue feather from a peacock's neck.

Considered an essential pattern, especially on the Isles of Lewis and Harris that have some wonderful salmon and sea trout lochs. One river/lake system on Lewis, Grimersta, holds the world record salmon catch: 54 salmon caught by one man (A. M. Naylor) in six hours on 23 August 1888. Mr Naylor and two other rods caught a total of 333 salmon in six consecutive days fishing. The GOAT'S TOE may be fished as either a bob fly or point-fly (see p. 228).

Lest it be thought that this category of flies has only been tied and fished in Europe, and mostly in Britain and Ireland, the following are from elsewhere in the world. Again, they are mostly very old, yet they are still worth tying and fishing.

PARMACHENEE BELLE

Hook: Wet fly, sizes 8–14.
Thread: Black or red.
Tails: 2–4 strands each of scarlet and white cock hackle fibres.
Body: Lemon-yellow mohair or yellow floss.
Rib: Oval silver tinsel.
Hackles: White and scarlet henny-cock.
Wings: White swan or goose with a strip of scarlet swan or goose in the middle.

Invented in the 1870s by Henry P. Wells, this was for years one of America's favourite wet flies. It was named after Maine's Parmachenee Lake. Originally the scarlet feather used was ibis.

There were arguments as to why a trout would take the PARMACHNEE BELLE. In which case the next two patterns might have evoked even greater argument!

SCARLET IBIS

Hook: Wet fly, sizes 8–14.
Thread: Black.
Tails: Strip of scarlet ibis.
Body: Scarlet floss.
Rib: Flat or oval gold tinsel.
Hackle: Scarlet henny-cock.
Wings: Scarlet ibis.

Duck or goose quills dyed scarlet are a good substitute. This was a very popular fly from the mid-1800s into the early 1900s. The following is a variant from this era.

In May 1992 the late Al Coen gave the present author a fly that had been tied by J. Shields of Brookline, Massachusetts, in 1880, which was designed for catching brook trout in tidal waters. It is very similar to the previous pattern. Note this fly is 'tied to gut', for it predates the eyed hook.

'NORTH AMERICAN FLY FOR SEA TROUT'

Hook: Wet fly, size 8.
Thread: Black.
Body: Round gold tinsel (faded on the example).
Hackle: Scarlet ibis.
Wings: Scarlet ibis.

When the scarlet ibis became protected, it was no longer possible to tie flies using their gorgeous feathers. Instead the following was devised. Note that the Northern Cardinal is a species of bird found in the United States in which the male has bright red plumage, and that both fly and bird take the name from the Catholic cardinals' brilliant red attire.

CARDINAL
Hook: Wet fly, sizes 8–14.
Thread: Black.
Tails: Fluorescent red hackle fibres.

Body: Fluorescent red floss.
Rib: Fine flat gold tinsel.
Hackle: Fluorescent red.
Wings: Duck quill slips dyed red.

The following pattern is from the same stable as the SCARLET IBIS and CARDINAL, but has a yellow body and a married yellow and red wing.

COLONEL FULLER

Hook: Wet fly, sizes 8–14.
Thread: Black.
Tail: Strip of scarlet ibis.
Body: Yellow floss.
Rib: Flat or oval gold tinsel.
Hackle: Scarlet cock.
Wings: Strips of dyed yellow duck or goose and scarlet ibis (use dyed duck or goose as substitute).

CLARET QUILL

Hook: Wet fly, sizes 8–14.
Thread: Black.
Tails: Claret hackle fibres.
Body: Claret floss.
Rib: Stripped peacock quill.
Hackle: Claret.
Wings: Mallard primary slips.

Claret was a colour commonly incorporated into many very effective salmon and trout flies (e.g. MALLARD AND CLARET, p. 237, CLARET BUMBLE, p. 232). Few more recent tyings include it.

CATSKILL

Hook: Wet fly, sizes 8–14.
Thread: Black.
Tails: Wood duck flank fibres.
Body: Brown floss.
Body hackle: Brown (natural red) hen with 2 turns at the front.
Wings: Wood duck flank fibres.

A fly that suggests a caddisfly – from the Catskills.

Orange Fish Hawk

Hook: Wet fly, sizes 8–14.
Thread: Cream.
Tag: Flat gold tinsel.
Body: Orange floss.
Rib: Flat gold tinsel.
Hackle: Light cream badger.

This very simple fly has, in recent years, caught migratory Arctic char in northern Iceland, trout in the Shetland Isles, and cutthroat trout in Washington State.

White Miller

Hook: Wet fly, sizes 8–14.
Thread: White.
Body: White floss.
Rib: Fine flat silver tinsel.
Hackle: White.
Wings: White duck quill.

Another now-neglected fly, but one that has two good uses. It is a very good pattern to use when small silver-white fry are on the trout menu, and it is excellent in size 8 at night, when trout are catching moths on the water surface.

The next two were once popular river wet flies in North America. In recent years they have scored on the eastern side of the Atlantic, having caught sea trout and salmon in the Hebrides and both brown and rainbow trout in British lakes.

Queen of Waters

Hook: Wet fly, sizes 8–14.
Thread: Black.
Tag: Flat gold tinsel.
Tails: Golden pheasant tippet fibres.

Body: Orange floss.
Rib: Fine flat or oval gold tinsel.
Hackle: Ginger henny-cock.
Wings: Mallard flank.

King of Waters

Hook: Wet fly, sizes 8–14.
Thread: Black.
Tails: Golden pheasant tippet fibres (sometimes omitted).
Body: Crimson floss.
Rib: Flat or oval gold tinsel.
Hackle: Brown (natural red) henny-cock.
Wings: Mallard flank.

Jerry-Ma-Didler

Hook: Wet fly, sizes 8–14.
Thread: Black.
Tail: Strip of scarlet duck quill.
Body: Green wool or floss.
Rib: Oval gold tinsel.
Hackle: Claret henny-cock.
Wings: Brown speckled turkey with a strip of scarlet duck on the side.

Note the two hot-spots on an otherwise fairly drab fly. This old American pattern has a curious and unique colour combination found in no other 'fancy fly': green, claret, scarlet, brown.

Murrumbidgee Wonder

Hook: Wet fly, sizes 8–12.
Thread: Yellow.
Tails: Fibres from scarlet duck or goose quill.
Body: Tip of tying thread, then yellow seal's fur (or substitute).
Rib: Oval gold tinsel.
Body hackle: Light ginger henny-cock wound over seal's fur body.
Hackle: Pale ginger henny-cock.

This is an Australian fancy wet fly that suggested a good imitation of a caddis emerger. Swedish grayling, feeding on hatching caddis in the twilight of a midsummer night, agreed!

Black And Yellow Devil

Hook: Wet fly, sizes 6–10.
Thread: Black.
Tails: Few black bucktail hairs.
Body: Rear ½: Yellow mohair or seal's fur (or substitute).

Middle hackle: Short-fibred black henny-cock (or a longer fibred, clipped short).
Body: Front ½: As rear half.
Hackle: Black cock.

A New Zealand fly that will catch trout anywhere in the world ... if tied and tried!

Claret Jessie

Hook: Wet fly, sizes 8–12.
Thread: Black.
Tails: Few claret hackle fibres.
Body: Peacock herl.
Hackle: Claret henny-cock.
Wings: Grouse tail.

Another New Zealand fly that would not look amiss in a fly-fisher's box on the other side of the world. It is virtually a Grouse and Claret (p. 235) with a peacock herl body, and trout love peacock herl!

African Belle

Hook: Wet fly, sizes 6–10.
Thread: Black.
Tails: Golden pheasant tippet fibres.
Body:
Rear ⅔: Red seal's fur (or substitute).
Front ⅓: Golden-yellow seal's fur (or substitute).
Rib: Oval gold tinsel.
Hackle: Gallina (guinea fowl).
Wings: Fibres cinnamon-tipped brown turkey.

This and the next two are old South African fancy wet flies.

Prince Charming

Hook: Wet fly, sizes 8–12.
Thread: Black.
Tails: Golden pheasant tippet fibres.
Body: Divided into 3 sections: peacock herl; flat silver tinsel; peacock herl.
Hackle: Blue jay.
Wings: White tipped blue slips from a mallard's speculum.

Rector's Fancy
Hook: Wet fly, sizes 8–12.
Thread: Black.
Tails: Golden pheasant tippet fibres.
Body: Flat silver tinsel (embossed if available).
Hackle: Hot orange henny-cock.
Wings: Blue slips from a mallard's speculum.

A South African Butcher (see p. 230).

And finally, for this section …

Last Chance
Hook: Wet fly, sizes 8–14.
Thread: Black.
Tag: Flat gold tinsel.
Tails: Scarlet hackle fibres.
Body: Yellow floss.
Rib: Black floss.
Hackle: Natural red (brown) henny-cock.
Wings: Black quill slips (e.g. crow).

Clearly this American fly was designed to be used when all else had failed, and it was nearly time to go home!

DAPPING FLIES

Dapping is one of the original ways of fly-fishing. It takes us far back, to the centuries before the development of the heavy, tapered fly-line that is used to cast the fly. Instead the fly-fisher uses the wind to carry the fly, at the end of a light line, out to the fish. The flies too are aboriginal in their roots, being mostly palmer-hackled flies similar to those described by writers such as Charles Cotton in the seventeen century.

Dapping does not necessarily need artificial flies. Today, in Ireland, the tradition of using real insects continues. At mayfly time (May-early June), mayflies are caught or bought. Young children throng the boat-jetties asking: 'Would you like some mayflies, Sir. Only one euro each, Sir. An' they're right lovely fresh mayflies, Sir!' In September daddy long-legs are caught for dapping. When dapping the mayfly and the daddy, it is usual to impale two on the hook. In summer grasshoppers are collected for dapping and, for greatest effect, two grasshoppers are fixed on the hook either side of a bright yellow gorse flower.

For those who have never dapped, a few words on the subject. Dapping is carried out from a drifting boat on lakes for salmon, sea trout and brown trout. It has also been used successfully on lakes that have a head of rainbow trout and Arctic char. The drift of the boat is controlled so that it is not too rapid down-wind and so that it also moves across the wind to cover the best lies. The angler sits in the boat, holding a long rod (minimum 14 feet) bearing a reel containing plenty of backing-line and a length (equivalent to 1½–2 times rod length) of dapping floss. Dapping floss is sometimes called a blow-line. A leader links dapping floss and dapping fly. The aim is to have just the right amount of dapping floss beyond the top ring of the rod, and to hold the rod at an appropriate angle (usually almost vertical) so that the wind puts a belly in the dapping floss enabling it to billow forth like a yacht's sail. This carries the leader and the fly out over the water. No part of line (dapping floss nor leader) should touch the water. Instead the fly should bounce from wave to wave as the boat drifts. So once the drift has commenced, the angler does nothing but hold the rod. A fish rises. It is essential not to strike too soon. Say, out loud, 'God save the Queen!' or 'God bless America!' and then lift the rod to set the hook.

Some people think that dapping is a boring exercise. Others take a novel to read and hope that the gillie will tell them when a fish has grabbed hold. But sometimes dapping is the most effective way of rising a fish.

Some dapping flies have been given names, others have not. Most follow a simple recipe that goes as follows.

Dapping Fly

Hook: Low water salmon, sizes 2–18.[†] It used to be the practice to have a 'flying' treble attached by a length of mono to the hook shank just behind the eye.

Thread: Black or brown.

Tail: A few fibres of hackle or bunch of hairs (e.g. squirrel, calf tail).

Body: Entirely made of palmered cock hackles, beginning at the end of the hook shank and ending just behind the eye. Four or many more may be needed.

† In the first half of the twentieth century, they were tied on the largest of hooks, but subsequently on smaller ones. This group of six were dis-

covered in a box in the dusty roof of a Sutherland cottage; their hooks indicate that they were probably dressed very early in the twentieth century. They really are a 'mop' of hackles.

Colours: The most popular dapping flies today have a black body with blue, or red, or yellow at the front. Also popular is one with a body of dark ginger (light natural red) hackles with white at the front; this is known as the **Loch Ordie** and Stan Headley suggests that it is improved by having a black hackle at the rear. The **Red Palmer Dap** has a red wool tail, and natural bright red hackles palmered over red seal's fur. The **Black Pennell Dap** is really a large ordinary **Black Pennell** (p. 230), with golden pheasant tippet tails, silver-ribbed black floss body and a heavy hackling over the front third of the hook shank with black cock hackles.

Streamers and Bucktails

... it is difficult to induce anglers to try new patterns if they are peculiar or display combinations not usually approved of.

John McDonald (ed.), *The Complete Fly Fisher: The notes and letters of Theodore Gordon*, 1947.

The earliest catalogue of North American fishing flies was *Favorite Flies and their Histories* by Mary Orvis Marbury. Daughter of Charles F. Orvis, founder of the company bearing his name, she was put in charge of fly production in 1856. She investigated her potential market by writing to anglers throughout the United States and Canada, asking them which were their favourite flies, where they used them, and what species of fish they used them for. Her mammoth 522-page tome was published in 1892.

A perusal of *Favorite Flies* raises three general points about the flies being used in North America during the late 1880s. The first is that many flies being used were based on the 'fancy fly/lake fly/sea trout wet fly' category that had been exported from the British Isles, including British flies like the Greenwell's Glory (p. 46), Soldier Palmer (p. 239) and Zulu (p. 243).

The second point is that this was a period when gaudy feathers from exotic birds from around the world were being exploited by fly-dressers: cock-of-the-rock, blue chatterer, macaw, Indian crow, bustard, scarlet ibis and so on. Their use in tying 'classic' salmon flies is well known, and continues today mainly as a demonstration of the fly-dresser's art (see p. 298). But these feathers were also used in flies designed to catch a host of other species, from trout to largemouth and smallmouth bass. Today flies that include such materials in their dressing are not used, and being on the CITES list these exotic materials may not be imported or sold.

This is a plate of bass flies from *Favorite Flies and their Histories*. Top left: Lake Edward; top right: Massas-aga; centre left: Frank Gray (which was also said to be also a good fly for walleye). Centre right: Mather; bottom left: Owner; bottom right: McCloud. Though the flies were named, no tying recipes were given by Mary Orvis Marbury, presumably because she wanted fly-fishers to purchase their flies from the Orvis Company, and not to tie their own.

The third point is that there is not a single streamer or bucktail mentioned in the book, yet today few river or lake fly-fishers in the United States and Canada would not carry at least a couple of patterns in this category. The reason is purely one of timing, for Mary Orvis Marbury produced her catalogue just before fly-tying and fly-fishing in North America 'came of age' and developed its own styles that were not based on those styles developed over several centuries in Europe. The first bucktail tying was not published in the United States until 1903, by Theodore Gordon (though in a letter to J. D. Bates Jr., Roy Steenrod stated that Gordon was tying his first bucktails in the early 1880s). This fly was the Bumblepuppy. Incidentally, It is clear from research carried out by J. D. Bates Jr. (see below) that American Indians were using simple bucktails in the early 1800s, if not earlier.

Bumblepuppy

Hook: Long shank streamer, sizes 2–10.
Thread: Black.
Tag: Flat silver tinsel and red floss.
Tails: 2 scarlet ibis feathers tied back to back (we would use a dyed substitute).
Butt: Yellow or red chenille.
Body: White chenille.
Rib: Flat silver tinsel.
Body hackle: Badger, long fibred.
Hackle: Barred wigeon, wound in front of wings.
Wing: White bucktail, with white swan or goose tied over.
Cheeks: Jungle cock.
Head: Black tying thread, or red or yellow chenille.

There were several other versions of this pioneering fly that was used to catch pike, largemouth and smallmouth bass, trout and salmon. It was also used to catch striped bass in the sea off Rhode Island and Cape Cod.

It seems that the feather-winged streamer originated on the banks of Grand Lake Stream, in the State of Maine, for catching sebago, a landlocked variety of the Atlantic salmon. The fly, Rooster's Regret, used 'long feathers picked up around the henhouses of the farms along the river' (J. D. Bates). No full tying recipe of such a fly has been published, so the one below is based on some guesswork:

The following is a selection of bucktails and streamers. It includes different styles of flies that will catch fish. The first flies are the oldest, and it is interesting to note how those devised in the first half of the twentieth century have far more complex tyings than later ones. As already noted, this early period was also the era of the use of exotic materials and fancy tyings, when fly-fishers really did believe that trout, salmon, pike and other fish they were trying to catch could distinguish between subtle shades of colour and would reject a fly that had not been tied precisely according to the complex recipe.

Alaska Mary Ann Bucktail
Thread: Black.
Tails: Red hairs, e.g. bucktail.
Body: Ivory or light tan floss.
Rib: Flat silver tinsel.
Wing: Polar bear (white bucktail as substitute) to end of tails.
Cheeks: Jungle cock, short.

This bucktail was designed by Frank Dufresne in 1922 and was based on a lure used by Eskimos in Alaska's Kobuk River, and has accounted for Pacific salmon, rainbow and cutthroat trout, dolly varden, Arctic char, sheefish and pike. It has caught sea bass and sea trout in estuaries and rocky inlets on the eastern side of the Atlantic (use a stainless hook for saltwater fishing).

Black Ghost
Thread: Black.
Tails: Bunch yellow hackle fibres.
Body: Black floss, tapering at both ends.
Rib: Medium flat silver tinsel.
Hackle: Bunch yellow hackle fibres, tied false.
Wing: 4 white saddle hackles.
Cheeks: Jungle cock.

An old but still great streamer, invented by Herbet L. Welch of Mooselookmeguntic in 1927. J. D. Bates Jr. notes that, 'it turned out to be one of the best streamers that ever developed'. Tie it and fish it today!

Blue and Silver Terror
Mount: 3 size 10 wet fly hooks.
Thread: Black.

Tails: Red floss or dyed goose quill slip.
Body: Flat silver tinsel.
Rib: Oval silver tinsel.
Wing: 4 blue cock hackles, with strip of mallard flank over.

This category of fly may have been slow to arrive in British fresh water, but not in salt water. This was advertised in Hardy Bros.' 1908 catalogue for sea trout fishing in bays and estuaries. For a simplified version, see p. 357.

Chief Needahbeh

Thread: Black.
Tag: Flat silver tinsel.
Tails: Red goose quill slip.
Body: Red floss.
Rib: Fine flat silver tinsel.
Hackle: Dyed red henny-cock wound in front of wings.
Wings: Red saddle hackles outside yellow saddle hackles.
Cheeks: Jungle cock, short.

Chief Needahbeh was leader of the Penobscot tribe in the State of Maine early in the twentieth century. His streamer was designed for catching sebago salmon in Moosehead Lake, but later he used it to catch trout and largemouth and smallmouth bass.

Gray Ghost

Thread: Black and red.
Tag: Narrow flat silver tinsel.
Body: Orange floss wound over white floss.
Rib: Narrow flat silver tinsel.
'Throat' (a sort of low wing extending under shank): 4–5 strands peacock herl, a bunch white bucktail and a golden pheasant crest feather.

Wings: Golden pheasant crest and 4 olive-grey or blue dun saddle hackles.
'Shoulder' (side of wing): Silver pheasant body feather, one third as long as wings.
Cheeks: Jungle cock.

Carrie Stephens was a great tyer of streamer patterns. She had a lodge by Mooselookmeguntic Lake, Maine, and there she tied the first Gray Ghost on 1 July 1924. In its first hour, J. D. Bates tells us, that fly had a brook trout weighing 6lb 13oz.

Improved Governor Bucktail

Hook: Wet fly, sizes 6–8.
Thread: Black.
Tag: Red floss.
Tails: Dyed red hackle fibres.
Body: Dark green chenille.
Rib: Fine oval gold tinsel.
Hackle: Natural red (red-brown) wound in front of wing.
Wing: Dark brown wolverine or bear.
Cheeks: Jungle cock.

The Governor is an old British fly, dating from the middle of the nineteenth century; this tying was designed for catching steelhead in the Klamath River.

Mickey Finn

Thread: Black.
Body: Flat silver tinsel.
Rib: Fine oval silver tinsel.
Wing:
Lower ¼: Yellow bucktail.
Middle ¼: Red bucktail.
Top ½: Yellow bucktail.

J. D. Bates Jr. stated that this was called the Assassin and was re-christened Mickey Finn in 1936. At the time it was so popular that professional tyers had difficulty keeping up with demand. One company even staved off bankruptcy by specialising in this one pattern! It is sometimes tied with a false hackle of yellow henny-cock, but it fishes just as well without. Still a great fly.

Umpqua Special Bucktail

Hook: Wet fly, sizes 6–10 for low water; larger sizes on long shank hooks for steelhead.
Thread: Red.
Tails: White bucktail.
Body:
Rear ⅓: Yellow wool or floss.
Front ⅔: Red chenille.
Rib: Fine oval silver tinsel.
Hackle: Dark brown henny-cock wound in front of the wings as a collar.
Wing: White bucktail to beyond end of tails; not too thick, with red goose slip at either side (later red bucktail).
Cheeks: Jungle cock (optional).
Head: Red.

Also known as the Rogue River Special, this is still a great bucktail for North American West Coast rivers. Both the Umpqua and Rogue Rivers rise in the Cascades and flow to the Pacific through Oregon.

Silver Garland Marabou Streamer

Thread: Black.
Body: Flat silver tinsel.
Wing: White marabou, slightly longer than hook length.
Topping: 4 green-blue ostrich herls with 4 black ostrich herls over them.
'Shoulders': 4 yellow-green ostrich herls on either side of the wing.
Cheeks: Jungle cock, long.

Polly Rosborough's Fuzzy Nymphs can be found on pp. 68–9; this is his best-known streamer. He fished the rivers of Oregon, and devised this there in 1936. The tying given was for chinook and silver (Pacific) salmon, Atlantic salmon (land-locked) and as an imitation of small silvery bait-fish. For steelhead he gave the fly a hot orange marabou wing with black ostrich herl topping or a black marabou wing. For largemouth and smallmouth bass, he tied in a yellow marabou wing with black ostrich herl topping.

The following is a typically complex tying from 1926. It was invented in the mid-1920s by Joseph S. Stickney of Saco, Maine, and was designed to catch sebago (land-locked) Atlantic salmon, trout and bass.

Lady Doctor Bucktail

Thread: Black.
Tag: 3–4 turns narrow flat gold tinsel.
Tails: 2 yellow cock hackle points tied back-to-back.

Butt: 2–3 turns bright red floss (today, use fluorescent).
Body: Bright yellow floss.
Rib: Fine flat gold tinsel.
Body hackle: Yellow henny-cock.
Hackle: Bunch yellow henny-cock hackle fibres, tied false.
Wing: White polar bear with brown bear over. Neither bunches of hair should be thick, and their tips should extend back only a fraction longer than the hook. At the sides a hen feather dyed red extending back one third of wing length.
Topping: Two back-to-back long jungle cock feathers, extending back half as long as wing.

Most of the rest of the bucktails and streamers described are more recent, or are modern dressings based on older flies. None are as complex as the last pattern.

Andy's Smelt

Thread: Black.
Tail: Dyed red goose quill slip.
Body: Flat silver tinsel.
Rib: Fine oval silver tinsel.
Wing: White calf tail, with mallard flank dyed blue over.

Though designed to match the smelt, a small fish that inhabits estuaries and the lower fresh reaches of rivers, it is a useful pattern for matching any tiny silvery bait-fish.

Aztec

Thread: Black or body colour.

Tail, body and wing: 4-ply knitting yarn; choose any colour you fancy.

Dick Nelson's Aztec is easy to tie. Have ready, a 5 in piece of 4-ply yarn for the tails, 8 separated 1½ in single-ply lengths of yarn for the wing, and a 6–8 in length of 4-ply yarn to tie the fly. Any colour will do: it's your choice!

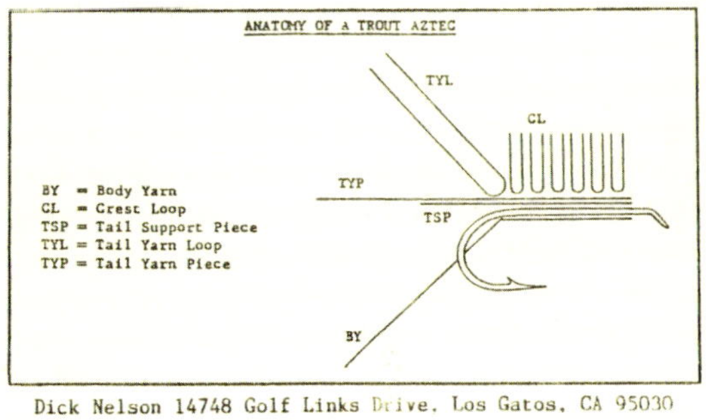

Bind the 6–8 in length of 4-ply wool along the underside of the hook shank, with the loose end to the front of the eye. Varnish the shank and twist the wool very tight and wind that back down the shank. Then varnish the wool underbody and shank. Now trap in the doubled 5 in length of 4-ply yarn with one turn of the tying wool. Make two touching turns forward with the tying wool and then trap in a piece of single-ply yarn. Continue forward, to the hook eye, with one turn of wool to trap in a wing length, followed by two turns before the next piece of wing wool is bound in. Tie off the tying wool with the thread and create a nice head. Using a dubbing needle and then a comb, tease out the tail and fibres to give a nice uniform tail and wing. Carefully trim these to the desired length.

Dick tied the fly illustrated and the back of his business card included instructions on how to tie his fly.

Badger Demon

Mount: Tandem mount of 2 size 10 wet fly hooks or a streamer/bucktail hook size 2–8.

Thread: Black.

Body: Orange wool.

Rib: Fine oval gold tinsel.

Hackle: Hot orange hackle fibres, tied false.
Wing: 2 badger cock hackles.
Cheeks: Jungle cock.

The BLACK DEMON is similar, but with black wool body, silver rib and black hackles for wings.

Marabou is a wonderful material for winging streamer patterns. It is light so that the fly is easy to cast, and it is highly mobile, pulsating with life as it swings across a river or is pulled through the still water of a lake. Note that, when wet, marabou is less bulky than when dry, so tie about 25 per cent more marabou in the wing than seems necessary and in the water it will be just right!

BLACK MARABOU
Thread: Black.
Tails: Black hackle fibres, or none.
Body: Flat silver tinsel.
Rib: Oval silver tinsel.
Hackle: Black, or red, or yellow, or orange hackle fibres, tied false.
Wing: Bunch black marabou, with 2–4 strands pearl Flashabou on either side.
Cheeks: Jungle cock (optional).
NOTE: Marabou is very soft and easily gets itself wrapped around the hook bend during casting. Do not tie the wing much longer than the hook.

By having some tied with coloured hackles, different 'trigger points' can be presented to the fish. This is a great streamer for marbled trout and huchen in Slovenia, big brown trout in Russia and Fenno-Scandinavia, rainbow trout in reservoirs, largemouth and smallmouth basses in Ontario's lakes, and cutthroats and rainbows in America's West.

The similarly tied WHITE MARABOU (with white marabou) makes an excellent bait-fish/fry imitation; YELLOW MARABOU (with yellow marabou) is a great pike fly in clear water, while ORANGE MARABOU (with orange marabou) is better in peaty water. Marabou

streamers, tied in sizes 2/0, 1/0 and 1, are outstanding flies for peacock bass in the Amazon tributaries (but be aware that one bite by a piranha will slice through the entire wing!).

There are many variations on this theme. For instance, Les Lewis's Christmas Tree has a tail of fluorescent green wool and a false hackle of a tuft of fluorescent red wool.

Black Matuku

Thread: Black.
Tails and back/wing: 4 black cock hackles tied 'matuku style'.
Body: Black chenille wool or fur dubbing.
Rib: Medium oval silver tinsel.
Hackle: Black henny-cock, as collar (optional).

The ribbing tinsel is tied in at the end of the hook shank, and then the body wound. Four identical black hackles are taken and, after basal fluff removed, arranged with two on two, concave surfaces together. The length of the tips needed to form the tails is measured, and then all the rest of the underside hackle fibres are removed. The feathers are then tied in securely at the front of the body. They are then held tightly in place along the back of the body and the tinsel rib wound tightly forward in open turns to the front of the body, at the same time binding down the back/wing. Take care not to tie down hackle fibres. The effect is something like a Mohican hairstyle extending along the top of the body.

This style of winging streamers originated in New Zealand. The Red Matuku is identical but has a red body and an oval gold tinsel rib. There are many variations on this theme.

Black Streamer
Thread: Black.
Body: Black chenille.
Rib: Oval silver tinsel.
Hackle: Black, or red, or yellow, or orange hackle fibres, tied false (see Black Marabou note).
Wing: 4 black cock hackles.
Cheeks: Jungle cock (optional).

This may also be tied on a tandem mount and is a good general streamer for trout, bass, sea trout etc.

Black-Nose Dace
Thread: Black.
Tails: Red wool or yarn, very short.
Body: Flat sliver tinsel.
Rib: Fine oval silver tinsel.
Wing:
Under: Polar bear or white bucktail.
Middle: Black bear or skunk (shorter than rest of wing).
Upper: Brown bucktail.

Art Flick's imitation of an American bait-fish works wherever there are small white-silvery minnows or other bait-fish. It has, for instance, caught trout in excess of five pounds in weight from rivers in Sweden and Russia.

Breatherliser
Thread: Black.
Tails: Black cock hackle fibres.
Body: Flat silver tinsel.
Rib: Finest oval silver tinsel.
Hackle: Badger, henny-cock tied as collar in front of wings.

Wings: 2 hot orange and 2 Green Highlander hackles.
Cheeks: Jungle cock.

A 1960s attempt by Alec Iles to imitate sticklebacks.

Dog Nobbler

Thread: Black.
Tail: Bunch marabou.
Body: Chenille.
Rib: Fine silver wire.
Body hackle: Grizzle cock palmered.
Head: BB shot pinched firmly behind eye. It was then painted black and then a black and white eye was painted on either side. Today use a black tungsten bead (see note on p. 56).

The Dog Nobbler was invented by Trevor Housby in 1980 and patented by Sid Knight. Tie any colour of tails and body … white, black, olive, brown. This is primarily a lake fly (black may suggest a big leach to smallmouth bass).

Frog Nobbler

Thread: Yellow.
Tails: Bunch yellow marabou.
Underbody: 2 layers of lead wire.
Overbody: Gold Mylar tube.

Devised by John Wilshaw in 1983, it is an alternative to the Dog Nobbler. Tie with different coloured tails.

Fuzzy Wuzzy

Thread: Black.
Tails: Black squirrel.
Body: Black chenille.†
Hackles: A black hackle palmered along the front half of the body, and another wound at the head.
† Is also tied with orange, red or yellow chenille body to give four flies with different body colours.

A New Zealand pattern. The similarly tied Red Setter has a red squirrel tail, a body of orange chenille, and a ginger hackle.

Hornberg Special
Hook: Wet fly, size 6.
Thread: Black.
Body: Flat silver tinsel.
Hackle: 4–5 turns grizzle hen in front of wings.
Wings: Two yellow cock hackle points with a drake mallard breast feather, 1½ in long, on either side.
Cheeks: Jungle cock.

Frank Hornberg was a Conservation Warden from Portage County, Wisconsin, when he invented this fly in the 1950s.

Joe's Smelt
Thread: Black.
Tails: Red calf tail, short.
Tag: Red thread used to tie down body at rear.
Body: Silver Mylar tubing, the front ¼ painted red.
Wing: Narrow drake pintail flank feather tied low over body.
Head: With black and white painted eyes.

Joe Sterling's imitation of a bait-fish for catching sebago and ouananiche (land-locked Atlantic salmon) and trout.

Laser Minnow
Hook: Wet fly, size 8.
Thread: Black.
Head: Goldhead pushed to eye of hook.
Underbody: Pearl sparkle (see below).
Overbody/wing: Sparkle synthetic winging material (see below).

Devised by Mick Hall, this Australian minnow pattern comes highly recommended for rainbow trout in lakes. It will catch fish in any lake or river. Mick uses Enrico Puglisi's synthetic materials in this fly – if Puglisi's are not available, use Antron, SLF or similar. Mick adds: 'the colours can be varied to suit and it works well in both fresh and brackish water'.

Leech Streamer
Thread: Black.
Body: Maroon or light claret wool.
Hackle: Bunch black cock hackle fibres, tied false.

Wings: 2 maroon or light claret saddle hackles with one black saddle hackle on either side.

Trout, bass, walleye and panfish feed on big swimming leeches and this pattern by Frier Gulline imitates these leeches.

Llama

Thread: Black.
Tails: Bunch grizzle hackle fibres.
Body: Red floss.
Rib: Flat gold tinsel.
Hackle: Grizzle henny-cock wound in front of wings.
Wing: Woodchuck (brown barred squirrel is a reasonable substitute).
Head: With painted black and white eyes.

This is a small bucktail, to be tied on size 8–12 hooks. It has also been tied with white and with black floss bodies.

Miracle Marabou Blacknose Dace

Thread: White.
Tails: Bunch cream hackle fibres.
Body: White fur, wider at front. A fine-textured synthetic fur is ideal.
Hackle: As tail, tied false.
Wing: White marabou with olive-brown marabou over. Along each side one length silver Mylar, the top half blackened (to suggest a lateral line) with permanent felt pen.
Head: Top brown, bottom white.

This was one of a series of flies designed in the 1960s to match the variety of minnows found in the northern United States and Canada.

Minnow

Thread: Black.
Tails: Tuft fluorescent red wool.
Body: Flat silver tinsel.
Rib: Fine oval silver tinsel.
'Throat': White and red bucktail.
Wing:
Under: White bucktail.
Over: Dark green bucktail.
Head: With painted black and white eyes.

A Taff Price fly that is very effective fished in the margins of rivers, where large numbers of minnows gather.

Minnow Streamer

Thread: Olive.
Tails: Bunch blue dun hackle fibres.
Body: White floss or wool.
Rib: Oval silver tinsel.
Hackle: Dyed red cock hackle fibres for male, blue dun for female, tied false.
Wing: Olive cock hackles, 2, back to back, with a strip of barred teal feather at either side.
Cheeks: Jungle cock.

Another pattern from the Taff Price stable. At mating time (which is the entire year save for winter) adult male minnows have red throats.

Missionary

Thread: Black.
Tails: Dyed red or natural red cock hackle fibres.
Body: White chenille.
Rib: Oval or flat silver tinsel.
Hackle: As tails, tied false.
Wing: One mallard feather, 1½ times length of body, tied low.

An excellent reservoir fly for rainbow trout, it is by Dick Shrive after an earlier pattern by J. J. Dunn.

Muddler Minnow

Thread: Black.
Tail: Turkey quill slip, slightly longer than hook gape.
Body: Flat gold tinsel (over rear half of hook shank).
Rib: Fine gold wire or finest oval gold tinsel (optional).
Wing: Large bunch grey squirrel tail, with wide slip of mottled turkey on either side.
Head and collar: Deer hair, spun on shank in front of wings and then trimmed to shape (see below).

This revolutionary pattern was developed by Don Gapen in the late 1940s or early 1950s, being first published in Al McClane's *The Practical Fly Fisherman* (1953). The name comes from a Cockatush minnow that lives in the Nipigon River of northern Ontario and has a nickname, 'Muddler'. J. D. Bates Jr. quotes from a letter sent to him by Gapen, listing all the fish species he had caught with his MUDDLER MINNOW: 'all trout, all bass, crappies, sunfish, snook, bonefish, and redfish [channel bass]. Also, at times, I have taken walleyes, pike, grayling, bonita, jacks, and even sharks.'

Fly-tying novices often have difficulty tying the fly's essential feature: its deer hair collar and head fly. There are four steps in doing this properly. First, take small bunches of deer hair; beginners tend to take too big a bunch. Two, comb out all basal fluff completely; with some sorts of deer hair it is worth cutting off the tips of the hairs unless they are needed for the collar. Three, hold the bunch at an angle over the hook shank, make two soft turns of thread around shank and hairs, and then pull steadily down, releasing the hairs as they start to splay. Four, make one or two hard turns of thread through the spun hairs and two turns in front; force the spun hairs back hard before tying and spinning the next bunch of hairs. Trim the head to a wedge shape, wider at the back, leaving rear-pointing hairs at the back untrimmed. Unless tying the fly for competition or demonstration, leave the head a bit untidy as this gives more life in the water.

Note that deer hair is hollow and very buoyant, so for fishing deep any fly with a muddler-style head must be heavily weighted (with two layers of lead). Note too that by trimming the head square, without the wedge taper, the Muddler Minnow makes an excellent popper pattern.

Not surprisingly, the muddler-style head has been used in many other patterns. A selection of some of the best is given below.

BLACK ANGUS

Hook: Long shank streamer, sizes 2–4.
Thread: Black.
Tails: 4 black cock hackles, tied flaring apart.
Underbody: Lead wire.
Body: Black floss (leave plenty of room for the head!).
Body hackle: A black marabou feather, tied in by its tip and wound up the body in open turns.
Head and collar: Black deer hair, muddler-style.

A fly devised for Alaskan waters by Angus Cameron and Eric Leiser. This has caught big brown trout in Fenno-Scandinavia, and when tied in yellow or olive is excellent for catching pike.

Kiwi Muddler

Thread: Tan.
Tails: Dark grey deer hair.
Underbody: Lead wire.
Body: Tan dubbing.
Rib: Oval gold tinsel.
Wing: Natural rabbit fur on a triangular piece of tanned (soft) skin.
Head and collar: Natural deer hair, muddler-style.

This is a modification of a New Zealand pattern where the wing was tied 'zonker-style' see p. 283. Like the next pattern, it was published by Jack Dennis in his *Western Trout Fly Tying Manual.*

Spruce Muddler

Thread: Black.
Tails: Tips of herls from a peacock's sword feather.
Underbody: Lead wire.
Body:
  Rear ½: Red floss, ribbed with embossed fine flat gold tinsel.
  Front ½: Peacock herl.
Wing: Grey squirrel tail, with 2 badger hackles at either side.
Collar: Dark moose, spun and clipped.
Head: Natural deer hair, spun and clipped.
Note: The muddler head has a bunch of spun moose hair to the rear of the deer hair. When trimming, leave the dark moose hairs to the rear unclipped, and leave the clipped moose hairs longer than the deer so that there will be a distinct dark collar.

This fly is a muddler version of the Spruce Fly Streamer, that lacks the muddler head.

Gartside's Muddler

Hook: Long shank or wet fly, sizes 6–10.
Thread: Black.
Tails: Cock pheasant tail fibres.
Body: Gold Mylar tube.

Wing: Yellow deer hair with 2 cock pheasant back feathers back-to-back on either side.
Head and collar: Natural deer hair, muddler-style.

Jack Gartside is one of the greatest eccentrics in the fly-tying world ... and a fine tyer. He has produced some very innovative flies for both Yellowstone and the Florida flats. His Muddler has caught trout in many parts of the world.

Marabou Muddler

Hook: Long shank, sizes 2–10, or 2 wet fly, sizes 6–10 in a tandem mount.
Thread: Black.
Underbody: Lead wire (optional).
Tail and body: Wool, with the end tuft as a tail, then the body wound (for colours see below).
Wing: Marabou (for colours see below).
Head and collar: Natural deer hair, or deer hair with colour as wing and body, muddler-style.
Colours: White, black, olive, brown, orange, yellow.

A very good pike fly, and when heavily weighted an excellent fly for big trout in brawling rivers.

Matuku Sculpin

Thread: Grey.
Tail and wings: 4 grizzle hackles, dyed brown or olive, tied 'matuku' style (see above).
Body: Tan wool.
Rib: Medium oval gold tinsel.
Gills: Red wool or floss (use fluorescent) wound between head/collar and body.
Head and collar: Deer hair, muddler-style (natural or dyed black, tan or olive).

Dave Whitlock has been one of the United States's leading fly-dressers since the 1970s. His sculpin will catch fish that eat real sculpins (also called miller's thumb and bullhead) anywhere.

AN EXAMPLE OF THE ART OF SPINNING AND STACKING DEER HAIR

Chris Helm, from Toledo, Ohio, is the leading exponent of using deer hair to create a range of splendid flies. He uses two techniques, spinning deer hair (as is used in muddler-style heads) and stacking deer hair. In the latter, bunches of hair are tied in without letting them flare and spin around the hook. Thus he can produce sculpin heads with bands and patches of hair of different colours. His sculpin and mouse imitations are works of art; sculptures in hair, fur and feather.

Mylar Minnow

Hook: Long shank, sizes 10–14.
Thread: Black.
Tails and back: 10–12 peacock herls.
Underbody: Fluorescent red wool or floss.
Body: Silver or pearl Mylar tube.

This very simple minnow or fry imitation is very effective when species like trout, perch and small pike are ambushing shoals in the river or lake margin.

Optic

Thread: Wet fly, sizes 4–10.
Thread: Black.
Body: Oval tinsel (see below).
Hackle: Henny-cock, wound in front of wing (optional).
Wing: Hair (bucktail, squirrel or calf tail etc.)

Head: A large split shop (swan in the larger sizes, BB in the smaller) clamped behind the hook eye and painted black.

California's Jim Pray came up with the Optic series of bucktails, using metal 'pins' from old-style radios for the bodies. These are no longer available, but oval gold and silver tinsel is more convenient and as effective.

He produced four colours of Optic:

Black Optic: Body gold; Hackle black; Wing black; Eye with yellow iris, black pupil.

Red Optic: Body silver; Wing mostly red with a little yellow under; Eye with yellow iris, black pupil.

Orange Optic: Body silver; Hackle red; Wing orange; Eye with white iris, red pupil.

Cock Robin Optic: Body silver; Hackle orange; Wing badger or grey squirrel; Eye with yellow iris, black pupil.

These were designed to catch steelhead and Pacific salmon and they remain very successful. The Red Optic and Orange Optic have proved their worth for summer salmon in European rivers. Simple, yet effective.

Perch Fry

Hook: Long shank, sizes 4–10.
Thread: Brown.
Tails: Bunch red-brown cock hackle fibres, cut square.
Underbody: Orange floss.
Body: Gold Mylar tube or embossed flat tinsel wound over the underbody, marked using permanent felt tip with dark brown or black vertical bars.
Wing: Brown marabou with a little orange marabou over.

'Throat' (i.e. belly of fish imitation): White marabou extending back ⅔ length of body.
Head: With painted black and white eyes.

Trout love to eat perch fry in both North America and the British Isles. When the perch fry hatch in the great limestone lakes of Ireland, the trout immediately stop feeding on mayflies etc. and turn entirely to one to two inch long fry. A fly by John Veniard.

Pintail Smelt

Hook: Long shank, sizes 6–8.
Thread: White.
Body: Embossed silver tinsel.
Underwing: Few fibres pink bucktail.
Wing: One pintail flank feather on either side, extending back about ¼ body length beyond hook bend.

This is David Goulet's imitation of small silvery baitfish, including smelt.

Polystickle

Hook: Wet fly or long shank, sizes 6–8 (silver if possible).
Thread: Black.
Tail and back: Originally brown raffine (see note below).
Underbody:
Rear ⅔: Black floss
Front ⅓: Fluorescent red floss.
Overbody: Strip from polythene bag.
Hackle: Bunch hot orange cock hackle fibres, tied false.
Head: With painted black and white eye.

A useful bait-fish imitation by Richard Walker. But note: though flies like the Mylar Minnow and Polystickle do 'look' to us like little fish, in the water they lack the action of real bucktails and streamers. So to the fish it is likely that they are not as deceiving. The fly is improved by using brown embroidery silk for back and tail, as the tail now moves in the water unlike the stiff raffine. The following is a similar sort of tying, but has a wing (back) that is free to move in the water and is therefore more suggestive of 'life'.

Sinfoil's Fry

Hook: Long shank, sizes 8–12.
Thread: Black.
Underbody:
Rear ⅔: Flat silver tinsel.
Front ⅓: Fluorescent red floss.
Overbody: Polythene strip.
Wing (back): Bronze mallard slip, rolled and tied in low.
Head: With painted black and white eye.

Sweeny Todd

Hook: Long shank 6–12, or 2 size 8–10 hooks in tandem.
Thread: Black.
Body: Black floss, with 2–3 turns of magenta floss in front.
Hackle: Bunch crimson hackle fibres, tied false.
Wing: Black squirrel tail.

By Richard Walker, this is a very good black bucktail for both freshwater resident and migratory trout.

Tadpole

Hook: Wet fly, sizes 10–12.
Thread: Black.
Tails: Black marabou.
Body: Black chenille wound over either lead wire or a tungsten bead.

Many species of fish will eat frog and toad tadpoles should they stray from cover into open water. This simple streamer is as good an imitation as there is.

THUNDERCREEK MINNOW

This is a series of eight bucktails by Keith C. Fulsher, and was devised in the 1960s. They are very easy to tie, provided basic rules are followed. Fulsher used 6X long, size 8 and 10 hooks with straight eyes. The latter point is most important, as the straight eye becomes part of the head. When tied the bucktail used in the dressing should extend back a faction beyond the hook bend. *But*, it is tied in the other way round, so that during tying the tips of the bunches of bucktail extend forward of the eye of the hook. The fly is completed by bringing all the bucktail back, with the fly finished off some distance behind the eye with several turns of red thread, suggesting gills. The folded-back bucktail immediately behind the eye looks like the rounded head of a minnow, and it is painted, with an eye.

Two or three bunches of bucktail were used. Brown bucktail was used to simulate the back of the minnow, white to simulate the belly of the minnow and, in two, a third sparse bunch was used to suggest a lateral line. The main differences between Fulsher's eight minnows was in the material used to cover the hook shank (what in most fly recipes would be called the 'body').

It is highly unlikely that even the most intelligent trout would notice the difference between at least some of the Thundercreek series. Nevertheless, they are still great flies and the four tyings given have caught trout in South America, New Zealand, Fenno-Scandinavia and the British Isles, as well as in North America.

The illustrated Thundercreek flies were tied on special Thundercreek hooks. These have a very long shank. From the fish-catching point-of-view, a flexible tandem mount would be more effective.

Thundercreek Blacknosed Dace
Thread: Red.
Body: Flat silver tinsel.
Wing:
Upper (back): Brown bucktail.
Middle (lateral line): Black bucktail.
Lower (belly): White bucktail.
Eye: Yellow iris, black pupil.

Thundercreek Golden Shiner
Thread: Red.
Body: Flat gold tinsel.
Wing:
Upper (back): Brown bucktail.
Middle (lateral line): Yellow bucktail.
Lower (belly): White bucktail.
Eye: Yellow iris, black pupil.

Thundercreek Red Fin Shiner

Thread: Red.
Body: Fluorescent pink floss.
Wing:
  Upper (back): Brown bucktail.
  Middle (lateral line): None.
  Lower (belly): White bucktail.
Eye: Yellow iris, black pupil.

Thundercreek Silver Shiner

Thread: Red.
Body: Flat silver tinsel.
Wing:
  Upper (back): Brown bucktail.
  Middle (lateral line): None.
  Lower (belly): White bucktail.
Eye: Yellow iris, black pupil.

Vulture

Thread: White.
Tails: Bunch hot orange cock hackle fibres.
Body: White chenille.
Rib: Fine oval silver tinsel.
Hackle: Bunch hot orange cock hackle fibres, tied false.
Underwing: White marabou.
Overwing: 2 vulturine gallina hackles.
Head: Red.

Vulturine gallina is a bird of the African savannah and on the CITES list. However it is bred in captivity for fly-tying. Its striking cobalt blue-striped feathers have long been used in Britain for sea trout flies (see also p. 352).

Walkers' Kitten

Thread: Black.
Tail: Black squirrel.
Body: Red chenille.
Wing: Brown speckled partridge hackles, 3 on each side.

A South African pattern very similar to New Zealand's Mrs Simpson (named after Wallis Simpson, who seduced King Edward VII). That has a yellow or red chenille or wool body and has cock pheasant rump feathers on either side instead of the partridge.

Whiskey Fly

Hook: Long shank, 6–10.
Thread: Orange.
Tag: Fluorescent hot orange floss.
Body: Flat silver tinsel.
Rib: Fluorescent hot orange floss.
Hackle: Hot orange henny-cock wound in front of wings.
Wing: Hot orange calf or goat.
Head: Orange.

Devised by Albert Willock, who initially used a pair of orange cock hackles as wing. Thus what is now a bucktail was at first a streamer. This has a great reputation in trout lakes where the fish are filter-feeding planktonic crustaceans (e.g. *Daphnia*) on hot summer days.

Woolly Bugger

Thread: Black, brown or red.
Tails: Marabou (preferably a blood feather), as long as hook shank. A very few fibres of pearl Flashabou or Crystal Hair may be added.
Body: Chenille.
Body hackle: A saddle hackle palmered along body in open, close turns.
Head: With painted black and white eye (optional).

This fly, devised by Russell Blessing, is one of the great bait-fish imitations. Grey, with a grizzle hackle, is outstanding; black, brown and white are excellent. But it doesn't look like a fish? In the water it is full of movement … so full of movement that predatory fish are fooled. And it is so easy to tie!

Dirty Harry

Hook: Streamer/bucktail, size 8.
Thread: Black.
Tail: Black marabou, plus 2 strands pearl Krystal Flash (or similar).
Body: Soft black fur, long in staple (e.g. BMS, SLF, arctic fox).
Rib: Red holographic tinsel.

This is Ray Brown's variation on the Woolly Bugger theme. He uses it when trout are feeding on frogs in the margins of Australia's lakes, though it would undoubtedly take predatory trout and char anywhere. Tied in bigger sizes (up to 2/0) will also catch big predators such as pike and peacock bass.

Zonker

A zonker strip is a length of narrow tanned rabbit skin, with fur attached, that is tied in either as a tail or as a wing. It is highly mobile in the water and, because it becomes heavy having absorbed water, it helps the fly sink quickly. Tied in a wide range of colours (black, white, white and red, olive, orange), Zonkers are simple to tie and effective, gaudy lures.

For example:

Thread: Same colour as zonker strip.
Tail: Zonker strip.
'Wing': Rabbit or arctic fox fur would around hook shank (ideally, use a dubbing loop), plus a few fibres pearl Flashabou.
Hackle: See above.
Head: Red.

Tie in a range of colours: white, black, yellow, orange, red, olive.

Fritz Streamers

These depend on the availability of the synthetic 'flashy' material Fritz for their construction. This is a chenille-like material in which short, Flashabou-like strands are trapped in plaited cotton thread. The tip of a length of fritz is tied in at the end of the hook shank and wound forward to create the body of the fly. The basic dressing is as follows:

Hook: Wet fly, sizes 6–10.
Thread: As body.
Tail: Bunch marabou, with 2–3 strands Flashabou each side.
Body: Fritz.
Head: Gold or tungsten head, or for snaggy-bottomed waters, bead-chain eyed tied to top of hook shank (the fly then swims upside-down).

These may be tied in a wide variety of colours and may be used to catch a variety of predatory fish from smallmouth bass to pike, from big brown trout to saltwater species (in the latter, white and chartreuse are the most useful colours).

And finally, for completeness … two outrageous flies!

The Blob

Blobs have enraged some fly-fishers because they are reputed to be catchers of any fish that swims, and have been lauded by others who enjoy catching fish! They are not catch-alls, though they are very efficient when it comes to catching trout newly stocked into lakes from the fish-farm.

Hook: Wide gape wet fly, sizes 6–10.
Thread: As body.
Body: Fritz (a flashy form of chenille) tightly wound to give a globular mass, plus a few short strands of Flashabou. Colours: red, orange, white, olive, green, black.

The aim is to cast them out and then strip them back quickly in front of a feeding fish, on a sinking or intermediate line. Alternatively, search the water by making very long casts, putting the rod under the arm, and stripping back as fast as possible using both hands. Like the next pattern, banned on some commercial fisheries because of its reputation.

The Booby

Boobies were devised for catching rainbow trout in English reservoirs and small pond fisheries. These fish can be very naive, especially just after they have been released into the water. Boobies float and are fished on very short leaders and fast-sinking fly-lines. The fly-line drags them under the surface and, when retrieved, they dive and when the retrieve is stopped they float upwards. They can be tied in the most garish colours and, like Blobs, have been outlawed by some fisheries.

Hook: Wet fly, sizes 10–12.
Thread: As eyes.
Tail and wing: Marabou, with a few strands of Flashabou (or similar).
Body: Fluorescent twinkly Fritz or similar.
'Eyes': Foam balls.

Three Boobies are illustrated. Those who wish to tie their own are free to use any colour they wish. Be as subtle or gaudy as you like!

Flies for Salmon, Sea Trout and Steelhead

> The Samon is the moost stately fyssh that ony man maye angle to in fresshe water.
>
> Anon., *The Treatyse of Fysshynge wyth an Angle*, 1496.

This section describes flies specially designed to catch Atlantic salmon, Pacific salmon, sea trout (sea-run brown trout) and steelhead (sea-run rainbow trout). At the end of this section are also some flies that are especially useful for catching sea-run cutthroat trout. Note that although a particular fly might have been designed for catching one species of migratory salmonid, it is quite likely to be useful for catching other species. For instance, Ally's Shrimp was designed to catch Atlantic salmon, but it is also a very effective steelhead pattern.

The previous two sections (on sea trout/lake flies and streamers/bucktails) also include many flies that can usefully be fished for migratory salmonids.

These migratory fish can be amongst the most frustrating to catch for one reason: when they return from their oceanic feeding grounds they *usually* have no interest in feeding. There are, of course, exceptions. Sea trout and sea-run cutthroats do feed in some rivers, and there they may be caught when they are feeding – like resident brown and cutthroat trout – on imitative nymphs and dry flies. But otherwise the situation is completely different. A pool may be full of beautiful sea-silver fish, but they all refuse to take the flies we cast to them. Are they the wrong flies? How can we know, for they cannot communicate with us? If they are not looking for food, we have nothing to imitate. What we tie on the leader is sheer guess work, or, at best, will be based on past experience or what others have recommended. When visiting a North American river, a guide, or on a river in the British Isles, a gillie will often recommend a particular fly. However such local experts can be fallible. 'You will never catch a salmon on this river with *that!*' said one guide, as he examined the fly knotted to a visitor's leader at lunchtime. The visiting fly-fisher replied that he had already caught three salmon on *that* fly in the hour just before lunch!

SO JUST WHY DO SALMON TAKE A FLY?

In his book *Salmon Fishing: A Practical Guide* (1984) Hugh Falkus suggested that salmon may take a fly for one of six reasons:

1. It takes the fly as an item of food. It has often been suggested that, when newly in from the sea, a shrimp/prawn or bait-fish imitation is then best, but, when the salmon has been long in the river, that a smaller fly resembling something that the fish ate before it went to sea is best.
2. It takes the fly because it might be food … the fly 'induces' the take because it looks edible to the salmon.
3. It takes out of aggression. The fly is invading its personal space so it grabs it hard, trying to kill it.
4. It takes because the fly is irritating it. This is likely to happen when one or more fish in a small lie are cast over time after time after time. Eventually, on the umpteenth cast, one of the salmon can take it no longer, and Bang!
5. The salmon finds the fly curious and wants to investigate a little more closely. Mammals use their paws or hands to hold and feel things that they are examining. Lacking these, the fish must use its mouth.
6. Playfulness.

Gary Anderson agreed with Falkus's assessment (in *Atlantic Salmon, Fact and Fantasy*). He also considered the feeding habit as being the main reason for salmon to take our flies, suggesting that it accounts 'for one-half to two-thirds of all rises'.

Alas, salmon refuse to confirm or deny the Falkus/Anderson assessment. What does seem the case is that salmon that do take the fly probably have a higher level of the hormone thyroxine that those that will not move to the fly (see Rod Sutterby and Malcolm Greenhalgh, *Atlantic Salmon*, 2005). This hormone renders a salmon more alert, and its level in the salmon's blood is higher on the return to the river than when the salmon has been resting for a few days in a lie. The thyroxine level is also higher when the salmon moves further upstream. Thus salmon that have just arrived in the river from the sea are more likely to take the fly than fish that have been settled in a lie for several days. Fish that have been forced to change lies, perhaps because of a spate, are more likely to take the fly before they have settled down in their new lies. Note that, in the old days, anglers used to arouse lethargic salmon by throwing boulders into a river or getting the dog to swim across the lies. Also, most upstream movement by salmon takes place around dusk and dawn, and it seems that thyroxine levels are raised at these changes of the light. Thus dawn and (especially) dusk are excellent times to catch salmon. Salmon, especially cock salmon, are also more likely to take a fly when they are close to spawning, for then the level of the masculine hormone testosterone as well as thyroxine is raised, making the fish very aggressive.

Thyroxine level is also higher in fish that have been injured (for example, scratched by a seal's claw or bitten by a sea lamprey). In the February 2003 issue of *Fly-Fishing & Fly-Tying* Malcolm Greenhalgh described one salmon from the Scottish Dee that took Mike Maughan's fly so violently that it ripped its gills and had to be killed. Its throat and stomach were packed with nymphs that the salmon had taken from the river-bed. Had it been feeding? The back of its stomach and in its intestines were crammed with parasitic tapeworms. That salmon was far from healthy. Its thyroxine level would have been high. It had grabbed nymphs crawling on the river-bed, and Mike's salmon fly. Yet there was no sign of any digestion of the nymphs it had taken. Had the salmon achieved some sort of palliative relief by cramming its stomach, already containing the parasitic tapeworms, with insects that it saw crawling on the river-bed? Perhaps.

So it is impossible to give a clear answer to the question of why salmon take, or refuse to take, our flies. From the fly-fishing point-of-view, for success the essential factors in a very complex equation are to fish when the fish are more likely to take the fly (see above) and to fish a fly of the correct size and perhaps colour (see below) in a way that the fish find irresistible. It is that easy!

HOOKS AND SIZES OF SALMON WET FLIES

In all fishing, the hook links fish and angler, and may make the difference between success and failure. This is more so in salmon fly-fishing than any other form of angling. First of all, hooks:

- **Single salmon hooks.** These can be usually be obtained in two weights, standard (thicker wire) and low water (thinner wire). Some have a long shank, and they should be shunned for, as Col. Esmond Drury put it (in J. D. Bates Jr., *Atlantic Salmon Flies and Fishing*, 1970), 'I regard flies tied on long-shanked flat singles (so popular in the United States) as the most inefficient hooking instruments of the lot. They look nice but are poor hookers and, because of leverage from the long shank, bad holders.'
- **Double salmon hooks.** Their advantage is that they are more likely to swim on an even keel and the two hooks enhance hooking and holding of the fish.
- **Treble salmon hooks.** They hook and hold salmon far better than single hooks.
- **Waddington mounts.** Invented by the great salmon angler Richard Waddington, the mount is a doubled length of wire. A treble hook is clipped in place at one end of the mount and at the other there is an eye for tying the fly to the leader. The mounts, that can be made easily from paperclips, come in a wide range of lengths, allowing a range of fly sizes to be tied.
- **Tubes.** These come in a range of lengths, and in plastic (lightest weight), aluminium (medium weight) and copper and brass (heavyweights). The leader is slipped through the tube, a treble hook is knotted to the end of the leader and the hook is kept in place by a short length of plastic tube.

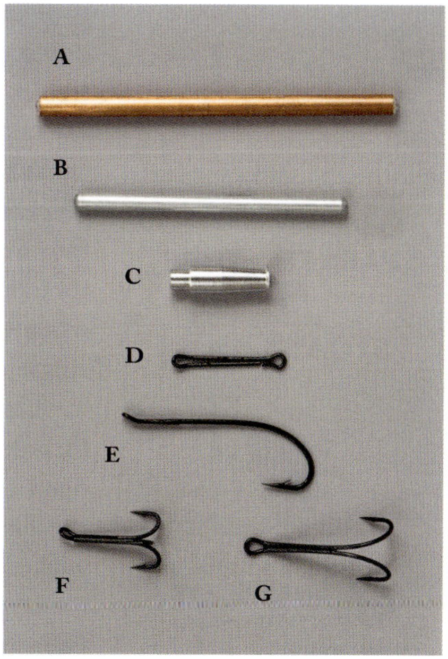

Hooks and mounts: (A) brass tube; (B) aluminium tube; (C) barrel tube; (D) Waddington shank; (E) low-water single; (F) treble fly; (G) low-water double.

In many parts of the world, rules prohibit the use of any but single hooks, and both Waddington shanks and tubes are fished with a single hook instead of a treble. The reason for this is that it is much easier to return a salmon alive to the water from a barbless single hook rather than a double or a treble, and in places with hook restrictions, catch-and-release is also often the rule. In his otherwise excellent *Steelhead Fly Tying Guide* (1994), H. Kent Helvie notes that, 'if you don't have an ethical problem with them, low water double hooks swim these flies well ... '. The use of double and treble hooks has nothing to do with ethics, for it is as ethical

are more likely to be attracted by lots of orange or red in the fly. In very clear water, light-coloured flies with blue in the dressing seem particularly effective, whereas in peat-stained rivers, or rivers that are coloured after heavy rain, orange attracts salmon. One interesting colour when it comes to salmon flies is green for, whilst it seems to be unattractive to salmon in most salmon rivers, in a few (some Norwegian and Canadian rivers) sometimes, but not always, it is an important component of the fly.

Recent years have seen the introduction of colour hot-spots and flash into salmon flies. There has, of course, always been some hot-spots and flash: for example, tinsel bodies and ribs, jungle cock eyes, the bright and almost iridescent crest feather of golden pheasant, the iridescent feather of the blue chatterer and of the Indian crow. Now, however, we have synthetic flashy materials such as Flashabou and Crystal (or Krystal) Hair (or Flash). And we have bright fluorescent flosses and wools. They are meant to catch the eye of the salmon. However they should be used in moderation. Between two and four strands of Crystal Hair in the tail or wing of the fly, and a short tip to the body of fluorescent red or orange floss is usually enough. If a fly pattern does not include such colour hot-spot or flash, include it if you want to. For this may give you more confidence in the fly …

CONFIDENCE IN THE FLY

When fishing an imitative fly for trout or bonefish or pike we have confidence in the fly because it matches what the fish are eating. It is not the same with salmon that (in the main) are not interested in food. After a fruitless hour of casting, the question arises in the little grey cells of: 'Am I using the right fly?' And then: 'Am I fishing the right size of fly?'

If you begin to doubt your choice of fly or if you lack confidence in the fly you are fishing, you will fish badly.

All the flies in this section have caught lots of fish, and notes with each fly or group of flies will help in making a correct choice. When you have made a choice of pattern, stick with it as you fish a pool through. However, instead of changing pattern, you would perhaps be better changing size of fly. Experience suggests, for Atlantic salmon at least, trying one a size smaller (for example, a size 6 instead of a size 4 hook). For sea trout and steelhead, going one size bigger will often improve catch rate. Or, as Hugh Falkus and Malcolm Greenhalgh pointed out in their *The Salmon and Sea Trout Fisher's Handbook*, if you double the size of your fly when fishing for sea trout and you will double your bag, and if you reduce the size of you fly when fishing for salmon and you will double your bag. For most anglers fish a too large fly for salmon, and too small a size when fishing for sea trout.

SALMON FLIES

Note that in many salmon flies, the pattern stipulates cock or rooster hackle. Today, when we think of such hackles we think of feathers from birds specially bred for tying dry flies. Their fibres are too stiff. Instead use a softer-fibred, or henny-cock, hackle from a non-genetic cape (Indian capes are excellent and inexpensive). Note also that these earlier flies would have been tied on blind hooks with gut eyes (as are the classic flies on pp. 298–304). Here they have been tied, as modern fishing flies, on eyed hooks.

EARLY SALMON FLIES

Some very old flies will still catch salmon in the twenty-first century. The first of these was described by an anonymous writer in *The North Country Angler* (1786). It has no name.

Thread: Black (?).
Tail: 5–6 strands peacock herl.
Body: Peacock herl.
Hackle: Black cock.
Wing: Bronze mallard or dark turkey tail.
Head: Yellow and brown pig's wool, well mixed.

In those days the wing was tied in first, forward over the eye, and brought back and tied in place when the head was formed. Pig's wool, shaved from the cottager's porker in autumn, was a popular material in early salmon flies.

Alexander MacIntosh published a second simple pattern in his book *The Driffield Angler* (1808).

Black Dog
Thread: Black (?).
Body: Lead-coloured pig's wool (later published as blue dun or grey seal's fur).
Rib: Gold tinsel (oval or flat?).
Hackle: Black cock.
Wing: Dark heron quill, plus a few fibres of turkey tail.
Head: Dark green mohair.

In *Trout and Salmon Fishing in Wales* (1834), George Hansard wrote that salmon fly patterns should be 'very sober in colour, and few in number'. His two flies would certainly catch salmon today … if they were tied and tried … and if we had some bittern feathers.

Spring Fly
Thread: Orange or black (?).
Body: Orange silk.
Rib: Oval gold tinsel.
Hackle: Grey (blue dun) cock.
Wing: Dark mottled bittern.

Summer Fly
Thread: Yellow or black (?).
Body: Yellow silk.
Rib: Oval gold tinsel.
Hackle: Deep blood-red cock.
Wing: Brown turkey with a few strands of green peacock herl (from the sword feather).

William Scrope wrote one of the greatest early books on salmon fishing in 1843, entitled *Days and Nights of Salmon Fishing in the Tweed*. He gave six dressings and was the first to recommend that the size of the fly should be changed as the speed and depth of the water changed. These flies would catch salmon today, though we would again have to find a substitute for the now rare and protected bittern.

Kinmount Willie
Thread: Black (?).
Tag: Red wool.
Tail: Yellow wool.

Body: Hare's ear.
Hackle: Black cock.
Wing: Teal flank.
Head: Crimson wool.

The Lady of Mertoun

Thread: Black (?).
Tag: Crimson wool.
Tail: Yellow wool.
Body: Water-rat fur.
Hackle: Red cock (natural, not dyed).
Wing: Teal flank.
Head: Crimson wool.

Mertoun is a beat on the great River Tweed.

Toppy

Thread: Black (?).
Tag: Crimson wool.
Tail: Yellow wool.
Body: Black bullock hair.
Hackle: Black cock.
Wing: White-tipped bronze turkey.
Head: Crimson wool.

That the flies described by Scrope were used elsewhere other than the Tweed is born out by this being the dressing for John Younger's Second Fly (in *River Angling*, 1840) and John Kirkbride calling this fly Topper (in *The Northern Angler*, 1837). See below!

Michael Scott

Thread: Black (?).
Tag: Hare's ear then crimson wool, with a short red gamecock hackle.
Tail: Yellow wool.
Body: Black wool.
Rib: Oval gold tinsel.
Hackle: Black cock.
Wing: Bronze mallard.
Head: Yellow wool with a little dubbed hare's ear.

Meg With a Muckle Mouth

Thread: Black (?).
Tag: Crimson wool, plus a red cock hackle.
Tail: Yellow or orange wool.
Body: Yellow floss silk.
Hackle: Dark natural red cock.
Wing: Brown turkey.
Head: Crimson wool.

Muckle, or mickle, is old Scottish for great or big. But who was Meg?

Meg in her Brawes

Thread: Black (?).
Tag: Green wool then crimson wool.
Tail: Yellow wool.
Body: Brown wool mixed with bullock hair.
Rib: Oval gold tinsel.
Hackle: Furnace cock.
Wing: Light brown bittern.
Head: Yellow wool.

'Brawe' is an old Scottish term for bravery. But again, who was Meg?

Scrope was not from the Tweed valley. He was a Lincolnshire squire who visited the Tweed valley to catch salmon and to shoot game. And while he has been praised by historians of the salmon fly for *his* six simple flies and their wild Scottish-sounding names, all is not as it seems. When Scrope was visiting Tweedsdale, the local expert and fly-dresser was one John Younger. And when Younger read Scropes's book he complained, in a letter published by Arthur Ransome (in *Mainly About Fishing*):

> His six flies are mine, of course, to a shade, they could indeed be properly no others, only that he has described them in other words, with perhaps more quaint punctuality in tufts and toppings, and under fanciful local names of designations, such as 'Meg in her braws', 'Kinmount Wille', 'The Lady of Mertoun' and so on.

Younger then goes on to explain that Scrope got the dressings wrong! The flies described by Scrope should have had bodies of soft wool. When bullock hair was used for bodies, the flies had no wound hackles. Instead, hairs were teased from the bullock hair body to create a sort of false hackle (as in the HARE'S EAR NYMPH, p. 61).

So, it seems, Scrope stole his flies from John Younger, and in the stealing he got them wrong!

A. H. Chaytor's *Letters to a Salmon Fisher's Sons* (1910) is one of the of the greatest 'reads' in salmon fishing literature. Chaytor recommended only three very simple flies for salmon fishing. Again, these would catch salmon today (and sea trout and steelhead), especially if a wing of brown squirrel or bucktail was used instead of the feather slip wing.

WHITE AND SILVER
Thread: Black (?).
Body: Oval silver tinsel.
Hackle: White cock, 2 turns.
Wings: Dark turkey.
Cheeks: Jungle cock.

CLARET
Thread: Black (?).
Body: Rough claret wool or seal's fur.
Rib: Broad oval silver tinsel.
Hackle: Claret cock.
Wings: Bronze mallard or brown turkey.

GIPPS
Thread: Black (?).
Body:
  Rear ½: Orange-brown seal's fur.
  Front ½: Black seal's fur.
Rib: Narrow oval silver tinsel.
Hackle: Black cock.
Wings: Brown turkey.

CLASSIC SALMON FLIES

When Chaytor's book was published, few salmon fishers anywhere in the world would then have fished such simple flies. During the latter half of the nineteenth century Britain had a vast empire on which 'the sun never set'. This coincided with the publication of Charles Darwin's theory of evolution and the collecting, from every corner of the Globe, of rare and unusual plants and animals. Not only were scientists fascinated by these collections, Victorian ladies embellished their hats with the feathers of flamingo, cock-of-the-rock, Indian crow, blue chatterer, birds of paradise, florican bustard, toucan and macaw. Chaytor's only brush with such exotic feathers was the incorporation of jungle cock eyes (brought from India) into one of his flies. But for other, professional, fly-dressers the advent of these bright and beautiful plumages was an opportunity to extract large amounts of cash from wealthy salmon anglers.

It all started in Ireland, where ships carrying cargoes back to Britain stopped off to top up their supply of drinking water having completed their voyage across the Atlantic from the West Indies or southern United States. Ballyshannon was then a small port at the mouth of the Erne, one of the greatest salmon rivers and visited by many wealthy anglers, and ruined in the 1950s by a hydroelectric dam. There Pat McKay founded a fly-dressing business in 1810, James Rogan in 1830 (which continued to produce flies up to the death of the last Rogan, Rita, in April 1989). They, and many others like them, began to produce flies based on these gaudy feathers. The tying of such ornate flies then spread to Britain, and from Britain to Scandinavia and North America. This was encouraged by wealthy salmon anglers who were influential writers, none more so than Francis Francis. Born Francis Morgan, he inherited his uncle's vast wealth by taking his uncle's surname, Francis, and he spent the rest of his life angling and promoting the exotic salmon fly. In his book *A Book on Angling* (1867, and several later editions) he wrote disparagingly of people like Scrope and Chaytor:

> There are many persons who hold that half a dozen flies are enough to kill salmon on any river … and who despise the notion of such an extended list of [gaudy] flies. To such irreverent scoffers and heretical unbelievers I have nothing to say. Let them indulge in their repertoire of a bit of old Turkey carpet and a live barn-door rooster.

Quickly the vast number of gaudy flies reached the United States, so that when Mary Orvis Marbury produced her book *Favorite Flies & their*

Histories in 1892 she could write that the brightly coloured fly Childers, that has red and blue macaw, Amherst pheasant, bustard and blue chatterer in its dressing, 'is well known to American fishermen'. And of the Jock Scott (that included 28 different materials in its dressing, including Indian crow, toucan, florican bustard, jungle cock, blue chatterer, and blue and yellow macaw) and Silver Doctor (that includes blue chatterer, bustard, and blue and yellow macaw) she wrote: 'these two flies [are] without doubt the prime favorites with salmon anglers the world over'.

The number of these gaudy salmon flies grew tremendously, and every moneyed angler worth his salt would have purchased the new patterns as they were produced, in several sizes, so that, with the cost at several times the cost of the old simple flies (up to ten shillings and six pence per fly early in the twentieth century, which is equal to 52½ pence or over US$1 in today's money) the fly-dressers did quite well out of the deal. An indication of the number of these flies can be gained from a review of the literature: Captain J. H. Hale (*How to Tie Salmon-Flies*, 1892) gave only 40 patterns; George M. Kelson (*The Salmon Fly*, 1895) gave 240 patterns; J. J. Hardy (*Salmon Fishing*, 1907) gave 402 patterns – and by 1919 another 18 were added; T. E. Pryce-Tannatt (*How to Dress Salmon-Flies*, 1914) gave 103 patterns.

This was by no means all. In *The Complete Salmon Fisher: Salmon on the Fly* (1996) Malcolm Greenhalgh noted that, 'Less famous writers contributed their patterns in minor books and magazines, and others never saw print! I have located the names of 47 salmon fly patterns from this era in fishing records from Norway, Canada, Scotland and northern England that I have been unable to trace in the literature, and I have examined flies dressed from this era that do not match any published pattern. Such was the explosion of salmon fly patterns in the nineteenth and early twentieth centuries.'

By the 1950s fly-fishers were beginning to see through the 'con-trick' of the complex gaudy salmon fly. Col. Esmond Drury, one of the leading post-Second World War salmon anglers put it this way in the *Journal of the Flyfishers' Club* (1960):

> The remarkable fact is that these Victorian relics have survived so long. The more particularly is this the case when one considers that they were, in the main, the product of ignorance and lack of scientific knowledge ... In his ignorance Kelson [one of the main inventors of such flies: see above] became a slave to ornate extravagance ... That he failed to include aspidistras and antimacassars in his fly-dressing was an oversight, although he nearly achieved the crinoline.

Instead salmon fly-fishers began once more to turn to simpler flies, using simpler materials. And the salmon seemed not to mind! A few anglers do still tie and fish these fancy flies (though CITES regulations prohibit the collection, transport and sale of the essential gaudy materials), but mostly these 'classic salmon flies' are popularly tied to illustrate the fly-dressers' art. For that they are ideal, as the perfect tying of just one fly will involve several tricky techniques and may take several hours. It has been said that the late Al Coen could spend up to ten hours in tying one fly, whilst Paul Little (who dressed the classic flies below) regularly spends three hours and more per fly.

CLASSIC SALMON FLIES

Because these are no longer fishing-flies, only a representative sample is included, dressed for this book by Paul Little. Admire their beautiful complexity and the skill in dressing them so perfectly. Note that Paul has used the precise materials as given in the dressing, including feathers from ancient collections where CITES species were used. Note also that the hooks used are from late nineteenth and early twentieth centuries and are 'blind', or eyeless. The eye was tied in at the start of dressing the fly, using catgut (made from sheep's, and *not* cat's intestines).

Green King

Body: Green Berlin wool.
Ribs: Flat silver and flat gold tinsel.
Body hackle: Red Spey cock.
Throat hackle: Teal.
Wings: Mallard slips.

This was a style of dressing known as the 'Spey style', named after the river of that name. The Green King was published by A. E. Knox in *Autumns on the Spey* (1872).

Tri-Colour

Tag: Oval silver tinsel.
Tail: Tip of red breast feather of golden pheasant.
Body: In three equal sections, of yellow, light blue and scarlet seal's fur.
Rib: Silver lace and flat silver tinsel.
Body hackle: Grey heron.
Throat hackle: Pintail.
Wings: Plain cinnamon turkey.

This is a Dee strip wing fly, taking its name from the famous Scottish salmon river. The long, flowing heron hackle is characteristic. This is a fly by G. M. Kelson.

Grub

Tip: Oval silver tinsel.
Tag: Red floss.
Tail: Yellow macaw and scarlet ibis.
Rear hackle (butt): Badger or silver coch-y-bonddu dyed yellow, and cheeked with jungle cock.
Body: Rear ½: Yellow seal's fur.
Rib: Oval silver tinsel.
Middle hackle: Badger or silver coch-y-bonddu dyed yellow, and cheeked with jungle cock.

Body: Front ½: Yellow seal's fur.
Rib: Oval silver tinsel.
Front hackles: Badger or silver coch-y-bonddu dyed yellow, and cheeked with jungle cock, with a guinea fowl hackle dyed hot orange in front.

These old grub flies were early forms of Shrimp-flies (see p. 322). This is another Kelson pattern.

Mar Lodge

Tag: Flat silver tinsel.
Tail: Golden pheasant topping, veiled with jungle cock.
Butt: Black ostrich herl.
Body: Flat silver tinsel with a band of black floss in the middle third.
Throat hackle: Guinea fowl.
Under wing: Golden pheasant tippets.
Main wing: Cinnamon turkey, florican bustard, grey mottled turkey, white swan, bustard, turkey tail and golden pheasant.
Cheeks: Large slip of summer duck and jungle cock.
Horns: Blue macaw.
Topping: Golden pheasant topping.

Many of the greatest classic salmon flies had 'married wings', where fibres from several different feathers were brought together and 'married' into a single wing. The effect is quite stunning. Mar Lodge comes from *How to Dress Salmon-Flies* by T. E. Pryce-Tannatt (1914).

Little Kelly

Tag: Gold twist.
Tail: Topping veiled with scarlet ibis.
Body: Dirty yellow seal's fur.
Rib: Oval gold tinsel.

Throat hackle: Coch-y-bonddu.
Wings: Peacock herl.
Horns: Blue and yellow macaw.

A 'simple' classic fly of the herl-winged style, but one that is difficult to tie perfectly. Another Kelson pattern.

The Badger
Tag: Flat silver tinsel.
Tail: Golden pheasant crest veiled with tippets.
Body: Red seal's fur.
Rib: Oval silver tinsel.
Hackle: Badger.
Wings: Grey mottled turkey.

This simple strip-wing fly is from J. H. Hale's *How to Tie Salmon-Flies* (1892). There is no doubt that this would catch salmon today; try it also with orange and yellow bodies.

Variegated Sun Fly
Tag: Oval silver tinsel and light blue floss.
Tail: Topping and cock-of-the-rock.
Body: Yellow, black and orange wool wound together.

Hackle: Black.
Wings: Six or more golden pheasant toppings.

This fabulous topping-winged pattern is by Pryce-Tannatt.

HAIR-WINGED SALMON FLIES

A sparsely dressed (top) and a more heavily dressed (above) hair-winged Black Bear.

Hair-winged flies are amongst the most popular and effective flies for all migratory salmonids, for hair is usually highly mobile in water and simulates flickering life. Amateur tyers tend to put too much hair in the wing; a good motto is – 'A little less is better than a little too much!' It is worth tying some of a particular pattern 'sparse' and some 'normal'. This is illustrated below. Fish the sparser tying in shallower, slower or very clear water, the normal in deeper, more turbulent or murkier water.

Bodies of salmon flies are normally tied to the very end of the hook shank, but it is worth tying some 'short' as in the Black Bear below. This is useful in times of low clear water, for then a small (= short) fly can be tied on a larger hook. This will help the fly sink and may result in a better hook hold.

It is always worth considering whether or not to add a little bright colour or flash to salmon flies. A tag or butt of fluorescent red, orange or yellow floss, and perhaps a very few strands of Crystal Hair, Flashabou or similar. But beware of 'over-egging the pudding', for too much of these might deter salmon from taking.

A Black Bear tied 'short' (in this case a size 8 dressing on a size 6 hook).

THE 'RAT' SERIES

Today we have some 'series' of salmon flies, such as Black Bear and Stoat's Tails. These series comprise several flies, all based on one type of wing material, that vary according to their body colour, hackle colour etc. One of the first such series are the Rats, the first four of which were devised by

Roy Angus Thomson (R. A. T.) in 1911. They are winged with the guard hairs of the grey fox, and have a hackle of grizzle cock wound in front of the wing. If grey fox is not available, a mix of black and white hairs will suffice, or even a well marked grey squirrel tail, for salmon are not experts in mammalology. Their heads are all of red thread, varnished with red tying cement.

The flies illustrated here were tied by Paul Little, using grey fox as wing.

Grey Rat (a)

Tag: Flat gold tinsel (use oval gold tinsel on double hooks).
Tail: Small golden pheasant crest feather.
Body: Dubbed under-fur of grey fox.
Rib: Flat gold tinsel.
Wing: Small bunch of grey fox guard-hairs.
Hackle: Grizzle, wound in front of wing.
Cheeks: Jungle cock, short (optional).
Head: Red.

A

Silver Rat (b)

With a body of flat silver tinsel, ribbed oval gold tinsel.

Gold Rat (c)

With a silver tag, tail of golden pheasant crest dyed red, and a body of flat gold tinsel ribbed oval silver tinsel.

Copper Rat (d)

With a copper tag, 2–3 peacock sword herls as tail, and body of flat copper tinsel ribbed oval copper tinsel.

B

C

BLACK RAT (E)
With a tag of flat silver tinsel, and a black seal's fur body ribbed with flat silver tinsel.

THE RAT (F)
With a silver tinsel tag, and body of peacock herl ribbed oval silver tinsel.

These were the first of the Rats, devised by R. A. T. together with his associates Herbert L. Howard (who gave R. A. T. his first grey fox fur), Colonel Ambrose Monell and Dr Orrin Summers, for fishing the rivers of New Brunswick and later Quebec. They are still great catchers of salmon, *in any salmon river*! Use the GREY RAT, BLACK RAT and THE RAT in most conditions. However in very clear water in bright light the SILVER RAT has the edge, the GOLD RAT in slightly coloured water, and the COPPER RAT in peaty water.

Later, other Rats were devised, based on the same wing, hackle and head.

RUSTY RAT (G)

Tag: Oval gold tinsel.
Tail: 3–4 peacock sword herls.
Body:
Rear ½: Bright yellow floss, with a strand of floss extending back over this part of the body..
Front ½: Peacock herl.
Rib: Oval silver tinsel.
Hackle: Grizzle, wound in front of wing.
Wing: Grey fox.
Cheeks: Jungle cock (optional).

The Blue Rat (h), devised by Poul Jorgensen for fishing the crystal clear Icelandic rivers, is tied like the Rusty Rat, but with blue floss instead of yellow floss as rear half of body and veil, and with the cheeks of blue kingfisher and jungle cock.

H

Red Rat (i)

Tag: Flat silver tinsel (use oval gold tinsel on double hooks).
Tail: 2 slips of wood duck.
Body: Dubbed red seal's fur.
Rib: Flat gold tinsel.
Wing: Small bunch of grey fox guard-hairs.
Hackle: Grizzle, wound in front of wing.
Cheeks: Jungle cock, short (optional).
Head: Red.

Brown Rat (j)

As Red Rat, but with a fiery brown seal's fur body. With the Red Rat, flies for rivers with some colour: a peat tinge, or silt content after heavy rain or sudden snow-melt.

I

J

BLACK HAIR-WINGS

Black hair-wings are the most popular and, although in two cases, they are named from the 'official' species from which the hair should be taken, almost any black hair will do. Thus, whilst in North America the Black Bear series should be tied with black bear hair, and in Europe the Stoat's Tail series should be tied with hairs from the black tip of a stoat's tail, black squirrel may be used as a substitute for either!

Red Butt Black Bear

Thread: Black.
Tag: Fine oval silver tinsel.

Butt: Fluorescent red floss.
Body: Black floss or wool.
Rib: Medium oval silver tinsel.
Hackle: Black cock (usually tied false as a beard).
Wing: Black bear (or substitute, in this case polar bear dyed black).

The Orange Butt Black Bear has a fluorescent orange floss butt, and the Green Butt Black Bear has a fluorescent green floss butt. Give the Black Bear a tail of black hackle fibres and it becomes the Black Conrad (do the salmon notice?). What they are more likely to notice is a difference in hackle colour. A fly with a yellow hackle seems to be more attractive to fresh-run salmon, whereas one with an orange hackle seem to have the edge in coloured water.

In the late 1980s Bill Taylor devised his Glitter Bear. This is tied as the Bear series, but has a body of peacock herl and a green Crystal Hair underwing. The example illustrated has an arctic fox wing.

Warren Duncan produced a pattern of Black Bear that has the tag as an interesting hot-spot. He called this the Undertaker.

Undertaker
Thread: Black.
Tag: Fine oval gold tinsel, then fluorescent green and red floss.
Body: Peacock herl.
Rib: Oval gold tinsel.
Hackle: Bunch black hackle fibres, tied false.
Wing: Black bear.
Cheeks: Jungle cock.

Besides Atlantic salmon, the Bear series are excellent steelhead and Pacific salmon flies. A range of tyings and sizes of either this or the next should be in every salmon fishers' fly-box.

Black Stoat's Tail
Thread: Black.
Tag: Fine oval silver tinsel or, in sizes smaller than #10, wire (optional).
Tail: Golden pheasant crest feather.
Butt: Fluorescent red, yellow or orange floss (optional).
Body: Black floss.

Rib: Oval silver tinsel.
Hackle: Black cock.
Wing: Stoat's tail or substitute (see Note; the example illustrated has a natural black squirrel wing).
NOTE: The black hairs at the tip of a stoat's tail are little more than ½-inch long and so cannot be used to wing a fly much bigger than a No. 12. Most Stoat's Tails are therefore tied with a wing of black squirrel, calf, skunk, bucktail or bear!

When tied with a hot orange hackle, this becomes the THUNDER STOAT, and is excellent in coloured water (the example illustrated has a dyed black squirrel wing).

The SILVER STOAT'S TAIL is identical, save for its body of flat silver tinsel (the illustrated example has a wing of dyed arctic fox with four strands of Crystal Hair). Dressed on 2–3 in tubes and Waddington shanks, this is a popular harling fly on the Namsen River. It is also an excellent sea trout/steelhead fly.

Far left: SILVER STOAT'S TAIL dressed on a heavy 1 in tube with added conehead, for harling or fly-fishing in deeper, turbulent rivers. *Left:* SILVER STOAT'S TAIL dressed on a size 6 single hook, for shallow, clear salmon and sea trout rivers.

BLUE STOAT'S TAIL
Thread: Black.
Body: Blue flat or embossed Mylar.
Hackle: Blue.
Wing: Black bear or squirrel tail, plus 4 strands blue Crystal Hair.

This is a fly for crystal clear water as, for example, in some Icelandic and Scottish rivers.

The following simple variation is excellent for night fishing for sea trout and daytime fishing for salmon.

Crimson-Hackled Stoat's Tail

Hook: Low water single or double, sizes 2–10.
Thread: Black.
Body: Black floss or wool.
Rib: Oval silver tinsel.
Hackle: Crimson cock, wound in front of the wing.
Wing: Black squirrel or bear, plus a few strands of pearl Flashabou or Crystal Hair.

When tied with a black seal's fur body and with jungle cock cheeks at either side of the wing, the Black Stoat's Tail becomes the Black Coltrin. The Icelandic Black Sheep is another variation on the theme of black hair-winged flies, the combination of blue hackle and red head seeming very attractive to salmon in that island's crystal clear rivers.

Black Sheep

Hook: Low water single, double or treble (the latter mostly used in Iceland), sizes 2–10.
Thread: Red.
Tag: Fine oval silver tinsel.
Body: Fine black wool.
Rib: None.
Hackle: Kingfisher blue, tied false.
Wing: Black hairs over yellow hairs, fairly sparse.
Cheeks: Jungle cock.

Note on using very small salmon flies: In low water conditions, in high summer when the water is very warm, it may be essential to use very small flies. These two flies are examples:

Silver Stoat's Tail
Hook: size 16 treble

Thunder Stoat
Hook: size 14 double

Both these flies have caught salmon, the Silver Stoat's Tail one of 4½ lbs in the River Spey, the Thunder Stoat one of 7 lbs in the Scottish Dee. When fishing such tiny flies, use a strong leader and tie the fly to it with a loop-knot so that the fly can move freely in the water.

Black Dose

Hook: Single, double or treble salmon, sizes 2–12.
Thread: Black.
Tag: Oval silver tinsel and fluorescent orange floss.
Tail: Golden pheasant crest feather.
Body:
  Rear ¼: Fluorescent blue floss.
  Front ¾: Black wool.
Rib: Oval silver tinsel.
Hackle: Black cock, palmered in open turns along the front (wool) part of the body.
Wing: 2 strands of fluorescent orange and green floss, under black squirrel tail.

This is a simplification of an old 'classic' Canadian fly for Atlantic salmon. As the old gaudy classics fell from favour, attempts were made to produce simpler hairwinged varieties with the same names. Thus came the hairwing Jock Scott, Thunder and Lightning and so on.

Black Bomber

Hook: Low water single or double, sizes 2–10.
Thread: Black.
Tag: Oval silver tinsel.
Tail: Golden pheasant crest feather.
Tip: Fluorescent yellow floss.
Body: Black wool.
Rib: Oval silver tinsel.
Hackle: Black hackle fibres, tied false.
Wing: Black squirrel with a golden pheasant topping over.
Cheeks: Jungle cock.

Another black hair-wing, this time designed for the Margaree River of Nova Scotia by Joe Aucoin.

Spencer Pool Fly

Thread: Black.
Tail: Orange calf-tail.
Body: Black seal's fur (or substitute).
Rib: Oval gold tinsel.
Hackle: Sparse bunch orange and brown calf-tail.
Wing: Orange under dark brown fox or calf-tail.

Spencer Pool is on Norway's wonderful Gaula River and its fly was devised by Hans P. Odegard. The combination of dark brown and orange is very effective anywhere when there is a touch of colour in the river.

Collie Dog

Hook: ½–1 in aluminium tube.
Thread: Black or red.
Wing: Black goat, up to 9 in long.

The original Collie Dog was tied, by George Ross in the early 1970s, with hair from the long 'feathers' trailing from the hind legs of a black sheep-dog. This is a fly for 'dibbling', where the fly is dibbled to and fro across the surface over known lies that hold salmon (a long rod is ideally used, for its use helps keep the angler out of view of the fish). The simple wing of long black hair swings enticingly over the fish time after time after time until … Bang!

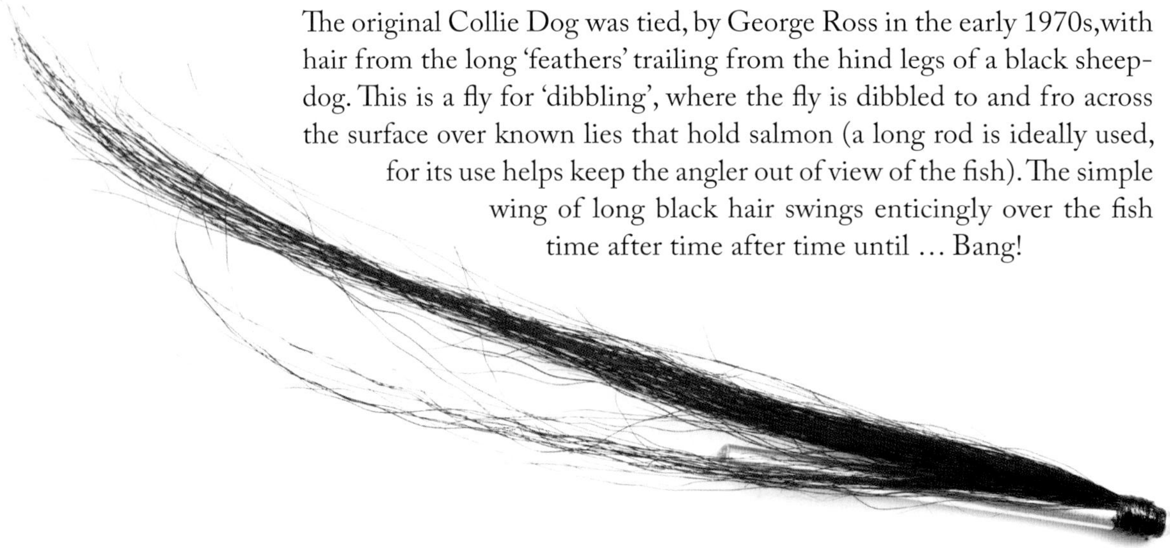

A completely different method of fishing the Collie Dog is as follows: fish the fly with a single-handed rod, a sinking fly-line and a fairly short leader. Cast across the flow and strip the fly back quickly. Salmon (and sea trout and steelhead) that have seen several more conventional flies being slowly drifted over their heads time after time sometimes respond violently to this quite different fly and presentation.

Black Silver Tip

Thread: Black.
Tag: Flat silver tinsel wound up rear third of shank.
Body: Black floss or wool.
Rib: Oval silver tinsel.
Wing: Dark moose (or black bucktail) tied long, low and sparse

First tied in the 1950s by Rocky Schulstad for Newfoundland salmon rivers, this will catch salmon anywhere.

Copper Smith

Hook: Low water single or double, sizes 2–10.
Thread: Black.
Tail: Bunch yellow calf-tail.
Body: Flat copper tinsel.
Rib: Fine gold wire or finest oval tinsel.
Hackle: Bunch yellow calf-tail.
Wing: Black calf-tail.

This is another salmon fly by Hans P. Odegard, who ties flies in the Norwegian copper-mining town of Røros. Hans acts as guide on the wonderful Gaula River in summer, and this fly catches many salmon there. It is excellent elsewhere in the salmon world.

Extra hotspots (e.g. a tag of fluorescent red floss) and a little flash (3–4 strands of Crystal Hair) may increase the effectiveness of this fly.

And Even More Hair-Wings, Some of Them Still Black

Skuli Kristinsen is Iceland's great salmon fly-dresser and in summer he guides on the Ranga River, one of the world's most prolific salmon rivers. For wing he uses the soft hair from Icelandic ponies. The two patterns below are outstanding in crystal clear rivers, as found in Iceland.

Hook: Low water double, sizes 8–12.
Thread: Black.
Tag: Fine oval silver tinsel.
Tail: Bunch blue hackle fibres.
Body: Flat silver tinsel.
Rib: Finest oval silver tinsel.
Hackle: Bunch blue hackle fibres, tied false.
Wing: Icelandic pony, dyed yellow.

Hook: Low water double, sizes 8–12.
Thread: Black.
Tag: Fine oval silver tinsel.
Tail: Bunch deep gentian blue hackle fibres.
Body: Flat silver tinsel.
Rib: Finest oval silver tinsel.
Hackle: Bunch deep gentian blue hackle fibres, tied false.
Wing: Black Icelandic pony.

Note: If Icelandic pony is not available, use arctic fox, and failing that, calf-tail.

Fox Fly

Hook: Preferably low water double (single, if rules insist), sizes 8–12.
Thread: Black.
Body: Silver or pearl flat tinsel.
Rib: Silver wire.
Hackle: Guinea fowl (gallina).
Wing: Golden pheasant breast feather, with black squirrel over, and with a topping of golden pheasant and pearl Crystal Hair (optional).

This is a Northern Ireland pattern specially designed for catching dollaghan as well as salmon. Dollaghan are trout that feed on whitefish in Lough Neagh, the largest lake in the British Isles. They grow large (to in excess of 20 lbs) and are caught, along with salmon, as they run their spawning streams in autumn. The Fox Fly was devised by Booby Bryans.

And from the simplest black and modern hair-wings, we go to a much older and more complex tying.

Night Hawk

Hook: Low water single or double, sizes 2–10.
Thread: Red.
Tag: Flat silver tinsel and yellow floss (today use fluorescent).
Tail: Golden pheasant crest feather.
Butt: Red wool.
Body: Flat silver tinsel.
Rib: Fine oval silver tinsel.
Hackle: Black hackle fibres, tied false.
Wing: Black squirrel tail.
Sides: Jungle cock, long.
Cheeks: Kingfisher.
Head: Red and black thread.

This was invented by a Mr Wright who later, in 1906, was shot dead after taking his assailant's wife out for dinner. J. D. Bates Jr. noted that: 'Fortunately these two events occurred in an order favourable to anglers.'

It is impossible to say which is 'the best' salmon fly, but the following is amongst the contenders.

Willie Gunn

Hook: Usually tied on tubes in a wide range of lengths and weights, but may also be tied on any hook.
Thread: Black.
Body: Black floss.
Rib: Oval silver tinsel.
Wing: Mix of yellow, orange and black hair.

Single size 8

4 in-long Waddington shank

Willie Gunn was head keeper on the magnificent Brora River in the Scottish Highlands. For spring fishing, or when the salmon are fresh in from the sea, or when the water is crystal clear, use far more yellow than orange (e.g. 40 per cent black, 50 per cent yellow, 10 per cent orange). For autumn fishing, or when the salmon have been in the river for two or three weeks, or the water is tinged brown with peat, use more orange (e.g. 40 per cent black, 50 per cent orange, 10 per cent yellow). For those who need a hot-spot and a bit of flash to give them confidence, give the body a fluorescent yellow floss tip and the wing a couple of strands of yellow Crystal Hair when yellow predominates in the dressing, and a tip of fluorescent orange floss and orange Crystal Hair when orange predominates. This fly will catch Atlantic salmon anywhere, as well as steelhead and Pacific salmon in the western rivers of North America.

Green Highlander

Thread: Black.
Hook: See below.
Tail: Yellow hackle fibres.
Tag: Yellow floss.
Body: Green floss.
Rib: Embossed narrow silver tinsel.

Wing: Mix of yellow, dark brown and green hairs (squirrel or bear), plus a few strands pearl Crystal Hair and/or Flashabou.

This is a more up-to-date version of a very important fly for rivers where green in the dressing attracts salmon. These are mainly North American and Scandinavian rivers. Tie this on a variety of hooks, the illustrated example being on an aluminium tube.

Comet

Thread: Black.
Hook: Tube (see below).
Tail or rear 'hackle': Yellow hair arranged around the rear of the tube.
Body: Rear ½: Deep ruby-red floss.
Centre 'hackle': Deep ruby-red hair.
Body: Front ½: Black floss.
Rib: Fine oval gold tinsel.
Front 'hackle' or wing: Black hair with a few strands red Crystal Hair.

This fly was devised for the big four Scottish salmon rivers (Dee, Spey, Tay and Tweed) when the water was high and cold in 'spring' (late January to March and October to the end of November). To get down to the fish, the Comet was invariably dressed on a metal tube.

Blue Charm

Hook: Low water single or double, sizes 2–12.
Thread: Black.
Tag: Fine oval silver tinsel and fluorescent yellow floss.
Tail: Golden pheasant crest feather.
Body: Black floss.
Rib: Oval silver tinsel.
Hackle: Blue hackle fibres, tied false.
Wing: Grey squirrel.

If tied with a brown squirrel wing the fly becomes the Hairy Mary. Both are hair-winged versions of old classic salmon flies and are still excellent catchers.

Crosfield

Hook: Low water single or double, sizes 2–12.
Thread: Black.
Tag: Fine oval silver tinsel.

Tail: Golden pheasant crest feather.
Body: Embossed silver tinsel.
Hackle: Blue, wound in front of the wing.
Wing: Originally mallard or teal, grey squirrel is far more mobile.

Feather-wing

Hair-wing

Designed by Ernest M. Crosfield, probably about 1920, for fishing clear Icelandic salmon rivers. To say that a salmon fly is improved by some modification is always fraught with danger, as one can not be certain that a salmon taking the improved version would not have taken the original unimproved one! But a Crosfield with a red head (using red tying thread) and a short red fluorescent tip to the body *has* caught many salmon in Iceland!

The SILVER BLUE is very similar, having a flat silver tinsel body, ribbed with fine oval silver tinsel. This is similar to the Medicine (p. 352) and is a great sea trout fly for night fishing as well as salmon fly in clear water.

The following two flies are Canadian in origin, but will travel. The second has caught salmon as far away from its native streams as Norway.

ORANGE BLOSSOM

Hook: Low water single or double, sizes 2–12.
Thread: Black.
Tag: Fine oval silver tinsel and orange floss.
Tail: Golden pheasant crest feather.
Body: Embossed silver tinsel.
Hackle: Bright orange, wound in front of the wing as a collar and tied back.
Wing: Light brown bucktail, sparse.

ROGER'S FANCY

Thread: Black.
Hook: Low water single or double, sizes 2–12.
Tag: Fine oval silver tinsel and fluorescent yellow floss.
Tail: Tips of four green herls from a peacock sword feather.
Body: Bright green seal's fur or wool.
Rib: Oval silver tinsel.

Hackle: Bunch bright yellow hackle fibres under a bunch of bright green hackle fibres, tied false.
Wing: Grey fox guard-hairs.
Cheeks: Jungle cock (optional).

Designed by the great Canadian fly-dresser Shirley Woods and named after Major-General Roger Rowley.

Green Butt Butterfly

Hook: Wet fly, sizes 6–10.
Thread: Black.
Tail: Red cock hackle fibres.
Butt: Fluorescent green wool.
Body: Bronze peacock herl.
Rib: Fine oval gold tinsel.
Hackle: Natural red (brown) wound in front of the wing.
Wing: White goat.

This is a fly designed for the Miramichi by Maurice Ingalls. Try it also with a fluorescent orange butt.

Yellow Dog

Hook: Low water single or double, sizes 2–12, or 1–2 in tubes.
Thread: Black.
Tag: Fine oval silver tinsel and fluorescent yellow floss (optional).
Tail: Golden pheasant crest feather.
Body: Black floss.
Rib: Oval silver tinsel.
Hackle: Blue cock or gallina dyed blue.
Wing: Yellow and red hair in ratio of 2:1.

This is an old pattern, having been designed in about 1860 by James Wright for the River Tweed. It is sometimes called Garry Dog and was once called the Minister's Dog. The reason for this is that the first tying used hairs from a golden labrador called Garry, who was owned by the village of Sprouston's minister! It is still an excellent fly for Atlantic and Pacific salmon and steelhead.

St Laurent

Hook: Low water single or double, sizes 2–12.
Thread: Black.
Body: Flat silver tinsel.
Rib: Fine oval silver tinsel.
Wing: Bright green and red calf-tail.
Cheek: Jungle cock.

By Roch St-Laurent of Quebec, this is a fly for bright sunny days when there is a bit of colour in the water.

Cosseboom

Hook: Low water single or double, sizes 2–12.
Thread: Red.
Tag: Embossed silver tinsel.
Tail: Short length pale olive floss.
Body: Pale olive floss.
Rib: Embossed silver tinsel.
Hackle: Lemon yellow cock, wound in front of the wings and tied back.
Wing: Red squirrel.
Head: Red.

An old pattern from about 1923 by John C. Cosseboom for the Miramichi River. There are over 30 variations but according to J. D. Bates Jr., this 'is by far the best one'.

The following two patterns have the green component that works well in some rivers (see note on p. 292) and incorporates the Muddler Minnow style. Though designed for catching Atlantic salmon, they are also great steelhead flies.

Green Muddler

Hook: Low water single, sizes 2–12.
Thread: Black or green.
Tail: Emerald-green hackle fibres.
Body: Flat gold tinsel.
Wing: 2 emerald-green hackles tied back and flaring.
Head: Green deer hair, spun and trimmed muddler fashion.

Green-Head Muddler
Hook: Low water single, sizes 2–12.
Thread: Black or green.
Tail: 3 golden pheasant crest feathers.
Body: Yellow Antron or similar synthetic sparkle fur.
Wing: Yellow marabou.
Head: Green deer hair, spun and trimmed muddler fashion.

Ray's Red
Thread: Red.
Tail: Hot orange floss cut square.
Body: Hot orange floss.
Rib: Medium embossed silver tinsel.
Wing: Grey squirrel dyed hot orange.

Many of the shrimp/prawn patterns (see pp. 322ff) are dominated by orange. This hot orange fly is excellent in very dark peat-stained water or in dirty water after heavy rain.

Hackles are an integral part of the majority of 'shrimp' flies (see below), but hackles may also be used to effect in other smaller salmon flies. The following are two examples.

Capercailiie and Purple
Thread: Black.
Tag: Fluorescent pink floss.
Body: Purple floss.
Rib: Fine oval silver tinsel.
Hackle: Cock capercaillie neck hackle, plus a couple of strands pink Crystal Hair.

Right: Capercaillie and Purple tied on a Waddington shank.
Far right: Capercaillie and Purple tied on an Esmond Drury treble fly hook.

The capercaillie is a grouse the size of a turkey that lives in the pine forests of northern Europe. It has lots of feathers that are potentially useful in fly-tying, but that have been ignored. This fly, by Malcolm Greenhalgh, has caught its inventor many salmon in Norway.

Silver Doctor (Hackled)

Hook: Waddington shank or Esmond Drury treble.
Thread: Red.
Tag: Fluorescent red floss.
Body: Flat silver tinsel.
Rib: Fine oval silver tinsel.
Hackles: Rear: blue henny-cock; front: barred teal flank; plus 2–3 strands smolt blue Crystal Hair.

Great for salmon in crystal clear rivers and for sea trout at night.

Salmon Shrimps and Prawns

Many salmon flies go under the banner of 'shrimp flies'. Their origins date to the time when gaudy flies were being invented and it has been suggested that the design of both Spey-flies and Dee-flies (p. 300–1) was based on marine shrimps. There is no direct evidence for this.

In the days when the gaudy salmon flies were being developed, several patterns were known as 'Grubs' (for examples, Spring Grub, Summer Grub, Tippet Grub, Wasp Grub and Wye Grub) though, to our eyes, they look nothing like grubs. The most famous of these was the Usk Grub. It takes its name from a major salmon river in South Wales. It is very similar to Kelson's Wye Bug, which was devised in the second half of the nineteenth century, and has three features that have been incorporated into many modern shrimp patterns:

- The use of a red golden pheasant breast feather as a tail hackle,
- The two-coloured body, and
- The use of jungle cock 'eyes' as wings.

Usk Grub

Hook: Low water single, double or treble, sizes 2–10.
Thread: Black.
Tag: Fine oval silver tinsel.
Rear hackle: Golden pheasant breast feather.

Body: Rear ½: Orange floss.
Rib: Fine oval silver tinsel.
Centre hackles: White and orange cock.
Body: Front ½: Black seal's fur.
Rib: Fine oval silver tinsel.
Wings: A pair of jungle cock eye feathers.
Front hackle: Furnace cock.
NOTE: Tie golden pheasant breast feathers in by the tip when using them as a hackle in shrimp patterns. The butt end of the stalk is very thick and adds ugly bulk to the fly.

By the 1930s the great salmon tyer Jimmy Younger was producing a very similar pattern that was marketed by Hardy Brothers. This was called a Shrimp.

Younger's Shrimp

Hook: Low water single, double or treble, sizes 2–8.
Thread: Black.
Tag: Fine oval gold tinsel.
Rear hackle: Golden pheasant breast feather.
Body: Rear ½: Yellow floss.
Rib: Fine oval gold tinsel.
Centre hackle: 3 turns golden pheasant breast feather with a fibre length ⅔ that of the rear hackle.
Body: Front ½: Black floss.
Rib: Fine oval gold tinsel.
Front hackle: As centre hackle.
Wings: A pair of jungle cock eye feathers.

Since then a huge number of shrimp flies have been designed. But why are they called 'Shrimps'?

In their oceanic feeding grounds salmon devour large numbers of shrimps and prawns. These flies imitate the shrimps and prawns that salmon ate whilst at sea. But do they? It is true that salmon can be caught on pink/orange boiled shrimps and prawns. They will also take shrimps that have been dyed purple. But the shrimps eaten by salmon out at sea are subtle translucent shades of grey, brown and olive. They are not a solid pink/orange or purple. At sea salmon also eat lots of fish, such as capelin and sand-eels, and squid. Surely, salmon flies closely imitating bait-fish and squid ought to catch salmon much better than, say, the hair-winged flies on pp. 304–20.

But they don't. It is likely that when a salmon grabs any shrimp fly the last thing that enters its tiny brain is that it is eating a real shrimp!

So what do salmon find so attractive in our shrimp flies? Visit a tackle shop in Ireland, where shrimp flies reign supreme, and look at their display of flies. It will glow orange, with some red and yellow. Alternatively, flick through the pages of Chris Mann and Robert Gillespie's *Shrimp and Spey Flies for Salmon* (2001). Almost every page will hit you with orange, red and yellow. And those are three colours that salmon see so clearly and find so attractive (see also p. 291).

Ireland is the true home of the shrimp fly with over 130 patterns, though England, Scotland, Iceland, Scandinavia and North America have developed their own patterns. Such flies are so effective that many salmon fly-fishers use nothing else other than their favourite shrimp and prawn patterns, and they catch a lot of fish. They are also excellent steelhead flies and have accounted for some very large sea trout.

IRISH SHRIMP FLIES

Note on hooks: Because Irish salmon rivers tend to be fairly shallow, especially on those lengths where fly-fishing is the norm, these are usually dressed on small hooks, sizes 10–12, occasionally 8 in cold or high water, 14 in summer droughts. Most fly-fishers prefer treble fly hooks (e.g. Esmond Drury), occasionally doubles. Of course, where double and trebles are not permitted these patterns must be fished on single hooks. In the big, cold and turbulent rivers of Norway and Canada, these patterns are effective tied on hooks up to size 1–2.

SHRIMPS WITH JUNGLE COCK WINGS (TIED AS A ROOF OVER THE BODY)

The late Pat Curry of Coleraine is considered the father of the modern Irish shrimp fly. His most famous, and still extremely effective, dressing is his Red Shrimp, which he first tied in the 1930s for fishing the River Bann.

Curry's Red Shrimp
Thread: Red.
Tag: Fine oval silver tinsel or flat silver tinsel.
Tail: A red breast feather from the golden pheasant, wound as a hackle.
Body: Rear ½: Red floss or wool.

Rib: Fine oval silver tinsel.
Veils over body: Crimson hackle tips or feathers from the white neck-ring of a cock pheasant dyed crimson.*
Middle hackle: Badger cock.
Body: Front ½: Black floss or wool.
Rib: Fine oval silver tinsel.
Veils over body: Crimson hackle tips or feathers from the white neck-ring of a cock pheasant dyed crimson.*
Front hackle: Long-fibred badger cock wound in front of wings.
Wings: A pair of jungle cock eye feathers tied over body.

* It was said that originally the veils were Indian crow (now a CITES species) but Mann and Gillespie found this never to have been the case. There are many colour variants of this fly, but the original is still the best.

Agivey Wye Bug

Thread: Black.
Tag: Fine oval silver tinsel.
Tail: A red breast feather from the golden pheasant, wound as a hackle.
Body: Rear ½: Orange seal's fur.
Rib: Fine oval silver tinsel.
Middle hackle: Hot orange.
Body: Front ½: Black seal's fur.
Rib: Fine oval silver tinsel.
Front hackle: Natural red or light brown cock, wound in front of wings.
Wings: A pair of jungle cock eye feathers tied over body.

This also is a very early Irish shrimp pattern based on the Wye and Usk Bugs, late-nineteenth/early-twentieth century patterns from South Wales. It was designed by E. C. Heaney.

Light Wilkinson Shrimp

Thread: Red.
Tag: Fine oval silver tinsel.
Tail: A red breast feather from the golden pheasant, wound as a hackle.
Body: Rear ½: Flat silver tinsel.
Rib: Fine oval silver tinsel.
Middle hackle: Magenta cock.
Body: Front ½: Flat silver tinsel.
Rib: Fine oval silver tinsel.

Front hackle: Blue cock tied in front of wings.
Wings: A pair of jungle cock eye feathers tied over body.

A third pattern with roots in the past, for it takes its name from the old salmon fly Silver Wilkinson.

Bann Special

Thread: Black.
Tag: Fine oval silver tinsel.
Tail: A red breast feather from the golden pheasant, wound as a hackle.
Body: Rear ½: Yellow floss or seal's fur.
Rib: Fine oval silver tinsel.
Middle hackle: Hot orange cock.
Body: Front ½: Black floss or seal's fur.
Rib: Fine oval silver tinsel.
Front hackle: Silver badger, wound in front of wings.
Wings: A pair of jungle cock eye feathers tied over body.

The River Bann is one of the most prolific grilse rivers in the world and this outstanding fly catches many of them.

NOTE: A grilse is a salmon that has spent only one winter (and only just over a full year) at sea feeding. They usually weight in the range 4–6 lbs, though many that return later in the autumn may attain weights in excess of 10 lbs. Catching ten or more grilse in a day on top Irish rivers is by no means exceptional.

Foxford Shrimp

Thread: Red.
Tag: Fine oval silver tinsel.
Tail: A red breast feather from the golden pheasant, wound as a hackle.
Body: Rear ½: Black seal's fur.
Rib: Fine oval silver tinsel.
Middle hackle: Badger cock.
Body: Front ½: Fiery-brown seal's fur.
Rib: Fine oval silver tinsel.
Front hackle: Natural red (brown) wound in front of wings.
Wings: A pair of jungle cock eye feathers tied over body.

Foxford is a village on the River Moy, one of the world's most prolific salmon rivers. Downstream of Foxford is the town of Ballina, and there one pool – the famous Ridge Pool – has yielded a thousand salmon to the fly in one year.

Yellow Shrimp

Thread: Black.
Tag: Fine oval silver tinsel.
Tail: A red breast feather from the golden pheasant, wound as a hackle.
Body: Rear ½: Yellow seal's fur.
Rib: Fine oval silver tinsel.
Middle hackle: Yellow cock.
Body: Front ½: Black seal's fur.
Rib: Fine oval silver tinsel.
Front hackle: Badger cock wound in front of the wings.
Wings: A pair of jungle cock eye feathers tied over body.

Salmon that have just run into the river from the sea appear to be more susceptible to flies with yellow in the dressing, whereas when they have been in the river for some time they appear more likely to fall for a fly with lots of orange in the dressing. Fish this then for fresh-run salmon. Stevie Munn also reports that it is an outstanding fly for catching dollaghan. These are trout that feed and grow large on pollan (a species of whitefish) that abound in the huge lake, Lough Neagh. They spawn in rivers flowing into the lough and, together with salmon, they are caught as they run into the rivers from the lough.

Orange and Gold Shrimp

Thread: Black.
Tag: Fine oval gold tinsel.
Tail: A red breast feather from the golden pheasant, wound as a hackle.
Body: Rear ½: Flat gold tinsel.
Rib: Fine oval gold tinsel.
Middle hackle: Orange cock.
Body: Front ½: Flat gold tinsel.
Rib: Fine oval gold tinsel.
Front hackle: Badger cock wound in front of the wings.
Wings: A pair of jungle cock eye feathers tied over body.

An outstanding fly in coloured water (peat-stained or with clay or silt washing through after a spate).

Black-Tailed Shrimp

Thread: Black.
Tag: Fine oval silver tinsel.
Tail: A red breast feather from the golden pheasant, wound as a hackle.
Body: Rear ½: Yellow floss or seal's fur.
Rib: Fine oval silver tinsel.
Middle hackle: Orange cock.
Body: Front ½: Black floss or seal's fur.
Rib: Fine oval silver tinsel.
Front hackle: Black cock wound in front of the wings.
Wings: A pair of jungle cock eye feathers tied over body.

SHRIMPS WITH JUNGLE COCK EYES

Thunder Shrimp

Thread: Black.
Tag: Fine oval gold tinsel.
Tail: A yellow breast feather from the golden pheasant, wound as a hackle.
Body: Rear ½: Black floss.
Rib: Fine oval gold tinsel.

Middle hackle: Orange cock.
Body: Front ½: Black seal's fur.
Rib: Fine oval gold tinsel.
Front hackle: Orange cock, with kingfisher blue hackle fibres tied false, as beard.
Eyes: Jungle cock.

This pattern is based on a very old classic salmon fly, the Thunder and Lightning, in which the dominant colours were black and orange. A good 'back-end' fly when the water is coloured.

Helmsdale Black Shrimp

Thread: Black.
Tag: Fine oval silver tinsel.
Tail: Black bucktail or squirrel.

Body: Rear ½: Flat silver tinsel.
Rib: Fine oval silver tinsel.
Middle hackle: Black cock.
Body: Front ½: Flat silver tinsel.
Rib: Fine oval silver tinsel.
Front hackle: Black cock.
Eyes: Jungle cock.

Black and silver has always been a useful combination in a salmon fly (e.g. SILVER STOAT'S TAIL, p. 309). Note that this is not an Irish pattern, but is based on the Irish style of tying Shrimp patterns. The Helmsdale is a first-class Scottish salmon river.

BLACK SHRIMP

Thread: Black.
Tag: Fine oval silver tinsel.
Tail: Long-fibres black cock hackle, wound as a rear hackle and tied back.
Body: Rear ½: Yellow floss.
Rib: Fine oval silver tinsel.
Middle hackle: Hot orange cock.
Body: Front ½: Black floss or seal's fur.
Rib: Fine oval silver tinsel.
Front hackle: Black cock.
Eyes: Jungle cock.

CLARET SHRIMP

Thread: Black.
Tag: Fine oval gold tinsel.
Tail: A red breast feather from the golden pheasant, wound as a hackle.
Body: Rear ½: Medium claret seal's fur.
Rib: Fine oval gold tinsel.
Middle hackle: Medium claret cock.
Body: Front ½: Dark claret seal's fur.
Rib: Fine oval gold tinsel.
Front hackles: Badger cock wound in front of a hot orange cock.
Eyes: Jungle cock.

By Robert McHaffie, this is rated as the best claret shrimp pattern.

Junction Shrimp

Thread: Red.
Tag: Fine oval gold tinsel.
Tail: Hot orange bucktail.
Body: Rear ½: Flat oval gold tinsel.
Rib: Fine oval gold tinsel.
Middle hackle: Orange bucktail.
Body: Front ½: Black floss.
Rib: Fine oval gold tinsel.
Front hackle: White bucktail.
Eyes: Jungle cock.

A Scottish shrimp fly that uses bucktail instead of bird feathers as hackles, but based on the Irish idea of tying shrimps. By Gavin Brown, this is named after the most famous salmon pool in the world, the Junction Pool on the River Tweed. Note that it is often dressed on tubes for rivers away from Ireland.

Kylie Shrimp

Thread: Red.
Tag: Fine oval gold tinsel.
Tail: Orange bucktail and a few strands of Crystal Hair.
Butt: Black floss.
Body: Rear ⅔: Flat copper tinsel (Mylar).
Rib: Fine gold wire.
Middle hackle: Hot orange cock.
Body: Front ⅓: Black floss.
Rib: Fine oval gold tinsel.
Front hackle: Hot orange cock with no more than 2 turns of blue cock in front.
Eyes: Jungle cock.

Irish in style, but again Scottish in origin, this pattern comes from the Kyle of Sutherland and was devised by Alan Donaldson. The rivers of the north of Scotland are mostly small and shallow, so they lend themselves to the Irish style.

Living Fire Shrimp

Thread: Red.
Tag: Flat silver Mylar tinsel.

Tail: Orange bucktail, plus a few strands orange Crystal Flash/Hair.
Body:
Rear ½: Flat silver Mylar tinsel.
Front ½: Mix fluorescent orange and crimson SLF (a synthetic seal's fur – equivalent to natural fur).

Rib: Fine oval silver tinsel.
Hackle: Hot orange wound in front of the wing.
Wing: 50:50 hot orange and crimson SLF hank (alternative, Antron or other synthetic hair), plus 5 strands orange Crystal Flash/Hair.
Eyes: Jungle cock.

Paddy Bonner devised this and the next fly in the 1990s, deliberately including synthetic materials and 'flash'.

Living Flame Red Shrimp

Thread: Red.
Tag: Flat gold Mylar tinsel.
Tail: Red bucktail, plus a few strands orange Crystal Flash/Hair.
Body:
Rear ½: Flat gold Mylar tinsel.
Front ½: 75:25 mix hot orange and crimson SLF.

Rib: Fine oval gold tinsel.
Hackle: Flame red wound in front of the wing.
Wing: 75:25 mix of hot orange and crimson SLF hank, plus 4–5 strands orange Crystal Flash/Hair.
Eyes: Jungle cock.

Both these flies are ideal for coloured water or autumn fishing.

IRISH SHRIMPS/SALMON FLIES LACKING JUNGLE COCK

Jungle cock is a CITES species and its export/import illegal. Jungle cocks are, however, specially bred for the fly-tying market, but they are expensive. There is no good substitute, for no one has been able to replicate the almost glowing orange-white enamel of the real jungle cock eye. So, for most fishing situations, leave out the jungle cock or dig deep into the pocket! The first three flies in this section, by Paddy Bonner, are such. They were invented for the Moy's Ridge Pool in the 1990s, but they do work on salmon (also steelhead) rivers throughout Europe and North America.

Orange And Gold Shadow Shrimp

Thread: Red.
Tail: Silver fox dyed deep orange, plus a few strands orange Crystal Flash/Hair.
Body: Rear ½: Flat gold Mylar tinsel.
Rib: Fine oval gold tinsel.
Veil: Golden pheasant tippet, with centre tip cut out and two remaining black tips varnished to suggest shrimp eyes (prepare several feathers in advance).
Middle hackle: Hot orange cock.
Body: Front ½: Flat gold Mylar tinsel.
Rib: Fine oval gold tinsel.
Front hackle: Silver badger dyed hot orange, wound in front of the wing.
Wing: Silver fox dyed hot orange.

Tail Fire Shadow Shrimp

Thread: Red.
Tail: Silver fox dyed yellow, plus a few strands yellow Crystal Flash/Hair.
Body: Rear ½: Flat gold Mylar tinsel.
Rib: Fine oval gold tinsel.
Veil: Golden pheasant tippet, with centre tip cut out and 2 remaining black tips varnished to suggest shrimp eyes.
Middle hackle: Hot orange cock.
Body: Front ½: Flat gold Mylar tinsel.
Rib: Fine oval gold tinsel.
Front hackle: Silver badger dyed hot yellow, wound in front of the wing.
Wing: Arctic fox dyed hot orange.

Cascade Shadow Shrimp

Thread: Black.
Tag: Flat silver Mylar tinsel.
Tail: Mix of black, orange and yellow squirrel tail, plus a few strands silver Crystal Flash/Hair.
Body: Rear ½: Flat silver Mylar tinsel.
Rib: Fine oval silver tinsel.
Veil: Golden pheasant tippet, with centre tip cut out and two remaining black tips varnished to suggest shrimp eyes.
Middle hackle: Silver badger dyed yellow.
Body: Front ½: Black seal's fur.

Rib: Fine oval silver tinsel.
Front hackle: Silver badger dyed hot yellow behind a similar hackle dyed hot orange, wound in front of the wing.
Wing: Black squirrel or arctic fox, plus four strands silver Crystal Flash/Hair.

Wee Davy

Thread: Red.
Body: Flat gold holographic tinsel.
Rib: Fine silver wire.
Hackle: Hot orange, wound in front of the wing.
Wing: Black squirrel.

A fly by Davy Telford for the dollaghan and salmon streams draining into Lough Neagh. A useful fly anywhere, and easy to tie.

Stevie's Shrimp

Thread: Red.
Tag: Fine oval silver tinsel or wire.
Tail: Hot orange hackle fibres, plus a few strands orange Crystal Flash/Hair.
Body: Rear ½: Pearl tinsel.
Rib: Fine oval silver tinsel or wire.
Middle hackle: Hot orange cock, long-fibred.
Body: Front ½: Red floss.
Rib: Fine oval silver tinsel or wire.
Front hackle: Kingfisher blue cock.

Stevie Munn is one of the world's leading fly-tyers. His Shrimp is a great all-round salmon fly that has caught salmon and steelhead in North America and salmon throughout Europe, as well as its native Northern Ireland.

THE WORLD OF SHRIMP FLIES

Many shrimp flies have been devised outside Ireland and they can now be seen, being fished throughout the salmon (and steelhead) world. The following is a selection of these.

Red Francis (or Frances)

Hook: Usually dressed on tubes or doubles or trebles, sizes 2–10.
Thread: Red.
Feelers: 3 white and 3 natural red stripped cock hackle stalks.
Head of shrimp/prawn: Warm brown fur (e.g. red fox).
Body: Red wool.
Rib: Oval gold tinsel.
Body hackle: Natural red cock, palmered along rear half of body.

Tied on size 14 treble (above and below); tied on 1-inch tube (right)

Invented by Peter Deane, this is an essential fly for Icelandic rivers. The Black Francis is tied similarly, with black wool, and has a yellow head.

These are heavy flies and they are fished quickly by casting across the river and, as the fly swings back across the flow, the rod tip is raised and lowed to produce extra life.

Orange Hackle Shrimp

Hook: Low water single, double or treble, sizes 10–14.
Thread: Red.
Tail: Bunch hot orange bucktail, plus few fibres Crystal Hair.
Body: Orange floss, with a ball of fluorescent orange floss at front.
Rib: Fine oval gold tinsel.
Hackle: Hot orange cock.

A fly by Malcolm Greenhalgh, who was trying to produce a simple, easy-to-tie but effective salmon fly. This has caught salmon of up to 37 lbs in Norway, and sea trout of 22 lbs in Sweden. It also catches steelhead (on single hooks, sizes 2–6); during the preparation of this book, an 18-pounder was caught on the Orange Hackle Shrimp from the Skeena River.

Yellow Mallard Shrimp

Hook: Low water single, double or treble, sizes 10–14.
Thread: Black.
Tail: Golden pheasant red breast feather, wound as a hackle.
Body: Rear ½: Red floss.
Front ½: Black floss.
Rib: Fine oval silver tinsel.
Hackle: Mallard drake breast or flank feather, dyed hot yellow.

The Orange Mallard Shrimp is tied in exactly the same way, but with a hackle of mallard dyed hot orange. Note that these, like many salmon flies, should be available *lightly dressed*, for clear, low, slow pools, and more *heavily dressed* for water with some colour, or very turbulent water.

Also by Malcolm Greenhalgh. The yellow version has the edge where salmon are fresh-run from the sea (has caught salmon in saltwater sea pools), whereas the orange version is better with fish that have been in the river for some time, or where the river is tinged with colour.

Little's Shrimps

The great tyer Paul Little fishes one of the greatest fly rivers (and best kept secrets) of the salmon world. That river is the Derwent in northwest England, where the annual catch is about 100 salmon per mile of river. It is a small river, where orange shrimp patterns are very successful.

Hook: Treble fly hook (silver or gold preferably).
Thread: Red.

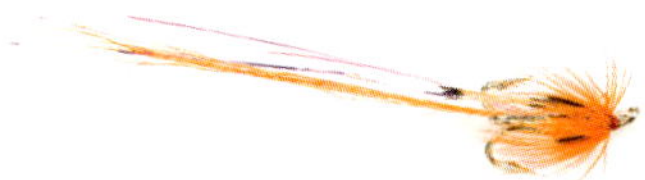

Note how the smaller hook was fixed to the leader with a loop-knot so that it could move freely in the water (see also p. 310). This actual fly caught a 15 lb salmon in September 2008 as this book was being prepared.

Tag: Finest oval gold tinsel.
Tail: Few strands of orange bucktail, plus fibres of Crystal Hair or Flashabou.
Body: Orange Mylar tinsel.
Rib: Finest oval gold tinsel.
'Wing'/hackle:
Either: Orange henny-cock, with two jungle cock eyes (above left).
Or: Few grey squirrel and golden pheasant tippets as wing, with orange henny-cock hackle wound in front (above right).

Chilimps

Hook: Low water single, double or treble, sizes 10–14.
Thread: Red.
Tail: 2 hot orange cock hackle points.
Body: Red wool, tapering to tail.
Rib: Fine flat tinsel.
Body hackle: Hot orange, wound with rib.
Hackle: Hot orange tied as collar.

Developed in Sweden in 1942, this is popular on the Morrum for catching big sea trout as well as salmon.

Ally's Shrimp
Hook: Low water single, double or treble, sizes 2–12.
Thread: Red.
Tail: Bunch hot orange bucktail.
Body:
Rear ½: Red floss.
Front ½: Black floss.
Rib: Fine oval silver tinsel.

Above left: A commercially tied Ally's Shrimp dressed on a treble fly-hook. *Above*: Tied on a single hook.

Hackle: Grey squirrel tail hairs.
Wing: Grey squirrel tail under golden pheasant tippet.
Collar hackle: Orange.

Ally Gowan's highly popular shrimp pattern that, over the last 20 years, has caught more salmon in Europe than any other one pattern. It also works well in North America. This is the original tying; other colours have been produced, but none is as good as the original!

Cascade

Hook: Low water single, double or treble, sizes 2–12.
Thread: Black.
Tag: Flat silver tinsel.
Tail: Bunch red and yellow bucktail, with 2–3 strands silver Crystal Hair.
Body:
  Rear ½: Flat silver tinsel.
  Front ½: Black floss.
Rib: Fine oval silver tinsel.
Hackle: Red and yellow, tied in front of wing.
Wing: Black squirrel tail, with very few strands silver Crystal Hair.

This is another fly by Ally Gowan and it is based on colours that, with

Below left: Cascade dressed on a treble fly-hook. *Below:* Cascade tied on a heavy tube for deep, and/or cold, and/or turbulent water.

orange, appear to be most attractive to salmon (see also Willie Gunn, p. 315). This is an outstanding fly for both salmon and steelhead. For those rivers in Canada and Norway where green is a very effective colour, Ally has produced the following version:

Green Cascade

Hook: Low water single, double or treble, sizes 2–12.
Thread: Black.

Tag: Flat gold tinsel.
Tail: Bunch green and yellow bucktail, with 2–3 strands gold Crystal Hair.
Body:
Rear half: Flat gold tinsel.
Front half: Black floss.
Rib: Fine oval gold tinsel.
Hackle: Green and yellow, tied in front of wing.
Wing: Black squirrel tail, with very few strands gold Crystal Hair.

Orange And Gold Sundown

Hook: Low water single, double or treble, sizes 2–12.
Thread: Orange.
Tag: Flat gold tinsel.
Tail: Bunch orange squirrel tail or bucktail, with 2–3 strands pearl Crystal Hair.
Body: Flat gold tinsel.
Rib: Fine oval gold tinsel or wire.
Eyes: Golden pheasant tippet feather with centre removed, and 2 outer black tips coated with clear cement. This is tied in to the rear of the middle hackle.
Hackles: Orange; one in middle of body, one at front.
Wing: Orange arctic fox.

Another useful salmon fly based on the effective orange. Highly effective in coloured water.

General Practitioner

Hook: Single, double and treble salmon hooks, sizes 2–10.
Thread: Red.
Tail (whiskers): Bunch of 10 hot orange bucktail hairs.
'Head': 2 red golden pheasant breast feathers.
Body: Orange seal's fur.
Rib: Fine oval gold tinsel.
Body hackle: Orange cock.
Wing: In 4 sections, from bottom to top: golden pheasant body feather; golden pheasant tippet, with centre removed; golden pheasant body feather, golden pheasant body feather.

This fly was invented by Col. Esmond Drury when fishing the real cooked prawn was banned from the beat of the Test (southern England) that he fished. The only clear difference between a boiled shrimp and prawn is one of size: prawns are bigger than shrimps. Shrimps may also be a bit pinker, but not necessarily so. Thus in larger sizes this makes a good prawn fly, in smaller a shrimp pattern. Like Ally's Shrimp, this has spawned many 'improved' variants.

Krabla

Hook: Single, double and treble salmon hooks, sizes 2–10.
Thread: Red.
Tail (Whiskers): 2 white and 2 pink stripped cock hackle stalks and a tuft of white marabou.
Body: 2 pink-red and 1 white cock hackles, palmered in touching turns and the fibres then trimmed to give a shrimpy body shape.
Rib: Fine oval silver tinsel.

A simple shrimp, the Krabla was invented for Icelandic rivers.

Ken's Pink Shrimp

Hook: Preferably treble fly hook, sizes 10–14.
Thread: Red.
Tail: Pink bucktail or squirrel, plus 2 strands Crystal Hair.
Body: Pearl Mylar tinsel.
Hackle: Pink, wound in front of wing and tied back.
Wing: Golden pheasant tippets, dyed pink, with jungle cock at sides.

Ken's Titchy Shrimp

Hook: Preferably treble fly hook, sizes 10–14.
Thread: Red.
Tail: Few fibres orange calf-tail, plus 2 strands Crystal Hair.
Body: Black floss.
Rib: Fine oval silver tinsel.
Hackle: Orange, wound in front of wing and tied back.
Wing: Golden pheasant tippets, with one jungle cock on top.

The last two small salmon flies are from Ken Maylor's stable. Ken fishes several small, shallow salmon rivers that have a good summer run when the water is very warm (in excess of 60F/17C). Then tiny flies are almost essential for success.

Latex Prawn

Hook: Single or double low water salmon, sizes 2–6.
Thread: Red.
Feelers (antennae): Strands of red, yellow and black pig's bristles.
Head: A red-brown golden pheasant breast feather.
Underbody: Orange seal's fur (or substitute).
Rib: Fine oval silver tinsel.
Exoskeleton ('shell'): Orange latex or fine plastic sheet.
Eyes: Black beads fixed in place with copper wire.

The first attempt to produce an ultra-realistic shrimp/prawn was by Dave and Steve Riding in the 1970s. Such creations look so perfect, and they are not too difficult to put together. However, the experience of many salmon anglers is that *Salmo salar* is not that impressed! Indeed, Steve Riding admitted that, although they had sold lots of their version of the LATEX PRAWN, he had yet to hear of a salmon falling for one. Of course, some idiot fish will have taken one of these somewhere, sometime, for as Arthur Oglesby once pointed out, some fool of a salmon will even take a wrist watch tied to the leader and cast into the river!

If salmon looked to taking flies that imitated real prawns and shrimps, then surely they would take the LATEX PRAWN before a GENERAL PRACTITIONER or ALLY'S SHRIMP? Which only seems to strengthen the theory that salmon shrimp patterns are really no such thing. In reality, they are flies that may suggest shrimps, to our eyes, provide we close them at least slightly.

HACKLE-POINT SHRIMPS

Hook: Low water salmon double (ideally, for balance), sizes 4–8.
Thread: Black, orange or red.
Feelers: 4 strands Crystal Hair plus a few hairs of black, orange or red bucktail.
Eyes: Orange bead.
Body: Built up with the tips of soft hen hackles in black, orange or red.

Terry Jenner came up with this idea and, whilst orange and red are commonest colours in shrimp patterns, his black version (as illustrated) is very effective in clear water.

Shrimp patterns – or flies with lots of orange or red in the dressing – cease to be as effective when the water loses all colour and becomes crystal clear. Then flies with black, blue and silver come into their own … things like the Black Bear and Stoat's Tail series.

JACK'S FLY

Hook: Treble fly hook, sizes 12–14.
Thread: Red.
Body: Prismatic purple tinsel.
Hackle: Dark grey (in the example, heron).

A most effective fly for when the river is low and running clear in summer, and is teaming with small salmon (grilse).

Salmon Dry Flies

Dry fly fishing in North America goes back a long way. In a letter dated 12 April 1906, to the great English chalk stream angler G. E. M. Skues, Theodore Gordon wrote:

> A friend of mine took a 14 pound salmon on a dry fly tied like a Coachman but dry fly style on a big Pennell hook. The line was slack, he broke his rod in striking the fish and was a long time in killing it. This was on the Restigouche and he got two more, a grilse and a small salmon in the same way out of the same pools in three days.
>
> J. D. McDonald, ed., *The Complete Fly Fisherman: The notes and letters of Theodore Gordon*, 1947.

Around the same time, as recalled by George M. L. La Branche in his *The Salmon and the Dry Fly* (1924): 'my friend [Colonel Monell] calmly announced that he had killed a fifteen-pound salmon two years before on a dry fly, and assumed that it was not an accident.' The Colonel had seen a salmon rising 'just like a trout' and it took his dry fly first cast. On the same day he also raised six or seven others, but failed to hook any of them. Colonel Monell will appear again in this section.

From the 1930s dry fly fishing for salmon became increasingly popular in North America, mainly through the writings of Lee Wulff, whose Wulff series of flies are still amongst the best dry flies for salmon. They are described on p. 139–40.

Things are different on the other side of the Atlantic for, as J. D. Bates Jr. put it in *Atlantic Salmon Flies and Fishing* (1970), 'Either salmon are much harder to take on the dry fly in the British Isles than in North America, or the British anglers are much harder to convince that it can be done consistently under favourable conditions.' That salmon can be taken on dry flies in Britain and Scandinavia is clear: for instance, Hans van Klinken caught many grilse in Norway on his first Klinkhammers (see p. 135), whilst Howard Croston and Malcolm Greenhalgh have caught salmon on dry Sedges (p. 193) and Oliver Edwards on a dry Daddy-long-legs (p. 218). However relatively few European salmon anglers have deliberately fished dry fly for salmon.

Hooks for salmon dry flies: While salmon have been caught on dry flies as small as a size 16 hook, the usual size range is sizes 4–10. Most are dressed on fine wire, low water singles (e.g. Partridge's Wilson Low Water) or a heavier wire trout dry fly hook (a big salmon will open up a fine wire hook).

In trout dry flies a tying that keeps the body close or touching the water, such as parachute hackled and no-hackled dry flies, is often more effective than a fly with a full wound hackle. In fact, often a fully hackled dry fly is made more effective when the lower hackle fibres are trimmed away (see, for example, p. 140). In contrast, effective dry flies for salmon (also steelhead and sea trout) are usually high floating and visible, with plenty of hackle.

The Bomber series, originated by the Rev. Elmer Smith, was first used on the Miramichi in 1967. They have proved their worth for steelhead as well as Atlantic salmon. The basic tying is as follows.

Bomber

Thread: Black or brown.
Tail: Brown bucktail, squirrel or woodchuck.
Body: Natural deer hair, spun along the hook shank and then trimmed to cigar shape, but making sure that the hook gape is left open to enhance hooking.
Body hackle: 2 natural red (brown) or grizzle cock hackles. In the trimming of the body one may accidentally get cut off or break, so one is a spare. Wind one in open turns around the deer-hair body.

Wing: As tail, tied forward over the hook eye (tie the wing in first, before tying the rest of the fly).

Most often tied on single salmon hooks in sizes 2–4, but a size 8–10 will take sea trout. Bombers are tied in a wide range of colours: orange, green, black etc.

Buck Bug

Hook: Trout wet or heavier wire dry fly, sizes 6–12.
Thread: Black or brown.
Butt: Green or orange fluorescent floss.
Tail: Deer hair.
Body: Natural deer hair, spun and trimmed to shape.
Body hackle: 2 natural red (brown) cock hackles palmered along the body.

This is a very small simpler version of the Bomber and may be tied in a range of body colours. For instance, the Green Machine has no tail, a fluorescent green butt, green deer-hair body and natural red cock body hackles; whereas the Shady Lady has a fine oval silver tinsel and fluorescent red floss butt, a body of black deer hair and black cock hackles. They are excellent for sea trout as well as salmon.

Brown Bivisible

Thread: Black or brown.
Tail: 2 natural red (brown) cock hackles tied in back-to-back so that they flare apart.
Body hackle: Up to six natural red (brown) cock hackles palmered in touching turns.
Hackle: In front of body hackle, white cock.

Bivisibles were devised in the 1930s by E. R. Hewitt (see p. 130). This tying is not only excellent for salmon in North America (and why not Europe?); it also is a great sea trout dry fly in Europe!

Dry Cosseboom

Thread: Yellow.
Tail: Grey squirrel or woodchuck tail.
Body: Green fur (either synthetic or natural) along the rear half of the hook shank.
Rib: Fine oval silver tinsel.

Hackle: Bright yellow wound in touching turns along the front half of the hook shank, either side of the wing.
Wing: Grey squirrel or woodchuck tail, tied upright and split.
Note: Tie the wings first, then go to the end of the hook shank and tie the rest of the fly.

The Cosseboom was originally tied as a wet fly (p. 319). Charles Lovelette first tied it as a dry fly for salmon in the late 1940s.

Dick Stewart and Farrow Allen give a variant of the Dry Cosseboom which sea trout and steelhead find attractive, as well as salmon.

Cosseboom Macintosh

Thread: Red.
Wing: Grey squirrel or woodchuck tail, tied halfway down the hook shank (it could be also called a tail).
Hackle: Up to 6 yellow cock hackles wound along the front half of the shank. Tie the first with the concave (undersurface) of the hackle pointing forwards, the next with the concave surface pointing backwards, and so on.

Others can be tied with dyed red, hot orange, purple and green hackles.

Grey Fly

Thread: Black.
Tail: White calf-tail.
Body: Natural grey rabbit fur.
Hackle: Medium blue dun (grey) cock.
Wing: White calf-tail, tied upright and split.

This is very similar to the Grey Wulff (p. 139), but the white wing makes the fly highly visible on rough water.

The Irresistible Series was designed by Joe Messinger Sr. in the late 1930s for trout fishing. In *The Complete Fly Tier* (1950) Rueben Cross reported: 'good success for salmon in sizes 10 to 4'. The deer-hair body contributes to the fly's near unsinkability.

Irresistible

Thread: Black or brown.
Tail: Brown bucktail.
Body: Natural deer hair spun and then clipped to a cone shape along the rear ⅔ of the hook shank.
Hackle: Grizzle or blue dun cock.
Wing: Brown bucktail.

The White Irresistible is tied similarly but with a white calf-tail tail and wing, white deer-hair body and a white or badger hackle. Harry Darbee's Rat-Faced McDougal is very similar to the Irresistible but has a pair of grizzle hackle points as wings. These are not very durable and not very visible on turbulent water. The White-Winged Rat-Faced McDougal is also very similar, but has a ginger hackle and white calf-tail wings.

Most dry flies are fished 'dead-drift', floating downstream over the heads of the fish with the current. As the name suggests, skaters are allowed to skate across the surface, creating a bit of a wake. They can, of course, also be fished dead-drift. The following are three skaters.

Skater

Hook: Trout dry fly, sizes 2–12.
Thread: Black or brown.
Tail: As hackle.
Body hackle: Long-fibred stiff cock hackle, wound in centre of hook-shank. Any colour of hackle will do, though brown, black, blue dun (grey) are most commonly used.

Skater

Hook: Trout up-eyed dry fly, sizes 8–12.
Thread: Black or brown.
Tail: 3 hot orange cock hackle points.
Body hackle: Black cock.
Wing: White bucktail or calf tied forwards at 45 degrees over the hook eye.

Dick Stewart and Farrow Allen described this skater pattern by Mack Strathdee in 1990.

Skitterbug

Thread: Black or brown.
Dressing: Two small bunches of natural deer hair. The first one is spun around the middle of the hook shank with hair tips forward and butts to rear. The second one is spun immediately in front of the first bunch around the middle of the hook shank with hair tips to the rear and butts forward. The butts are trimmed and the two flared bunches pushed together to give a narrow wheel-like circle of deer-hair fibres.

Invented by Dick Stewart in the 1970s – this is another good skater pattern.

A greased-up Muddler Minnow (see p. 272) will fish in the surface and can be fished dead-drift or skated across the surface as a 'wake fly'. Used as a wake fly it is also terrific for sea trout at night. Dick Stewart and Farrow Allen introduced a simple series – the Excel Series – by Mack Strathdee, designed especially for salmon and steelhead. Just vary the colour.

Orange Excel

Thread: Black or brown.
Body: Fluorescent hot orange wool.
Wing: Dark bucktail, dyed hot orange.
Head and collar: Deer-hair dyed fluorescent hot orange, spun and clipped to shape.

This version is excellent on many rivers, especially those with a slight peat tinge; on some a bright green version works well.

Soldier Palmer

Hook: Trout wet or heavier wire dry fly, sizes 6–12.
Thread: Red.
Tail: Red wool, short.
Body: Red wool.
Body hackle: Natural red (brown) cock, wound in close turns along the body.
Rib: Fine oval gold tinsel.
Hackle: As body hackle.

The Soldier Palmer is an ancient wet fly for lake and sea trout. Dressed more heavily and treated with floatant, it makes an excellent dry fly for bright conditions (especially where the water has a peaty tinge) for grilse and sea trout. Colonel Ambrose Monell devised a fly of similar style for catching Atlantic salmon in Canadian rivers.

Colonel Monell

Thread: Black or brown.
Tail: Sparse bunch Plymouth Rock cock hackle fibres (use grizzle if Plymouth Rock not available ... the salmon will not notice!)
Body: Peacock herl.
Body hackle: Plymouth Rock (or grizzle) cock.

Many salmon have fallen for trout dry flies, though few anglers would deliberately go out trying to catch the King of Fish on a size 20 Black Gnat! Daddy-long-legs are always worth trying (see p. 218) for both salmon and sea trout/steelhead. So too are big caddisfly (sedge) imitations. However, for trout fishing these are usually more effective minus the hackle. The following were designed on the eastern side of the Atlantic. The first works equally well on the western side, and has caught salmon, sea trout and steelhead. They were described by Hugh Falkus and Malcolm Greenhalgh in *The Salmon and Sea Trout Fisher's Handbook* (1997).

Salmon and Sea Trout Sedge

Hook: Trout dry fly, size 8–10.
Thread: Black or brown.
Body: Brown or olive fine synthetic fur.

Body hackle: Natural red (brown) cock in close turns.
Rib: Finest oval gold tinsel.
Hackle: Natural red (brown) cock.
Wing: Speckled turkey.
Antennae: 2 long cock pheasant tail fibres.

The second was found amongst Hugh Falkus's papers shortly after he died and as the aforementioned book was being completed. It is of Irish origin.

Fore and Aft

Hook: Trout dry fly, size 8–12.
Thread: Black or brown.
Tail: Few black cock hackle fibres.
Body: Hare's ear (originally the belly fur from a hedgehog).
Rib: Fine gold wire.
Hackles: Long-fibred black cock, one at either end of the body.

The aim is to have the fly bobble about on its hackle points.

Steelhead Bee

Thread: Black or brown.
Tail: Red squirrel or calf tail.
Body: Seal's fur (or substitute) in 3 equal sections, tied full and a bit scruffy: brown/yellow/brown.
Hackle: 3 turns brown (natural red) cock.
Wing: Red squirrel or calf tail tied over hook eye.
Note: Tie the wing in first, then the rest of the fly.

This is a Roderick Haig-Brown invention. Haig-Brown was from a wealthy English family who seems to have blotted his copybook. He was sent to British Columbia where he worked in the logging industry, fished and wrote some splendid books on fly-fishing. This is a 'moist fly' that fishes in the surface film.

SALMON NYMPHS

Few people have gone out especially to design nymphs for catching salmon (and sea trout and steelhead). Frank Sawyer described catching salmon to 15 lb on his Killer Bug (p. 119) in *Nymphs and the Trout* (1958). Chris Hosker accidentally devised a consistent taker of salmon (named here the Salmon Bug, p. 101) when he was trying to find a weighted fly that would take grayling in cold, high, coloured rivers. Oliver Edwards once hooked a salmon on a Hare's Ear Goldhead (p. 57) when grayling fishing on the Piddle, a small English chalk stream. Malcolm Greenhalgh has caught grilse in Norway on the Montana Nymph (p. 74). And Raymond Rocher caught salmon on his Faisan et Orange (p. 71). Those five weighted flies are well worth fishing for salmon. So too are the following, designed for catching salmon. Tie them on low water salmon singles, size 8–10.

Black Nymph

Thread: Black.
Tag: Fine flat gold tinsel and orange floss (fluorescent may be best).
Tail: 3–4 fibres bronze mallard.
Butt: Peacock herl.
Body: Black seal's fur.
Rib: Fine oval gold tinsel.
Hackle: Bronze mallard fibres, tied false.
Wing: A jungle cock hackle tied on top of the body and extending back as far as the butt.

Charles De Feo designed a series of nymphs in the 1950s, of which this is just one.

Salmon March Brown Nymph

Thread: Brown.
Tail: 3 cock pheasant tail fibres, separated.
Body: Blend of tan fox and amber seal's fur (or substitute).
Rib: Dark brown thread.
Legs: Brown speckled partridge.
Wing case: Dark brown turkey, lacquered.

This was designed by W. J. Keane.

It is likely that nymph fishing deliberately for salmon is unlikely to develop much further as, when fishing below the surface, we have so many very effective wet flies, shrimps, streamers and bucktails.

Flies for Sea-Run Trout: Sea Trout, Steelhead, Cutthroat and Char

Sea trout are the sea-run brown trout of northwest Europe; they can also be found in many places where brown trout were introduced, such as Tierra del Fuego and the Falkland Islands. Steelhead are the sea-run rainbow trout of North America west of the Rockies. They too occur in places where rainbow trout were introduced, such as the Great Lakes of the northeast United States and Canada, and rivers running into them. Both sea trout and steelhead can attain great, salmon-like size, in excess of twenty pounds. Sea-run cutthroat trout, which share the same natural range as the steelhead, and most sea-run char, rarely exceed five pounds. In Arctic Norway and Russia, Iceland and Greenland, for instance, sea-run Arctic char average about three pounds. These migratory salmonids are highly prized, for they take the fly more readily than most salmon, they make long swift runs when hooked, and gourmets rate them more highly than salmon.

Many flies previously described in the sections on Fancy Flies and Bucktails and Streamers are excellent catchers of migratory trout. Many also are caught by salmon anglers on salmon flies (for instance, the ORANGE HACKLED SHRIMP caught two sea trout in excess of 20 lbs in Sweden's River Morum in 1993 and a 24 lbs steelhead in the North

Umpqua in 1992). The flies in this section are specially designed to catch migratory trout (though they *will* take salmon!). Note too that some of the sea trout flies will catch steelhead, and vice versa.

SEA TROUT FLIES

Often the best fishing for sea trout in rivers is at night and that is what the flies described below were designed for (see Hugh Falkus, *Sea Trout Fishing*, enlarged edition 1975 [1962]). For daytime fishing use wet flies in sizes 8–14, such as Mallard and Claret, Teal, Blue and Silver, Silver Invicta, Black Pennell, Peter Ross etc. Dry fly can also be effective on some rivers; imitative flies may be used, though a bushier or larger fly such as Salmon and Sea Trout Sedge or Daddy long-legs will bring up the sea trout and not the smaller, unwanted brown trout.

Secret Weapons

Falkus gave tying recipes for what he called Secret Weapons, but any wet fly can be turned into a Secret Weapon. Take a small treble hook (sizes 12–16, the larger the front hook [see below] the larger the treble) and fix it to a doubled strand of about 10 lb test monofilament fishing line. Now fix the doubled monofilament to a single trout wet fly or salmon hook, so that the front of the eye of the treble is only a very short distance behind the end of the bend of the single hook. Tie what ever wet fly you like on the front hook, but omitting any tail in the tying recipe. The idea is that a sea trout trying to nip the end of the wet fly will be hooked on the treble. See also wake lures, below.

Where the use of treble hooks, or tandem mounts is prohibited, Secret Weapons are also prohibited.

Medicine

Hook: Low-water salmon, sizes 2–8.
Thread: Black or red.
Body: Flat silver tinsel (Falkus used metallic silver paint, but this must be allowed to dry for two days).
Hackle: Blue henny-cock.
Wing: Earlier in the season, drake mallard flank – later bronze mallard or wigeon. A wide slip is cut from the feather and folded twice, to give a slender wing. A couple of strands of pearl or light blue Crystal Hair may be tied in at the sides of the wing.

Tied with mallard flank

Tied with bronze mallard

This is a renamed large MALLARD AND SILVER, long known as a great fly for night fishing. A very old angler said that, in the 1940s and 1950s, it was practice on the rivers fished by Falkus to impale as many maggots as possible around the bend of the hook or to seek big white docken grubs and stick one of them on the hook. Using just one or two maggots on the fly was common practice in most sea trout rivers; today that is usually against the fishery rules. The maggots were probably not what the sea trout wanted to eat, but it is likely that the maggots at the hook bend caused the fly to wobble in the water as it moved across the stream. A small piece of chamois-leather impaled on the hook bend has the same effect without contravening any rules. The very similar Norwegian fly, Telemarkskongen, has a tail of red ibis (substitute).

Many other fancy wet flies can be tied 'Medicine style' on big hooks. PETER ROSS, SILVER INVICTA, BUTCHER and ALEXANDRA are ideal. Fish from dusk and well into the night. Great for summer grilse.

PETER ROSS (MEDICINE STYLE)

Hook: Low-water salmon, sizes 2–6.
Thread: Black.
Body:
Rear ½: Flat silver or gold tinsel.
Front ½: Red seal's fur (or substitute).
Rib: Fine oval silver or gold tinsel.
Hackle: Black henny-cock, sparse.
Wing: Grey squirrel tail, plus 2–3 strands pearl Crystal Hair.

Use the gold version in coloured/peat-stained water, the silver one in clear water. See p. 241 for standard PETER ROSS.

Elver (Elverine) Lure

Hook: Low-water salmon, sizes 1/0–8.
Thread: Red.
Body: Flat silver tinsel.
Rib: Oval silver tinsel.
Hackle: Cobalt-blue feather fibres from vulturine gallina (or deep blue dyed hen), tied false.
Wing: 2 well-marked vulturine gallina hackles, tied back to back.
Cheeks: Jungle cock.

A fly by Arthur Ransome (see Wake Lures, below) that is exceedingly useful also in salt water (use stainless steel hooks). It can also be tied on a tandem mount. Vulturine gallina is a CITES species, but is bred in captivity for fly-tying (the feathers are relatively expensive).

Black Shark

Hook: Low-water salmon, sizes 2–8.
Thread: Black.
Body: None
'Hackle': Bunch black squirrel tail hairs.
Wing: Red and black squirrel tail hairs well mixed, with 4–6 peacock herls over.

This Swedish fly is one of several black flies that will catch sea trout and steelhead. Try also the Bear or Stoat's Tail series (pp. 307–11).

Morum

Hook: Low-water salmon, sizes 2–8.
Thread: Black.
Tag: Fine oval silver tinsel, then fluorescent red floss.

Body: Black floss.
Rib: Oval silver tinsel.
Body hackle: Red golden pheasant breast feather, palmered. †
Hackle: Barred teal fibres, tied false.
Wing: Golden pheasant tippet and golden pheasant body feather.
† Tie the feather in by its tip. The butt of this feather is very thick and if tied in by the butt makes a bulky rear end of the fly.

A great sea trout fly, for Sweden's River Morum, by Jan Grunwald. This could be considered a 'shrimp' fly.

Sun Ray Shadow

Hook: Trout or low-water salmon double, sizes 6–8.
Thread: Black.
Body: Olive, or white, or orange dubbing (natural or synthetic).
Wing: Black goat, plus pearl and/or red Flashabou, tied long. For variation, try also a yellow underwing and brown overwing.

See p. 312 for Collie Dog. The aim here is movement within the fly. Fish in low water, by day or night, in streamier, shallower water. Cast the fly up and across the flow, and strip it back quickly. Takes are vicious! This is catching more sea trout every year, and is also useful for salmon and steelhead. Where doubles are prohibited, use a single, but add some extra weight (such as a tungsten bead at the head) to get the fly down quickly.

Rogan's Gadget

Hook: Streamer hook, sizes 2–10.
Thread: Black.
Body: Flat silver tinsel or silver mylar tube.
Tail and back: Peacock herl.
Head: Peacock herl.

The method of tying is easy: tie a bunch of peacock herls in at the end of the hook shank with plenty trailing at the back; then tie the body; bring the herls over the back and tie them in behind the hook eye; wind peacock herl behind the hook eye to create the head; cut the trailing ends of herl square to form a tail.

This is by the famous but now sadly defunct Irish fly-tying family of Rogans of Ballyshannon. It was originally dressed for catching sea trout in the nearby Erne estuary but will also take sea trout in fresh water. The Gadget is a simple fry pattern and has caught sea bass, striped bass, bluefish and pollock in the sea.

Sea Trout Fry

Hook: Streamer, sizes 2–6.
Thread: Black.
Underbody: Flat silver tinsel, with turns of fluorescent red floss at front.
Overbody: Clear polythene strip, wound.
Wing: Barred teal (or wigeon).
Head: Black thread with a painted eye.

Sea trout fresh from the sea, or still in the brackish water of their native estuary, find this pattern very attractive. It can also be used for catching species like big browns and perch that seek fry.

TANDEM SUNK LURES

Flies tied on tandem or three-hook mounts have been used for catching sea trout, especially in estuaries, for very many years. The simplest was two wet-fly hooks, linked by a strand of monofilament. This simple mount was then painted with metallic silver paint, and when the paint was dry a couple of blue hackles were tied in at the front. Such flies were called Terrors or Demons. Falkus's Sunk Lure is an old standard Terror that he named after himself.

Mount: Two size 4–8 single trout or 8–12 low-water, single or double salmon hooks fixed in tandem; the total length of the mounts to be 2½–3½ inches. There are a couple of ways of linking the hooks. The original was to use a doubled or trebled strand of fairly thick monofilament (at least 12 lb test). The other is to use a length of braided backing-line. Whichever is used, always test that the link is secure.

Falkus's Sunk Lure

Body: Metallic silver paint. Allow at least two days to dry.
Thread: Red or black.
Wing: 2 pairs blue cock hackles tied back to back so that their natural curve flares outwards, with a few peacock herls over the top. For a modern touch, add 3–4 strands blue or pearl Crystal Hair. Note that the wing tip should not protrude beyond the bend of the rear hook.

Grizzle Sunk Lure

Body: Metallic silver paint. Allow at least two days to dry.
Thread: Red.
Wing: 2 pairs grizzle cock hackles tied back to back so that their natural curve flares outwards, with a few peacock herls and 3–4 strands pearl Crystal Hair on top. Note that the wing tip should not protrude beyond the bend of the rear hook.

By Malcolm Greenhalgh, who believes that this out-fishes the first tying. It is also effective in estuaries and bays for sea trout and sea bass (use sizes 4–6 stainless steel hooks).

Blackie

Mount: As above, but not painted.
Thread: Black.
Body: Black seal's fur (or substitute).
Rib: Oval silver tinsel.
Hackle: Black hackle fibres, tied false.
Wing: Black squirrel tail.
Cheeks: Jungle cock (optional).

This is, of course, simply a tandem Black Stoats's Tail (see p. 308). Great for night fishing.

Marchog Du

Mount: A size 2–4 single in front of a size 8–10 treble at the rear, the 2 hooks being linked by plaiting 3 strands of 20 lb test mono. All the dressing is on the front hook, the end of the wing being level with the bend of the treble hook.
Thread: Black.
Butt: Fluorescent orange floss.
Body: Flat silver tinsel.
Hackle: Hot orange hackle fibres, tied false.
Wing: 2 black hackles tied back to back, with a shorter grizzle hackle on either side.

Wales has some of the most outstanding of the world's sea-trout rivers. In Welsh, sea trout are called 'sewin' and the names of their flies are all in the Welsh tongue. MARCHOG DU means Black Knight. Change the black hackles for yellow and you have MARCHOG MELYN, with red hackles MARCHOG GOCH, with blue hackles MARCHOG GLAS and with brown hackles MARCHOG DBU.

Marchog Melyyn

Marchog Glas

WORM FLY

Mount: 2 size 8–12 single trout hooks, in tandem, the rear of the front hook only a short distance in front of the eye of the rear hook.
Thread: Red or black.
Tails: Tuft red wool (on both hooks).
Body: Peacock herl (on both hooks).
Hackle: Natural red (brown) hen (on both hooks).

This is simply two Wet Red Tags (see p. 226) tied in tandem. It is very good for catching sea trout that have been in the river for some time.

Sunk Lures should be fished deep and will catch sea trout in rivers all night. Note, though, that they may not be used where tandem mounts are prohibited. In which case, cut off the point and bend of the front hook to produce a flexible one-hook mount.

WAKE LURES

During the 1930s F. M. Warhurst from Ulverston, at the edge of the English Lake District National Park, had his own fishing beat on the River Duddon. One night he cast a bit too far and hooked a hawthorn bush on the far bank. He pulled on the line and his hook broke free, but impaled on it was a piece of dead twig. As he pulled his fly back, he noticed, in the moonlight, that it made a wake on the surface. Then his fly vanished in an almighty swirl as a sea trout took hold. Mr Warhurst took the hint. The following day he tied a piece of cork to a hook and that night, accompanied by the famous writer Arthur Ransome (author of children's books such as *Swallows and Amazons* and great angling books such as *Rod and Line*), he returned to the river. His Wake Lure was so successful that it featured in the catalogues of Hardy Bros. Falkus renamed it the Surface Lure.

Mount: A tandem consisting of a large single hook (low-water salmon or streamer, sizes 2–8) with a size 8–12 treble at the rear. Length of mount: 2–4 inches.

Dressing: The following may be used (all on the front hook).

CORK WAKE LURE (painted silver)

1. Cork, cut to bullet shape and lashed to the tip of the hook shank. This may be painted (Falkus usually painted his red with his long-suffering wife's nail varnish).
2. A piece of goose or swan quill, with the hole plugged with plastic wood, as Cork (1).
3. A piece of balsa wood, as Cork (1).
4. A piece of ethafoam, as Cork (1).
5. As 1–4 but made more 'fly-like' by lashing the hackles of woodcock, snipe etc. to the sides and top of the body. Such adornments do not enhance the catching quality.
6. Deer hair. Malcolm Greenhalgh came up with this idea in 1988, and he and Falkus fished it that summer. Simply spin deer hair, muddler-style, along the shank of the front hook, and then trim it to shape, leaving a few strands at the back untrimmed. Natural and black deer hair work well. The addition of a few trailing strands of pearl Flashabou may enhance the angler's confidence, but it seems that the sea trout do not notice! Greenhalgh called his fly the NIGHT MUDDLER (see Hugh Falkus and Malcolm Greenhalgh, *The Salmon and Sea Trout Fisher's Handbook*, 1997). Others have also come up with this idea

NIGHT MUDDLER, OR THE MOUSE

Tag: Fine oval silver tinsel.
Body: Orange floss.
Rib: Fine oval silver tinsel.
Hackle: White arctic fox under orange arctic fox.

Autumn Run

Hook: Low-water salmon, sizes 2–4.
Thread: Black.
Tag: Fine oval gold tinsel.
Body: Orange floss.
Rib: Fine oval gold tinsel.
Hackle: White arctic fox. fix in a dubbing loop, spin and then wind as a hackle.
Wing: Orange arctic fox.

Deschutes Passion

Hook: Low-water salmon, sizes 2–4.
Thread: Black.
Body: Several strands of pearl Flashabou or Crystal Hair (or similar flashy synthetic fibre) tied in and wound along shank.
Hackle: Hot pink arctic fox. This is best fixed in a dubbing loop, spun and then wound.
Wing: Purple arctic fox and pearl Flashabou or Crystal Hair.

A

B

Lunar Mist [a]

Hook: Low-water salmon, sizes 2–6.
Thread: Black.
Tag: Fine oval silver tinsel.
Body: Bright green floss.
Rib: Fine oval silver tinsel.
Hackle: Chartreuse arctic fox in front of white arctic fox.

Lunar Run [b]

Hook: Low-water salmon, sizes 2–6.
Thread: Black.
Tag: Fine oval silver tinsel.
Body: Flat silver tinsel.
Rib: Fine oval silver tinsel.
Hackle: Black arctic fox.
Wing: Chartreuse arctic fox.

Tied in smaller sizes (down to size 12) these five flies would also be potentially excellent salmon flies, the first four of the 'Shrimp school'.

Bill Black and Ken Ferguson of Roseburg, Oregon devised a series of steelhead flies, weighted with metal eyes so that they would get deep in fast turbulent flows. Their tyings insisted on the use of Dazl-Eyes and a synthetic sparkling material called Lite Brite Mylar for the bodies. As with all synthetic materials, if these are no longer produced, what happens to the flies that use them? Alternatives will have to be found. These flies use rabbit zonker strip as wings; these give the fly movement and life.

These flies are tied on a wide range of hook sizes, 2/0–6.

Soft Candy Cain

Thread: Red.
Tag: Flat gold tinsel.
Body: Salmon-pink Lite Brite Mylar (or any synthetic dubbing with sparkle). Don't dub too tightly and tease out a few fibres; light should pass through the material.
Rib: Flat gold tinsel.

Hackle: Red hen, wound in front of wing.
Wing: White rabbit zonker strip.
Eyes: Heavy, brass, gold or silver.
Head: As body.

Bumble Bee Bunny

Thread: Black.
Tag: Flat gold tinsel.
Body: Hot yellow Lite Brite Mylar (or any synthetic dubbing with sparkle). See note above.
Rib: Flat gold tinsel.
Hackle: Black hen, wound in front of wing.
Wing: Black rabbit zonker strip.
Eyes: Heavy, brass, gold or silver.
Head: as body.

Besides these two patterns, other tyings include grizzle, pink, purple, yellow and orange zonker strip.

Black Prince

Hook: Low-water salmon, sizes 2–6.
Thread: Black.
Tag: Fine oval silver tinsel.
Tail: Bunch red hackle fibres.
Body:
Rear ⅓: Yellow wool.
Front ⅔: Black wool.
Rib: Oval silver tinsel.
Hackle: Black hen wound as a collar in front of the wing.
Wing: Black bear, squirrel etc.

The Black Prince is one of the oldest steelhead flies and is also useful for sea trout and salmon (see above). It was probably first fished in the Umpqua River system.

Blue Moon
Hook: Low-water salmon, sizes 2/0–4.
Thread: Black.

Hackle: Kingfisher blue schlappen hackle wound as collar in front of wing.
Wing: Black marabou with strands of pearl and/or blue Crystal Hair or Flashabou.

Invented by George Cook for the rivers of British Columbia, this fly has lots of built-in 'life'.

Bosquito

Hook: Low-water salmon, sizes 2–6.
Thread: White.
Tail: Bunch red hackle fibres.
Body: Yellow wool or chenille.
Rib: Fine flat gold tinsel.
Hackle: Black, tied as collar in front of wings.
Wing: White polar bear (or bucktail).
Head: White.

Many steelhead flies have been designed with white hair wings. These are rare in salmon and sea trout flies.

Boss

Hook: Low-water salmon, sizes 2–6.
Thread: Fluorescent orange.
Tail: Black squirrel or bucktail.
Body: Black chenille.
Rib: Fine flat or oval silver tinsel.
Hackle: Hot orange, fully wound as a collar.
Eyes: Silver bead chain or silver bumbell eyes.

The Boss is the most popular of the Comet series of flies that have silver bead chain eyes, a long tail and a hackle but no wing. It is a fairly old fly, originating in the 1940s.

The following three flies illustrate the two extremes in steelhead flies, the bright and gaudy, and the dull and drab. All are very good takers of steelhead.

Brad's Brat

Hook: Low-water salmon, sizes 2–6.
Thread: Black.
Tail: A bunch of white bucktail over a bunch of orange bucktail, tied fairly short.
Body:
Rear ½ : Orange wool.
Front ½ : Red wool.
Hackle: Brown, tied as a collar in front of wing.
Wing: Orange bucktail with a few white bucktail fibres on top.

Indian Fly

Hook: Low-water salmon, sizes 2–8.
Thread: Black.
Tail: Bunch white hackle fibres.
Body: Rear ½: Yellow wool.
Rib: Front ½: Red wool.
Hackle: Brown, wound as collar in front of wing.
Wing: Black squirrel tail.

Burlap

Hook: Low-water salmon, sizes 2–8.
Thread: Brown.
Tail: Bunch natural deer hair.
Body: Burlap sacking material.
Hackle: Grizzle hen or henny-cock.

Marabou Streamer

Hook: Low-water salmon, sizes 2–6.
Thread: Black.
Body: None.
Hackles:
Rear: Cerise, chartreuse, olive, orange, pink, purple or red marabou, wound as a hackle so that the fibres radiate around the hook shank.
Front: Black marabou, tied as rear hackle, with a few strands of Crystal Hair (pearl or as rear hackle).

This is a modification of a pattern by Jack Gartside. It is simple to tie (note that blood marabou is easier to use as a hackle than the usual marabou, it is highly mobile in the water, and it has taken many steelhead and sea trout in fast water during the day.

Yellow is always good for attracting fresh-run fish to the fly. The next fly is an example of this.

Kalama Special

Hook: Low-water salmon, sizes 2–8.
Thread: Black.
Body: Yellow wool.
Body hackle: A golden badger, palmered along the body, with two full turns at the front.
Wing: White bucktail.

Polar Shrimp

Hook: Low-water salmon, sizes 2–8.
Thread: Black.
Tag: Flat gold tinsel.
Tail: Bunch red hackle fibres.
Body: Fluorescent orange chenille.
Hackle: Orange.
Wing: White polar bear or bucktail.

This is one of the oldest steelhead flies, and still very effective throughout steelhead range.

There are relatively few purple flies for steelhead and salmon, though the latter readily take real shrimps and prawns that have been dyed purple more readily than the boiled pink/orange prawns. The Purple Peril and Rick's Revenge are two such flies that might also be used for catching salmon.

Purple Peril

Hook: Low-water salmon, sizes 2–6.
Thread: Black.
Tag: Flat silver tinsel.
Body: Purple chenille or wool.

Rib: Oval silver tinsel.
Hackle: Purple.
Wing: Brown squirrel or bucktail.
Note: A hackle made from very soft hair such as arctic fox, using a dubbing loop, is more mobile than a conventional feather hackle.

Rick's Revenge

Hook: Low-water salmon, sizes 2–8.
Thread: Purple.
Tail: Fluorescent pink floss.
Body:
Rear ½: Fluorescent pink floss. Tie a short length of the front 'waste' of the floss back as a veil over the rear half of the body.
Front ½: Purple seal's fur (or substitute).
Rib: Fine oval gold tinsel, over front half of body.
Hackle: Purple hen or arctic fox (see note above).
Wing: White polar bear or bucktail, with few purple strands over.

Skunk

Hook: Low-water salmon, sizes 2–8.
Thread: Black.
Tail: Bunch red hackle fibres.
Body: Black chenille.
Rib: Oval silver tinsel.
Hackle: Black.
Wing: White polar bear or bucktail.

This is one of the most widely used of steelhead flies and it has spawned many variant tyings. Its origins go back to the 1930s.

Spade

Hook: Low-water salmon, sizes 2–8.
Thread: Black.
Tail: Bunch natural deer hair.
Body: Black chenille.
Hackle: Grizzle.

Another widely used steelhead fly that was first fished by Bob Arnold in the Stillaguamish River in the 1960s. Again, as with many successful flies, there have been variant tyings that, their inventors argue, are better than the original. The truth may be that the original tying was so simple that even the most novice could tie it. Professional tyers thus had to produce more complex variants that they could tie and sell!

Umpqua Special
Hook: Low-water salmon, sizes 2–6.
Thread: Red.
Tail: White bucktail.
Body:
  Rear ⅓: Yellow wool.
  Front ⅔: Red wool.
Rib: Medium oval silver tinsel.
Hackle: Brown, wound as collar in front of wing.
Wing: White polar bear, calf or bucktail, with a strip of red goose on either side.
Cheeks: Jungle cock (optional, without the jungle cock is simply the Umpqua).

An old steelhead fly, going back to the 1930s, with lots of variants.

A VISIT TO BRITISH COLUMBIA

Wally Nowak and his son Trevor live at Courtennay, British Columbia, where they tie flies and fish for steelhead, char (Arctic and the big-lake trout *Salvelinus namaycush*) and Pacific salmon. Their flies are tied solely for fishing, and often they have no names. The first Nowak fly has roots from over a hundred years ago in the Atlantic salmon rivers of Scotland.

Nowak's Dee Strip
Hook: Long shank salmon single, sizes 1/0–4.
Thread: Black.
Tag: Red Mylar tinsel.
Tail: Golden pheasant crest.
Butt: Peacock herl.
Body – Rear: Flat silver tinsel.
Rib: Fine oval silver tinsel.

Veils: Blue hackle points.
Butt of front ½ of body: Peacock herl.
Body – Front ½: Yellow seal's fur.
Body hackle (over front ½ of body): Light blue cock.
Rib: Fine oval silver tinsel.
Throat hackle: Black and white barred, e.g. gallina or black francolin.
Wings: Black quill slips.
Head: Green.

Though involved in the tying, Dee- and Spey-strip flies based on the old classics still have some fans on the Pacific side of the Rockies, where they are fished for steelhead.

The following three flies, also nameless, are more straightforward in the dressing.

No Name 1

Hook: Salmon single, sizes 2–6.
Thread: Fluorescent bright red.
Tag: Blue pearlescent Mylar tinsel.
Tail: Fluorescent flame red floss, long.
Body: Lime-green seal's fur.
Rib: Oval green Mylar tinsel.
Hackle: Blue cock, wound in front of wing.
Wing: Polar bear (or substitute).

No Name 2

Hook: Salmon single, sizes 2–6.
Thread: Fluorescent bright red.
Tag: Flat silver Mylar tinsel.
Tail: Orange-yellow fluorscent floss, long.
Body: Yellow seal's fur.
Rib: Oval silver Mylar tinsel.
Hackle: Yellow cock, wound in front of wing.
Wing: Red bucktail, or squirrel or calftail.

No Name 3

Hook: Salmon single, sizes 2–6.
Thread: Fluorescent bright red.
Tag: Flat red Mylar tinsel.
Tail: Fluorescent yellow floss, long.

Body: Pink synthetic dubbing.
Rib: Oval silver Mylar tinsel.
Hackle: Badger dyed purple, wound in front of wing.
Wing: Light purple under light claret bucktail.

The following three flies were developed for catching steelhead and Arctic char.

Spuddler (Wally Nowak).
Hook: Salmon or long shank trout streamer, sizes 2–6.
Thread: Red.
Tail: Bright lime floss.
Body: Flat gold tinsel.
Wing: A pair of cree hackles dyed olive, with one undyed on either side.
Head: Red chenille or dubbed seal's fur, then a small spun and clipped deer-hair head, with the fibres trailing back unclipped as a collar.

Spuddler (Trevor Nowak)
Hook: Salmon or long shank trout streamer, sizes 2–6.
Thread: Olive.
Tail: Ginger hair (e.g. calftail), sparse.
Body: Olive seal's fur.
Body hackle: Light olive cock.
Rib: Oval gold tinsel.
Hackle: Soft black spade or Schlappen, wound in front of wing.
Wing: Two pairs cree hackles
Eyes: Jungle cock.

Spuddler (Dec Hogan)
Hook: Salmon or long shank trout streamer, sizes 2–6.
Thread: Pink.
Tail: Light orange hair (e.g. dyed polar bear or squirrel).
Body: Orange seal's fur.
Body hackle: Yellow-gold cock.
Rib: Oval gold tinsel.
Hackle: Soft orange spade or Schlappen, wound in front of wing.
Wing: Two pairs cree hackles dyed orange.

Hot Glue Egg Flies

These are not really tied – they are put together!

- Take a brass bead that has been enamelled orange or pink and slide it up to the eye of a wide-gape size 10–12 short-shank hook.
- Take red tying thread and make several turns behind the bead. This thread base should allow the bead to bed down tightly when pushed back.
- Using a glue-gun, as the vice head is carefully rotated, squeeze over the bead a nice sphere of clear glue. Keep rotating as the glue hardens and, if not spherical, use a cigarette lighter to soften the glue.

Chris Hosker devised this quick-sinking pattern for catching grayling that are devouring washed-out salmon eggs in the winter months.

FLIES FOR SEA-RUN CUTTHROAT

Sea-run cutthroat can be caught on many fancy wet flies, streamers, bucktails and salmon and steelhead flies, though usually tied in smaller sizes (8–12). The following are a selection of more traditional dressings. These are also very good catchers of sea-run Arctic char in northern Canada, Greenland and Iceland.

American Coachman

Hook: Trout wet fly, sizes 6–12.
Thread: Black.
Tail: Red bucktail.
Body: Yellow wool.
Hackle: Brown (natural red).
Wing: White polar bear or bucktail.

Cutthroat (Doc Baker's Tying)

Hook: Trout wet fly, sizes 6–12.
Thread: Black.
Tail: 6–8 mallard flank feather fibres.
Body: Fluorescent hot orange floss.
Rib: Oval silver tinsel.
Hackle: Yellow.
Wing: White marabou.

Cutthroat (Al Knudsen's Tying)

Hook: Trout wet fly, sizes 6–12.
Thread: Black.
Tail: Sparse bunch red hackle fibres.
Body: Yellow wool.
Rib: Oval silver tinsel.
Hackle: Red hackle fibres, tied false.
Wing: Bunch red bucktail under bunch of white bucktail (to end of body).

Red Cutthroat

Hook: Trout wet fly, sizes 6–12.
Thread: Black.
Tail: Sparse bunch black hackle fibres.
Body: Red chenille (sometimes tied with red wool).
Rib: Oval silver tinsel.
Hackle: Black.
Wing: White polar bear or bucktail.

The Black Cutthroat and Yellow Cutthroat are similarly tied; the first has a black body and hackle and a white wing, the second a yellow body and hackle and white wing.

Cutthroat Minnow

Hook: Trout wet fly, sizes 6–10.
Thread: Black.
Tail: Very bright red wool.
Body: Flat silver tinsel.
Hackle: Grizzle.
Wing: Bunch of fibres from mallard drake flank, with 4–6 strands peacock herl over.

Invented by Bruce Ferguson of Washington State, this pattern is often used in estuaries.

Beach Fly
Hook: Trout wet fly, sizes 6–10.
Thread: Hot orange.
Tail: Bunch hot orange hackle fibres.
Body: Light fluorescent orange floss.
Hackle: Medium brown (natural red).
Wing: White Polar bear or bucktail.

By Les Johnson, for inshore saltwater fishing. Johnson has also caught Pacific salmon on this fly.

Sea-Run Special
Hook: Trout wet fly, sizes 6–10.
Thread: Black.
Tail: Sparse bunch yellow hackle fibres.
Body: Orange wool.
Rib: Oval gold tinsel.
Hackle: Grizzle (2 turns).
Wing: Deer hair – to end of body.

Stillaguamish Special
Hook: Trout streamer, sizes 8–12.
Thread: Black.
Butt: Fine oval silver tinsel.
Tail: Mix of red and white hackle fibres.
Body: Yellow wool.
Rib: Oval silver tinsel.
Body hackle: Yellow, palmered in wide turns.
Hackle: Red, 3–4 turns.
Wing: White bucktail with a few fibres red bucktail.
Head: Peacock herl.

Coho Fly
Hook: Long shank streamer fly, sizes 6–12.
Thread: Black.
Body: Flat silver tinsel.
Rib: Oval silver tinsel.
Wing: Bucktail or polar bear, in the following colour combinations:

	A	B	C	D	E	F	G
Upper:	Blue	Yellow	Orange	Brown	Red	Green	Blue
Middle:	Red	Red	–	–	–	Red	Olive
Lower (next to hook):	White	Yellow	White	White	White	White	White

A

B

C

D

E

F

G

These are usually fished in saltwater (bays, estuaries) or in freshwater at the head of the tide.

Finally, a simple fly for catching coho and small king salmon from the beaches of Vancouver Island by the British Columbia master, Roderick L. Haig-Brown. In his book *Fisherman's Summer* (1959) he wrote: 'a heavily dressed polar bear wing with a silver body on a No. 1 hook does very well'.

Simple yet effective: the perfect fishing fly!

Flies for Freshwater Predators

The vast majority of fly-fishers seek resident trout (brown, rainbow, cutthroat and golden), migratory trout (sea trout and steelhead), char (Arctic, speckled/brook trout, dolly varden), grayling and salmon when they go fishing. Thus far all the flies described and illustrated were designed for these fish. There are, however, many other species of freshwater fish that are eagerly sought.

Some of these other species (e.g. whitefish, chub) do feed on insects and other invertebrates and can be caught on nymphs, bugs and dry flies. Others are predatory species and they seek larger prey: lesser fish (sometimes including their own kind), frogs, and even mice that fall into the water.

Pike are the archetypical circumpolar predator, occurring widely in parts of North America (where they are called, 'northern pike') and across Europe. Then there are the closely related zander of Europe, walleye of North America that feed primarily on tiny fish. The largemouth and smallmouth basses are very popular sport fish in North America; so popular are they that they have been introduced into parts of Europe. Several smaller species of fish are termed 'panfish' in North America, and they will all take the fly and provide a tasty breakfast. Likewise perch and ide in Europe.

Head to tropical freshwaters and the variety of predators increases along with their sizes. The most popular in African lakes is the Nile perch, that can attain sizes well in excess of 200 lbs. Do you need flies specially tied to catch them? No. In their book *Nile Perch* (2008), Barrie Rickards and Tim Baily report that:

> … any [fly] resembling tilapia fry are good, and tarpon flies have also proved to work well, especially with size 3/0 and 4/0 hooks. The range of pike flies now available seems to work well, but it is worth noting that the fly does not need to be big. Pikers tend to use flies up to 6in long, and whilst these do work with Nile perch quite well, you seem to get just as many takes on flies half that length – and the latter are much easier to cast, of course.

The most popular tourist's quarry species in the Amazonian rivers is the peacock bass. This comes in a variety of colours, from deep red to bright yellow to grey, with a distinct 'peacock eye' on its tail, and it takes the fly powerfully. Yet these rivers are full of a host of other predatory fish, including the toothy piranha and even toothier payara.

All these predatory fish will take bucktails and streamers (pp. 255–85), though many of those were devised for catching trout. But note: trout themselves are freshwater predators and, as many fishery biologists have pointed out, big trout would much rather eat a small fish than a tiny insect!

The following is therefore a selection of flies that freshwater predators will take. Add these to the streamers and bucktails already described. All these will also take saltwater predators (see p. 400), and many saltwater patterns, notably things like Clouser Minnows and Lefty's Deceivers, can be used to catch freshwater as well as saltwater fish.

Hooks for tying flies for freshwater predators: Strong wire, streamer hooks are ideal, in sizes 5/0 to 4. It is worth tying those that will be used for catching very large fish (pike, Nile perch, peacock bass) on stainless steel saltwater hooks as they are usually stronger than ordinary bronzed streamer hooks.

FLOATING FLIES

Many predatory fish cannot resist grabbing some semblance of life that is struggling about on the surface. This category includes 'poppers'.

Deer Hair Mouse

Thread: Black.
Tail and legs: Grey-buff wool.
Body: Natural deer hair, spun and clipped to mouse shape, with a nose of black deer hair.
Eyes: Any prominent artificial eyes.

Deer Hair Thing … Is It a Mouse? Is It a Frog?

Thread: Black.

Tail and two hind legs: Brown rabbit zonker strip.

Body: Deer hair, spun and clipped to shape. Use all brown or natural deer hair, or use a mix of colours.

These two flies are great for largemouth and smallmouth bass, pike, perch and even large trout. The great pleasure comes from creating these little mice or whatever; the same method can be used to produce Deer Hair Frogs. Cast them out, tweak them back ... Bang!

Deer Hair Popper

Thread: Black.

Tail: Barred olive blood marabou, plus a few strands red and pearl Flashabou.

Body: Deer hair, spun and clipped to shape. The example has bands of different coloured deer hair – olive, black, orange, olive, orange and natural – and it does work. But are the different colours essential? Probably not.

Deer Hair Popper

Thread: Black.

Tail: Four natural red (brown) cock hackles, flaring out.

Body: Deer hair, spun and clipped to shape.

Eyes: Any prominent artificial eyes.

Again, tie these in a range of colours, though colour may not matter as far as the fish are concerned. Of far more importance are the size of the fly and the way it is worked in the surface.

Dahlberg Diver (Modified Version)
Thread: Black.
Wing: A mix of hairs (synthetic or natural), flashy fibres (Crystal Hair, Crystal Flash, Flashabou etc.), saddle hackles and peacock herl.
Collar and head: Deer hair (see Note), with glued-on eyes.

Note: Tie these up in a wide range of lengths and colour variations. The example has a wing of (beginning at the base), pearl Crystal Hair, yellow and blue goat's hair, peacock herl at the top, and a few strands red Crystal Hair at the sides. What you are after is either a general small fish coloration (darker on the back, paler underneath) or a coloration that shows out in poor visibility (lots of orange, red or yellow). The deer hair is spun in small bunches along the hook shank and then trimmed to give a fairly narrow head leading back to a flared collar. Using plenty of clear head cement, use fingers and thumb to mould the collar into shape. When cast out, this sits on the water; when line is stripped back, it dives under, but will pop back to the surface when the retrieve is stopped.

Great for pike, peacock bass, largemouth and smallmouth bass, and in the salt for striped and sea bass, bluefish, false albacore and other species in fairly shallow water.

Polystyrene Popper

Thread: Black.

Tail: Bucktail. White and green, or olive and grey, or brown and chartreuse, or …

Butt: Fritz (a multi-thread strand incorporating flashy fibres that comes in a variety of shocking colours).

Body: Foam popper body, slipped over the eye of the hook and prevented in sliding further back by the Fritz butt. Self-adhesive flashy tape is stuck around the popper body, and eyes stuck on at the sides.

These are (2009) being commercially produced under the name, 'Bob's Banger'.

The teeth of a pike or the powerful (though toothless) jaws of a peacock bass can destroy a popper body as though it were a piece of overripe banana. When that happens, slide a new body over the hook shank. These are also outstanding in saltwater.

BALSA-BODIED POPPERS

Whilst carving and sanding popper bodies from very light, buoyant woods like balsa, it is far more convenient to purchase them; preformed balsa popper bodies come in a wide range of sizes, and it is simply a matter of fixing them to an appropriately sized hook using Superglue and then adding the rest of the fly. Such poppers are indispensable for both fresh- and saltwater predators.

The important feature of these – and all poppers – is the way they are fished, for a gentle approach (as may be essential when trying to catch a trout in a clear stream) is useless. From the first cast, and a splashing, eruptive retrieve, the aim is to let the fish 'feel', through the sensory system of the lateral lines, the fact that some commotion is occurring at the surface. You can see this in a clear Amazonian stream. Cast carefully from the boat to the edge of the tangle of stranded trees and other debris that lines the riverbank, retrieve gently and you will get little in the way of response. Now cast so that the fly lands with a splash at the surface, and pull so that the popper creates a right commotion and you will see the predators (peacock bass, mostly) emerging from cover. If the first cast doesn't catch, the second usually will.

The poppers illustrated are ideal for small to medium species such as largemouth and smallmouth bass, perch and small pike. The one on the left has a tail of black synthetic hairs, white rubber legs (to enhance movement) and a black balsa body with white eyes. The one on the right has a fluorescent lime wool tail, a black hackle wound as a 'skirt', rubber legs and a yellow balsa body with red eyes.

Sickly Sculpin

Thread: Olive or brown.
Tail and back: Mottle brown blood marabou.
Belly: Cream wool.
Rib: Oval gold tinsel.
Gills: Fluorescent red floss.
Pectoral fins: Woodcock upper wing cover (or speckled brown partridge).
Head: Deer hair, spun and clipped to shape.

This simple but highly mobile pattern can be tweaked in the surface to match a real sculpin (or miller's thumb) in its death throes. Note that the bulky dry marabou becomes slender when wet.

SINKING FLIES

Woolhead Minnow

Thread: Olive or brown.
'Tail and body': Brown or olive and white bucktail. This is tied in midway down the hook shank. The bunch of bucktail should not be too thick, for it is essential that each fibre should be able to move in the water. The white is tied in on top of the brown or olive and will simulate the belly of the fly, which swims with the hook point uppermost.
'Underhead': Lead or tungsten strip lashed to the top of the front half of the hook shank. This will weight the fly and make it fish with the hook point uppermost. Thus it is less likely to snag bottom.
Head: Wool; light olive or light brown on the lower side, dark on the upper.
Eyes: Lead dumb-bell tied in on top of hook shank, and painted white with black or red pupil.

Excellent for all small- to medium-sized predators, but dressed on 4/0 and 5/0 hooks will take the biggest.

Hackle Streamers

Thread: See below.

'Wing': Up to 8 long hackles, tied on either side of the hook shank, with a bunch of silver or pearl Crystal Hair or Flashabou in the middle.

Use a neutral-coloured thread or a bright fluorescent one to give extra flash. Grizzle or white cock dyed yellow, pink or chartreuse are useful colours. Three are illustrated, the middle one showing the effect of one bite by an unknown Amazonian set of teeth!

Weighted Eye Streamers

Thread: Bright red, pink or yellow.
Eyes: Heavy silver dumb-bell, tied on top of hook shank.
'Wing': Up to 8 long hackles, tied on either side of the hook shank, with a bunch of similarly coloured bucktail.

Great for pike, Nile perch, peacock bass etc. Tie in a range of colours and sizes.

Marabou Hackle Streamers

Thread: Grey, cream or tan.
'Wing': Blood marabou, tied in and wound as a hackle, with 2 or 4 strands silver or pearl Crystal Hair.
Eyes: Stick-on (optional).

A Jack Gartside idea that is so easy! Use a comb to encourage the marabou fibres to radiate around the hook. You can use one or several colours of marabou. Alternatively, one or two colours of blood marabou (yellow and orange in the illustrated example) and then, in front, a wound bronze mallard feather. These flies really move when pulled back, and are great for largemouth and smallmouth bass, 'jack' pike and perch.

Mylar Tube Fry

Thread: Black.
Body: Silver Mylar tube.
Belly: Soft white hair (arctic fox or Icelandic pony).
Back: Soft hair (arctic fox or Icelandic pony) in purple, olive, grey, warm brown.

Elver

Thread: Black.
Body: Wide oval silver tinsel.
Rib: Wide oval silver tinsel.
Back and tail: Black rabbit zonker strip.
'Hackle': Few fibres pearl or silver Crystal Hair.
Head: Black deer hair, spun and clipped.
Eyes: 'Stick-on', prominent.

Pike love to eat eels. This is understandable for, despite their sliminess, eels are rich in protein and oils. Fish in slow pulls on a sinking line close to the bottom of canals, slow river pools or lake margins.

PIKE STREAMERS

Fly fishing for pike is very popular in Finland (an across much of southern Scandinavia and the Low Countries). One type of streamer has been developed in Finland in which the fly is dressed on flexible tubing. The leader is threaded through this tubing, a hook tied to the end of the leader, and the hook fixed in place by pushing the eye into the rear of the tube.

The dressing is based on long synthetic hair, which is coloured with permanent markers as desired. The head is of clear epoxy, with an eye fixed underneath.

Because the hair and tubes used in the dressing are so relatively light, this style of fly is easy to cast on a #9–10 rod, and because the structure is so flexible (compared with a rigid long-shank hook) the hook does not easily lever out of a pike's jaw.

Besides pike, these large flies can also be used to catch a wide variety of predators, including saltwater species (use a stainless steel hook).

Note tube arrangement.

Fly-fishing for pike is very popular throughout the Low Countries, in reed-lined lakes and meandering canals. The following originate in the Netherlands and are great for all large freshwater predators.

Pike Flies

Hook: Plastic tube up to 2½ inches long. A single or treble hook is fixed at the end of this when fishing.

Wing: 2–4 inch length of rabbit zonker strip tied at end of tube, then 6–8 long cock saddle hackles tied so that they flare outwards to add mobility to the fly, and a bunch of bucktail and pearl Crystal Hair/ Krystal Flash.

Collar: Mix of long coloured bucktail, with shorter bucktail in front.

Total length: 6–8 inches.

These flies are a mix of colours: orange or white zonker, grizzle hackles dyed yellow or white hackles dyed yellow or orange, and bucktail dyed yellow, orange, pink and black. No pike could overlook one of these, fished through its lair!

CLOUSER DEEP MINNOW VARIANTS

(For Bob Clouser's Deep Minnows for salt water, see p. 408.)

The following two patterns are useful for catching pike, Nile perch and peacock bass, especially when tied in large sizes or length (4–5 inches). As in all Clousers, the eyes are lashed to the underside of the shank so that the hook fishes point-up and therefore avoids snags.

Green and White Clouser
Thread: Blue or green.
Belly: White bucktail.
Back: Green bucktail, plus a few strands green Flashabou.

Blue and White Clouser

Thread: Blue or green.
Belly: White bucktail or synthetic hair.
Back: Blue Crystal Hair.

MP Flies

MP stands for 'modular predator' or for Marc Petitjean who came up with this splendid idea. Several hooks are taken, in a wide range of sizes, and clips are whipped to the tip of the shank, with the end of the clip just behind the end of the hook bend. Now you dress the hook with whatever streamer-type dressing you like. In the illustrated examples, the dressing included cul de canard, Crystal Hair and Fritz, but soft hair (such as arctic fox) or marabou are also ideal. Several of these dressed hooks, or modules, can be clipped together to give different lengths of fly, in the illustrated version, three hooks of decreasing length, with a terminal module dressed on a short piece of wire. Note that by decreasing module size the overall fly is more likely to land straight, with each module in line, than when all modules are of the same size.

In some places it is illegal to fish more than one hook. There have a modular arrangement, but with only the front module tied on a hook, the rest to lengths of wire (such as hook shanks, with the bend and point of the fly cut away).

Weed guards: Note that the illustrated examples have also been fitted with a 'weed guard'. This consists of two lengths of very thick monofilament fishing-line tied in just behind the head and at the bend of the hook, with its curve extending a fraction beyond the hook point. This deflects any weed and prevents snagging, but when the powerful predator jaws close on the fly the weed guard is forced out of the way. Weed guards are easily fitted to most streamers, bucktails, and to fresh- and saltwater predator flies, and it is well worth carrying some flies with them fitted. Remember that some of the biggest predators live in a jungle of weed and other debris and that if you are to catch them, your fly must not get caught up.

Arctic Fox Sculpin

Hook: 2/0–8.
Thread: Black.
Tail: Two colours of arctic fox tied in three bunches (see Note) plus a few strands pearl Crystal Hair.
Body: Flat or embossed gold or silver tinsel.

Back (or wing): Bunch arctic fox (see Note).
'Hackle': Bunch arctic fox (see Note).
Head: Arctic fox stacked and trimmed, with yellow and black eyes.
Note: In the left-hand example, the tail is of orange and brown arctic fox, the back brown, and the hackle orange and the head brown arctic fox trimmed to shape. In the right-hand example, the tail is of green and black arctic fox, the back green, the hackle black and the head is a mix of stacked and trimmed green and black arctic fox.

Great for small- to medium-sized predators such as perch, largemouth and smallmouth bass, large trout, small pike etc.

Chenille Sculpin

Hook: Short-shank wet fly, sizes 1/0–6.
Thread: As tail.
Tail: Four layers – olive, brown, olive, brown – of a soft natural hair such as Icelandic pony or goat or (in small sizes) arctic fox.
Pectoral fins: Bunches of mottled brown blood marabou.
Body/head: Green-olive and brown chenille, with yellow and black eyes.
Especially useful for catching large trout in big rivers.

Perch Fry

Hook: Wide gape streamer, sizes 1/0–4.
Thread: Green.
Tail (in fact, the majority of the perch's body): 2 pairs olive hackles with black vertical bars added with felt-tip pen.
Body: Olive chenille.

'Hackle': Olive bucktail, plus few fibres pearl Flashabou.
Back: Olive bucktail, with few peacock herls over. Note that the bucktail in both hackle and back as marked similarly to the olive hackles making up the tail.
Eyes: White with black pupils, prominent.

Perch are abundant fish especially in temperate lakes in both Europe and North America. They spawn in early spring, and from the time that their fry hatch a few weeks later perch fry are favourite bait-fish for species like trout, walleye, zander, ide and smaller pike. As they grow, so the provide food for larger predators. Perch are extremely good to eat, and not only for predatory fish. They can be caught on fly (small fancy wet flies and streamers are good) and fried they taste delicious. In the Second World War they were canned in England and sold under the brand name, 'Perchines'!

Mudeye

Hook: Streamer, sizes 2–6.
Thread: Black or brown.
Wing and body: Dull medium brown soft fur (e.g. arctic fox), tied around hook shank and clipped to shape.
Head: As body, but small and round, with black burnt mono or tiny bead eyes.

Mudeyes are small sculpin-like fish found in Australia. This pattern also works well in northern rivers, where trout are feeding on sculpins and loaches.

Saltwater Flies

> I think that the most important yet rarely discussed feature of a fly is its castability.
>
> Lefty Kreh, *Fly Fishing in Salt Water*, 1986.

Only twice, thus far, has reference been made to a fly design that has inbuilt problems when it comes to casting: the fan-winged style of dry fly (p. 178) and the cut-winged dry fly when badly tied, with the wings too far apart (p. 158). It was also noted that one of the virtues of cul de canard in dry flies is the way that CDC collapses in the cast, thus aiding in the streamlining of the fly during the cast (see p. 164). Generally, most trout and salmon flies are easy to cast, provided that a reasonable rod and line rating is used. However, in fishing saltwater, it is absolutely essential that the fly is easy to cast. This is partly because the flies being used are often huge in comparison with trout and salmon flies, and partly because when saltwater fly-fishing the wind is almost always blowing and the flies have to be cast into or across a stiff breeze. It is for this reason why the great saltwater fly-fishers – people like Ed Jaworowski, Lefty Kreh and Bob Popovics – place great emphasis on the ability to cast well, in all weather conditions.

Most saltwater fish have a feeding depth that may vary through the day or according to the depth of water, and they are often reluctant to move up or down from this depth to take our artificial flies. For instance, a permit or bonefish may be feeding on crabs or shrimps close to or on the bottom, and it will not rise higher to take our fly. So our fly must sink quickly to the bottom. But the water may be almost still and two feet deep, or it may be four feet deep with a distinct current. So it follows that we need to have the same patterns of flies with different sinking rates if we are to tackle both types of water. Similarly, when fishing the flooding tide in an estuary, an unweighted sand-eel imitation may be fine just as the tide begins its flood, but half an hour later as it rushes in with a loud hissing noise, a heavily weighted fly may be essential to get down to where the fish are hunting real sand-eels, just above the sandbanks. So, besides being castable, the fly should be appropriately sinkable … most flies should be tied in at least two weights, or sinking-rates.

Weight may be added in several ways. One is by using lightweight hooks and heavyweight hooks. Lead wire (or other heavy wires or foils such as tungsten) may be wrapped around the hook shank; to hinder the rapid oxidization of lead, after creating the heavy underbody, give the thing a couple of coats of clear tying cement. But probably the best way of weighting a saltwater fly is by the use of heavy eyes. For lightweight versions, simply glue cut-out or peel-off eyes onto the thread head. For heavier versions, use bead-chain, lead, brass, stainless steel or tungsten dumb-bell eyes, lashing these firmly down behind the hook eye. Note that this is the key to success in Bob Clouser's Minnow (p. 408), where the eyes lashed on top of the hook shank tend to make the fly swim upside-down (i.e. point-upwards), reducing the chance of snagging the bottom.

Most of the species of saltwater fish sought by saltwater fly-fishers are dedicated piscivores. They eat other, lesser fish. And provided the artificial fly is at their depth and is roughly the size of the fish they are eating, they don't seem to worry too much about the finer points of fly-tying. In fact, sometimes their feeding-frenzy doesn't give them time to examine carefully the real fry and the fry imitation. Stand on a beach in New Jersey or on Martha's Vineyard when the striped bass and bluefish are in. A narrow darker band stretches in the shallows along the water's edge, with the blue-green beyond. That narrow band is a mass of bait-fish, keeping as close to shore and in as shallow water as possible. Suddenly the water erupts as a school of big predators arrives, chomping its way through the shallows. The little fish try to avoid getting eaten by jumping out of the water. Some may land high-and-dry on the beach where waiting gulls, who have seen this all too often, stroll slowly along, gathering the dying morsels. Put any fry imitation, between four and six inches long, in front of one of these feeding fish and you will get a tremendous strike. So the third point to consider when choosing a fly for catching fish that are eating smaller fish is the length of the fly. And it should roughly match the length of the bait-fish being eaten. There are exceptions …

Bonefish are bottom feeders (their underslung mouth indicates this) and they love to eat shrimps. So the most effective bonefish flies are either imitations of or suggestions of shrimps. Permit, perhaps the most difficult of the fly-fisher's fishes to catch on a fly, love to eat crabs that are on or close to the bottom. So the most effective permit flies are either imitations of or suggestions of crabs. Sometimes other species of saltwater fish may *appear* to be feeding selectively on shrimps or crabs, simply because shrimps or crabs are so abundant. For instance, in one English estuary, the sea bass and sea trout feed on brown shrimps over the shallow sandbanks and on crabs in the deeper, silt-bottomed shipping channel. Here shrimp or crab imitations are *sometimes* more effective than bait-fish imitations.

Mullet are another exception for, despite the size they can attain (in excess of 10 lbs), their main foods are particles.

MULLET AND THE FLIES TO CATCH THEM

From the base of the cliff of Europa Point, the southernmost tip of Gibraltar is (or at least *was* in 1998) the biggest raw sewage outfall imaginable. From here a huge brown stream meanders into the Strait, towards the continent of Africa. And on either side of this pollution are millions of mullet, their mouths sucking down this noxious soup.

Once a dead cow became stranded in two feet of water and there, over many tides, its carcase slowly rotted. At every high tide, mullet came to suck down bits of rotting flesh (and perhaps some washed-out maggots).

For particle-feeding mullet, soft-hackled spider wet flies (pp. 45–54) are ideal in shallower water up to three feet in depth, tied on size 14–16 wet fly hooks. Successful patterns include ORANGE PARTRIDGE, YELLOW PARTRIDGE, WATERHEN BLOA, DARK NEEDLE. For deeper water (as in harbours), KILLER BUG (p. 119) and HARE'S EAR GOLDHEAD (p. 57) are useful, again in sizes 14–16. Note that fine tippets must be used when fishing these small flies, and that 3–5 lb mullet make tremendous runs on being hooked. So either treat the fish gently or use some power-gum in the leader to prevent the tippet shattering.

Stable estuary sandflats often are covered with growths of fine, filamentous green algae, and as the tide floods the flats, fragments of algae are broken off and drift out on the ebb. David Burnett was fishing the Cumbrian Esk for sea trout but the river was low and there had been no run of fish. So he went to the estuary and there watched mullet taking tiny particles of alga. He tied some ALGA FLIES, returned to the estuary and caught mullet, including one weighing 7 lb.

ALGA FLY

Hook: Wet fly, size 14.
Thread: Green.
Alga: A short length of green wool.

Mullet are opportunistic feeders, in that they will take any small item of food that appears in or on the water. They will frequently take land-bred flies that have been blown of coastal pastures. Then they can be taken on dry flies, such as LA PETITE MERDE (p. 205) and BLACK GNATS (p. 216) in sizes 14–16.

Mullet are reputedly difficult to catch on fly, and many fly-fishers have quickly grown frustrated as they cast and cast and cast to feeding fish only a few yards away. The clue is to fish tiny flies at the depth the mullet are feeding, and to fish the fly very slowly (allow the current to work the fly). To catch a big mullet in this way is as rewarding as catching a permit on fly!

Another way of catching mullet is with the bread-imitating fly, Mother's Pride. This was invented for catching trout that were rising to take bread thrown into a stretch of river by picnickers; it also would have caught ducks that were also feeding on the hatch of bread if the fly had not been pulled away when the ducks tried to grab it! Perfect imitation.

MOTHER'S PRIDE

Hook: Dry fly, sizes 14–16.
Thread: White.
Body: White deer hair, spun muddler-fashion and then trimmed to 'piece-of-bread' shape. Note that some purists add a little brown deer hair at the front to match the bread crust.

Throw a slice of bread onto the water. Mullet will appear from nowhere and begin to suck down the soggy mass. Cast Mother's Pride alongside the bread and a mullet is bound to suck it down!

FLIES THAT IMITATE BAIT-FISH

Tie these on a range of hook sizes (stainless steel or coated saltwater resistant) and in lengths that will match any bait-fish your predator might try to eat. Several of the 'flies' described are really styles or series of flies, so that colour may be varied to match bait-fish or whim of the fly-fisher. Sometimes even materials may be changed, for instance, a bunch of white bucktail instead of long white hackles in a wing. It is important to note that all these bait-fish imitations are also excellent flies for catching freshwater predators, such as pike, Nile perch and peacock bass. It is just that they are best known as saltwater flies and were invented for catching saltwater fish.

Note that these often include synthetic materials, which may or may not be readily available. These include 'flash', strands of material that includes Crystal Hair, Krystal Flash, Flashabou, Mylar and so on. Natural hairs are frequently used, but often synthetic hair used instead, such as FisHair and UltraHair. Use what is available *to you* remembering that fish have no materials catalogues to check your tying before deciding whether or not to grab hold!

Joe Brooks was, with Stue Apte, Dan Blanton, Chico Fernandez, Lefty Kreh and Billy Pate, one of the great pioneers of modern saltwater fly-fishing. He passed on to the great heavenly ocean in 1974. His Blonde series is as simple a set of bait-fish imitations that you might tie; they are still very effective.

Argentine Blonde

Hook: Standard shank, sizes 4/0–6.
Thread: Black.
Tail: White bucktail.
Body: Flat silver tinsel (Mylar).
Wing: Blue bucktail.
Note: The tip of the wing should extend back to the tip of the tail.

Vary the colour of the wing, for example chartreuse, yellow, olive and black are all useful. Today we might also add a few strands of twinkle, such as Crystal Hair. The Platinum Blonde has a white wing.

Lefty Kreh has, perhaps, had more impact on the saltwater fly-fishing scene than any other person. He is also an outstanding caster and catcher of freshwater fish. His book *Fly Fishing in Salt Water* was first published in 1974 and is still in print. His fly, the DECEIVER, is famed around the world. In his book he tells us that: 'I designed it so that it would resemble the shape and size of various swimming baitfish, but when lifted from the water it offers a sleek missile that casts easily.'

Lefty's Deceiver

Hook: Standard shank, sizes 7/0–6.
Thread: White.
Wing (tied at end hook shank): 2 pairs white saddle hackles, on either side of a bunch of white bucktail, and with about 6 strands silver Mylar each side.
Body: None.
Collar: White bucktail, long.

This great bait-fish pattern is now tied in a wide range of colours. For instance, Ed Jaworowski's tying has a collar of black bucktail dorsally, olive bucktail at the sides and has a throat of red Mylar tinsel (*top opposite*). Another tying has a wing of white bucktail, lacking the saddle hackles, and has black and silver stick-on eyes (*opposite*). A third variant has a wing of olive saddle hackles and several strands of olive Crystal Hair, a collar of olive bucktail and yellow and black stick-on eyes (not shown).

Slimey Mack Deceivers
Thread: White.
Wing (tied at end hook shank): 2 pairs white saddle hackles on either side of several strands pearl Crystal Hair.
Body: None.
Collar: White bucktail with a topping of one pair grizzle hackles dyed blue and one pair dyed green.
Head: Silicone, with either stick on eyes (lightweight) or chrome bead eyes (heavyweight).

This gives two weights of flies based of the different eyes. Again, vary length/hook size and colour to match various bait-fish.

Bob Clouser devised what is perhaps now the most-used bait-fish imitation, the Clouser Minnow. By using a range of weights of eyes the fly sinks quickly to the required depth. By lashing the eyes to the top of the hook shank the fly fishes point-up so that there is less chance of the fly snagging on a rocky or weedy bottom. By tying Bob's fly in a range of lengths (and hook sizes) and in a range of colours, all potential bait-fish, both in the sea and in fresh water, can be imitated. The basic tying is as follows:

Clouser Minnow

Hook: Any saltwater fly hook.

Eyes: A pair of dumb-bell eyes securely lashed to the top of the hook shank well back from the eye.

Wing: Darker bucktail over pearl Crystal Hair/Krystal Flash over white bucktail (note that the fly is tied upside-down, with point uppermost).

Colour of darker bucktail: Chartreuse (most essential), olive, green, blue, grey, yellow, orange (least essential). Four variations shown below have olive bucktail wing (top left), synthetic hair wing (top right), and a mix of synthetic hairs plus very heavy eyes for very deep water (above left) and, tied by Ed Jaworowski, perhaps the most useful colour combination, chartreuse and yellow (above right).

Many recent flies have incorporated heavy eyes and fixed them on the top of the hook as in the Clouser Minnow. For example, the Half-And-Half. Also by Bob Clouser, this includes the eyes and part of the wing from his Minnow with a heavily dressed wing of a Lefty's Deceiver.

Half-And-Half

Thread: White.

'Tail' Wing (tied at end hook shank): 12 white saddle hackles, with several strands silver Flashabou on either side. This will be the belly of the bait-fish imitation.

Body: None.
Eyes: Tied on top of shank.
'Front' wing: Olive bucktail with a topping of red bucktail, tied under hook shank so that, with the fly swimming upside-down, it is on top when fishing and is the back of the bait-fish imitation.

Again, vary the colour and length of the fly: brown back, olive belly; olive back, yellow belly; chartreuse back, white belly; olive or brown back, chartreuse belly; blue back, white belly; and so on.

Bob Popovics has become a major name in the world of saltwater fly-fishing. He lives on the shores of New Jersey and fishes mostly his home waters of the coast there, and north to Cape Cod and Martha's Vineyard for striped bass, bluefish and false albacore. Bob's Surf Candy is one of the best bait-fish/fry imitations.

Surf Candy

Hook: Standard shank, sizes 3/0–4.
Thread: Finest white or transparent.
Underbody: Flat silver Mylar tinsel.
Body and wing: UltraHair or similar fine synthetic hair with a touch of flash. Underneath smoke or pale grey UltraHair, top (back of fly) green UltraHair; about 8 strands of 'flash' (e.g. pearl Crystal Hair) are tied on either side.

The head and front of the fly are coated with 5-minute clear epoxy and, as this is nearly set, body/wing are pulled back to give a slender head. When this first epoxy coat is fully dry, silver and black stick-on eyes are fixed in place, and a bright red permanent felt-tip used to mark gill openings. The fly is then given at least two more thin coats of clear epoxy. If tying several of these (or other flies with epoxy coats) it is worth investing in a rotating machine that will prevent the epoxy running.

Other colours should be tied: with backs of grey, chartreuse, olive, green.

Ed Jaworowski has provided a variant:

SURF CANDY (JAWOROWSKI)
Hook: Short shank, sizes 3/0–4.
Thread: Transparent.
Body: Pearl Mylar tube with the tip of a grizzle hackle epoxied in place as tail fin. Around this UltraHair, tan dorsally, white ventrally. The head and front of body are epoxied (see above).

Again, tie in a range of lengths and colours.

The DEEP CANDY is tied as above, but with a very heavy silver/chrome head. The SCHOOLIE consists of two small CANDIES, tied on a keel-hook.

DEEP CANDY

Schoolie

Gibb's Striper

Hook: Standard shank, sizes 3/0–4.
Thread: White.
Body: Flat silver Mylar tinsel.
Throat: Red Flashabou or Crystal Hair/Krystal Flash or red hackle fibres.
Wing: White bucktail with a band of blue bucktail in the centre.
Sides: Jungle cock.

The use of jungle cock to suggest eyes in this fly indicates that it is an old pattern. It was devised by Harold Gibbs in the late 1940s for catching striped bass off Rhode Island.

Rattle Rouser

Hook: 1/0 or larger (to accommodate the 15 mm rattle).

Thread: Black.

Body: A plastic rattle is lashed beneath the hook shank and pearl Mylar tube pulled over. This is then coated with a thin coat of quick-drying epoxy.

Wing: Bucktail – white under cerise, blue, olive or tan, or yellow under chartreuse. Also incorporated a few strands of 'flash' (e.g. pearl Crystal Hair) and a topping of peacock herl.

Head: With stick-on eyes.

Invented by John Cave, this is more effective than other, silent patterns in cloudy water of estuaries. Specialist suppliers of tying materials can provide the tiny rattles that, of course, may be added to any large bait-fish fly for both fresh- and saltwater.

Antron Fry

Hook: Saltwater long shank, 3/0–4.

Thread: White or black.

Body: None.

Wing: Antron or similar synthetic yarn. Top, blue or green Antron, bottom white Antron with a few strands of pearl or silver 'flash' (e.g. Crystal Hair).

Head: With stick-on eyes – coated with clear epoxy.

This is a very simply yet effective bait-fish imitation.

White Hi-Tie

Hook: To match the length of bait-fish being imitated, size usually in the range 4/0–1.

Thread: White.

Wing: Small bunches of white bucktail and pearl 'flash' tied in on top of the hook shank as the thread is being wound in touching turns from end of shank back to eye.

One great problem with having a long, soft, mobile wing tied at the front of the hook is that the wing often gets twisted and trapped in the hook bend. This problem is overcome with wings tied at the end of the shank (as in Deceivers and Keys-style tarpon flies) or by tying the wing Hi-Tie style.

Hi-Ties can also be dressed upside-down (with the point of the hook upwards when the fly is being fished). Simply tie the wing bunches in under the shank of the hook.

Other useful colours include yellow thread with a chartreuse wing, red thread with a white wing and white thread with a blue wing.

Sand-eels are very important bait-fish and the previous patterns, tied slender and long, can be used to match them. However, the following flies are more precise imitations.

Basic Sand-Eel

Hook: Saltwater streamer, sizes 2/0–4.
Thread: Transparent.
Body: Olive over white bucktail, tied long and slender. Coat the front part and head with clear epoxy and, when dry, add eyes before giving it a second coat of epoxy.

This is as simple as it comes, but this has caught stripers and bluefish on Martha's Vineyard and sea trout and sea bass in the estuaries of western Ireland. Add a few strands of 'flash if you like.

Flashy Sand-Eel

Hook: Saltwater streamer, sizes 2/0–4.
Thread: White or transparent.
Body: Underside, white bucktail. Middle and sides, mix of silver, green and gold 'flash' (e.g. Crystal Hair or Fashabou). Top (back), blue flash. Epoxy front and add stick-on eyes and red gill openings before adding final coat of epoxy.

Sand-Eel (Eric Peterson)
Hook: Saltwater streamer, sizes 2/0–4.
Thread: White.
Wing: FisHair or UltraHair, tan over white, with a few strands of pearl 'flash'.
Body: Pearl Mylar overwound with clear 15 lb BS monofilament.
Head: With stick-on eyes.

Sand-Eel
Hook: Saltwater streamer, sizes 2/0–4.
Thread: White.
Wing: White bucktail, with a few strands of pearl 'flash'.

Body: Pearl Mylar tube over a foundation of tying thread.
Head: With stick-on eyes and a very thin coat of clear epoxy.

Jack Gartside had devised many flies for freshwater fishing, such as his HOPPER (p. 223). His three sand-eel imitations are based on a synthetic tube called Corsair.

GARTSIDES'S SAND-EEL

Hook: Saltwater Streamer, Sizes 2/0–1.
Thread: White.
Body: Length of Corsair tube, the end of which is teased apart to create a tail. The tube is then coloured as required with permanent felt-tip pens.

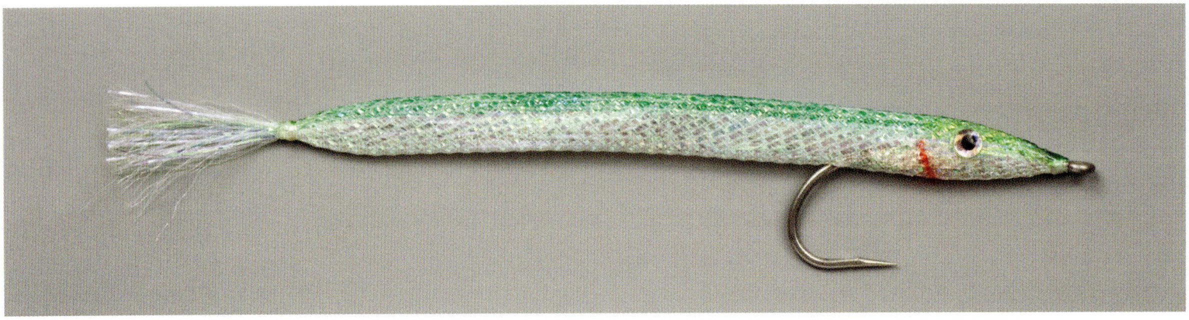

GARTSIDE'S FLOATING SAND-EEL is tied in exactly the same way, but has a slither of dense foam inserted into the tube.

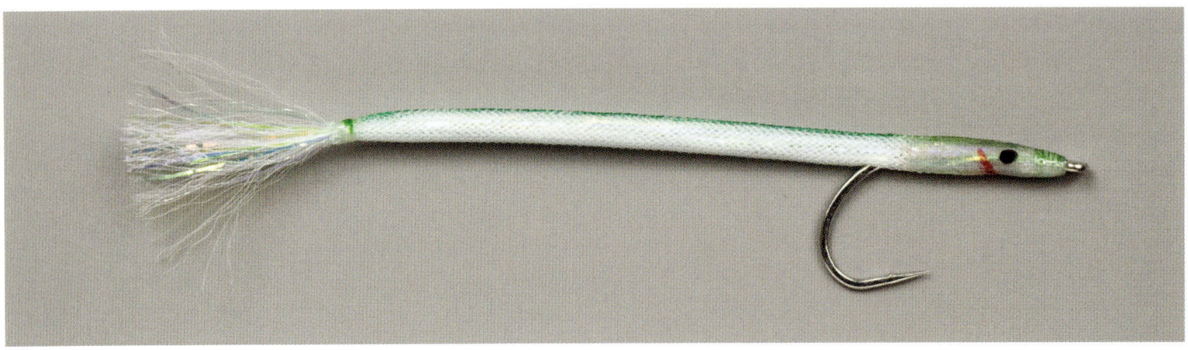

GARTSIDE'S BLACK SAND-EEL has an underbody of silver Corsair tube and an overbody of black Corsair tube. Jack devised this for night fishing for inshore species like striped bass, the idea being that it gives a strong silhouette.

Reverse-Tied bucktail

Hook: Standard shank, sizes 1/0–6.
Thread: White.
Wing: Both top and bottom (back and belly of the bait-fish fly) are white bucktail, the middle blue and pearl 'flash' (e.g. Crystal Hair). These are all tied with the tips forward, extending far in front of the eye of the hook. Then pull these back into their final resting position, and lash them down to create a head. Give the head a couple of coats of clear epoxy, adding eyes before the last coat.

This is a modernisation of a much older style developed for trout fishing by Carrie Stevens and then Keith Fulscher in the Thundercreek Series (see p. 278). Again, tie in a range of sizes and colours, especially the hair used for the back.

Mylar Tube Sand-Eel

Hook: Standard shank or streamer, sizes 4/0–1.
Thread: Green.
Wing: Olive bucktail and strands from body material.
Body: Mylar tube – reflective green/olive, with red markings added for gill openings and stick-on eyes. After adding eyes, give a coat of clear epoxy.

Mylar Tube Sand-Eel

Hook: Standard shank or streamer, sizes 4/0–1.
Thread: White.
Body: Silver Mylar tube with core left in. The end of the tube is teased out to give a silvery tail. Add eyes at the head and coat with clear epoxy.

Anchovies and sardines are amongst many small bait-fish that are eagerly gulped down by big predators.

Electric Anchovy

Hook: Short shank, sizes 1/0–4.
Thread: White or transparent.
Body: Embossed silver Mylar tinsel.
Wing: A 'belly' of white bucktail is tied in under the hook shank. The back and sides are tied above the belly
Belly: White bucktail and pearl 'flash', with yellow bucktail over, then red bucktail, then light blue bucktail and finally the back of deep blue bucktail.
Head: With silver and black eyes, and a coat of clear epoxy.

The very many species of tiny bait-fish are often clumped under the heading of 'whitebait'. This may include the fry of, for example, herring, sprat and pilchard. It also includes some species with very small adults, for example, glass minnows.

Olive and White Glass Minnow

Hook: Standard shank, sizes 2/0–4.
Thread: White.
Underbody: Flat silver Mylar tinsel.
Body: Clear 15 lb BS monofilament.
Wing: Olive bucktail with a few strands of olive 'flash' (Crystal Hair).
Head: With silver-and-black eye and a layer of clear epoxy.

Also useful is a **Grey And White Glass Minnow** with a wing of pearl Crystal Hair and grey bucktail.

Tasmanian Whitebait (White-Wing) [a]
Hook: Standard shank, sizes 4–8.
Thread: White.
Body: Pearl Mylar tinsel over tying thread.
Wing: White polar bear or similar, with a few strands pearl Crystal Hair.
Head: With silver and black eye and a layer of clear epoxy.

A

Useful alternatives have an **Olive-Wing [b]** and a **Grey-Wing [c]**.

B

C

Jenner's Irish Whitebait

Terry Jenner produced a variant of the Tasmanian Whitebait for catching sea bass in Irish bays and estuaries. It has a Microbrite body (use pearl Flashabou or Crystal Hair as alternative) and an olive arctic fox wing.

Bob Popovics devised the Jiggy for use in snaggy water. It fishes upside-down (hook point uppermost) and the hook point is masked by the wing, so it can be fished through (light) weed. Vary size and colours. Note that the fly should be fixed to the leader with a loop-knot to give greater movement.

Jiggy

Hook: Streamer, with shank bent to 'bend-back' style, sizes 2/0–2.
Thread: Clear monofilament.
Head: Heavy bead – silver, red, gold, orange, brass.
Wing: Bunches of white and brown bucktail, with pearl and silver 'flash'.
Eyes: Stick-on, covered with clear epoxy.

To bend the hook, take a pair of snipe-nosed pliers and bend the shank midway on the opposite side to the hook bend and point as shown.

Australian Chris Beech came up with a similar fly, the Jiggy Habit. This has a pearl Sparkle Braid Body (use embossed silver Mylar tinsel if Braid Body unavailable).

Tunnel Fly

Hook: Streamer, sizes 4/0–2/0.
Thread: Clear monofilament.
Tunnel: A length of clear plastic tube lashed on top of hook shank and fixed in place with epoxy.

Wing: White Krystal Flash, then pearl Sparkle Flash or Crystal Hair, then pearl Gliss 'N' Glow, then, on top, grey (smoke) Super Hair.
Eyes: Silver and black, covered with a coat of clear epoxy.

A fly by Ken Culgin of New South Wales, the idea being that, as the fly is pulled back through the water, water gurgles through the 'tunnel', adding an extra attraction. Catches a wide range of predators, including barracuda, jacks and golden and giant trevally. The wing may provide problems in that some or all of the synthetics may not be available. Use substitutes, including the very available bucktail. This idea of having a tube tied on top of the hook shank to make some kind of noise as the fly is retrieved could be adopted by all large flies for fresh- and saltwater fishing.

Pink Thing

Hook: Streamer, sizes 4/0–1.
Thread: Orange.
Eyes: Bead chain, fixed in place before the rest of the fly is tied.
Wing: White bucktail, with a few strands of copper 'flash', and, on each side, a grizzle hackle.
Collar: Pink marabou.

An Australian pattern tied by Prof. Chris Paris.

Bead chain eyes are popular is saltwater flies for, besides helping the fly to sink, it is said that as the water flows past them they emit a whistling sound that the fish may detect. This feature led to Dan Blanton devising his Whistler.

Whistler

Hook: Standard shank, sizes 4/0–2 (the fly should by up to 6 inches long).
Thread: Red.
Wing (tail): White bucktail, silver 'flash' and grizzle hackles, tied long and mobile.
Body: red wool or fur dubbing.
Collar: Dyed red or white saddle hackle.
Eyes: Bead chain.

Seaducer

Hook: Standard shank, sizes 4/0–1/0.
Thread: Flat white or clear monofilament.
Wing: Saddle hackles tied in long and flaring out for extra movement, plus a few strands of 'flash'.

Hackle: Cock or saddle, palmered in touching turns along the hook shank.

This is a fairly old fly, but still a great catcher of fish. Useful in lengths 4–6 inches. Colours: red and white, chartreuse and yellow, black and purple, brown and olive.

Balao

Hook: Short shank or circle hooks, sizes 7/0–1/0.
Thread: Flat white or clear monofilament.
Wing: Several bunches of long white, pearl, pale grey or palest pink FisHair or similar crimped synthetic hair, plus a few strands of 'flash'.

These bunches are tied on top of each other to give depth to the body of the fly and not width. On top of these, a back of blue or medium olive or green hairs.

Head: With large black and white (or silver) eyes, fixed in place with two layers of clear epoxy.

Bream Weaver

Hook: Streamer, sizes 4/0–2.

Thread: White.

Wing: White bucktail, with strands of silver and pearl 'flash' (Mylar, Crystal Hair, Flashabou etc.).

Underbody: White acrylic yarn, built up to shape. Colour blue along back.

Overbody: Wide silver Mylar tube brought over the body so that the Mylar mesh opens up to suggest silver scaling and reveals the underbody.

Eyes: Stick-on silver and black, with a smear of clear epoxy.

An attractive style of bait-fish imitation by Bruce Porter. The underbody may be variously coloured.

Bend-Backs

Hook: Streamer, 4/0–1. Bent midway down shank as in Jiggy (see p. 423).

Thread: Black.

Body: Chenille.

Wing: Pairs of hackles or bunch of bucktail, with a few fibres of 'flash', and with (optional) a few fibres peacock herl over.

Head: Black with a painted eye (optional).

Bend-Backs fish upside-down, so they are useful in shallow, snaggy-bottomed water.

Streaker

Hook: Standard or streamer, sizes 3/0–2.

Thread: Orange.

Wing: 8 strands of silver Flashabou; outside them a pair of grizzle saddle hackles. On top and sides a pair of peacock swords, and under peacock swords a sparse bunch of yellow bucktail.

Body: Orange thread with black and white eyes. Several thin coats of clear tying cement or epoxy over.

Other body colours are useful (olive, grey, chartreuse etc.). Also tie with different weights of eyes for different water depths. This is a good barracuda fly.

Braided FisHair Needlefish Fly

Hook: Standard shank, sizes 3/0–1/0.
Thread: Lime-green.
Wing/body: Braided strands of FisHair (or similar long synthetic hair); dark olive and green; alternatively red and white, orange and white, chartreuse and yellow.
Head: FisHair from body, with large eyes; coat with clear epoxy.

A good barracuda fly. Beware of using brightly coloured fly-lines in 'cuda infested waters. They will grab the fly-line ('thinking' that it is a huge needlefish) and cut it to shreds.

TARPON FLIES

Many tarpon flies are dressed 'Keys style', with the dressing at the end of the hook shank and with either the shank bare or covered with wrappings of tying thread coated with clear epoxy. Keys, of course, means the Florida Keys. These two types are illustrated with the first fly, the Cockroach.

Hooks for tarpon flies: Tarpon are very big fish that put an immense amount of strain on the entire fishing rig, from rod and reel, through line and leader, to the hook. Some very strong hooks have been designed with tarpon in mind. The thickness of the wire in these hooks does hinder hook penetration, so it is essential to flatten the barb completely and to use a fine file to make the point needle-sharp. Also, when a big tarpon does take, strike hard to set the hook because its jaws are seemingly steel-plated! Size 4/0–2/0.

Cockroach

Thread: Black.
Wing: 6–8 grizzle saddle hackles, flaring out.
Collar: Dark brown or black bear.

Bare-shanked (above left); covered shank (above right).

Black Death

Thread: Black.
Wing: 4–6 red saddle hackles, flaring out.
Collar: Black marabou.

Bushy's Bongo
Thread: Red.
Wing: 2–6 grizzle saddle hackles, flaring out.
Collar: 2 grizzle hackles wound at end of hook shank around eyes.
Eyes: Bead chain.

Devised by Australian 'Bushy' Bush, this is often tied in small sizes for lesser species as well as larger sizes for tarpon.

Apte's Tarpon Fly
Thread: Red-orange.
Wing: Red-orange saddle hackles, flaring out.
Collar: Red and yellow hackles wound at end of hook shank.

Stu Apte was a great pioneer of tarpon fishing in the Keys. May be tied in a range of colours.

Summer Blues

Thread: Red.
Wing: Blue bucktail over white bucktail, plus a few strands of 'flash'.

A very simple pattern by Greg Derr, this may be tied in a wide range of colours.

Tarpon Bunny

Thread: Same colour as wing (see Note).
Wing: Rabbit zonker strip.
Collar: 2 saddle hackles wound at end of hook shank.
Note: Rabbit zonker strip is highly mobile (far more so than the bucktail of Summer Blues, for instance). Tie in black, white, yellow, chartreuse, green, or a mix of these.

Tarpon Toad

Thread: As wing and body.
Wing: Bunch marabou.
Collar: Either a piece of rabbit zonker wound around the hook shank, or a long-fibred Schlappen hackle.
Body: Wool yarn.
Eyes: See below.

Tie in black, black and purple, chartreuse and yellow, tan and orange. Have some with lightweight stick-on eyes (cover with clear epoxy) and with heavy dumb-bell eyes for different depths of water.

POP FLEYES

Pop Fleyes is the title of a book written by Bob Popovics and Ed Jaworowski that includes several flies devised by Bob that use sheep fleece and silicone. The sheep's fleece is stacked along the hook shank rather like deer hair in Muddler Minnows (p. 273). It is then trimmed to shape before being impregnated with silicone sealant. It is now moulded and further trimmed as necessary to the precise shape and size required. The result is a soft but seemingly bulky structure that is very light to cast.

Silicone Silver Mullet

Hook: Standard shank or streamer, sizes 4/0–2.
Thread: White.
Wing: 8 white spade hackles plus strands of silver Mylar or Flashabou.
Body and head: White fleece treated with silicone and trimmed carefully to shape. A final thin coat of silicone is applied after the eyes have been stuck in place.

This is an excellent baitfish imitation.

Silicone Squid

Hook: Standard shank or streamer, sizes 4/0–2/0.
Thread: Buff or very light tan.
Tentacles: 8–9 narrow ginger-buff cock hackles, marked with a permanent black felt-tip pen, or 4 long and 12 short rubber legs speckled with silver dust.
Body and head: Very pale ginger or buff sheep's fleece, treated with silicone and trimmed/moulded to the shape of a squid's body. A final smear of silicone is applied after the eyes have been stuck in place.

Squid are a favourite food of many pelagic species, including several tuna species (see also p. 440). An excellent fly for these species.

Pop-Lips (Terry Jenner)
Hook: Streamer, sizes 4/0–2/0.
Thread: White.
Tentacles: 6 white cock hackles, plus a few strands of silver or pearl 'flash' (Crystal Hair, Krystal Flash, Flashabou, Mylar etc.), and with a few short strands white ostrich.

Body and head: White fleece, treated with silicone and trimmed/moulded to shape. This includes a diving vane at the front, so that when retrieved the fly dives deep. Red and black or silver and black stick-on eyes are put in place before a final thin smear of silicone.

Pop-Lips (Bob Popovics)

Hook: Streamer, sizes 4/0–2/0.
Thread: White.
Tentacles: 6 grizzle cock hackles dyed golden-olive, plus a bunch tan bucktail.
Collar (at rear of shank): Cock hackle dyed golden-olive.
Body and head: As above.

Codger

Hook: Streamer, sizes 4/0–1.
Thread: Clear monofilament.
Body and head: Fleece with pearl 'flash', treated with silicone and trimmed/moulded to shape.

This bait-fish imitation by Australian Shaun Ash may be coloured olive back, white belly, or green back, white or yellow belly, or chartreuse back, buff belly, etc. to suit the bait-fish being imitated. This can be used for both saltwater and freshwater predators.

POPPERS

These are often used when predators are hunting bait-fish in the surface of the sea. The time to try one is when the bait-fish are leaping from the water, trying to evade the gnashing teeth just below them. Cast the popper out and pull it back with sharp tugs on the line so that it splashes and gurgles in the surface. These are useful for all predatory fish (see pp. 384ff).

Bob's Banger

Hook: Long shank, 6/0–2/0.
Thread: White.
Wing: Marabou, bucktail, cock or spade hackles, plus some 'flash'.
Body: Flashy synthetic chenille (e.g. Fritz).
Head: Bob's Banger Head.

Vary the colour of wing and body. The heads, devised by Bob Popovics, are preformed white foam, and they slide over the hook eye back to the short body. They are coloured either with felt-tip pen or, sold with them, metallic strips of various colours and patterns. If a fish destroys a Banger Head, simply slide a new one in place.

Foam Poppers

Hook: Long shank, sizes 6/0–1/0

Thread: White.

Wing: Marabou, bucktail, cock or spade hackles, plus some 'flash'.

Head: Commercially produced popper heads (available from all good suppliers of tying materials). These are coloured as required, using either pain or permanent felt-tip. Add stick-on eyes. Coat the completed head with clear tying cement.

Tie these in a range of sizes, for they can be used to catch smaller species, like sea bass, stripers, bluefish and false albacore, and larger pelagic species like dorado and billfish.

Slider

Hook: Long shank, sizes 6/0–1/0.

Thread: White.

Wing: Saddle hackles, plus some 'flash'.

Collar: 2 saddle or Schlappen hackles.

Head: Commercially produced foam popper heads, as above. In the case of the Slider the head is fixed in place the other way round, i.e. with the tapering narrow side to the fore. The idea is that this acts as a quieter 'popper', the argument being that some fish may be deterred from taking a loud popper, but will grab a less splashy one. Again, tie in a wide range of colours.

Crease Fly

Hook: Long shank, sizes 3/0–1/0.
Thread: White or clear.
Wing: Bucktail, plus some 'flash'.
Body: Cut from a section of white foam sheet, folded over the shank and fixed in place with Superglue. When dry, trim to shape and then colour with felt-tip pens to match any bait-fish. Add stick-on eyes and give the body a very thin coat of clear epoxy.

Devised by Joe Blades for catching striped bass, bluefish and false albacore off Long Island, this is a good estuary/inshore water fly anywhere in the world. Cast it out and it will lie on its side like a dead or dying fish. Pull it back and it acts like a popper.

Slab Side

Hook: Streamer, sizes 4/0–1/0.
Thread: White or clear monofilament.
Wing: Mix of bucktail and 'flash', with a topping of peacock herl.
Head: Deer hair, spun and trimmed Muddler-style (p. 272), with large plastic doll's eyes glued in place.

Lou Tarbory devised this pattern for use along the coast of New England. Vary length and colour.

SQUID

Squid and cuttlefish are eaten by many species of pelagic fish. Tie them in a wide range of lengths, up to 12 inches long.

Jenner's Baby Squid

Hook: Sea streamer, sizes 2/0–1.
Thread: White.
Tentacles: 2 long and 8 short rubber legs.
Body: 'Sili-Kin' or latex or other similar flexible thin cream or buff sheet, wound to create a squid-shaped body. Fix stick-on yellow and black eyes in place and give the body a coat of clear epoxy.

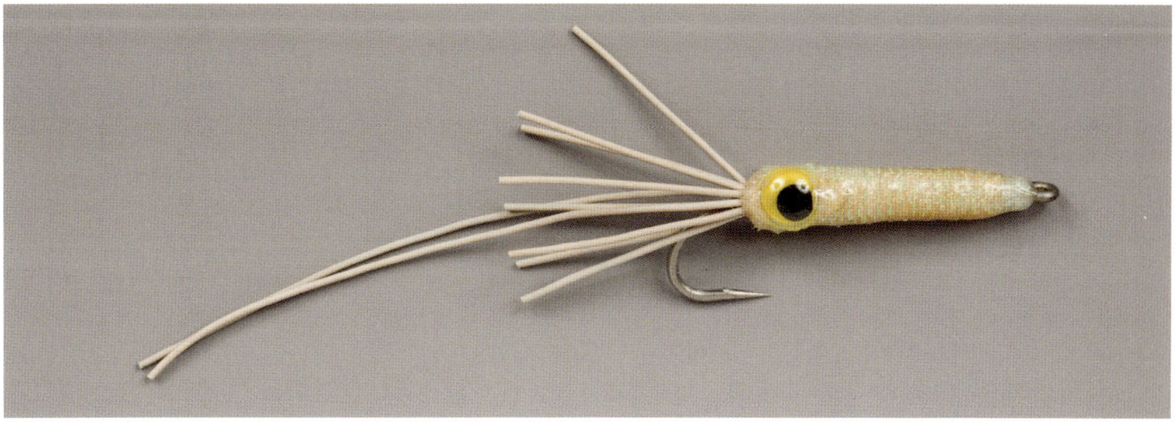

Silicone Squid (Terry Jenner)

Hook: Sea streamer, sizes 2/0–1.
Thread: Pale grey.
Tentacles: 2 long and 6 short buff hackle with black markings.
Body: Creamy-buff lamb's fleece, coated with silicone, and trimmed to shape. Fix a pair of doll's eyes in place and give the body a coat of silicone with silver dust mixed in.

This is a variant of Bob Popovics's Silicone Squid (p. 434).

Baltic Squid

Hook: Sea streamer, sizes 2/0–4.
Thread: White.
Tentacles: Soft white hair and two strands silver Flashabou, surrounded by the tips of cream-buff ostrich herl.
Body: Transparent pearl tubing. Fix stick-on silver and black eyes in place and give the body a coat of clear epoxy.

Devised by Peter Joest for catching sea trout in the Baltic and predatory freshwater fish in the rivers, lakes and canals of mainland Europe (where there are no squid!).

Squimp

Hook: Standard or long shank, sizes 2–10.
Thread: Olive.
Eyes: Lead dumb-bell, tied on top of shank so that the fly fishes upside-down (see Clouser Minnow, p. 408).
Tail: Bunch calf-tail or synthetic hair.
Body: Suede chenille.
Wing: As tail.
Legs: Silicone rubber, 2 pairs for tails, 2 tied in 'X' arrangement at head.
Colours: Tan, olive, yellow, orange, hot-pink, white.

According to Chris Beech, this is a hybrid pattern, matching both a shrimp and a small squid. It has proved outstanding for catching bonefish in places like Christmas Island and Belize and for species such as cobia, black- and yellow-fin bream, trevally and snook.

SHRIMPS AND CRABS

Many inshore water fish devour crabs and shrimps. However the mention of shrimps immediately brings to mind days out on the flats after bonefish, and of crabs, days trying to tempt a permit. But do not forget that members of the bass family, in the temperate waters of both Europe and North America love to eat these crustaceans and that at least sometimes they will select them from a wide range of other sea animals.

Grizzle Shrimp

Hook: Standard shank, sizes 2–4.
Thread: Grey.
Feelers: Stripped grizzle hackle stalks, a grizzle hackle point and a sparse bunch grey fox guard hairs.
Body: Palmered grizzle hackles in touching turns down hook shank, then trimmed to give shrimp shape.

This is like the Krabla in style (see p. 339) and was devised by Ken Abrames. Use natural red (brown) hackles to tie a Brown Shrimp or grey to create a Grey Shrimp (below). 'Mono' is monofilament or nylon fishing line.

Grey Shrimp

Hook: Curved shank shrimp hook, sizes 2–6.
Thread: White.
Feelers: 8 grey heron feather fibres taken from neck feather (long and soft), plus 4 strands Crystal Hair or Krystal Flash.
Eyes: Tiny black beads or very thick mono, burnt.
Body: Light blue dun (grey) henny-cock hackle palmered in touching turns down hook shank, and trimmed short except below shank where the fibres represent shrimp legs.

The following two flies imitate members of one of the commonest genera of shrimps in all temperate estuaries and salt-marsh creeks, *Palaemonetes*. Species in this genus are almost transparent.

Bend-Back Shrimp

Hook: Standard shank, sizes 2–4, with the hook bent back a short distance behind the eye.
Thread: White.
Feelers: 4 strands of pearl Crystal Hair or Krystal Flash.
Eyes: Tiny black beads or very thick mono, burnt.
Body: Pearl Flashabou or similar 'flash' wound over tying thread foundation.
Wing: Black-tipped white arctic fox.

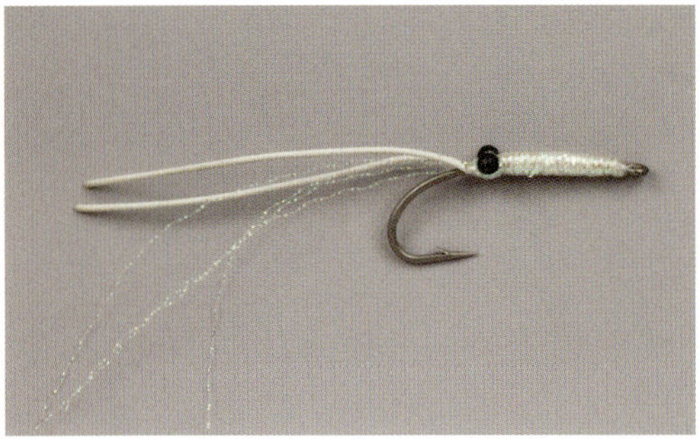

Rubber-Leg Shrimp
Hook: Standard shank, sizes 2–4.
Thread: White.
Feelers: 2 white rubber legs and 4 strands Crystal Hair or similar 'flash'.
Eyes: Tiny black beads or very thick mono, burnt.
Body: Pearl Flashabou or similar 'flash' wound over tying thread foundation.

The next two flies are by Germany's Peter Joest, who uses them in the Baltic to catch sea trout. His Pink Shrimp has lots of 'life', but as a fishing fly Peter rates the Brown Shrimp more highly.

Pink Shrimp
Hook: Standard shank, sizes 2–4.
Thread: Pale pink.
Feelers: 2 grizzle hackle stalks, with feather cut at tip, plus bunch of fine pale pink hackle fibres.
Eyes: Tiny black beads or very thick mono, burnt.
Body: Pink seal's fur or synthetic substitute.
Body hackle (legs): Long-fibred pink hackle, wound in open turns along body.
Back: Pink Antron yarn or similar.
Rib: Pale pink thread.

Brown Shrimp

Hook: Standard shank, sizes 2–4.
Thread: Olive or brown.
Feelers: 2 strands copper or brown Crystal hair or Krystal Flash.
Eyes: Tiny black beads or very thick mono, burnt.
Body: Sandy-brown Antron or similar synthetic fur, spun and wound in a dubbing loop. The straggly fibres that stick down below the hook shank represent the legs and add movement when the fly is being fished.

Ego

Hook: Curved shank shrimp hook, sizes 2–4.
Thread: Clear mono.
Feelers: 2 long and 4 short lengths of very fine clear mono.
Eyes: Tiny black beads or very thick mono, burnt.
Body: Mono wound over a foundation of tying thread, thicker at thorax.
Legs: Very fine clear mono, marked with black permanent marker.

Terry Jenner's shrimp pattern is tied using different thicknesses of clear mono.

Minipuff

Hook: Standard shank, sizes 4–8.
Thread: Tan.
Wing: Tan calf-tail with a grizzle hackle point on each side.
Eyes: Silver bead chain.
Head: Pink or tan chenille.

This is a great bonefish fly, especially with a pink head. It has also caught permit, stripers, sea bass and other inshore shrimp- and crab-eating fish.

Swimming Shrimp

Hook: Standard shank, sizes 2–6.
Thread: White.

Tail: Tan calf and gold Crystal Hair or Krystal Flash.
Wing: Grizzle hackle point.
Body: Tan deer hair, trimmed to shape at front but left as a collar in front of wing.
Eyes: Lead, painted.

Designed by Tim Borski, this might represent and small swimming crustacean such as squat lobsters, as well as shrimps.

Gotcha

Hook: Standard shank, sizes 2–6.
Thread: Pink.
Tail: Pearl Flashabou or Mylar tube.
Body: Pearl braid or pearl Mylar wound over foundation of tying thread.
Wing: Light tan hair (e.g. calf-tail or synthetic).
Eyes: Silver bead-chain.

This is a very popular fly for catching bonefish on the flats. In the original (*above left*) the eyes are tied on just behind the hook eye, but Terry Jenner suggests that a better place to tie them is at the end of the hook shank (*above right*).

The following might be taken as small squat shrimps or crabs by a host of species including bonefish and permit. The originals came from Jerry Martin and, though the tyings commonly used vary, the basic method remains the same, using epoxy resins.

Epoxy Moes

Hook: Standard shank, sizes 2–6.
Thread: Clear mono.

Tail: Tan deer hair plus two grizzle points.
Eyes: Very thick mono a little wider than the fly will be, with both ends burnt to create eyes. This length is tied in at right angles to the hook shank.
Body: This mono is tied to create a kite-shaped outline between bases of eyes and hook shank just behind the eye and at the end of the shank (see illustration). This is then filled in, a little at a time, with clear epoxy that has been coloured with water-colour paint powder and a little gold or other flashy 'dust'.

Foundation (above left); completed fly (above right).

An Epoxy Crab is produced similarly with rubber legs attached and either with plastic or burnt mono eyes or with lead eyes. In shallow water use the lighter version, but in water more than a three feet deep the lead-eyed version will be essential.

Crazy Charlie

Hook: Standard shank, sizes 2–6.
Thread: White or clear mono.
Tail: Silver Flashabou or similar 'flash'.
Body: Clear mono or stretch tubing.
Wing: White hackle points.
Eyes: Silver bead-chain.

Suggests a glass-minnow or a translucent shrimp. This was first tied by Bob Nauheim but has subsequently been tied in all sorts of colours and with all sorts of materials. A pink or tan version is excellent for bonefish.

Chernobyl Crab

Hook: Standard shank, sizes 2–4.
Thread: White.
Tail (or claws): White and tan calf-tail and 'flash', with grizzle hackles flaring out on the outside.
Body: Deer hair, spun and then clipped to a flattened crab shape.
Legs: A grizzle or furnace hackle wound in open turns through the body and trimmed on top.
Eyes: Silver bead-chain or lead.

Designed by Tim Borski. Of this fly and Del Brown's Crab, Ed Jaworowski stated (in *Essential Saltwater Flies*), that 'if you can't take a bonefish, permit, striped bass, or redfish' on these flies, 'they aren't eating crabs'.

Del Brown's Wool Yarn Crab

Hook: Standard shank, sizes 1/0–4.
Thread: White or clear mono.
Eyes: Lead or bead chain, tied behind hook eye before tying the rest of the fly.
Tail (pincers etc. from of a real crab's body): Sparse bunch tan or brown hair, plus a couple of strands of Flashabou, plus two cree or furnace hackle points.
Body: Rug yarn. Strands are tied at right angles to the hook shank and, when the shank is full, trimmed to a crab-like shape.
Legs: Rubber, tied in as body is being tied.

Chum Flies

It is common practice, especially when fishing for pelagic fish, to bring them close to the boat by 'chumming'. Lots of potential prey fish, especially oily species such as mackerel, are chopped up and mixed in a bucket with extra fish oils. This is then thrown into the sea, down-current of the boat, a bit at a time. The stench can be quite disgusting! Given enough chum and time, this will bring fish from several miles away and, as they chomp on the free offerings, a CHUM FLY is cast to them. The two imitations, illustrated below, of fish-heads from the chum bucket are very effective.

Hook: Short shank, preferably red, sizes 6/0–4/0 or larger.
Thread: Red.
Body: Lamb's fleece spun on the shank, treated with silicone (see p. 433) and trimmed and moulded to shape. The body is then coloured using permanent felt-tip pens, stick-on eyes put in position, and a final coat of clear silicone seals everything in place.
Blood: A bunch of bright red wool or marabou.

The Art of Fly-Dressing … or Why People Tie Flies

If we discount the hundreds of women who work in fly-tying factories in the Far East and Africa, and who probably have little or no idea of what fly-fishing is about and the difference between trout, salmon and saltwater fly-fishing, there are two main categories of fly-tyer.

The first, and most abundant, are fly-fishers who need flies so that they can go fishing, and who tie their own. They tie their own partly because they think that they can tie a better fly than they can buy (this is not always the case!), partly because they can add their own little variations to their flies, and partly because they think that it is less expensive to tie your own. For the vast majority, the latter is untrue simply because, when let loose in a fly-fishing shop, show, fair or conclave, the credit card takes over from the brain and a vast array of materials, 'that might come in useful', is purchased and doesn't come in useful! Nevertheless, it is great fun tying your own. Long winter nights, with the wind whistling in the eaves and snow drifting against the side wall of the house, are spent tying the very flies that will, in the warmth of next spring, summer or fall, catch a trout in such-and-such a river, a char in so-and-so a lake, and some bass from the shore at What'sit-by-the-Sea. When we cannot go fly-fishing, there is nothing better than reading about it, talking about it, and tying flies for next season. And as the fly boxes are replenished, so the days before the start of the next season diminish.

Some of this category of fly-dressers enjoy tying flies so much that they become semi-professional, tying a few extra flies to sell to friends and other club members who, for some inexplicable reason, have never learnt to tie flies. A few even give up gainful employment by becoming full-time professional tyers. But that can be a dangerous move because, during the fishing season, urgent orders of so many hundreds of flies may have to be completed and fly-fishing may have to be temporarily abandoned. One well-known American professional described how, after tying for ten hours per day for three weeks solid to get an important order out of the way, he sent off the boxes of flies. A week later an envelope arrived. Great!' I exclaimed. 'Honey,' I shouted to the wife as I started to open the envelope, 'I think that this is the cheque for those flies I sent off last week. Let's go an have a few days in the Catskills!' It wasn't that cheque. It was another order for hundreds more flies!

The second category of fly-dressers consists of people for whom fly-tying is the crux or *raison d'etre* of life. For them, fly-fishing is either irrelevant or almost so, as far as their fly-tying is concerned. Their flies are not for fishing. They are the outcome of a craft or, rather, an art form that is the equal of any piece of meat pickled in formalin by Damien Hirst or abandoned bed by Tracey Emin!

You think that this is an exaggeration? If you want to buy a framed ultra-imitative stonefly nymph tied by Oliver Edwards, or a fully dressed classic salmon fly by Paul Little or Marvin Nolte, you will have to dig deep into your pocket.

Yet today few would go salmon fishing with a perfectly tied classic salmon fly that has, in its dressing, feathers that were obtained from Victorian collections and that may no longer be sold under CITES regulations. And surely no one would cast into a rocky, turbulent stream an imitation of a nymph that took 50 hours to tie ...? A fly that took 50 hours to tie ... !

There are a small number of fly-dressers who specialise in the tying of the old, classic salmon flies. Flies that were described briefly on pp. 298–304 and that have, in their dressing, things like the feathers of bustard, cock-of-the-rock, blue chatterer, Indian crow (that is not a crow and does not come from India!), macaw, toucan and so on. There are many more fly-dressers who happily use substitutes for these exotic feathers, but the real specialists seek the real thing. Every so often some real feathers will be unearthed, perhaps in a dusty old drawer belonging to a long-deceased fly-tyer, and they will go onto the market. These few specialists will jostle to buy them, whatever the cost. Bustard feathers at

$120 (£80) each. Blue chatterer feathers at $8 (£5) each or you might prefer to buy a full skin for about $600 (£500). Indian crow feathers at $15 (£12) each, and two of each are needed in a fly. Those are 2009 prices and the cost is rising faster than the rate of inflation!

These tyers of classic salmon flies seek perfection, and they have honed the techniques of tying the old flies far beyond those of the people who invented them, a hundred and more years ago. They can tie Kelson's flies better than Kelson and Captain Hale's flies better than Captain Hale ever could! But it takes time. If one fibre is out of place, say during the tying in of a wing, then the tying in of the wing begins again from scratch. 'It will do!' or 'It's not perfect, but it will catch fish!' are never used as an excuse in the same way that many tyers of the first category excuse the imperfection in their flies. The materials going into the fly are perfect and were expensive to buy. Time is given to match this perfection and expense.

On the last day of a fly-tying show, Paul Little began to tie a new fly at 1.30pm. When the show ended three hours later, he hadn't quite got round to tying in the wings! But that's nothing. The late Al Coen took up to ten hours to dress one classic salmon fly! They sought perfection, and achieved it. Examples of Paul's tying are shown on pp. 300–7.

But even more time may be taken by a very small category of fly-dressers who produce 'ultra-imitation' flies. These are imitations of the

You are never too young to learn how to tie a fly: Paul Little with the potentially great fly-tyer Dylan Hooley.

The perfect stonefly imitation … but it takes time!

various stages of the insect life cycle, or crustaceans such as crayfish, shrimps and crabs. Earlier in this book are described some 'imitations' of adult stoneflies that are used for fishing, but none are imitations in the same league as the stonefly imitation dressed by Paul van den Driesche. This is a precise, ultra-imitation. Everything perfectly matches the real insect; even the legs have the sections coxa, trochanter, femur, tibia, tarsus, and the tarsus has the correct number of segments! And that is a 50-hour fly.

These ultra-imitations are tied to give the tyer pleasure and a sense of achievement. No one would ever dream of tying this pair of mating mayflies to a leader, or the perfect dragonfly (every vein in the wings is correct). The ultra-imitation dragonfly can even be identified to species: *Aeshna isoceles*, the green-eyed hawker, which occurs

Mating mayflies – perfect imitation.

Earring fly by Faiza Weillenmann (above); ultra-imitation … the dragonfly, green-eyed hawker (above right).

throughout central and south-eastern Europe, with a toe-hold in south-east England. One tyer of an ultra-imitation dragonfly explained how the abdomen had taken twelve hours, the thorax twelve hours, the legs a full weekend and the wings another full weekend to tie; the head had already taken four hours but was far from complete! He had spent 70 hours in the tying, and still the fly was not finished! And what fly is being tied here? Not a fly, but ear-rings!

Oh! And will the mouse take the cheese?

Mousetrap by André Miegies.

Many of those who belong to the first category of tyers, those who tie flies solely for fishing, argue that those in the second category are merely model-makers and wasting time.

That is grossly unfair, for what is fly-tying (unless one is a professional) other than a hobby and a pastime. It is done for pleasure.

Yet all who tie flies for fishing might learn much that would improve their fly-tying by watching those who seek to tie complex and perfect flies. For, good fly-tying being the art of handling thread, those who tie these seemingly outlandish creations are the greatest handlers of tying thread. Watch them select and prepare some material for tying into the fly. Watch how the material is manipulated and tied in with the minimum number of turns. Note how, if it is not quite right, the thread wraps are reversed and the material tied in again until it is right.

There are now fly-fishing and fly-tying shows, fairs and conclaves throughout Europe, the United States and in Japan. Such events are spreading to other places, like Australia. There will be the world's best tyers, of both categories of fly-tying. Visit them. There you will be able to purchase the best tying tools and materials as well as learn much by watching the experts tie their flies.

The line between fishing flies and flies tied solely for their beauty is a hazy one. The three flies above *could* be fished, for they don't take hours to tie. They are semi-realistic imitative flies. Marc Petitjean's Heptagenid Nymph (above left) is tied almost entirely with cul de canard; Oliver Edward's Stonefly Nymph (above centre) has all the main features of a real stonefly nymph; and Duns involve weaving a realistic body on wire detached from the hook (that takes time) and burnt wings (above right).

Select Bibliography

The following is not a complete list of all the books and booklets ever written about fishing flies, nor is it a list of all those books about fly-fishing that include a selection of flies. It is, however, a full list of all those books used in the preparation of this book and a selection of other important volumes on fishing flies. Many of these books are out-of-print, but they are usually readily available from secondhand/antiquarian book dealers, or exist in new editions. Readers wishing to purchase any of the books below are recommended to go to Paul Morgan, Coch-y-bonddu Books, Machynlleth, West Wales for he always has a vast collection for purchase.

Alaska Flyfishers, *Fly Patterns of Alaska* (Portland, OR: Frank Amato Publications, rev. edn, 1993).

Almy, Gerald, *Tying and Fishing Terrestrials* (Mechanicsburg, PA: Stackpole Books, 1978).

Anderson, Gary, *Atlantic Salmon, Fact and Fantasy* (Quebec: Salar Publications, 1990). Includes an interesting section as to why salmon take the fly.

Atherton, John, *The Fly and the Fish* (Mineola, NY: Dover Publications, reprinted, 2006 [1951]).

Bainbridge, G. C. *The Fly Fisher's Guide* (Liverpool, 1816). Early/modern trout and salmon flies.

Barker, Thomas, *Barker's Delight, or The Art of Angling* (1651). An important reference for those interested in the history of the fly.

Bates, Joseph D., Jr., *Streamer Fly Tying and Fishing* (Mechanicsburg, PA: Stackpole Books, reprinted 1995 [1950]).

Bates, Joseph D., Jr., *Atlantic Salmon Flies and Fishing* (Mechanicsburg, PA: Stackpole Books, 2nd edn, 1995 [1970]).

Bates, Joseph D., Jr., *The Art of the Atlantic Salmon Fly* (Boston, MA: David R. Godine, 1987). Written by a great American student of fishing flies, these are three very important works of reference for fly-fishers on both sides of the Atlantic.

Bergera, Juan de, *El Manuscrito de Astorga* (1624. Translated by Preben Torp Jacobsen in 1984 (see page 21).

Best, A. K., *A. K.'s Fly Box* (Guilford, CT: The Lyons Press, reprinted 1996). An excellent book on tying trout flies. A. K.'s *Advanced Fly Tying* and *Production Fly Tying* are also very useful.

Betts, John, *Synthetic Flies* (privately published by the author, 1980).

Blacker, T., *The Art of Fly-Making* (Lanham, MD: Derrydale Press, reprinted 1994 [1855]).
Blades, W., *Fishing Flies and Fly Tying* (Mechanicsburg, PA: Stackpole Books, new edn, 1980 [1950])
Boisset, L. de., *Les Mouches de Pêcheur de Truite* (Paris: Librairie des Champs-Elysees, 1939.
Bondoreu, Tom, *Fly Fishing the Gulf Coast*, 1997.
Borger, Gary A., *Nymphing: A Basic Book* (Mechanicsburg, PA: Stackpole Books, 1979).
Borger, Gary A., *Naturals: A Guide to Food Organisms of the Trout* (Harrisburg, PA: Stackpole Books, new edn, 2002 [1980]).
Bowkler, R. and C. , *The Art of Angling* (1747).
Brooks, Joe, *Saltwater Fly Fishing* (Lanham, MD: Derrydale Press, new edn, 2002 [1950]).
Brooks, Joe, *Salt Water Game Fishing* (New York: Harper & Row, Book Club Edition, 1968). Two books by a modern saltwater pioneer.
Brown, Dick, *Fly Fishing for Bonefish* (Guilford, CT: The Lyons Press, rev. edn, 2008 [1993]). An essential reference for this very important tropical flats species.
Buckland, John, *The Pocket Guide to Trout and Salmon Flies*, (London: Mitchell Beazley, reprinted 1997 [1986]). Photographs of many flies, including black bass and saltwater, but no tying recipes.
Buckland, John and Oglesby, Arthur, *A Guide to Salmon Flies*, (Marlborough, UK: The Crowood Press Ltd, 1990). A very comprehensive reference of old and new flies, from around the 'salmon world'.
Buller, Fred and Falkus, Hugh, *Dame Juliana, The Angling Treatyse and its Mysteries* (Moretonhampstead, UK: Flyfisher's Classic Library, 2001). The best work on the 1496 angling *Treatyse*, includes a side-by-side facsimile and translation of the original.
Burke, Edgar, *American Dry Flies and How to Tie Them* (Privately printed, The Anglers' Club of New York, 1931).
Carnill, Bob, and Robson, Kenneth, *Dressed to Kill: Seventy Successful Trout Lures* (Henlow Camp, UK: Beekay International, 1987). British streamers and bucktails ('lures').
Carrere, J., *La Pesca de la Trucha con mosca artificial* (1934).
Caucci, Al, and Nastasi, Bob, *Hatches I* (New York: Comparahatch Ltd, 1975).
Caucci, Al, and Nastasi, Bob, *Hatches II* (Guilford, CT: The Lyons Press, 3rd rev. edn., 1990). Matching the hatch in North America.
Chaytor, A. J., *Letters to a Salmon Fisher's Sons* (London: John Murray, 1910).
Chetham, J. *The Angler's Vade Mecum* (1681). Adds to the information given by Walton and Cotton about seventeenth-century fly-tying.
Clouser, Bob, *Clouser's Flies: : Tying and Fishing the Fly Patterns of Bob Clouser* (Mechanicsburg, PA: Stackpole Books, 2006).
Collyer, D., *Fly Dressing*, (Newton Abbot, UK: David and Charles, 1975).
Combs, Trey, *Steelhead Fly Fishing and Flies* (Portland, OR: Frank Amato Publications, reprint 1986 [1971]).
Combs, Trey, *The Steelhead Trout* (Portland, OR: Frank Amato Publications, 1988 [1976]).
Combs, Trey, *Steelhead Fly Fishing* (Guilford, CT: The Lyons Press, new edn 1999).
Combs, Trey, *Bluewater Fly Fishing* (Guilford, CT: The Lyons Press, new edn 2005). Standard works for flies for catching steelhead and oceanic species like marlin.
Curcione, Nick, *The Orvis Guide to Saltwater Fly Fishing* (Guilford, CT: The Lyons Press, rev. edn, 2008 [1993]).
Denis, Jack, *Western Trout Fly Tying Manual I and II* (Jackson Hole, WY: Snake River Books, 1991 [1980]).
Dimmock, A.W., *The Book of the Tarpon*, (Far Hills, NY: Meadow Run Press, 1990 [1912]). Essential reading for those wanting to catch a big tarpon.
Du Bois, Daniel, *The Fisherman's Handbook of Trout Flies*, (New York: A. S. Barnes & Co, 1960. Thousands of patterns listed half a century ago!
Dunham, Judith, *The Art of the Trout Fly*, (San Francisco: Chronicle Books, 1989).
Dunne, J. W., *Sunshine and the Dry Fly* (London: Adam and Charles Black, 2nd edn, 1950).
Earnhardt, Tom, *Flyfishing the Tidewaters* (Guilford, CT: The Lyons Press, rev. edn , 2001[1995]). Flies for the United States coast.
Edwards, Oliver, *Flytyers Masterclass* (Ludlow, UK: Merlin Unwin Books, 1994). How to tie some very imitative trout flies by a master.

Elder, Frank, *The Book of the Hackle*, (Edinburgh: Scottish Academic Press Ltd, 1979).

Engle, Ed, *Tying Small Flies* (Mechanicsburg, PA: Stackpole Books, 2004). The best book on tying tiny trout flies.

Falkus, Hugh, *Sea Trout Fishing* (London: Cassell Illustrated, new edn, 2004 [1962, 1975]).

Falkus, Hugh, *Salmon Fishing* (London: Cassell Illustrated, new edn, 2002 [1982]). The two classic textbooks.

Falkus, Hugh, and Greenhalgh, Malcolm, *The Salmon and Sea Trout Fisher's Handbook* (Ludlow, UK: Excellent Press, 1997). A précis of the two Falkus books, plus dry fly and nymph fishing.

Fauceglia, Ted, *Mayflies* (Mechanicsburg, PA: Stackpole Books, 2005). A beautiful book on North American mayflies.

Ferguson, Bruce, Johnson, Les, and Trotter, Pat, *Fly Fishing for Pacific Salmon* (Portland, OR: Frank Amato Publications, 1985).

Flick, Art, *New Streamside Guide* (Guilford, CT: The Lyons Press, 2nd rev. edn, 1983 [1969]).

Flick, Art, *et al.*, *Art Flick's Master Fly-Tying Guide* (New York: Crown Publishers, 1972).

Fogg, W. S. Roger, *The Art of the Wet Fly* (London: A & C Black Publishers, 1979). A standard reference to mainly British wet flies. Fogg also produced a slim volume *A Handbook of North Country Flies.*

Francis, Francis, *A Book on Angling* (1867).

Frodin, Mikael, *Classic salmon Flies: History and Patterns* (New York: Bonanza Books, 1991).

Fulsher, Keith, and Krom, Charles, *Hair-winged Atlantic Salmon Flies* (North Conway, NH: Fly Tyer, reprint 1982 [1981]).

Goddard, John, *Trout Fly Recognition* (London: A & C Black Publishers, 1966).

Goddard, John, *Trout Flies of Stillwater: The Natural Fly, Its Matching Artificial and Fishing Technique* (London: A & C Black Publishers, 1969). Matching the hatch in the UK

Goddard, John, *The Super Flies of Stillwater* (London: A & C Black Publishers, 1977).

Goddard, John, *Stillwater Flies: How and When to Fish Them*. (London: Ernest Benn, 1982.

Goddard, John and Clarke, Brian, *The Trout and the Fly* (Guilford, CT: The Lyons Press, 2005 [1980]).

Grant, George E., *Montana Trout Flies* (privately published, 1972).

Greenhalgh, Malcolm, *Trout Fishing in Rivers: Fly and Its Presentation*, (London: Cassell Illustrated, 1987).

Greenhalgh, Malcolm, *The Complete Salmon Fisher (Vol. 2): Salmon on the Fly* (London: Cassell Illustrated, 1996).

Greenhalgh, Malcolm, *The Floating Fly* (Ellesmere, UK: Medlar Press, 2008).

Greenhalgh, Malcolm, *The Mayfly and the Trout* (Ellesmere, UK: Medlar Press, 2009).

Greenhalgh, Malcolm, and Jaworowski, Ed. (eds), *The Complete Book of Fly-Fishing* (London: Mitchell Beazley, 1998). Fresh and saltwater fly-fishing from around the world, with contributions by great fly-fishers including Trey Combs, Nick Curcione, Oliver Edwards, John Goddard, Lefty Kreh, Ernest Schweibert, Dave Whitlock and Joan Wulff.

Greenhalgh, Malcolm, and Ovenden, Denys, *The Flyfisher's Handbook: The Natural Foods of Trout and Grayling and Their Artificial Imitations*, (Machynlleth, UK: Coch-y-Bonddu Books, 2nd rev. edn, 2004). Matching the hatch in Europe.

Hale, (J. H.) Capt., *How to Tie Salmon Flies* (1892). The centenary edition (1992) by the Flyfishers' Classic Library also contains J. J. Hardy's recipes for 361 classics.

Halford, F. M., *Floating Flies and How to Dress Them* (Winchester, UK: Barry Shurlock: 2nd rev. edn, 1974 [1886]).

Halford, F. M., *Modern Development of the Dry Fly: The New Dry Fly Patterns,the Manipulation of Dressing Them and Practical Experiences of Their Use* (London: Routledge, 1910). The two major works by the 'High Priest' of the dry fly.

Harris, Graeme, and Morgan, Moc, *Successful Sea Trout Angling* (Machynlleth, UK: Coch-y-Bonddu Books, 2nd rev. edn, 1996 [1989]). More complete than the classic work of Hugh Falkus.

Headley, Stan, *Trout and Salmon Flies of Scotland*, (Ludlow, UK: Merlin Unwin Books, 1997).

Hellekson, Terry, *Popular Fly Patterns* (Salt Lake City, UT: Peregrine Smith Inc, 1977).

Helvie, H. Kent, *Steelhead Fly Tying Guide* (Portland, OR: Frank Amato Publications, 1994).

Herd, Andrew, *The Fly* (Ellesmere, UK: Medlar Press, 2003). By far the best work on the history of fly-fishing and fishing flies.

Hewitt, Edward R., *A Trout and Salmon Fisherman for Seventy-Five Years* (1948). An important hitorical account from the United States.

Hughes, Dave, *Wet Flies* (Mechanicsburg, PA: Stackpole Books, 1995).

Hughes, Dave, *Trout Flies: The Tier's Reference* (Mechanicsburg, PA: Stackpole Books, 1999). Excellent on fly-tying, from the United States.

Jacobsen, Preben Torp, *Torfluefiskeri* (1965).

Jacobsen, Preben Torp, *Nymfeskeri* (1972).

Jacobsen, Preben Torp, *Fluebinding* (1976). Danish flies for catching trout and grayling.

Jaques, D. *Fisherman's Fly and Other Studies*, (London: A & C Black Publishers, 1965.

Jaworowski, Ed and Popovics, Bob, *Pop Fleyes: Bob Popovich's Approach to Saltwater Fly Design* (Mechanicsburg, PA: Stackpole Books, 2001). Saltwater flies. The title could be extended to 'Popovics' flies with eyes'!

Jaworowski, Ed, *Essential Saltwater Flies: Step-by-Step Typing Instructions - 38 Indispensable Designs and Their Most Useful Variations* (Mechanicsburg, PA: Stackpole Books, 2008). The best book or anyone starting off tying flies for saltwater.

Jennings, Preston, *A Book of Trout Flies: Containing a List of the Most Important American Stream Insects and Their Imitations* (New York: Crown Publishers, 1970 [1935]). A classic.

Johnson, L., *Sea Run: Complete Guide to Fishing for Sea-Run Cutthroat Trout* (1979).

Jorgensen, Poul, *Dressing Flies for Fresh and Salt Water* (Freshet Press, 1973).

Jorgensen, Poul, *Modern Fly Dressings for the Practical Angler* (New York: Winchester Press, 1976).

Jorgensen, Poul, *Modern Trout Flies*, (London: Doubleday, 1979).

Jorgensen, Poul, *Salmon Flies: Their Character, Style and Dressing*, (Mechanicsburg, PA: Stackpole Books, 2nd rev. edn, 1999).

Jorgensen, Poul, *Dry Fly Patterns for the New Millennium* (Portland, OR: Frank Amato Publications, 2002).
– Six works by one of the grestest fly-tyers of the second half of the twentieth century.

Kaufmann, Randall, *Bonefishing with a Fly* (Portland, OR: Frank Amato Publications, 1992).

Kaufmann, Randall, *Tying Nymphs* (Moose, WY: Western Fishermans Press, 1994).
– Essential references on two completely different aspects of fly-tying by a master.

Keith, Tom, *Fly Tying and Fishing for Panfish and Bass* (Portland, OR: Frank Amato Publications, 1989).

Kelson, G. M., *The Salmon Fly* (1895). One of the classic works on the classic salmon fly.

Kite, Oliver, *Nymph Fishing in Practice* (Shrewsbury, UK: Swan Hill Press, 2nd rev. edn, 2000 [1963]).

Koch, Ed, *Fishing the Midge: A New and Revised Edition of an Angling Classic* (Mechanicsburg, PA: Stackpole Books, 2002 [1972]).

Kreh, Lefty, *Fly Fishing in Salt Water* (Guilford, CT: The Lyons Press, 3rd rev. edn, 1998 [1974]). The definitive work, including a basic collection of flies.

Kreh, Lefty, *Saltwater Fly Patterns* (Guilford, CT: The Lyons Press, 2nd rev. edn, 1996). The essential textbook of saltwater flies.

Kugach, Gene, *Fly Fisher's Pattern Book* (Mechanicsburg, PA: Stackpole Books, 2000).

La Branche, George M. L., *The Salmon and the Dry Fly* (Lyon, MS: The Derrydale Press, new edn, 1994 [1924]). The pioneering book on the subject.

LaFontaine, Gary, *Caddisflies* (Guilford, CT: The Lyons Press, rev edn, 2006 [1981]). Though the American textbook, relevant everywhere.

LaFontaine, Gary, *Trout Flies: Proven Patterns* (Guilford, CT: The Lyons Pres, rev edn, 2001 [1993]).

Lawrie, W. H., *Scottish Trout Flies* (London: Frederick Muller Ltd, 1966).

Lawrie, W. H., *All-fur Flies and How to Dress Them* (New York: A. S. Barnes & Co., 1967).

Lawrie, W. H., *English and Welsh Trout Flies* (London: Frederick Muller Ltd, 1967).

Lawrie, W. H., *International Trout Flies* (London: Frederick Muller Ltd,1969).

Leighton, Michael, *Trout Flies of Shropshire and the Welsh Borderlands* (privately published, 1987).

Leiser, Eric, *The Book of Fly Patterns* (New York: Random House, 1988). A most useful reference for tying traditional, proven fishing-flies.

Leiser, Eric, and Boyle, Robert H., *Stoneflies for the Angler* (New York: Alfred A. Knopf, 1982).

Leiser, Eric, and Solomon, Larry, *The Caddis and the Angler* (Mechanicsburg, PA: Stackpole Books, 1977). Matching nymphs and adults of two important food groups in North America.

Leisenring, James, *The Art of the Wet Fly* (New York: Dodd, Mead & Co., 1941).

Leisenring, James, and Hidy, V.S., *The Art of Tying the Wet Fly and Fishing the Flymph* (New York: Crown Publishers, 1971).

Leonard, J. Edson, *Flies* (New York: A. S. Barnes & Co., 1950).

Light, Tom, and Humphrey, Neal, *Steelhead Fly Tying Manual* (Portland, OR: Frank Amato Publications, 1985).

Lingren, Art, *Fly Patterns of British Columbia* (Portland, OR: Frank Amato Publications, 1999).

Links, Leon, *Tying Flies with CDC: The Fisherman's Miracle Feather* (Ludlow, UK: Merlin Unwin Books, 2002). The major reference to tying trout flies with cul de canard.

Lively, Chauncy K., *Chauncy Lively's Flybox: A Portfolio of Modern Trout Flies* (Mechanicsburg, PA: Stackpole Books, 1980).

Lumini, Piero, *Imitazione di Effimere* (n.d.)

Lumini, Piero, *Imitazione di Tricotteri* (n.d.)

Mackintosh, Alexander, *The Driffield Angler* (privately published, sold by H. Mozley, 1806).

McDonald, John, (ed.) *The Complete Fly Fisherman: The Notes and Letters of Theodore Gordon* (1947).

McDowell, Hugh, *New Zealand Fly-Tying: The Ten-Thumbed Beginner's Guide* (Wellington, New Zealand: A. H. & A. W. Reed, 1984).

Malone, E. J., *Irish Trout and Salmon Flies* (Machynlleth, UK: Coch-y-Bonddu Books, 1984).

Malone, E. J., *Tying Flies in the Irish Style: Trout and Sea Trout Patterns* (Yeadon, UK: Smith Settle, 2000).

Mann, Chris, and Gillespie, Robert, *Shrimp and Spey Flies for Salmon* (Ludlow, UK: Merlin Unwin Books, 2001). For Atlantic salmon on both sides of the ocean; also useful for steelhead and Pacific salmon.

Marbury, Mary Orvis, *Favorite Flies and their Histories* (1892).

Marinaro, Vincent C., *A Modern Dry-Fly Code* (Guilford, CT: The Lyons Press, new edn, 1998 [1950]).

Marinaro, Vincent C., *In the Ring of the Rise* (Guilford, CT: The Lyons Press, new edn, 2001 [1976]). Two classics on dry flies.

Marriner, Paul C., *Modern Atlantic Salmon Flies* (Portland, OR: Frank Amato Publications, 1998).

Marsh, Norman, *Trout Stream Insects of New Zealand* (Mechanicsburg, PA: Stackpole Books, 2005). With imitative flies.

Martin, Darrel, *Imitations: Methods in Tying and Trouting* (Seattle, WA: SunKing Publishing, 1980).

Martin, Darrel, *Fly-Tying Methods*, (Newton Abbot, UK: David and Charles, 1987).

Martin, Darrel, *Micropatterns*, (Guilford, CT: The Lyons Press, new edn, 1999 [1994]). Three excellent books on tying by one of the United States's greatest technical tyers.

Mascall, L., *A Booke of Fishing with Hooke and Line* (1590).

Migel, J. Michael, and Wright, Leonard, (eds) *The Masters on the Nymph* (Guilford, CT: The Lyons Press, new edn, 2003 [1979]).

Mitchell, Ed, *Fly Rodding the Coast* (Mechanicsburg, PA: Stackpole Books, 1995). Though written from the view-point of the New England coast, a useful guide for any temperate shore.

Moore, T. C. Kingsmill, *A Man May Fish* (Gerrards Cross, UK: Colin Smythe Ltd, new edn, 2003 [1979]). Essential for any fly-fisher intending to visit Ireland.

Morgan, Moc, *Fly Patterns for the Rivers and Lakes of Wales* (Llandysul, UK: Gomer Press, 1984).

Morgan, Moc, *Trout and Salmon Flies of Wales* (Ludlow, UK: Merlin Unwin Books, 1996).

Morris, Skip, *The Art of Tying the Dry Fly* (Portland, OR: Frank Amato Publications, 1993).

Nemes, Sylvester, *The Soft-hackled Fly* (Greenwich, CT: Chatham Press, 1975).

Nemes, Sylvester, *The Soft-hackled Fly Addict* (Mechanicsburg, PA: Stackpole Books, new edn, 1993 [1981]).

O'Reilly, Pat, *Matching the Hatch: Stillwater, River and Stream* (Shrewsbury, UK: Swan Hill Press, 1997).

O'Reilly, Peter, *Trout and Salmon Flies of Ireland* (Ludlow, UK: Merlin Unwin Books, 1995).
Overfield, T. D., *Famous Flies and Their Originators* (London: A & C Black Publishers, 1972).
Overfield, T. D., *G.E.M. Skues, The Way of a Man with a Trout* (London: Ernest Benn, 1977).
Pequegnot, Jean-Paul, *French Fishing Flies* (Guilford, CT: The Lyons Press, 1984).
Price, S. D. Taff, *Stillwater Flies I, II, III* (London: Ernest Benn, 1981).
Price, S. D. Taff, *Lures for Game, Coarse and Sea Fishing*, (London: A & C Black Publishers, 1972). For 'lures' read bucktails and streamers.
Price, S. D. Taff, *Rough Stream Trout Flies* (Random House, 1976).
Price, Taff, *Fly Patterns: an International Guide* (London: Cassell Illustrated, 2nd rev. edn, 1992 [1986]). A useful collection of fly-tying recipes from around the world.
Price, Taff, *The Angler's Sedge: Tying and Fishing the Caddis* (London: Cassell Illustrated, 1989). Primarily flies for European trout, but has recipes from around the world.
Pritt, T. E., *North Country Trout Flies* (Yeadon, UK: Smith Settle, facsimile edition, 1995 [1886]).
Proper, Datus, *What the Trout Said: About the Design of Trout Flies and Other Mysteries* (Guilford, CT: The Lyons Press, 2nd rev. edn, 1990 [1982]). The answer was Nothing! Fly-fishing from the trout's point-of-view.
Pryce-Tannatt, Thomas, *How to Dress Salmon Flies: A Handbook for Amateurs* (London: A & C Black Publishers, 1914). Classic flies.
Reynolds, John, *Flyfishing for Sailfish* (Machynlleth, UK: Coch-y-Bonddu Books, 1997).
Rice, F. A., *Fly-Tying Illustrated for Nymphs and Lures* (Newton Abbot, UK: David and Charles, 1976). 'Lures' = 'streamers and bucktails'.
Rice, F.A., *Fly-Tying Illustrated: Wet and Dry Patterns* (London: B. T. Batsford, 1981).
Richards, Carl, Swisher, Doug, and Arbona, Fred, *Stoneflies* (1983).
Ritz, Charles, *A Fly Fisher's Life* (London: Robert Hale Ltd, new edn, 1996 [1959]).
Roberts, John, *The New Illustrated Dictionary of Trout Flies* (London: George Allen & Unwin, 1986). Mainly flies from the British Isles.
Roberts, John, *A Guide to River Trout Flies* (Marlborough, UK: The Crowood Press, 1989). Primarily European and North American flies.
Roberts, John, *Flyfishing for Grayling* (Ludlow, UK: Excellent Press, 1999). The essential reference.
Robson, K., *Robson's Guide* (Henlow Camp, UK: Beekay International, 1985). The title does not tell what a useful reference this is!
Ronalds, A. *The Fly-Fisher's Entomology* (1836). Many later editions.
Rosborough, E.H. 'Polly', *Tying and Fishing the Fuzzy Nymphs* (Mechanicsburg, PA: Stackpole Books, 4th rev. edn, 1988).
Sawyer, F., *Nymphs and the Trout* (London: A & C Black Publishers, 2nd rev. edn, 1970 [1958]). The classic text; many later editions.
Schullery, Paul, *American Fly Fishing: A History* (Guilford, CT: The Lyons Press, 1987).
Schweibert, Ernest, *Matching the Hatch*, (New York: MacMillan Publishing, 1955).
Schweibert, Ernest, *Nymphs* (Winchester, 1973).
Scrope, William, *Days and Nights of Salmon Fishing on the Tweed* (1843).
Shaw, Helen, *Fly-Tying: Materials, Tools, Technique* (Guilford, CT: The Lyons Press, 4th rev. edn, 1996 [1963]).
Skues, G.E.M., *Nymph Fishing for Chalk Stream Trout* (London: A & C Black Publishers, 1939). Skues wrote several other useful pioneering books on this subject.
Stewart, Dick, and Allen, Farrow, *Flies for Atlantic Salmon* (Guilford, CT: The Lyons Press, 1991).
Stewart, T., *Two Hundred Popular Flies*, (London: A & C Black Publishers, new edn, 1991 [1979]).
Swisher, Doug, and Richards, Carl, *Selective Trout*, (Guilford, CT: The Lyons Press, 1996 [1971]).
Swisher, Doug, and Richards, Carl, *Emergers* (Guilford, CT: The Lyons Press, new edn, 2000 [1991]). Essential reference works for those who want to 'match the hatch'. American, but useful elsewhere.
Talleur, Richard W., *Mastering the Art of Fly Tying* (Mechanicsburg, PA: Stackpole Books, 1979).
Talleur, Richard W., *The Fly Tyer's Primer* (New York: Nick Lyons Books, 1988). Two useful books on tying techniques by one of the United States' finest tyers.

Tashiro, Nori, and Tashiro, Tada, *The Tashiro Nymphs and Naturals* (1981 [Japan]).

Thornton, Barry M., *Saltwater Fly Fishing for Pacific Salmon* (Surrey, BC, Canada: Hancock House Publishers, 1995).

Venables, R., *The Experienc'd Angler* (1662).

Veniard, J., *Fly Dressers Guide* (London: A & C Black Publishers, 1952).

Veniard, J., *Further Guide to Fly Dressing* (London: A & C Black Publishers, 1964).

Veniard, J., *Reservoir and Lake Flies* (London: A & C Black Publishers, 1970. Three essential volumes on tying flies, with many tying recipes.

Walker, C. F., *Lake Flies and their Imitations*, (London: Herbert Jenkins, 1960).

Walker, Richard (Dick), *Fly Dressing Innovations* (London: Ernest Benn, 1974).

Walker, Richard (Dick), *Modern Fly Dressings* (London: Ernest Benn, 1980).

Walton, Izaak and Cotton, Charles, *The Compleat Angler*, 5th edn (1676). This was the first edition to have Cotton's supplement that gave the first good instruction for tying a trout fly.

West, Leonard, *The Natural Trout Fly and Its Imitation* (St Helen's: 1912).

Whitlock, Dave, *Guide to Aquatic Trout Foods* (Guilford, CT: The Lyons Press, 2nd rev. edn, 2007 [1982]).

Williams, A. C., *A Dictionary of Trout Flies* (London: A & C Black Publishers, 5th edn, 1973).

Wilson, Bob, and Parks, Richard, *Tying and Fishing the West's Best Dry Flies* (Portland, OR: Frank Amato Publications, 1978).

Woolley, R., *Modern Trout Fly Dressings* (London: The Fishing Gazette, 2nd edn, 1939 [1932]). The adjective 'Modern' ought never to be used in such titles! Woolley's is a useful guide to trout and grayling flies, mainly in the UK, midway through the twentieth century.

Wulff, Lee, *Lee Wulff on Flies* (Mechanicsburg, PA: Stackpole Books, 1980).

Wulff, Lee, *The Atlantic Salmon* (Guilford, CT: The Lyons Press, 1983). Wulff was the great pioneer into catching salmon on dry fly consistently; his Wulff series is now world famous.

Index

AUBERGE DE L'ANGE